Ironies of Faith

Ironies of Faith

The Laughter at the Heart of Christian Literature

Anthony Esolen

ISI BOOKS
WILMINGTON, DELAWARE
2007

Esolen, Anthony M.

 Ironies of faith / Anthony M. Esolen.—1st ed.—Wilmington, Del. : ISI Books, c2007

  p. ; cm.

  ISBN-13: 978-1-933859-21-7
  ISBN-10: 1-933859-21-0

  1. Religion and literature. I. Title.

PN49 .E86 2007   2006935900
809/.93382—DC22   0707

Published in the United States by:

 ISI Books
 Intercollegiate Studies Institute
 3901 Centerville Road
 Wilmington, Delaware 19807
 www.isibooks.org

Book design by Jennifer M. Connolly

Contents

Part Four: The Irony of Love

Part Five: The Mighty Child

DEDICATION

For Rodney Delasanta (1932–2007)
Teacher, Colleague, and Friend

"Now I send thee, to open their eyes,
and to turn them from darkness to light."

Preface

> But all human efforts, all the lavish gifts of the emperor, and the propitiations of the gods, did not banish the sinister belief that the conflagration was the result of an order. Consequently, to get rid of the report, Nero fastened the guilt and inflicted the most exquisite tortures on a class hated for their abominations, called Christians by the populace. Christus, from whom the name had its origin, suffered the extreme penalty during the reign of Tiberius at the hands of one of our procurators, Pontius Pilatus, and a most mischievous superstition, thus checked for the moment, again broke out not only in Judaea, the first source of the evil, but even in Rome, where all things hideous and shameful from every part of the world find their center and become popular. Accordingly, an arrest was first made of all who pleaded guilty; then, upon their information, an immense multitude was convicted, not so much of the crime of firing the city, as of hatred against mankind.
>
> Tacitus, *Annals* 15.44

How pleasant it is to forgive the errors of historians. Here we have Tacitus, the great chronicler of decadence among the Roman aristocracy of the first century. He is explaining how the tyrant Nero deflected suspicion from himself by blaming the Christians in Rome not merely for setting the city on fire, but for perfect monstrosity—"hatred against mankind." Tacitus sees the technical injustice of the charge, but does not shed a tear for the Christians, whose abominations (Christians were typically accused of cannibalism) deserve no compassion. Nor do they stir his curiosity. They are footnotes in his epic account of Roman history.

Tacitus could not know that that small sect, whose beliefs were other than what he supposed, would survive to overcome the Romans, and that two thousand years later, Christianity would be the dominant religious and cultural force in the world, while his pagan Rome would be no more. With the assistance of Tacitus himself, Nero would become the imbecilic emblem of all that was ignoble and debased in the great city; while the chief Christians whom Nero executed, Peter and Paul, would be revered as saints. Needless to say, the otherwise clear-sighted Tacitus could not see exactly what was going on. He was but a man of his day.

What of the men of our day? Can they see Christianity any the more clearly? Tacitus's mistake was born of unfamiliarity; ours are born of overfamiliarity. We are like people who live in the shadow of a great and rugged mountain, who never notice how it alters even the light of the day, from the rising to the setting sun.

Specifically, many people who teach and write about European literature do not understand the heart of Christianity. That is a problem—as great as if one attempted to discuss the poetry of Islam, without knowing what it was like, from the heart, to be a Muslim. It is compounded by the pervasiveness of Christian images and ideas in our culture. They give one a self-deceptive ease in talking about Christianity. Then, when the faith proves more subtle than one's caricature, that same overfamiliarity tempts one to patter about "contradictions" and "tensions." The critic sees holes where there are but spaces in a most intricate lacework.

Along with overfamiliarity steals a weariness of the intellect and the imagination. Man abhors an empty altar. He longs to lay his will at the feet of one worthy to be obeyed. But when he detaches himself from the ground of his being, and when his idols prove to be the cheats of his own fancy, he retires into skepticism. Henryk Sienkiewicz captures the mood in the first sentence of his epic *Quo Vadis?* He reveals the lassitude of a world deprived of the wonder of worship: "Petronius woke only about midday and as usual greatly wearied." The master of Nero's games requires the ministrations of bath attendants, slaves all, to rouse his "slothful blood" and quicken him, "as if he had risen from the dead." But Petronius has not risen from the dead, and is not yet suited to see the One who has. For now, when he hears of a certain Paul preaching the resurrection, he smiles, as if he had heard it all before.

Whether a book like this can win a hearing from our contemporary Petronii and Petroniae who teach literature, I cannot tell. But I have a more important motive. Esteeming the experts too highly, many Christians have abandoned their literature to the mainly secular scholars that inhabit our universities. But Shakespeare, Herbert, Dickens, and Hopkins did not write for scholars in universities. What would have been the point? For the sake of the literature itself, meant to be loved by anyone who could read or attend a play, Christians should reclaim their heritage. This book is written to assist them in their quest.

Finally, I am writing to meditate upon the mysteries of the Christian faith. I have chosen irony as my organizing principle, partly because the subject interests me, and partly because it is often assumed that irony and faith are incompatible. Irony corrodes any stable supposition of truth, say some; but I think it is rather skepticism that corrodes the possibilities for irony. I do not think that irony must lead to nihilism. If one examines the evidence of Christian literature, one might conclude quite the opposite: that the richest irony presupposes truth and order. Be that as it may, in this book I hope to save irony from its worst friends. In doing so, I pray that I may be touched by the Christian mysteries of incarnation and transcendence, free will and design, sin and redemption, blindness and vision, freedom and submission, and, most of all, the subtle strand that links human love to the love that moves the sun and the other stars.

Part One

Humility & Vision

1

To Be Pompilia, Not the Fisc:
Browning and the Irony of Humility

B efore I define what irony is, let us examine what habits of mind are necessary for understanding so subtle a feature of language. Those habits are all
the more necessary as the language of Christendom grows more distant and
the culture more foreign.

Cleverness is not the answer. I would like to illustrate why by turning to a
masterpiece of Christian poetry. Robert Browning wrote his longest and most
difficult work, *The Ring and the Book*, precisely to show human beings failing
to interpret correctly the actions and motives of one another. They fail not
because they are dim-witted, but because their moral compromises limit their
vision. Pride — and its concomitant assumption that everyone must be just like
oneself, only not quite so intelligent or strong-willed — is the problem.

Browning derives his plot from the account of a notorious series of trials
in late-seventeenth-century Rome. Violante, a childless wife, finds a woman
of the streets who has recently given birth to a girl. She pays her for the baby
and passes it off to her husband Pietro as their own. They christen her Pompilia, and together they live well enough for people with no hereditary title.
Worried that the secret of the birth will come out, Violante seeks to marry
Pompilia away as soon as she can to someone with the title they lack. She finds

one Guido, an Aretine and hanger-on at the cardinal's court, no priest but enough of a cleric to claim ecclesiastical privilege. He is a short, middle-aged, cowardly, ugly, embittered, and poverty-stricken aristocrat. The marriage is a hugger-mugger affair, Pietro not even present. Guido expects a large dowry; Pietro imagines the wealth of Guido's ancestral home. When that castle in Arezzo proves dilapidated and cold, and when Guido treats the parents with brute tyranny, they flee to their old home in Rome, leaving Pompilia behind.

There she bides, patient and unhappy, subjected to Guido's tyrannical whims and to the obscenity of his brother, a canon of the church. When the parents suddenly turn about and attack their attacker, testifying that Pompilia was not their daughter (and that therefore Guido was not entitled to her dowry), Guido counters by attempting to tar her as an adulteress. He uses maids and "friends" to try to press Pompilia into compromising herself with a local priest, the dashing Giuseppe Caponsacchi. He goes so far as to compel her to "write" letters at his instruction: he holds her hand and forces the pen along, as she can neither read nor write, nor does she know the content of what he has her compose! Caponsacchi, however, who has never spoken with or met Pompilia but only looked upon her sad, strange beauty once and from afar, sees through the ruse and resists.

Pompilia entreats first the governor of Arezzo, then the archbishop, while weeping like a child, pleading to be rescued from the evil that threatens her, body and soul. But they are worldly men and cronies of her husband. They know better. They wink at the wickedness and tell her to go home. They have no ears to hear.

At that, Pompilia turns to her last hope. She has never spoken to Caponsacchi. By all rights she should know nothing about him. But she does know. She has looked into his eyes once and seen—her knight.

Browning dares the reader to play the archbishop or the governor, to smile and shake his head and say that such "knowledge" is for fairy tales and not for real life (whatever that is). But a true man is what Pompilia sees. She manages to send him a plea to come take her away. After some days of hesitation, for he knows that no one will understand, and that he is about to destroy the churchly career his superiors have chiseled out for him, Caponsacchi submits to the promptings of a holy love. He sweeps her away to Rome. Just before they arrive, they are overtaken by Guido and his henchmen—Pompilia sleeping in a bedroom in a wayside inn, the priest watching over her.

So incriminating are the appearances that Guido might have slain her on the spot and been pardoned. But he is a coward; the priest raises a sword to defend Pompilia, and when the henchmen pinion his arms, the girl herself seizes a sword and raises it against Guido. At this point he retreats and decides to take legal action. The trial of charge and countercharge ends in stalemate: Guido is allowed to keep the dowry, Caponsacchi is removed to a retreat house, and Pompilia is committed to a convent outside Rome. When, a few weeks later, she is found pregnant, the court mercifully remands her to the home of her mother and father, under provision that she not leave. There she gives birth to a son, whom she names Gaetano, after a recently canonized saint, for as she sees it, Guido has no part in this son—only heaven.

Infuriated by the perceived insult to his honor, Guido steals to Rome during Christmastide and knocks at the door where the family dwells. When they ask who is there, he utters the magic word, "Caponsacchi." When Violante opens, he slashes her in the face. He and his fellows cut her mother and father to pieces, and give Pompilia what should have been a dozen death-stabs. But Pompilia does not die, not yet. Guido is discovered fleeing back to Arezzo and is brought to Rome to stand trial. Pompilia gives her full testimony from the bed where she will soon die—the testimony of a young woman in love, chaste love, with her champion, the gallant Caponsacchi! The priest and Guido testify; and Browning provides us with the "opinions" of the half of Rome that is for Guido, and of the half of Rome that is for Pompilia, and also of what he calls "Tertium Quid," the sophisticates who see more keenly, so they think, than does either side of the rabble. We are likewise presented with the trial preparations of the prosecutor (the grandly titled Fisc) and the defense attorney—worldly men, not exactly bad and not exactly good, full of themselves, and cutting a partly comic figure in their pretending to know everything.

When Guido is convicted and sentenced to death, he appeals to the pope, Innocent XII, himself old and dying. The pope responds that while, everyone might have expected Guido to long outlive him, as it is, in all his weakness the pope will live another day, while Guido shall not see the sun set again.

What Browning shows us in this tangle of purity and wickedness, and half-virtue and shadowy half-vice, is not only how difficult it is for us to "read." That is what critics of Browning put forth: he is the poet, they say, of multiple points of view, himself coolly distant from judgment. We are granted the irony of seeing that the same events might be viewed in a variety of ways, with all kinds of arguments to justify them.

But the irony Browning relishes is deeper than that. The spokesman for "Tertium Quid," a cool aristocratic skeptic, dismisses Pompilia's claim of innocence as incredible and dismisses Guido as a coward who in part got what he deserved. And he expects the pope to do the "reasonable" thing, to commute the sentence. Tertium might well be a modern trader in literary criticism. He is well-heeled, smiling at outrageous claims either to surpassing virtue or to surpassing wickedness. He pretends to a careful examination of evidence, but actually he works for self-advancement, whispering into the ear of his lordly master just what his lordly master is to believe of all the brouhaha. Yet the irony cuts against him and against all skeptics: for Browning reveals that Pompilia was not only innocent but miraculously pure. We who cannot believe are the ultimate objects of his admonition.

Pompilia is also the most acute "critic" in the poem—she, barely seventeen, who can neither read nor write, and who was married, as she says, "hardly knowing what a husband meant" (7.410). What makes her wise? Browning identifies it unhesitatingly. Pompilia's *humility* enables her to move outside herself, to imagine what it might be like to be someone else. So she is the only one in the poem, aside from the similarly humble pope, to excuse the whore who sold her away:

> Well, since she had to bear this brand—let me!
> The rather do I understand her now,—
> From my experience of what hate calls love,—
> Much love might be in what their love called hate. (874–77)

So too she reads the virtue in Caponsacchi, though he—trained for worldly expectations, and having priested it so far among the gentry—struggles honestly and abashedly to find the same. And, ironically, she knows that others will "know" better:

> So we are made, such difference in minds,
> Such difference too in eyes that see the minds!
> That man, you misinterpret and misprise—
> The glory of his nature, I had thought,
> Shot itself out in white light, blazed the truth
> Through every atom of his act with me:
> Yet where I point you, through the crystal shrine,
> Purity in quintessence, one dew-drop,
> You all descry a spider in the midst.

> One says, "The head of it is plain to see,"
> And one, "They are the feet by which I judge,"
> All say, "Those films were spun by nothing else." (7.918–29)

We judge by what we see, and unless we love deeply, we see ourselves. So will a cheat watch the fingers of everyone else at the card table.

What do the Romans make of the evidence? Most often, Browning shows, evidence is a motley thing, patched up with fads, half-heard news, clichés, smug assumptions about how all people must be, self-satisfaction, and, in the case of the professional Fisc and his hilariously slick-talking opponent Lord Hyacinth of the Archangels, the false alleys provided by a little learning and a heap of rhetorical trash. Pompilia, Caponsacchi, and the pope also have to weigh evidence; but humility opens their hearts to insight. Here is Pompilia, trying to express a joy in bearing a child who will never know his mother, but who will probably hear the lies:

> Who is it makes the soft gold hair turn black,
> And sets the tongue, might lie so long at rest,
> Trying to talk? Let us leave God alone!
> Why should I doubt He will explain in time
> What I feel now, but fail to find the words? (7.1756–61)

Her words profess incapacity—and speak to the heart. God, who unties the tongue of the infant, will reveal to Gaetano the truth. An innocent child will hear when all the world is deaf.

The pope hears and understands. We meet him in his chambers, pondering the mystery of evil, knowing he is not long for this world, and wondering what fruit of all his shepherding he will have to show in the end. The world regards him as powerful, but the world is wrong. Consider with what humility and love he regards Pompilia:

> Everywhere
> I see in the world the intellect of man,
> That sword, the energy his subtle spear,
> The knowledge which defends him like a shield—
> Everywhere; but they make not up, I think,
> The marvel of a soul like thine, earth's flower
> She holds up to the softened gaze of God!
> It was not given Pompilia to know much,
> Speak much, to write a book, to move mankind,

> Be memorized by who records my time.
> Yet if in purity and patience, if
> In faith held fast despite the plucking fiend,
> Safe like the signet-stone with the new name
> That saints are known by,— if in right returned
> For wrong, most pardon for worst injury,
> If there be any virtue, any praise,—
> Then will this woman-child have proved—who knows?—
> Just the one prize vouchsafed unworthy me. (10.1019–29)

No one sees what is really going on, says the pope; no one can read the narrative of the world from God's point of view. Yet he sees, humbly enough, that the finest harvest from his priesthood may be just this one poor soul, the illiterate Pompilia, a "woman-child," of whose virtue and sanctity Innocent considers himself unworthy. She never wrote a book, or even her own name. The papal historian will not remember her. But the Recording Angel will. Does that assertion strike the reader as credulous sentiment? Beware. The problem with skeptics and cynics is not only the faith they lose, but the faith they gain. It is what the pope identifies as Guido's telltale mark, "That he believes in just the vile of life" (10.511). On the night before his execution Guido can "see through," with what he thinks is ironical acuity, the façade of the pope's goodness:

> The Pope moreover, this old Innocent,
> Being so meek and mild and merciful,
> So fond o' the poor and so fatigued of earth,
> So . . . fifty thousand plagues in deepest hell! (11.55–58)

So the spokesman for "Half-Rome" can also "know" what a curly-haired young priest is all about, "Apollos turned Apollo" (2.794)! He'll not "prejudge the case" (680), he insists, yet so far does prejudge it that he pieces events out with his own sly imagination, picturing the contretemps between Pompilia and Caponsacchi, things that never happened at all: "Now he pressed close till his foot touched her gown, / His hand touched hers" (803–4).

If we must be blind, would it not be better to be dazzled by a piercing light? In this way Pompilia is blind, and therefore she sees—and it is actually there—the virtue of a man, Caponsacchi, who is yet to become the man she imagines. If she is blind to the faults of a less-than-chastely spent youth, it is because she is dazzled by the greater light. These are her dying words, spoken as if even now Caponsacchi were her saving knight, and not she his saving damsel:

> So, let him wait God's instant men call years;
> Meantime hold hard by truth and his great soul,
> Do out the duty! Through such souls alone
> God stooping shows sufficient of His light
> For us i' the dark to rise by. And I rise. (7.1841–45)

Criticism and Gossip

THE RING AND THE BOOK is a storm of irony, currents and crosscurrents of knowledge and ignorance, surefire plans foiled, certitudes that wither away, and impossibilities come to pass. To understand the irony we must adopt the stance of Socrates, who in humility, perhaps in mock humility, insisted that he was the only man in Athens who did not know anything. For irony, as we shall see, has to do with what people think they know, or what they think they can expect. All criticism that does not begin in the humility of wonder must end up as the one or the other half of Rome: when correct, correct by happenstance; pretending to analyze, yet studying nothing with that patience that invites us to learn from what is beyond us; mired in gossip, and often gossip with a clear incentive in money or prestige.

From gossip we learn nothing new. If Mrs. Jones flirts with the delivery-man, we may find it shameless; but we know nothing more from our self-pleasing gossip than that she has done what we would not (usually, let it be noted, because we happen not to be tempted that way). But of what it might be like to be Mrs. Jones, or the poor workman, nothing. Gossip preempts, then deadens, our half-hearted attempts to enter imaginatively into the life of another. If we could glimpse the world for a moment through something distantly like Mrs. Jones's eyes, our understanding of her action might be very different. We might then be ready to invite her to tea, or to lock her up. There is no logical reason to suppose that our imaginative entry into her world must make us think the better of her; the pope saw into Guido, and found the lizards of our lower nature. Consider how uncomfortable you would feel if your admirers could enter your thoughts for the twinkling of an eye.

But perhaps I have miscast the action. Most of us are not endowed with what Keats called "negative capability," the imaginative power whereby we empty ourselves and assume the minds and souls of others. If *we* are to work

7

our imaginations, we must love or hate. If we hate, we will, from our position of moral superiority, see our own vices smiling back at us, as Browning's Romans do, the vices we would possess if we were like the people we judge; but, thanks be to almighty God or to a sound education, we are not like them. He whom I imagine is no better than I am. So the Fisc, to win his case for Pompilia, will not concede that she had any love affair with the priest, nor that she committed adultery (unless the priest took his importunate way with her while she slept). Fine; but see how his "defense" patronizes her supposed weakness of character and turns her into a common flirt:

> And what is beauty's sure concomitant,
> Nay, intimate essential character,
> But melting wiles, deliciousest deceits,
> The whole redoubted armoury of love? (9.229–32)

No beauty that reflects the grandeur of God, this. The Fisc's vision is imaginative indeed, drearily so, and many "truths" of the petty and misleading variety can be derived from such a thing. We can happily note the small wickedness of others, and miss the darkness that is our own.

The truly educative act of imagination is spurred by love: that turn of the mind towards the fellow sufferer on his way to the grave. It may be tinged with pity; it need not be, and may be better if not. I turn towards him because he means something to me—he is as I am. Such an act of imagination begins in humility. I am no better than is he whom I imagine. I may be worse. In any case, I will be more apt to aspire to assume his virtues than to assign to him my vices. My understanding of him will thus be far subtler and far richer, far more fulfilling than if I were moved by hate. For virtue is to vice as manliness is to machismo, as womanliness is to effeminacy, as any full-blooded reality is to its caricature. In this vision, by an act of humble imagination, I recast my inner world in the image of someone else.

Unfortunately, much of what passes for criticism is little better than idle gossip. Its initial spur is often not honor for the work of genius at hand, but the desire to say something clever. That is not fertile ground for love; thus, neither for the imagination. Yet the result can be impressive in a perverse way. Milton's Satan, hating Eve, saw his own vices potentially in her, and thus could squat like a toad at her ear, imaginatively entering her and attempting to pollute her. Nor could Nietzsche have misunderstood the Bible so well had he not hated it so thoroughly.

With far less of fallen glory the same can be said of many a critic of Shake-speare, Chaucer, or Milton. Their words all but confess that they dislike the deepest beliefs these men either possessed or struggled vainly not to possess. Having delivered beauty, sex, love, sport, religion, education, youth, age, family life, and even the care of newborns to an obsession with politics, the modern critic sees his own political face everywhere. Lorenzo and Jessica in *The Merchant of Venice* sing their rallying love-hymn to the night; the critic sees a tiresome struggle for power. The traitor Macbeth is beheaded; the critic snickers and says that Malcolm will probably prove worse.

2

Emptying Ourselves of What We Think We Know

Is it possible to come to wrong conclusions on every important point? If our criticism were subject to random chance, we would be bound to get many things right. But the more intelligent we are, the more consistent our conclusions will be, and if we start from false principles, the more consistently wrong they will be. Take for example a young critic of medieval and Renaissance English poetry. Suppose that he is thoroughly conversant with the language of those old texts. Suppose also that he knows the history of England—and not just the wool trade or the tin mines or other now fashionable niches of economic history. Grant that he knows it well enough to place the poetry in its historic context, the better to understand what the words on the page mean. Grant him the rare knack for catching the well-turned phrase or the well-hewn line. Such a critic must still fail if he does not also understand what it might be like to believe in the Christianity which was the shared faith of Chaucer, Spenser, Donne, Shakespeare, Jonson, Herrick, Herbert, and Milton.

Can such an understanding be attained? If not, why read books? I am a great lover of the poet Lucretius, though he is a materialist and, for all practical purposes, an atheist, while I am not. When I read Lucretius, the skeptic, the satirist, and the scientist in me can relish his attack upon superstition. So could the ancient Christian polemicist Lactantius, who enjoyed the poetry and then used it as a sabre against paganism. But Lactantius could hardly have done so had he not entered into the spirit of Lucretius.

For the sake of understanding materialist poetry, then, I become provisionally and temporarily a materialist. As C. S. Lewis says, what the critic requires is not so often a suspension of disbelief as a suspension of *belief*. It is too easy to respond that such self-transformation is an illusion. Of course we cannot leave our minds behind. The point is that our minds possess myriads of possibilities, usually dormant, inactive, unrealized. Good reading sets them in motion. For the sake of Lucretius's great poetry I allow the materialist in me to take the stage and declaim. That Lucretius' voice is still bound up with my own does not matter. It could not be otherwise; nor do I require it. All I require is that humbling release of what I am and what I believe now, surrendering to what I might have been or to what I might have believed had I been more like Lucretius. I say with Alyosha Karamazov, who tries to understand his brother Ivan, "I want to suffer too" (*The Brothers Karamazov*, 287). I surrender in imaginative love.

Now there is a catch to this surrender. The farther you are from the faith of the author you are reading, the more readily you will acknowledge the need to surrender yourself, but the more difficult it will be. The closer you are to the author's faith, the easier the surrender would be, could you ever be prevailed upon to see the need. In the case of Christianity, it is as Chesterton puts it. You had better be in the faith completely or out of it completely. The worst position, if you want to understand it, is to be partly in and partly out, or to have a passing, culturally based familiarity with its surface. You are neither so familiar with it as to probe its depths, nor is it so strange that you are moved to approach it with care. You take the attitude of Petronius, or of "Tertium Quid." You've seen it all before.

Apply a two-dimensional Christianity to the mature allegories of Spenser and Milton, and at once you will discover discrepancies and incoherence. Why don't Spenser's Guyon and the Palmer kill the witch Acrasia? Are they still tempted by her Bower of Bliss? Why do the devils in hell discourse on philosophy? Has Milton rejected his classical education? Are faith and reason to part forever? Many such false dilemmas arise because the critic has failed to understand the subtleties of the Christian faith.

And Christianity is the subtlest of faiths, yet of a wondrous simplicity. "I thank thee," Jesus observes with biting irony, "O Father, Lord of heaven and earth, because thou hast hid these things from the wise and prudent, and hast revealed them unto babes" (Matt. 11:25). The kernel of the faith can be grasped by a child. We are sinners. The Lord who created us not to sin sent his obedient Son to die for us. That Son rose from the dead to sit at the right hand of the Father. We may join him in heaven if we have faith.

Christianity is the opposite of a mystery religion: the creed is short and openly professed. Yet its simple tenets belie unfathomable depth. "Matter is a form of energy." We all know this Einsteinian truth—a child could be taught it, and, to the limits of his capacity, really believe it. But what does it imply? What does it mean? "There are three persons in one God: Father, Son, and Holy Spirit." Again, a child could learn the formula, but what does the Trinity imply? The wise and prudent are struck dumb. A religious anthropologist may chatter about the symbolism of three, and how all cultures attach a mystical importance to it, and on and learnedly on. But to the clean of heart it may reveal the mystery of existence itself. So Dante implies in his invocation to God:

> O Light that dwell within Thyself alone,
>   who alone know Thyself, are known, and smile
>   with Love upon the Knowing and the Known! (*Paradise*, 33.124–26)

Merely to exist, to be a knowable object, is to have been made by the God of knowledge who knows and is known, whose being is love, and who has loved into being all things that have been, are, and are to come.

Pride is blinding; the moral problem becomes epistemological. Suppose we assume that the lanky fellow across the table is a dullard. When he remarks of someone else's immorality, "For them as likes that sort of thing, that is the sort of thing they likes," we will find our prejudice confirmed. The statement is tautological and evasive. But if we knew that the man was Lincoln, we might see the wry condemnation hiding beneath the hayseed humor. We will know, when he assumes the self-deprecatory air, not to take him at his word. When we later discover the same man condemning that behavior, we will know that it is not he who is inconsistent, but we who underestimated him.

Irony and Knowledge

WHAT DOES THIS HAVE to do with irony and faith? Much, if we consider what irony is.

Until fairly recently, most writers on irony have defined it as speech that means something other than (or opposite to) what is literally said. The problem with this definition is that it is at once too narrow, too broad, and beside the point. Liars mean other than what they say, but the lie is not in itself ironic; and you may, with irony, mean exactly what you say, but in a way that your audience (or perhaps a putative audience, more foolish than those who are actually listening to you) will not understand. The definition is beside the point, since moments of dramatic irony, or what some have called "irony of event," may not involve speech at all, but only strange turns of fate.

Contemporary literary theorists have attempted to distill the essence of irony, that which underlies both the winking assertions of ignorance made by Socrates, and concatenations of events that seem (but only seem) to suggest design, or that demolish any sense of design. Irony, they assert, is a universal solvent: no theology or epistemology can contain it. It dissolves—it "deconstructs"—every assertion of absolute truth.[1]

The trouble with this view of irony now prevalent in the academy is that it enshrines one sort of ironic statement or event and ignores the rest. Worse, the kind of irony it enshrines is destructive, and the first thing it destroys is irony. If there is no objective truth—if irony must undermine and destabilize—then, once we have noticed the fact, there is no more point for irony, just as it makes no sense for the skeptic to embark on a quest for knowledge, when there is no knowledge to be had. How, after all, does one then proceed, by irony, to undermine the "truth" that every truth can be undermined? If all speech is inherently slippery, why trouble oneself with the subtleties of irony? Why pour oil on a sheet of ice?

But in fact, irony commonly is used to exalt rather than undermine. It can stun us with wonder and raise our eyes to behold a truth we had missed. All kinds of unsuspected truths, particularly those combined in paradoxes, await our attention, but we are too dulled by habit to notice. Then irony—verbal or dramatic—awakes us. Consider:

1. A bystander watches as a professor, holding forth to his suffering companion on the epistemological subtleties of irony, steps dangerously near a banana peel.

---

1. For my money, the best and still most evenhanded discussion of irony per se is Wayne Booth's *A Rhetoric of Irony* (Chicago: Chicago University Press, 1974); I am indebted to his insight into the relationship between irony and knowledge.

2. In *King Lear*, Gloucester tries to refuse the help of his son Edgar, whom he cannot see and does not know: "I have no way and therefore want no eyes; / I stumbled when I saw." (4.1. 18–19)

3. In *II Henry IV* (and apparently in real life, too) the usurper King Henry, who had wanted to atone for his sin by fighting in the Crusades, removes to die in a room called "Jerusalem," noting that it had been foretold to him that he would die in Jerusalem. (4.5. 236–40)

4. St. Paul sings a hymn of Christ's Atonement:

> Let this mind be in you, which was also in Christ Jesus: Who, being in the form of God, thought it not robbery to equal with God: But made himself of no reputation, and took upon him the form of a servant, and was made in the likeness of men: And being found in fashion as a man, he humbled himself, and became obedient unto death, even the death of the cross. Wherefore God also hath highly exalted him, and given him a name which is above every name: That at the name of Jesus every knee should bow, of things in heaven, and things in earth, and things under the earth; And that every tongue should confess that Jesus Christ is Lord, to the glory of God the Father. (Phil. 2:5–11)

5. In Molière's comedy *Tartuffe*, the jealous husband Orgon squirms under the table where his wife Elmire has put him, listening as his protégé Tartuffe, the one man he is amazingly *not* suspicious of, attempts to seduce her. (4.5)

What do the cases have in common? The first verges upon slapstick; the second involves a lesson learned in an unusual way; the third hinges upon a play on words; the fourth is a theological reversal of expectations; the fifth is a piece of staged ignorance. Each involves a problem of knowing. The irony lies in a stark clash between what a character thinks he knows and what he really knows. This clash is staged to let the reader or the audience in on the secret. We are, then, not merely watching ignorance, but ignorance unaware of itself and about to learn better, or at least about to teach by way of its own incorrigibility. The irony reveals, with a kind of electric shock, order where randomness was expected, or complexity and subtlety where simplicity was expected.

Each case involves a staged clash of incompatible levels of knowledge:

1. The professor thinks he knows a lot about the subtlest things, but misses the humble and material banana at his feet. The bystander probably knows a great deal less about irony, but he does see the hazard and, if he possesses either a profound moral sensibility or none at all, will stand back to enjoy the tumble. The apparent intellectual hierarchy belies a richer order: the great intellect is not so wise. He "deserves" to slip, falling victim to the very thing, irony, about which he declaims so proudly. Had he known less about it, he might have looked to the sidewalk in time.

2. Only after Gloucester loses his eyes does he "see" how rashly and unjustly he has treated his son Edgar. The irony, a reversal of expectations accompanied by a deepening knowledge, is richly theological as well. For there is an order at work, bringing about Gloucester's sight through blindness, and his reconciliation with his son through suffering. The man before him is that wronged son, whom he has seen in disguise and taken for one Tom-a-Bedlam, the "poor, bare, forked animal" that "unaccommodated man" is (*King Lear*, 3.4. 105–106). Now it is the wronged Gloucester reduced to misery who requires assistance from Mad Tom. Gloucester does not yet understand what his "way" is, why he has been blinded and what he must suffer still. He says he has no way, yet his meeting with Edgar shows that a way has been designed for him nonetheless. He will walk towards a final, terrible resignation to his punishment and reconciliation with his son. And Edgar will be his eyes—his spiritual guide—along this way.

3. We "know" that Henry might have died in any room or might have died falling from a horse on a holiday hunt. He had hoped to die in the Holy Land, and when he learns the name of the room, he finally sees the design and resigns himself to its justice. For us, that death feels right—better than if he had died a-crusading, better than if he had been hanged at the Tower of London. The usurper should not be granted a martyr's death; better that he should be disappointed by his hope to expiate the crime. The place of his death reveals a more subtle order than either he or we had expected.

4. The chasm between human expectations and divine will has never been sung more powerfully. The prophet cries, "For my thoughts are not your thoughts, neither are your ways my ways, saith the Lord" (Isa., 55:8), but here Saint Paul fleshes out that cry with specifics that seem impossible to hold

simultaneously. If Christ is equal with God, why should he, or how can he, empty himself, making himself of no reputation? How can God become obedient to God, obedient unto the shameful death on a cross? How can submission exalt? For Christ is not exalted despite his humility, but in it and through it. For the believer, then, Paul's hymn reveals complexities in the notions of equality and hierarchy: because Christ was the Son of God, he set aside that equality, and in his obedience he is set above all things in heaven, on earth, and under the earth. He is equal to the Father *because* he obeys.

5. This brilliant stage business shows dramatic irony at its purest. Of this double-plot no one, not even the audience, can see everything. Elmire knows she is chaste, but as she leads Tartuffe on, to prove to her husband under the table what a fool he has been to trust the charlatan, she must worry lest her trick backfire and Tartuffe ravish her before Orgon manages to get out from under there. For she cannot see him, and cannot be sure that he will come to his senses even when he hears Tartuffe making love to her. Meanwhile Orgon can only fry in imagination: he hears but cannot see the couple, and must restrain his wrath and jealousy long enough to let Tartuffe hang himself for certain. The audience, too, can see Tartuffe and Elmire, and so they know what Orgon must learn; but they cannot see Orgon, and must guess, from his awkward and frantic movements under the table, what must be going through his mind. Finally, there is Tartuffe, master trickster, steeped in ignorance, believing himself so clever yet missing so obvious a trick—for I do not think Orgon can remain as still as a churchmouse!

It is, then, not the unexpectedness of a thing that produces irony—a violin flung at a man's head is unexpected, but not ironic—nor is it ignorance that produces irony—after all, if he saw the violin he would duck. Irony arises, rather, from the ignorance of unseen or unexpected order (or, as it may happen, disorder), from the failure to note subtleties, or from seeing subtleties that are not there, especially when the ignorance and the failure are highlighted before observers in a better position to see the truth. That is the sort of thing we feel as ironic. A violin flung at a man's head is not ironic. A man missing a sharp as he tries to hum the Kreutzer sonata is not ironic. The same man botching Beethoven as the violin sails his way—now that is ironic.

3

Christian Irony and the Image of the Invisible God

How, then, do the teachings of Christianity bring forth irony—as a high-lighted disjunction between planes of knowledge? I will focus on three wellsprings for irony in Christian literature: the providence that binds together the histories of men; the visionary strength of man when he responds to God with love; and the God who so loves man as to have created him, to reveal himself to him, to redeem him by taking on flesh, and to order his loves aright, giving him not only the command to love but the grace to fulfill it. I will call these, in subsequent chapters, the Ironies of Time, the Ironies of Power, and the Ironies of Love.

How Do the Gods Teach? Sophocles' *King Oedipus*

EVERY SOCIETY PORTRAYS ITS gods as knowing what men do not. They may hoard up their knowledge to punish the wicked, or to bring innocent men to destruction; or they may parcel it out, little by little, to teach men the hard lessons of humility and wisdom. A few examples from ancient Greece will il-lustrate the point.

One day on the road to Thebes a young man fell into a quarrel at a three-way intersection, and killed the man in the chariot who had struck him and tried to hustle him aside. As the play by Sophocles opens, this same passionate Oedipus, who freed the Thebans by solving the riddle of their nemesis the Sphinx, now plies his considerable power of mind and his almost unruly energy to solve a new riddle. Why are his beloved Thebans dying of the plague? Says he to the people who come crying out to him:

> I grieve for you, my children. Believe me, I know
> All that you desire of me, all that you suffer;
> And while you suffer, none suffers more than I.
> You have your several griefs, each for himself;
> But my heart bears the weight of my own, and yours
> And all my people's sorrows. I am not asleep.
> I weep; and walk through endless ways of thought.
>   But I have not been idle; one thing I have already done—
> The only thing that promised hope. My kinsman
> Creon, the son of Menoeceus, has been sent
> To the Pythian house of Apollo, to learn what act
> Or word of mine could help you. (27)

Let us pause to note the king's tragic virtue. Though Oedipus is a man from the ancient myths, Sophocles has him speak with the fervor of an Athenian of his own time, one for whom the city is an object of religious devotion. Were it not for Oedipus's intellectual acuity and restlessness, and his care for the people, the tragedy would not unfold; he would never learn that he himself was the cause of the plague. Nor should we wriggle out of the difficulty by attributing to Oedipus a haughty overvaluing of human knowledge, a refusal to submit to the wisdom of the gods. Here at least we learn that he has admitted being stumped, and has sent to the oracle of Apollo at Delphi to find out what he can.

When the messenger Creon returns with word that the plague is a punishment for the unavenged murder of the late King Laius, Oedipus determines to ferret out the murderer. We in the audience know—we are Greeks, and have heard the tale before—that Oedipus is himself the killer. Thus when he delivers his first proclamation to the people, we are aware, as we are throughout the play, of a web of irony, a trap that will close upon him and catch him by his own words:

> And it is my solemn prayer
> That the unknown murderer, and his accomplices,

If such there be, may wear the brand of shame
For their shameful act, unfriended, to their life's end.
Nor do I exempt myself from the imprecation;
If, with my knowledge, house or hearth of mine
Receive the guilty man, upon my head
Lie all the curses I have laid on others. (32)

We are aware, after the fact, of what the gods know and what Oedipus does not know; and we also know that, were we in Oedipus's place, we would know as little as he. Man is a marvel, says Sophocles, taming the waves and furrowing the land with wheat, tracking the paths of the stars and building his gleaming cities of marble; but eternal laws bind us, and the gods who know the future and seldom tell it will deal out their justice as they please, and not as we determine.

Sophocles' play is a tissue of ironies of knowledge and of the dreadful plotting of the unseen gods. Were it not for the equivocations of the oracle at Delphi (a notoriously anti-democratic oracle, hostile to Sophocles' Athens), there would have been no tragedy. The gods begin by playing with, meddling with, the incomplete knowledge of men. They seem to enlighten, yet bring darkness. For Laius and his wife Jocasta had learned from Delphi that the son she bore would kill his father and marry his mother. To avert this unspeakable wickedness, they committed wickedness of their own, laming the child (hence his name Oedipus, or "Swollenfoot") and instructing a trusted servant to expose him in the mountains nearby. Such exposure was thought of as returning the child to the gods—a perilous chance, it seems, when the gods are malign, leading you on to commit the deed for which they will crush you. For Oedipus did not die; he was taken up by a shepherd and brought to Corinth, where he was adopted into the home of Polybus and Merope, whom he took for his father and mother.

But people will talk. Young Oedipus, hearing it whispered that those good people were not his parents, went in person to Delphi—as always, impetuous to know. The oracle, however (as oracles will), did not exactly reply. Instead, the priestess informed Oedipus that he would kill his father and marry his mother. Horrified by the prospect of this sin, Oedipus leaves Corinth. If he is to be blamed for thinking he could avert the evil, he is also to be credited with wanting so much to avert it that he would sentence himself to exile. However we judge his flight, it is clear that the gods have put him in the way of the sin: had he been less pious, less desirous to know the truth, and less courageous,

21

he never would have left Corinth, and therefore never would have sinned. They have given him what he thinks is reliable knowledge, knowing that he would misinterpret it and believe he knew what he did not know. We in the audience know this, and watch the plot unfold, and know that the gods may do the same to us.

Many and subtle are the changes that Sophocles rings on the fundamental irony of Oedipus's situation: his accusing the blind seer Tiresias with conspiracy, when all along it is he who is blind; Jocasta's impious attempt to comfort him with the unreliability of oracles, telling him about how she and Laius averted a prophecy by doing what (as she has yet to learn) would fulfill it; how Oedipus rejects her womanish advice to leave bad enough alone, once she has seen what he does not yet see; how for his crime he puts out his eyes, the egg-like organs that refer symbolically to the testicles, his instruments for the great crime against nature—as he himself puts it, for sowing the field of his own mother. Yet it is one moment I wish to examine, early in the play. Tiresias, a prophet of Apollo, has been summoned. He knows what Oedipus does not know, but in his desire to spare him (no matter for the plague that devastates the city) he will not speak.

Oedipus, naturally enough, accuses Tiresias of hiding knowledge for his own sake:

> I tell you I believe you had a hand
> In plotting, and all but doing, this very act.
> If you had eyes to see with, I would have said
> Your hand, and yours alone, had done it all. (35)

To which the seer replies with the most devastating line in the play:

> You would so? Then hear this: upon your head
> Is the ban your lips have uttered—from this day forth
> Never to speak to me or any here.
> You are the cursed polluter of this land. (35)

"You are the man!" Oedipus will not believe it—why should he? What reasons has Tiresias alleged? The accusation only enrages the king, drawing from his lips the condemnations that will come thundering down upon him when the truth, the how and where and why of it, is finally revealed. We watch in amazement and comprehending horror as the ruler of Thebes does what we know we might do, denying what he cannot understand, in his ever greater stridency pressing against the truth he cannot help but suspect, the truth that cannot be but is. Indeed, Oedipus learns nothing from his contentious meeting with Tiresias, and is meant to learn nothing; the clue rather leads him to pursue false suppositions, as for instance that Tiresias has connived with Creon to steal the throne.

The man is being crushed by the gods.

The moral that the chorus draws from the terrible finale is one of resignation, even despair. The lofty will fall, not necessarily because they are proud (though they usually are), but because they are lofty. Best to keep to the unobtrusive middle; best to know when to duck. We live in relative ignorance, and do not even know, as Oedipus certainly did not, whether we shall escape this twilight life with something like happiness. Only the end makes us sure: and at that end we do not rejoice but breathe a sigh of relief:

> Sons and daughters of Thebes, behold: this was Oedipus,
> Greatest of men: he held the key to the deepest mysteries;
> Was envied by all his fellow-men for his great prosperity;
> Behold, what a full tide of misfortune swept over his head.
> Then learn that mortal man must always look to his ending,
> And none can be called happy until that day when he carries
> His happiness down to the grave in peace. (68)

The Instruction of David

Now compare the Oedipus story with this account from the Old Testament. David, King of Israel, is a married man; once, and not happily, to Michal, daughter of the late King Saul; then again to Abigail, a woman who had assisted him when he fled Saul's wrath. And there were at least two others. Then one evening David, rich in wives, "arose from off his bed, and walked upon the roof of the king's house: and from the roof he saw a woman washing herself; and the woman was very beautiful to look on" (2 Sam. 11:2).

The king learns that she is Bathsheba, wife of his loyal soldier, Uriah the Hittite. He sends for her, and lies with her, "for she was purified from her uncleanness" (11:4); that is to say, she was past the time of her menstrual period. The inspired author does not need to mention that neither she nor David is purified of the uncleanness of adultery; and the sly detail leads us to suspect that the good and clean time for a husband to have relations with his wife is not exactly the best time for David to have relations with Bathsheba. For "the woman conceived, and sent and told David, and said, I am with child" (2 Sam. 11:5).

Now David finds himself in difficulties. He schemes; he knows a secret, and thinks he can keep it hidden. Immediately he summons Uriah from the battlefield, asking him pertinent (but to David quite unimportant) questions about the war. Then he commands Uriah to go home and "wash his feet" (11:8), a euphemism for bathing the genitals, as prelude to more delightful battle with his wife. David even sends a rich meal down to Uriah's house, hoping that a full belly will set the man to it.

That should have been enough. David wants Uriah to lie with Bathsheba, that the child already conceived may be passed off as Uriah's own, given the vagaries of gestation and reckoning the calendar. But he does not reckon on Uriah's great loyalty: the soldier knows his duty, and will not go home: "The ark, and Israel, and Judah, abide in tents; and my lord Joab, and the servants of my lord, are encamped in the open fields; shall I then go into mine house, to eat and drink, and to lie with my wife? as thou livest, and as thy soul liveth, I will not do this thing" (11:11). The hearer of these words in the synagogue must consider the irony. Here we have David, who danced for joy as he brought the sacred ark of the covenant into Jerusalem—dancing with such abandon that his skirts rose up over his shame, as his dour wife Michal duly noted later, looking upon him from a window and despising him in her heart. But David has forgotten about that covenant. Uriah has not forgotten—and he is Uriah *the Hittite*, an alien, one who has chosen to worship the God of Israel and to fight as a soldier for Israel's king. He is to be loved as an Israelite, for they themselves "were strangers in the land of Egypt," says the Lord (Lev., 19:34); and this stranger is moreover one who, like David's own great-grandmother Ruth, has piously united himself with God and God's people.

David's hand is forced—so he thinks. He's given Uriah a decent chance; now there is nothing to do but shoulder the husband out of the way: "And it came to pass in the morning, that David wrote a letter to [his general] Joab, and sent it by the hand of Uriah. And he wrote in the letter, saying, Set ye Uriah in the foremost of the hottest battle, and retire ye from him, that he may be smitten, and die" (11:14–15). The letter, in politic fashion, leaves the means to Joab. That general—who made a virtue of placing political considerations above piety, even though he knew right from wrong—obeys. But obedience exacts a price, taking the lives of others besides Uriah: for Joab has had to engage in a "blunder" to expose him. Joab knows that David will understand.

Thus he instructs his messenger: "When thou hast made an end of telling the matters of the war unto the king, And if so be that the king's wrath arise, and he say unto thee, Wherefore approached ye so nigh unto the city when ye did fight? knew ye not that they would shoot from the wall? Who smote Abimelech the son of Jerubbesheth? did not a woman cast a piece of a millstone upon him from the wall, that he died in Thebez? why went ye nigh the wall? then say thou, Thy servant Uriah the Hittite is dead also" (19–21). Joab washes his hands of the blame. Yet he wants David to know that the action was shameful; so shameful, that one Abimelech must die by a woman's hand, all so that David's "servant"—fine word, "servant"—would never return alive.

By comparison with the gods of the Greek play, the God of Israel seems to have kept free of the scene. He does not meddle, nor use oracular chicanery to elicit the wickedness he will punish. David's sin has its birth in David's mind alone. But in another sense God is all the more intimately involved by his apparent absence. Uriah's reference to the ark reveals God's presence: that precious box, so humble that David thought it unworthy, was the dwelling place of the Lord among his people. How the Creator of all things seen and unseen could take up special habitation in a cedar chest, we are never told; not until, as Christians believe, that same Creator would take flesh of the Virgin and dwell within her womb, whereof the ark was but a type and a shadow. However it may be, the Lord is near, as David of all people ought to know. He and Joab know what the messenger does not, but the Lord knows all, and will bring it to light.

And here marks one critical difference between the classical irony of Sophocles and the ironies of the Jewish and the Christian faith. The Greek gods know many things that men do not; they do not know everything; they too submit to a mysterious Fate. One of the things they do not know, or do not care to know, is the human heart. But the Lord does know the heart, because there is the temple where the Lord wishes to dwell, pleased with the only sacrifice that means anything: the burnt offerings of love. So the Lord sends a messenger to David.

The king does not send for the prophet; the prophet comes to the king. Tiresias speaks in riddles almost perversely designed to enrage Oedipus and check his understanding; Nathan speaks in a parable designed to capture the heart of David before he is aware. We who are aware watch as the scene builds to its climactic irony:

> And the Lord sent Nathan unto David. And he came unto him, and said unto him,

There were two men in one city; the one rich, and the other poor.

The rich man had exceeding many flocks and herds:

But the poor man had nothing, save one little ewe lamb, which he had bought and nourished up: and it grew up together with him, and with his children; it did eat of his own meat, and drank of his own cup, and lay in his bosom, and was unto him as a daughter.

And there came a traveller unto the rich man, and he spared to take of his own flock and of his own herd, to dress for the wayfaring man that was come unto him; but took the poor man's lamb, and dressed it for the man that was come to him.

And David's anger was greatly kindled against the man; and he said to Nathan, As the Lord liveth, the man that hath done this thing shall surely die:

And he shall restore the lamb fourfold, because he did this thing, and because he had no pity.

And Nathan said to David, Thou art the man. (12:1–7)

"You are the man!" That accusation again—with a difference. The parable has summoned David's sympathies. He feels in his heart the betrayal of the poor man, what he did not feel in Uriah's case, as he shuffled and connived and ducked. The vision he is granted, by the mercy of God, and by God's justice which does not veer from his mercy, is meant to convict him, and, by convicting him, to redeem him. Nathan does deliver a terrible prophecy of punishment to come, duly levied upon David's offspring, in that David had violated the womb of another man's wife. War shall fall upon David's house, and the child conceived by Bathsheba shall die. What David did in secret, the Lord will ironically and appropriately enough do in the open, to David's shame, before all the people. But even as he hears the punishment David is struck to the heart, not urging excuse, but saying simply, "I have sinned against the Lord" (12:13).

That is the key moment, right there. For God works to bring David to life again; he is God of the living, not the dying. Nathan replies at once: "The Lord also hath put away thy sin; thou shalt not die" (12:13).

And David does penance, fasting, lying prostrate upon the earth, praying to no avail that the Lord will alter his punishment and let his child live. The half-understanding counselors see this and try to advise the king to be reasonable, but he, wiser than they, refuses. Then the child dies, and David lifts himself from the ground and bathes and changes his clothes, to the astonishment of those same counselors who still do not see. Why mourn now, says David?

What good will that do? The king's trust is once again like a child's. He has submitted to the Lord. And so far from believing that Bathsheba is unclean territory, he understands not only his sin but the Lord's forgiveness. After night comes the morning: "And David comforted Bathsheba his wife, and went in unto her, and lay with her; and she bare a son, and he called his name Solomon: and the Lord loved him" (12:25).

How strange that the son of the adulterers should become the next and most glorious king of Israel! But he is the son not of the adultery, but of the repentance and the forgiveness. He is the son of the new knowledge, not simply that mankind is nothing before the gods, but that man who is nothing before God is, by the grace of God, "a little lower than the angels" (Ps. 8:5), crowned with glory and honor. Nathan ratifies the event, for David sends for that good prophet, who looks upon the baby and "called his name Jedidiah [beloved of the Lord]" (2 Sam. 12:25).

That story of David and Bathsheba reveals the workings of a God whose ways are not our ways, whose thoughts are not our thoughts, but who made us to walk in his ways, and to be fulfilled in the intellectual vision of his glory. If it is not irreverent to say so, he is a God who swindles man into his restoration. He dupes man into truth. He becomes flesh, to raise man to himself.

Revelation Opens the Field of Play

WE SEE THAT IN the biblical account of David's sin and in Sophocles' play of Oedipus, the ironies result from a dramatic severance between what God or the gods know and what man knows. The sinner makes much of his cunning (David) or intellect (Oedipus), only to find with a shock that he has already been found out, and that not only does he know less than he thought he did, but the truth is other than what he had suspected. In both cases the sinner comes to a humiliating (for Oedipus, also horrifying) knowledge of who he is, and how small he is before the divine. In both, the punishment will extend into future generations: Israel will be divided into two kingdoms, reflecting the division foretold for David's family. Thebes will fall to civil war when each of the incest-born sons of Oedipus attempts to oust the other.

Yet Oedipus is the archetypal tragic hero, while David is celebrated as a great king. David's sins and unhappy old age could never, for the Jewish people and their prophets, efface his glory as Israel's greatest ruler and the progenitor of the Messiah. Why the divergence? One reason is that the irony instructs David in a way it cannot instruct Oedipus. The sinner gains knowledge of himself, true. But he also gains knowledge of God, and of God not as an external and mystifying will, but as a person, a Being to whom one can pray, before whom one can dance. He is a God who reveals himself because he wishes to be known.

So for Jews and Christians there is an added dimension to the irony of incomplete knowledge, a liberating depth, where otherwise all would have been flat confinement. A single act of love from the heart of the Almighty explodes the tense yet static confrontation between the classical heroes and the gods. For no matter how heroic or pious the man was, he could never know more about the gods than was already given him to know: they were immortal, powerful, beautiful, ruthless. Greek philosophy serves rather to highlight what man cannot know for certain about the gods than what he can know or even suppose with a fair probability. The alley is blind.

By the time of the Roman poet Lucretius (ca. 60 B.C.), many looked to be liberated by admitting defeat. Everyone supposes that the gods exist, says Lucretius, so it is reasonable to concede that minor point. But we cannot know anything else about them. They can neither touch nor be touched:

> For by necessity the gods above
> Enjoy eternity in highest peace,
> Withdrawn and far removed from our affairs.
> Free of all trouble, free of all care, the gods
> Thrive in their own works and need nothing from us,
> Not won with virtuous deeds nor touched by prayers.
> (*On the Nature of Things*, 1.44–49)

Even the gods bow to the necessity of their limitation, their utter removal from our world. Then we might as well spend our brief lives seeking a few modest pleasures of the body, and the sweeter pleasures of the mind. These latter, of course, will be severely restricted in scope, since we can know nothing of the divine. We bide our time in the antechamber of death, persuading ourselves that we do not care:

> Death, then, is nothing to us, no concern,
> Once we grant that the soul will also die. (3.827–28)

How to wait while the slow stroke falls, that is the object of the true philosopher. A benignant calm is all we can ever know, all it will ever profit us to know.

So the terrible irony is that man, whose mind can search the stars, "raiding the fields of the unmeasured All," as Lucretius says in overpraise of his master Epicurus (1.74), is the single being in creation whose faculties are quite in vain. It is as if a malign fate had ordered it so. We long to seize the fulfillment of our intellects, finite though we are, but because we are finite yet can apprehend the infinite, we neither can nor will. That, say the grim sages, ought to teach us a lesson.

But what if the One we wish to know knows us and wishes to be known by us? That is no idle fancy but the startling claim that Judaism and Christianity make: it is an assertion of a fact. Such a God either exists or he does not. There is no third possibility. And if he does exist? Suddenly and with a fearful abandon he may free us from our resigning and comfortable limitations. He may knock loose the iron fetters forged by what we think we know and what we think we cannot know.

4

The Meek Do Inherit the Earth

To whom should God reveal himself? To the learned, we expect: to theologians, lawyers, politicians, and quacks. But such people are often tight-
fisted with their precious knowledge, so miserly that they shut themselves off
from knowledge that would come to them purely as a gift. It is fitting, then,
bespeaking a wisdom and order that we the inattentive had not expected, that
a God who in his mercy and love of the smallest buds of life created lilies and
sparrows and mustard seeds (and who saw, unlike thunderous Jove, that they
were good), would approach first the unconsidered trifles of the world, the
nobodies, the fools.

Jesus lifts his heart in jubilation to think of it, this wisdom granted unto
babes (Matt. 11:25–26). He consummates the whole pattern of God's dramatic
self-revelation in scripture and in the history of the Hebrews. For God confused the cosmopolitan builders of Babel, but allowed the mysterious and
solitary Enoch to walk with him (Gen. 5:24; 11:1–9). God allowed the proud
hearts of Jacob's elder sons to be hardened, but to Joseph he granted dreams
and interpretations of dreams. He ignores the sycophantic "prophets" who
hang upon the courts of the last kings of Judah, no doubt reading the latest wire-releases and plying their imaginations to tell the kings they have a
lock on God's favor, as they possess God's capital, Jerusalem, and God's holy

temple. But he reveals himself to Jeremiah, who foretells destruction and captivity and is flung down a cistern for his pains (Jer. 26–28). God appears not to the sophisticated he-woman Jezebel, but to Elijah and Elisha, ruffians from the outback; not to that self-styled god and guarantor of good harvests, Lord Pharaoh of the Nile (who is apparently too weak to fight gnats, locusts, hail, frogs, boils, plague, and the silent shadow of death), but to Moses, an exiled homicide and stutterer.

Christians believe that this pattern continues. God wills it, to give us a clue as to who he is. So Anthony of Egypt wanders into church and hears the gospel of the rich young man who would not sell all he had to follow Jesus. Anthony, young and impetuous and large-hearted, learns the lesson well. He sells all he has and strides alone into the desert to fast and pray. There, through no plan of his own, he inspires the eremitical movement in the East: and thousands of people journey into the deserts of Egypt and Syria and Anatolia to see holy men like Anthony and to learn what God had revealed to them. Theologians sometimes express a sour amazement for the lowliness of such people: a Bernadette at Lourdes, the unlettered half-breed Juan Diego, the failed student John Vianney, the spoiled bourgeois girl Thérèse of Lisieux, the teetotaling ballplayer Billy Sunday. What bad taste God has! But "God hath chosen the foolish things of the world to confound the wise; and God hath chosen the weak things of the world to confound the things which are mighty; And base things of the world, and things which are despised, hath God chosen, yea, and things which are not, to bring to nought things that are" (1 Cor. 1:27–28).

About Some Gods It Is Better Not to Know

SOMEONE MAY OBJECT THAT the Greek gods did reveal themselves to men: witness the divinities dinning sword and shield around the ringing walls of Troy. But it is one thing for a god to appear in human form (often for the god's own devious or selfish purposes, as for instance to seduce a fair maid). It is another for the god to reveal his nature as god. What is missing from the Greek accounts of such revelation is any desire on the part of the gods that a man be brought into the life of the god *as* god. The gods do play favorites, may even apotheosize a Hercules here or a Perseus there, raising them to the stars. But they do not love.

Watch out when a god reveals himself. Paradigmatic is the sly Dionysus. When King Pentheus of Athens denounces him as an alien (that is, a suspicious eastern invasion of irrationality), effeminate, drunken, and destructive, the god shows up to take his revenge. He appears in the guise of a handsome boy and allows himself to be found out. Pentheus thinks he's got him cornered, but as surely as ivy creeps round a post, so does Dionysus entangle Pentheus in a plot of vicious irony and poetic injustice. Since Pentheus had scoffed at the mad females of the city, including his own mother, raving through the forests in a Bacchanalian narcosis, Dionysus turns the poor young swaggerer inside-out, revealing the king's own timidity and suppressed effeminacy. He drives Pentheus mad, dresses him in female garb, and lashes him into the woods as one of his own orgiastic worshipers. There the other Dionysian frenetics, that horde of madwomen, are tricked by the god into mistaking Pentheus for a deer. They dismember him. His mother Agape—yes, that is her name!—bears the head aloft, not yet knowing it is her son's (Euripides, *The Bacchae*).

Hardly less cruel is the most celebrated "revealer" among the Greek gods, the farshooting doubletalker Apollo. As he did to Oedipus, he will riddle you to your destruction if he pleases, and will rack the laurel-toking priestess with epileptic spasms to do it:

> Here, as the men approached the entrance way,
> The Sibyl cried out: "Now is the time to ask
> Your destinies!"
>
> And then: "The god! Look there!
> The god!"
> And as she spoke neither her face
> Nor hue went untransformed, nor did her hair
> Stay neatly bound: her breast heaved, her wild heart
> Grew large with passion. (Virgil, *Aeneid*, 6.70–80)

The contrast with scripture is stunning. One day an old man, a shepherd living in the fruitful land of the Chaldees, a nobody, hears a voice. We are told nothing—and it is a remarkable omission—about the manner of the voice. No vision accompanies it, no thunderbolt, no dragon. Apparently the voice does not convulse the man. It says, matter-of-factly, "Get thee out of thy country, and from thy kindred, and from thy father's house, unto a land that I will shew thee" (Gen. 12:1). Leave everything and everyone you know and love, it says, and promises the reward of a great nation to spring from the old man's progeny. Now an expert in the malice of the gods might have a few things to say about this summons. He might know the right sacrifice to lift the curse about to fall upon Nobody's head.

Happily, Nobody is Nobody, not a demonologist. So he believes and acts. And God will reveal to Abram one simple and profound truth about himself: that he is a giver of gifts, even the gift of a new name and identity, as he raises Abram to *Abraham*, "father of a great multitude" (Gen. 17:5).

We will learn that the gifts are good gifts, because this is a God who loves. Do the Greek gods give gifts? Indeed they do. Consider the legend of Cleobis and Biton, recounted by Herodotus.

It was the day of the city festival, but all the horses on the farm were in the fields. The grand lady of the house wanted to attend in style; it would be a shame for her to walk the five miles to town, and missing the feast was too great a disappointment. So her sons Cleobis and Biton told their mother to climb into the chariot. Then they hitched themselves up like draft horses, conveying their mother into town in a magnificent display of youthful strength and filial piety. They were celebrated by all the townspeople, who congratulated their mother for having raised such splendid sons.

That evening, filled with elation and gratitude, the mother besought the gods to give her deserving sons the greatest gift they had to offer man. The gods answered her prayer, and the next morning Cleobis and Biton were found dead in their sleep. Never would their limbs grow slack and their manly voices feeble and shrill. They died at the peak of their lives, having won a renown that could never be undone by misfortune or by sliding into wickedness. Some unknown sculptor has fashioned their youthful forms in marble, broad-shouldered, nude, captured forever in one fleeting moment of honor.

Perhaps we feel no more than a shadow of sympathy for the overweening mother. She loved her sons, but she also loved her glory, and the answer to her prayers ironically punished her in a cruelly appropriate way. But examine again the deep and desperate irony. The mother assumed that the gods have good things to give. She was right, they do. But the best thing they have to give is what we least want, and what they themselves hate: "For Death is the one immortal who can never be moved, and therefore he is most hated of gods and men" (*Iliad*, 9.158–59). Nor do we reject this gift of Death because we are sinners. We reject it because we are men, longing to live and to see and to know.

No such reversal awaits Abraham: God's gifts are genuinely good. But God is no straightforward fulfiller of what we think are our desires. No being who truly loves would substitute what we think we want for what we really want.

God visits Abraham in the persons of three heralds (representing, say the church fathers, the three persons of the Trinity). Abraham treats them with great courtesy, inviting them to sit and eat. While he waits upon them—with his wife Sarah in the nearby hut, busily preparing the lamb—they announce that one year later his wife will have borne him a son (Gen. 18:1–15).

Scripture tells us that Abraham and Sarah were about a hundred years old. That Abraham could have begotten a son was exceedingly doubtful; that Sarah could not have conceived one was certain. She must best have known that. So Sarah did the appropriate thing. She thought about the absurdity of doing that old prerequisite for producing a son: "After I am waxed old shall I have pleasure, my lord being old also?" (18:12). She laughed.

We shouldn't blame her. Abraham himself has already received the same word from the Lord, at which he too laughs (after falling upon his face; God does not mind the occasional lightheartedness in worship [17:17]). And he does more. He dickers with the Lord, urging him, wistfully, to accept as the bringer of the promised nation Ishmael, his son by the concubine Hagar: "O that Ishmael might live before thee!" (17:18). It is almost as if Abraham credited God with good intentions, but was willing to accept instead a son ready-begotten. His response is like that of the good-hearted old Shunammite woman, who centuries later would assist the prophet Elisha with food and drink. When, in return for her generosity, Elisha prophesies that one year later she and her husband will embrace a son, she replies, "Nay, my lord, thou man of God, do not lie unto thine handmaid" (2 Kgs. 4:16).

She and Abraham must be the patrons of all of us who judge by our own limited means and limited love, and would be content with God if he would but put forth a decent showing. But God loves better than we can imagine. He is as outlandish in his insistence that Sarah shall bear a son as he was in urging old Nobody to leave his kin and home in the first place. He will bless Ishmael, in answer to Abraham's prayer, but his covenant he will establish with Isaac (Gen. 17:20), a sign whereof shall be the circumcision of every male in Abraham's household. The symbolism is clear: even in the ordinary way of men before they are ninety years old, it is not they who do the begetting, but God. He is the one who makes us to increase and multiply.

And when Abraham's son is born, the gentle irony of this chapter receives its crowning moment. They call him Isaac, from the Hebrew verb *to laugh*. He is a child through whom laughter shall come to others: "And Sarah said, God hath made me to laugh, so that all that hear me shall laugh with me" (21:6).

"She Has Loved Much"

I WILL SOON TOUCH upon the scene that looms over Sarah's laughter, that mysterious incident on the slopes of Mount Moriah. In the meantime let us note that if God is a God of love—or, in Saint John's revolutionary claim, if "God is love" (1 John 4:8)—then those who do not know that God is love dwell in a troubling night. And those who separate themselves from love, hardening their hearts as they grasp for power or wealth or fame, must separate themselves from the ground of their being. To fail to love is to destroy oneself.

The world has been deeply ambivalent about love, as to what it is, and whether and under what conditions it is good. The Buddha severed the passion of love from a distanced benevolence. Indeed, he preached, since there is nothing of everlasting good in this life, it is folly to love anything so as to desire to possess it forever. Stoicisms of all kinds are suspicious of love, considering it an unmanly illusion. For Lucretius the clear-sighted Epicurean, love is madness, belied by the materially unattainable desire to immerse oneself wholly in the body of the other:

> As a thirsty man will dream of drinking, but
> No water is there to quench his parching body—
> He strives for the shadow of water and struggles for nothing,
> Gulping the rush of the river and yet still thirsty,
> So lovers are fooled by Venus and her shadows,
> Never having their fill of seeing the nude beside them
> Nor able to glean the sleekness from its limbs,
> Their vague hands roaming wildly over the body.
> (*On the Nature of Things*, 4.1088–95)

The Epicurean from outside the illusion can see the irony that the lover cannot. In such love, he says, we thirst for mere phantasms, specters. We think we have what we still cannot grasp: the vague hands roam and gain nothing.

Cicero, who detested Epicureans for encouraging men to withdraw from the trouble of state affairs, agreed with them on the worthlessness of sexual passion. In the soaring dialogues *Phaedrus* and the *Symposium*, Plato's Socrates, while exalting man's love for the True, the Good, and the Beautiful, and arguing for a distant relationship between such love and the love of man and woman that comes to fruition in marriage, still associates love with a kind of weakness, a deficiency, albeit a deficiency that spurs us on to seek what transcends us:

> Now Contrivance was drunk with nectar . . . and went out into the gar-
> den of Zeus, and was overcome by sleep. So Poverty, thinking to alleviate
> her wretched condition by bearing a child on Contrivance, lay with him
> and conceived Love. Since Love was begotten on Aphrodite's birthday,
> and since he has also an innate passion for the beautiful, and so for the
> beauty of Aphrodite herself, he became her follower and servant. Again,
> having Contrivance for his father and Poverty for his mother, he bears the
> following character. He is always poor, and, far from being sensitive and
> beautiful, as most people imagine, he is hard and weather-beaten, shoeless
> and homeless, always sleeping out for want of a bed, on the ground, on
> doorsteps, and in the street. (*Symposium*, 203 b–d)

Note that if Love is, on one side anyhow, born of Poverty, then it makes no
sense to say that God can love, since by his very being God can need nothing.
God may be the object of our loving contemplation, but when it comes to
his loving us, that is no more to be expected from Plato's God than from the
shadowy gods of the Epicureans, who dwell in perpetual aloofness, or from
the "One" of the Neoplatonist Plotinus, eternally brimming forth in Being,
but impersonal and bound by the necessity of its superabundance. Against
such worldly wisdom it seems absurd, even blasphemous, to say with Jesus that
"God so loved the world, that he gave his only begotten Son, that whosoever
believeth in him should not perish, but have everlasting life" (John 3:16).

In fact, a world made by a God who loves—God, who needs nothing, yet
desires, and without suffering wills that man, his creature, be one with him, for
"you arouse him to take joy in praising you, for you have made us for yourself,
and our heart is restless until it rests in you" (Augustine, *Confessions*, 1.1)—is
an infinitely more perilous and interesting world than that imagined even by
Plato. Dramatic things happen in it, prompted by God himself—things that
need not have happened at all. The world is not the necessitated overflow of
Being from the One; it is not the complex but finally static interplay of the
forces of Strife and Love, as Empedocles taught, with Strife tending to pull
everything apart into chaos, and Love tending to merge them all back together
into chaos; it is not even the fated stage, as the Stoic Epictetus says, for the
drama of men's actions, as conforming or not conforming to some universal,
providential, but wholly impersonal plan. It is, the Christians say, an act of
God's love, as all of history is the drama of man's response to that love.

Now the Stoic vision of the world does lend itself to irony, of that classical disillusioning sort. The rich and powerful man walks through life brazen,

self-assured, unaware of the net waiting to catch him. But the net has always been there. It is a feature of the universe, part of the play, if it makes sense to attribute authorial choices to a mind bound by necessity. But suppose the net is placed by loving intent. Suppose what the proud man feels as a snare is an invitation to be taken up, caught in love; and suppose that what he and the world see as a fall is his first painful lurch towards exaltation and freedom?

Imagine then this scene. The teacher is sitting at table with a very important man, and a holy one, too, one of the leaders in the religious community. He has invited the teacher to his house for a few ambiguous reasons. He is drawn to the teacher; not all of his fellow leaders have bothered to extend such an invitation. More to the purpose, the teacher loves *him*, as we shall see. He wants to sift the teacher, to see whether he can glean any new and brilliant exposition of scripture (for some men are afficionados of worship just as others are of brothels or the combats of gladiators). Perhaps even more to be desired, he may catch the teacher in a tic of blasphemy that will allow him to assume the pleasant role of Wise Protector of the People. It is no ordinary invitation to dinner.

Into the house comes a long-haired woman, the trash of the town. Simon the Pharisee is stunned into embarrassment, and probably a shiver of self-satisfaction, as he sees the woman break open a jar of costly perfume, anoint the teacher's feet, wash them with her tears, and dry them with her hair.

Simon believes he understands the scene before him perfectly. He sees and relishes the irony: "Now when the Pharisee which had bidden him saw it, he spake within himself, saying, This man, if he were a prophet, would have known who and what manner of woman this is that toucheth him: for she is a sinner" (Luke 7:39). Simon simply interprets by what he sees, and what he mainly sees is that the teacher does not see.

But the irony is that Simon's sight depends upon Simon's desire to see — that is, upon his love. Since he does not truly love the teacher, and since he bears nothing but contempt for the woman, he is in a bad position for understanding what is going on in front of him. He thinks the scene reveals who this teacher is not, when actually it reveals who he *is*. And the revelation comes in a way that Simon could not have expected. It also reveals who Simon is, at least as yet: a small man important in his own mind, but a very fool.

The teacher reads Simon's thoughts. As often, he uses a parable to defuse the interlocutor's automatic responses, so that the man's own words will show him the truth, like it or not:

And Jesus answering said unto him, Simon, I have somewhat to say unto thee. And he saith, Master, say on.

There was a certain creditor which had two debtors: the one owed five hundred pence, and the other fifty.

And when they had nothing to pay, he frankly forgave them both. Tell me therefore, which of them will love him most? (Luke 7:40–42)

Until this point Simon thinks he is in control. The teacher's story calls for an obvious answer, and Simon gives it: "I suppose that he, to whom he forgave most" (7:43). But the teacher now calls upon Simon to open his eyes and see things as they are. All Simon knows about the woman is that she is a sinner; the teacher shows him more. All Simon knows about himself is that he is a righteous man; the teacher shows him more. All that anyone at table knows about Jesus is that he is an interesting, possibly dangerous, itinerant rabbi. Jesus' actions show that he claims to be far more:

And he turned to the woman, and said unto Simon, Seest thou this woman? I entered into thine house, thou gavest me no water for my feet: but she hath washed my feet with tears, and wiped them with the hairs of her head.

Thou gavest me no kiss: but this woman since the time I came in hath not ceased to kiss my feet.

My head with oil thou didst not anoint: but this woman hath anointed my feet with ointment.

Wherefore I say unto thee, Her sins, which are many, are forgiven; for she loved much: but to whom little is forgiven, the same loveth little.

And he said unto her, Thy sins are forgiven.

And they that sat at meat with him began to say within themselves, Who is this that forgiveth sins also? (7:44–49)

We are not told of Simon's response. His friends run for the shelter of religious truism. This man, they think (and they think that their thoughts cannot be read, but it is clear that Jesus says what he says precisely because he does read their thoughts), claims to forgive sins. But only God can forgive sins. Therefore this man is a blasphemer. Naturally, their reasoning presumes that Jesus is not divine. If instead they had said, "This man claims to forgive sins; but only God can forgive sins; therefore this man claims to be one with God," the reasoning would have been correct, and the next step would have been to determine whether the astonishing claim were true. But the woman, whose thoughts we know by her actions, sees what they do not see. They think they know her, but she knows Jesus, whom they do not know. Her outpouring of love wins for her the grace of vision: "And he said to the woman, Thy faith hath saved thee; go in peace" (50).

For whose benefit has the drama been played, if not for Simon's and that of his poor important friends, who cannot see how many sins of their own must be forgiven? They are debtors too, after all. They, the powerful, think they have been forgiven little, or maybe even think that in their relationship with God they stand rather on the side of creditor! Therefore they love little. Therefore they do not see. Worse, in their persistent claim to see, they are truly blind: "If ye were blind, ye should have no sin: but now ye say, We see; therefore your sin remaineth" (John 9:41).

"Dost Thou Love Me?"

LOVE IS STRONGER THAN all the powers of the world. It is hard to remember, after our familiarity with Christianity, how startling an assertion that is. But love is essential to man as a being made for God, and, in God, for his fellow man. So true is this that even what look like feats of wondrous faith—impressive churchliness, we might say—are nothing at all without love: "And though I have the gift of wondrous prophecy, and understand all mysteries, and all knowledge; and though I have all faith, so that I could remove mountains, and have not charity, I am nothing" (1 Cor. 13:2).

Consider another scene. Jesus has been speaking to the Jews about a manna come down from heaven, bringing life everlasting: "I am the bread of life: he that cometh to me shall never hunger, and he that believeth on me shall never thirst" (John 6:35). But the Jews say to themselves (again we witness man's small-hearted refusal to see) that they know better. They interpret Jesus' words not literally (for surely they are familiar with figures of speech) so much as contemptuously: "Is not this Jesus, the son of Joseph, whose father and mother we know? how is it then that he saith, I came down from heaven?" (6:42).

Jesus gives them no quarter. He does not say, "I was using a metaphor," as indeed he was not, but goes on to assert that the bread "is my flesh, which I will give for the life of the world" (6:51). When the Jews again snort—insisting upon a literal interpretation for its absurdity, so that they can dismiss Jesus and his claims—Jesus goes them one better, asserting that "except ye eat the flesh of the Son of man, and drink his blood, ye have no life in you" (6:53).

At this point it is not Jesus' enemies alone who leave, but many of his disciples, muttering, "This is a hard saying: who can hear it?" (6:60). When finally Jesus turns to the twelve, his chosen apostles, he asks them whether they will leave, too. Peter replies. Note that by his own light Peter understands no more of what Jesus has said than does anyone else. He too must feel mystified and disappointed. But he does know one thing: he loves. Beyond all rational argument, he knows that he wants to stand beside the teacher: "Then Simon Peter answered him, Lord, to whom shall we go? thou hast the words of everlasting life" (6:68).

Peter's life is a history of love, of wanting to be beside Jesus. We are told that John was the disciple whom Jesus in his humanity loved most, but it was Peter, not John, who said atop the mount of Transfiguration, "Master, it is good for us to be here: and let us make three tabernacles; one for thee, and one for Moses, and one for Elias" (Mk., 9:5), wanting to pitch some tents so that the prophets of old could tarry with them awhile. It was Peter, not John, who so loved Jesus that at first he did not want to sully him with his presence: "Depart from me; for I am a sinful man, O Lord" (Luke 5:8). It was Peter, not John, who tried to walk on the water to be near Jesus in the storm (Matt. 14:24–31). It was Peter, not the younger and fleeter John, who was first to enter the tomb on Easter morning (John 20:3–6). And after the Resurrection, to soothe the pain of Peter's having denied that he knew him—a caustic and salutary penance, this—Jesus asks Peter three times, once for each denial, "Simon, son of Jonas, lovest thou me more than these?" When Peter replies that he does, Jesus assigns to him again the loving care for his brothers: "Feed my lambs" (21:15).

Note that in choosing the chief of the apostles, Jesus does not ask Peter whether he is courageous and self-denying. That is what a good Stoic would take pride in. Nor does he ask whether Peter is fully conversant with scripture. That is what a good rabbi would take pride in. Nor does he ask whether Peter has attended the lectures of the wisest men and read the works of Plato and Aristotle. That is what a Greek would take pride in. Jesus rather wants to confirm Peter in love. It is this love that will confer upon Peter both knowledge and more strength of character than any Stoic could boast, not through Peter's grim determination but through the gladsome ministrations of the Holy Spirit.

But this passage in John's gospel, taking as given what the early church knew about Peter's leadership after the Resurrection, focuses on Peter's crucifixion in Rome, a slave's death that conformed him to the One he loved, who set him free. For when Peter, sad and exasperated, says for the third time, "Lord, thou knowest all things; thou knowest that I love thee" (21:17), Jesus replies by predicting what would look to the world like weakness and shameful defeat:

> When thou wast young, thou girdedst thyself, and walkedst whither thou wouldest: but when thou shalt be old, thou shalt stretch forth thy hands, and another shall gird thee, and carry thee whither thou wouldest not.
> This spake he, signifying by what death he should glorify God.
> (21:18–19)

It is well here to touch upon that death—it is the climactic event of Sienkiewicz's *Quo Vadis?* (The Latin title means, Where are you going?) Legend had it that Peter was advised by his friends to leave Rome before Nero could lay hands upon him. They were thinking practically: the chief of the apostles must not lose his life. They needed him. Those friends loved Peter, and genuinely strove to build the church. But God's love is dangerous and brings to bear upon man's life a power from which he yearns to hide. On his way out of the city, along the Appian Way, Peter sees a vision, a figure emerging from the gleam of the sun. His disciple Nazarius does not see it; but Peter falls to the ground in adoration. The following scene is a small masterpiece of irony, as Peter is confirmed in love:

> He fell with his face to the earth, as if kissing some one's feet.
> The silence continued long; then were heard the words of the aged man, broken by sobs—"Quo vadis, Domine?"
> Nazarius did not hear the answer; but to Peter's ears came a sad and sweet voice, which said,—"If thou desert my people, I am going to Rome to be crucified a second time."
> The Apostle lay on the ground, his face in the dust, without motion or speech. It seemed to Nazarius that he had fainted or was dead; but he rose at last, seized the staff with trembling hands, and turned without a word toward the seven hills of the city.
> The boy, seeing this, repeated as an echo,—"Quo vadis, Domine?"
> "To Rome," said the Apostle, in a low voice.
> And he returned. (402)

Sienkiewicz understands and presents with keen insight the irony of the event that follows. Rome is about to be stormed and taken by force: its gates will not prevail. No one sees it. Not the debauched Nero, with reason afraid of his sycophants. Not the weary libertine Petronius, who will die by his own hand, witty and sad to the end. Not the soldiers who wait their chance to send the effeminate and cruel emperor to his deserved apotheosis—who would make a god of him with all speed, that they might set up a puppet more to their liking! But the Christians are even now conquering. Tertullian would say, two hundred years later, that the blood of the martyrs is the seed of the church. And that same Peter who sheds his last blood in an act of communion with the teacher he once denied but never ceased to love, that same Peter, we Christians say, will be the savior of Rome herself. As a stranger he did not merit beheading within the city walls; but on his tomb will be built the great basilica, as upon the ruins of Rome will be built a new center of Christendom. Who remembers Ctesiphon or Susa or Ecbatana, the capitals of once great empires? Carthage is a desert plain sowed with salt. Memphis is a vast sand-rippled tomb. Rome remains; but it was the "criminal" Peter, true to the last to his love for the master, who saved her. A Christian of any persuasion can relish the irony of a redemption that no one but an old Jewish fisherman, about to be executed, could see:

> The Apostle, with his head in the sun-rays and golden light, turned for the last time towards the city. At a distance lower down was seen the gleaming Tiber; beyond was the Campus Martius; higher up, the Mauso-leum of Augustus; below that, the gigantic baths just begun by Nero; still lower, Pompey's theatre; and beyond them were visible in places, and in places hidden by other buildings, the Septa Julia, a multitude of porticos, temples, columns, great edifices; and, finally, far in the distance, hills cov-ered with houses, a gigantic resort of people, the borders of which vanished in the blue haze,—an abode of crime, but of power; of madness, but of order,—which had become the head of the world, its oppressor, but its law and its peace, almighty, invincible, eternal.
>
> But Peter, surrounded by soldiers, looked at the city as a ruler and king looks at his inheritance. And he said to it, "Thou art redeemed and mine!" And no one, not merely among the soldiers digging the hole in which to plant the cross, but even among true believers, could divine that standing there among them was the true ruler of that moving life. (404–5)

5

What Is the Meaning of the Turning Years?
Virgil's Aeneid

Here we stand at the shore of a great sea. Christians proclaim that it was ordained by God that the just man unjustly condemned should redeem a city that had long since lost its soul. Agnostics demur and say that the irony lies in a coincidence that looks purposive, as if a blind world for once worked so as to deliver a poetic "justice" to the Rome of Nero. The mystery of divine providence stands before us, and demands a response. If providence is an illusion, then we are presented with the irony as if it had been part of a superimposed design, as we pretend that a concatenation of events is interesting, even as we know that it means nothing and leads nowhere. But if, as I have suggested, the essence of irony is dramatic and not merely verbal—if it involves a sudden revelation of unexpected yet fitting truth, even truth that had been firmly denied—then the Christian belief in the providence of God allows for both the artful design and the clash between levels of knowledge that irony requires.

The classical belief in fate provided, for Christian artists, both a model and a foreshadowing of this kind of irony. Take the example of Troy, rich and towered, queen of Asia, ruled by the happy king Priam, he of the fifty valiant sons and the fifty lovely daughters. But Troy was proud, and therefore Troy must fall. Pride goeth before a fall, Saint Paul will say; but for Troy there will be no subsequent redemption. Her walls and towers are burnt to dust, as Dante puts it.

The history of the Trojan War is full of events that seem wholly inappropriate but also within the design of fate, ironically fitting and instructive. Consider one scene from the *Aeneid* of Virgil, the poet whose notion of fate or destiny sometimes seems, but only seems, to approach the rich Christian faith in a guiding providence.

The war has been going on for ten wearisome years. Most of Priam's sons have died in battle. That includes the noble Hector, slain by Achilles, who then desecrated his body by boring holes through his ankles, strapping him by thongs to his chariot, and dragging him through the dust three times round the city walls in full view of the man's royal father and mother, his kin and his grieving countrymen. Yet even then, Troy did not fall. Achilles himself is dead, slain by a wound in the foot inflicted by the arrow of Paris, that malingering womanizer whose abduction of Helen caused the war. And now Paris is dead, too, and Helen handed along to another husband.

Troy must fall. The sin deserves its punishment. But on one terrible morning the plains beyond her walls are empty, silent in the beautiful sunlight. Tentatively, the people leave the gates to see what is going on:

> We thought the Greeks had gone,
> Sailing home to Mycenae before the wind,
> So Teucer's town is freed of her long anguish,
> Gates thrown wide! And out we go in joy
> To see the Dorian campsites, all deserted,
> The beach they left behind. Here the Dolopians
> Pitched their tents, here cruel Achilles lodged,
> There lay the ships. (*Aeneid*, 2.34–41)

No Greeks nearby. There lie the pools in the rock where the women and girls used to go on washing day, making a happy picnic of it, long ago before the Greek ships came. There lap the waters in the harbor where the Greeks were moored. There is the spot where Achilles slew Hector. All now as it used to be, ten years ago. All, except for a gigantic wooden horse, solitary in the plain. Its head nearly reaches the battlements of the city walls.

What to do about this horse? In the darkness of our minds, says Aeneas, who is telling the story, some of us said we ought to destroy it, and some, fools or traitors we do not know, said we ought to bring it into the city.

In the midst of the argument the priest of Apollo, Laocoon, comes running and hollering. He tries desperately to remind the Trojans of the impiety, the fraud, of the Greeks, particularly of their arch-strategist:

> O my poor people,
> Men of Troy, what madness has come over you?
> Can you believe the enemy truly gone?
> A gift from the Danaans, and no ruse?
> Is that Ulysses' way, as you have known him?
> Achaeans must be hiding in this timber,
> Or it was built to butt against our walls,
> Peer over them into our houses, pelt
> The city from the sky. Some crookedness
> Is in this thing. Have no faith in the horse!
> Whatever it is, even when Greeks bring gifts
> I fear them, gifts and all. (2.59–70)

The priest hurls his lance at the side of the horse's belly, and it sticks there, with a hollow ring. But somehow the Trojans do not hear it.

They are distracted by a commotion. A posse of taunting boys is leading a Greek soldier in bonds. His name is Sinon. He has allowed himself to be captured so that he can tell the most brilliant lie in all of classical literature.

Now there is nothing ironic in being fooled by a lie—unless the lie is just what the liar knows you are bound to believe, given the weaknesses (or the strengths!) of your character. Sinon pretends to have fled the impious treachery of Ulysses, who has hated him ever since Sinon's beloved commander railed against the stupidity of the war. That commander now deceased, Ulysses has directed his vengeance against the lieutenant.

So says Sinon. He has the advantage of knowing both Trojan piety and Greek impiety; and he knows that the Trojans know of that impiety, too. He knows that the Trojans have heard that the Greeks were required to perform a human sacrifice to gain fair winds before sailing for Troy. The victim was Iphigenia, eldest daughter of the Greek chieftain, Agamemnon. Lucretius, Virgil's predecessor, would present the scene in all its repulsive irony:

> As soon as they tressed her hair with the ritual fillet,
> The tassels spilling neatly upon each cheek,
> And she sensed her grieving father beside the altar
> With the acolytes nearby, hiding the knife,
> And countrymen weeping to look upon her—mute

> With fear, she fell to her knees, she groped for the earth.
> Poor girl, what good did it do her then, that she
> Was the first to give the king the name of "father"?
> Up to the altar the men escorted her, trembling;
> Not so that when her solemn rites were finished
> She might be cheered in the ringing wedding-hymn,
> But filthily, at the marrying age, unblemished
> Victim, she fell by her father's slaughter-stroke
> To shove his fleet off on a *bon voyage!* (1.87–100)

They who would mock the maiden Iphigenia with such a marriage would be capable of much besides.

So at this juncture, with the war mired in indecision, says Sinon, Ulysses pretended to require another human sacrifice. He bribed the prophet Calchas (a plausible event in the career of a Greek prophet, to be bribed or browbeaten), sequestering him in his tent for ten days. There Calchas asked the god who should be sacrificed. In the meantime the brave Greek warriors all hoped it would be the next fellow and not themselves. At last, to almost everyone's relief and no one's surprise, Sinon was named; but he foiled their plans by escaping. And in the midst of this terrible memory, overcome by despair and loathing for his former comrades the Greeks, he interrupts his story with a plea for quick execution, and concludes it with a plea for mercy:

> Now no hope is left for me
> Of seeing my home country ever again,
> My sweet children, my father, missed for years.
> Perhaps the army will demand they pay
> For my escape, my crime here, and their death,
> Poor things, will be my punishment. Ah, sir,
> I beg you by the gods above, the powers
> In whom truth lies, and by what faith remains
> Uncontaminated to men, take pity
> On pain so great and so unmerited. (2.185–95)

Master rhetorician, that Sinon.

Let us pause to appreciate the craftsmanship of the lie. Sinon knows that the Trojans take their piety seriously, especially in their devotion to fathers and their care for children. If they did not, they would find out what they could from him, then kill him anyway, supplication or no; and so the gambit would fail. Sinon also knows that the Trojans will be quick to believe Ulysses capable of a bottomless depth of wickedness: he is the "inventor of impieties," as Virgil calls him. Of course, we know what the Trojans on the scene do not know, and what Aeneas, sadder and wiser, now knows full well. It was Ulysses himself who devised this lie! He who helped design the Trojan horse has turned and fitted and sanded an even more polished work of art. Its success depends upon Trojan virtue and his own reputation for evil. And only Ulysses could think to save the most critical part of the lie for the end, almost as an afterthought. The Greeks have sailed back to the mainland, Sinon says, to retrieve new omens for the war. If, when they have returned, the horse still stands outside the city, they will use it to crush Troy. But if Troy takes the horse inside, the city will be queen of Asia forever.

Here we are taken up short by another dramatic interruption. Two huge serpents rise up out of the sea. They have been sent, as Aeneas learns only much later, by the goddess Athena, implacable in her anger against the Trojans (for Paris had chosen Aphrodite and not herself as the fairest of the goddesses, bribed by the prospect of enjoying the most beautiful woman in the world, namely Helen). Laocoon and his two sons are innocently offering a heifer at the altar of Apollo, when the serpents wind themselves about them, turning priest into horrible victim:

> Twice about his throat
> They whipped their back-scales, and their heads towered,
> While with both hands he fought to break the knots,
> Drenched in slime, his head-bands black with venom,
> Sending to heaven his appalling cries
> Like a slashed bull escaping from an altar,
> The fumbled axe shrugged off. (2.296–302)

That would seem to decide the issue—Sinon himself could not have timed it better. The Trojans, after all, honor the gods, whom Laocoon, it appears, has dishonored by insisting that the horse be destroyed. They witness Laocoon's death and attribute it to justice; and they find Sinon's story plausible, and attribute his escape to justice, too. Says Priam to the young man: "You shall be one of us" (2.202).

No more discussion. With boys cheering and girls dancing, the men drag the horse on rollers into the city, straining to accomplish their own destruction. The Greeks in fact are skulking behind the shelter of an island a few miles from the harbor. That night while the Trojans celebrate they row silently to shore. Sinon opens a hatch in the horse's belly, letting out Ulysses and other picked warriors. They throw open the gates of the city, and all is lost. So Aeneas remarks upon the bitter irony of it:

> This fraud of Sinon, this accomplished lying,
> Won us over; a tall tale and faked tears
> Had captured us, whom neither Diomedes
> Nor Larisean Achilles overpowered,
> Nor ten long years, nor all their thousand ships. (2.268–72)

Troy sinned, therefore Troy must fall, even by means of its humanity and reverence for the gods. But the irony extends further than Aeneas knows. For Virgil is enshrining the Roman legend that claimed that the city was founded by Aeneas, an exile from fallen Troy. There is no historical truth to that legend; Virgil's contemporary Livy treats it as a pious and useful fairy tale. Yet it once served to place Rome on a level with the more culturally advanced Greeks; and now, after the Greek world has been vitiated by wealth and squabbling, and has been conquered by Rome, it seems to vindicate the Trojan cause after all. So Sinon spoke more truly than he knew. If the Trojans would only bring the horse into the city, they would be—as Romans, not Trojans—the masters of Asia.

But that sunny interpretation of Rome's perpetual power—*imperium sine fine,* says Jupiter (10.375)—is not exactly warranted by Virgil's poem. For Virgil will take away the assurance he seems to have given. In the second half of the *Aeneid,* his hero, the pious Aeneas, will be compelled by circumstances to stand in the role of the hated Achilles. One example, the most powerful, will suffice. As Hector lies dying outside the walls of Troy, he begs Achilles to consider his father far across the Aegean Sea in Phthia. By your father's memory, he says to his victor, give my body back to the Trojans for burial; pity my mother and father. But Achilles cannot be moved. He sees gleaming upon Hector's body the armor that Hector had stripped from Patroclus, Achilles' bosom friend. How the victor of that day could wish he had hung back from the battle! No matter that Patroclus's death was Achilles' own fault—that Patroclus had gone too far out into the battle only because Achilles was still sulking in his ship, angered by the affront of Agamemnon. That it was his own fault enrages Achilles all the more. So he replies to Hector brutishly, assuring him that no ransom will suffice:

"Not if Priam son of Dardanus should offer to weigh out
your bulk in gold, not even so shall the lady your mother
who herself bore you lay you on the death-bed and mourn you
no, but the dogs and the birds will have you all for their feasting."
(*Iliad*, 22.351–54)

Aeneas's situation is even more acutely painful. It is a noble young man who lies before him: Turnus, prince of the Rutulians, who has led the Italian tribes opposing Aeneas's settling among them. He has a legitimate grievance against Aeneas, as Aeneas well knows. Turnus had been promised the daughter of King Latinus in marriage, but Latinus, learning of the arrival of the Trojan Aeneas and recalling a prophecy that his blood should be united with the blood of foreigners, breaks the promise and gives her to Aeneas instead. Thus Aeneas is forced, against his inclinations, into the role of the woman-stealing Paris. Turnus also is brave and valiant: all the considerations of person are in his favor. He is wounded, but he may survive. He asks Aeneas to return him to his father, Daunus, and begs it in the memory of the one human being in the world dearest to Aeneas, his own father, Anchises.

That should be enough to move Aeneas. He is a man of profound humanity who struggles, in this twilight life, to do the right thing. But the whole poem, apparently a work in praise of Roman pietas, duty to one's father, one's fatherland, and the gods, now sets pietas against pietas in an insoluble dilemma. For Aeneas sees on Turnus's waist the belt of Pallas, a young native Italian who had allied his forces with Aeneas. The lad had looked up to him as a father, and Aeneas had promised the boy's aged father, Evander, that he would bring Pallas back to him safe and sound. In vain: for on his great virgin morning of battle Pallas cut down all before him, till he came to Turnus. And when, with the funeral cortege proceeding before him, Aeneas encountered the poor old Evander, that good man swore him to vengeance.

Achilles saw Patroclus's armor on the dying Hector, and steeled himself in ruthlessness. Aeneas sees Pallas's belt, and what can he do? Piety and impiety pull him apart—and Aeneas, *insignis pietate vir*, the man who has strived with more determination than flair to hold to what is good and proper, and who has reaped not happiness but loss after loss, his path strewed with the bodies of one beloved or noble human being after another, this Aeneas falls into a rage and despatches Turnus thus:

> "You in your plunder, torn from one of mine,
> Shall I be robbed of you? This wound will come
> From Pallas: Pallas makes this offering
> And from your criminal blood exacts his due."
> He sank his blade in fury in Turnus' chest.
> Then all the body slackened in death's chill,
> And with a groan for the indignity
> His spirit fled into the gloom below. (*Aeneid*, 12.1291–98)

And that is how the poem ends.

If there is a providence in Virgil's world, it is surely ambiguous: a flicker of hope, perhaps, that in the great scheme of history, events will work according to a benign plan. But the poem does not end with the dynastic marriage of Aeneas and Latinus's daughter, Lavinia. It ends with a confused and disappointed man in the grip of wrath. The irony of the Greek victory at Troy was that it would seal their own defeat; yet the irony of the Roman conquest of the Greeks might well have been their consequent abandonment of piety. The Greeks came bearing cultural gifts, dangerous gifts; and, as Livy saw it, the Romans were corrupted by the Greeks they had conquered. All paganism ends in despair: even in Virgil we have not left the iron cycle of birth and death, and rise and fall, wherein one state succeeds upon another, and the only design in it all serves to reveal our littleness. And in this littleness there is nothing redeeming. So writes the Renaissance poet Tommaso Campanella, reverting to the gray Stoicism of the ancient Romans:

> Thus are we in this earth, great animal
> Within the greatest; we are like to lice
> On our own bodies, ignorant and foul.
> Proud race of man, I bid you raise your eyes,
> And measure what you're worth against the all:
> Then learn your true position and be wise.
> ("The World and its Parts," 9–14)

The Son Bore the Wood

SUCH IRONY — WHICH shows man, who thinks he knows things, to be a counter in a game played out by fate or impersonal law or design — in a strange fashion presupposes the providence it denies. It is parasitic upon a suppressed belief in One who foresees. For there either is a plan, or there is not. If there is not, then all man's attempts to divine meaning in his history are vain. One irony of a flat and uninteresting sort pervades all: man thinks he knows, then learns that he knows nothing, if he can even be said to learn that. Yet hidden deep within a belief in a disillusioning fate is a belief that there ought to be a providence: that, despite all we see to the contrary, history ought to be a stage for justice, however dimly perceived and incomplete, and that man is made to know, however straitened that knowledge must be on this side of the grave.

So believers in providence have more, not fewer, opportunities to see irony at play than have the disbelievers. For, granting providence, the artist may illustrate man's movement from ignorance to knowledge; or from perception of one kind of order to perception of order of a wholly different magnitude, not contradicting but comprehending the former. The artist may attend to knowledge gained in surprising ways that yet are most suitable for the knower, for the thing known, and for the God who grants the knowledge; or he may attend to those who can have no pretensions to knowledge, for instance to children and fools, who yet prove wiser than their betters. And the artist may see these ironies at work not only in the life of one person, but in mankind's long and meandering history.

Augustine was the first, in his *City of God*, to outline a Christian theory of history. But the notion that history had a meaning (other than providing object lessons in valor and, more commonly, folly or vice) was implicit in scripture and was a cornerstone of the Jewish tradition at the time of Christ. History was going somewhere: events of old not only prepared the way for events to come but foreshadowed them, concealing their full meanings until the time for complete revelation should come. The Jews held, for instance, the mysterious belief that the prophet Elijah would precede the coming of the Messiah — yet the same Jews were deeply divided on the question of the survival of the soul after death. Evidently they expected someone who was *not* Elijah's soul reincarnate, but who was Elijah in more than an analogical sense: someone who fulfilled the meaning of Elijah, who was, and had always been meant to be, Elijah come again. Thus the Jews ask Jesus, "Are you Elijah?", they do not mean, "What can you tell us about King Ahab, who lived back in your day?" or "Are you playing the role of Elijah?" but rather "Is Elijah fulfilled in you? *Are you Elijah?*"

If you do not understand this belief in a history-ordaining God, you cannot understand scripture, Old Testament or New or both together. Nor can you understand the rich ironies of Christian literary works that model their own "history" after the pattern of God's revelation not only *in* history but *by means of it*. Let us return now to the story of father Abraham.

Despite his old age—and his laughter!—Abraham has been granted a son of laughter, Isaac. He has circumcised him by his own hand and has thereby dedicated him to God. Through the loins of Isaac shall come the promise, the descendants as numerous as the stars.

Then one night God delivers a startling command:

> And it came to pass after these things, that God did tempt Abraham: and he said unto him, Abraham: and he said, Behold, here I am.
> And he said, Take now thy son, thine only son Isaac, whom thou lovest, and get thee into the land of Moriah; and offer him there for a burnt offering upon one of the mountains which I will tell thee of. (Gen. 22:1–2)

It is important to remember the darkness surrounding Abraham. He must have been crushed by God's command—led so soon from unexpected joy to despair. Nor is there a convenient detour. For, with the Lord's consent, Abraham has allowed his wife Sarah to banish the concubine Hagar and their son Ishmael, a boy whom Abraham loved dearly. God reconciled Abraham to the banishment by promising care for Ishmael (which he does provide, miraculously and tenderly [Gen. 21:14–21]; but for all Abraham knows, their bones are bleaching in the desert). And God reasserted his covenant, to be fulfilled through Isaac and his sons: "Let it not be grievous in thy sight because of the lad, and because of thy bondwoman; in all that Sarah hath said unto thee, hearken unto her voice, for in Isaac shall thy seed be called" (21:12). Now all has been snatched away. Abraham has left his kin forever; he has banished his son, at the command of this strange God. He has won victory in battle, with this God's assistance, and has witnessed the destruction of the wicked cities Sodom and Gomorrah, at the hands of this God; and he was allowed to plead for the lives of the few just people living there, namely his nephew Lot and his household. Beyond these things Abraham knows nothing about God, or at least nothing we are told.

So he is crushed, but I think not entirely surprised. He is the victim of a god's practical joke. That is how gods are. They set you up and knock you down. There is no reason to trust them, except that refusal to trust might end up even worse. Yet on that grim morning, Abraham trusts. It is no myth he follows, but the voice of the living God. He does not know why he trusts; we are granted no revelation regarding his thoughts. If he could reason his way into a proof of God's trustworthiness, that would derogate from his trust. God speaks to him—not a theological proposition, not a mythical father of might, but God in truth—and Abraham responds.

Man and son climb the mountain alone. Abraham has left two young companions at the base, saying, "Abide ye here with the ass; and I and the lad will go yonder and worship, and come again unto you" (22:5). Of course, Abraham is lying, in part. Worship there will be, but as far as he knows, Isaac will never return. Yet we who know the story (and "we" includes all the Hebrews, who told and retold with reverence this foundational story of their race) know that Abraham speaks the truth unwittingly. He thinks he has been fooled by God, and does not suspect that he *is being* fooled by God. He thinks he knows that God is capricious, like all the gods; he will find that God is faithful, like none of those shams.

The innocence of the boy makes the climb all the more terrible. Abraham carries the knife and, carefully, in both hands, a pot of glowing coals for the fire. Isaac bears the wood strapped to his back—for Mount Moriah is bleak and bare, with no decent firewood to be found. Isaac unsuspectingly asks the obvious question: "Behold the fire and the wood: but where is a lamb for the burnt offering?" (22:7).

With what hardly controlled agony the father replies! "My son, God will provide himself a lamb for a burnt offering" (22:8). He dissembles; he believes that God has already provided the lamb, the son Isaac born by God's miraculous intervention. Perhaps Abraham hopes against hope that another lamb will be provided—if so, it is surely a great example of his faith. Yet such a "perhaps" must be gray and flickering. Abraham hears the steps of his young and harmless boy beside him, knows what Isaac does not know, and must imagine the black loneliness of returning down the accursed mountain without him.

Again, however, Abraham has spoken the truth he did not see. For as he raises his knife to slay Isaac, bound upon the same stone altar his own young hands have helped his father build, Abraham is stopped by a herald of the Lord: "Lay not thine hand upon the lad, neither do thou any thing unto him: for now I know that thou fearest God, seeing thou hast not withheld thy son, thine only son from me" (22:12). Such is the language God uses to present truth to the finite mind of man. God has known Abraham all along; it is rather Abraham here who learns. He learns about his own faith, and he learns, should he ever doubt it, that God will not break his word. He is not a god like the other gods.

As for those other gods—fertility gods especially, the Baals of the Canaan-ites and Moloch (Melkor) of the Phoenicians—they demanded human sac-rifice as the filthily ironic price of good harvests and large families. Abraham knew as much, as did the Hebrews who told the story. The gods, in malevolent control of everything, require that you slay your child (which seems, to the ignorant, a counterproductive thing to do), so as to secure more children (as everyone as sophisticated as the Phoenicians knows will happen, for that is the cruel yet necessary bargain). But it is not so.

Or it is so, in a way the surrounding peoples do not understand. Their sacrifices form part of an iron economy, a rigid rule for the universe. They give up, to gain. They kill, but they do not yield; they allow the wailing infant to pass through the fire to Moloch, on condition that Moloch uphold his end of the deal. Abraham must have thought that God was requiring something similar from him. It is remarkable that God has, however, given Abraham no hint of a recompense, and yet Abraham obeys anyway.

The message, then, is that God does not want Abraham to sacrifice Isaac *in that way.* God is no rewarder of mercenaries, nor does a mercenary really offer a sacrifice. Abraham has slain the choice of his heart, and for making that sacrifice God rewards him with the return of Isaac, and a ram for the offering: "And Abraham lifted up his eyes, and looked, and behold behind him a ram caught in a thicket by his horns: and Abraham went and took the ram, and of-fered him up for a burnt offering in the stead of his son. And Abraham called the name of that place Jehovah-jireh: as it is said to this day, In the mount of the Lord it shall be seen" (22:13–14).

What has providence to do with this episode, beyond fashioning a narrow escape for the heroic Abraham? Consider the ram tangled in the thicket. It is slain in place of Abraham's first-born son. *God has provided* is now the name of the fateful spot; Abraham names it, recalling his words to Isaac as they climbed the mountain. The lesson would not be lost on the Hebrews, who owed their survival as a free people to another such sacrificial lamb: the Pasch, the Passover lamb, whose blood besprinkled upon the lintel and the doorposts would cause the Destroying Angel to pass by their homes on that dread night when God smote the first-born of Egypt and of all her bleating gods.

It is pointless for the critic, and blasphemous for the Christian, to say that the similarity is accidental. Pointless, because what matters is how the Chris-tian faith, and that includes Christian habits of reading scripture, helped de-termine the ironies built into the Christian vision of the world, as given color and form in Christian literature. Blasphemous, because it denies the providence of God, implying that the Creator of the universe could never have willed from all eternity the foreshadowing of the Passover in the sacrifice upon Mount Moriah.

But the providential wisdom does not end there. Examine the celebrated icon of the Holy Trinity by the fifteenth-century Russian artist, Andrey Rublev (see figure below). The genius of the icon lies in a profound theological insight. The Father, the Son, and the Holy Spirit, distinct yet as one, are the three angelic visitors to Abraham, sitting at table, while Sarah prepares the lamb. But the outlines of their robes form, in a kind of absent presence, the negative of a chalice: the cup of wine consecrated to become the blood of Christ, given for all. They are the ones invited to a feast, as Abraham thinks; but the truth is that they are inviting to their feast Abraham and all his descendants in faith. And since they are announcing the conception and birth of Isaac, the artist has implied a long arc of providential meaning, extending from this moment under the terebinth trees of Mamre, to the birth of Isaac, to the "sacrifice," to the true Passover lamb, the Christ. God gives himself wholly to man, that man may rise to enjoy the life of God.

Andrey Rublev, The Holy Trinity

The ram provided by God to spare the life of Isaac, the firstlings of the Passover feast to spare the lives of the Hebrews in bondage what were they, say the ancient Christians, but shadows of Christ? He it is who gives his body not merely in place of ours, to suffer death, but to redeem us from sin and the death that is sin's wages. Isaac lived another day, to sin and die and await his Redeemer. So did the Hebrews who followed Moses across the Red Sea. But the true Lamb that the Lord provides is no substitute simply, but his own Son, his only beloved Son, that is to say his very self, that all who believe may be cleansed of sin and may live forever. They will enjoy the wedding feast of the Lamb, himself, his own life, given as food to those he loves (Rev. 19:9).

A world governed by so playful—I can find no better word—a providence abounds in meaning, a cascade of it, from every least word or action. If God is no miser of his blessings, neither is he a miser of meanings: they burst from every tree and leaf. It follows that we cannot know the full significance of what we say and do, but that God does know and can choose to reveal that significance to others, especially by means of events that reenact the past and reveal it to have been far more, or far other, than what the actors themselves supposed.

A charming instance of this cascade is given unwittingly by the inspired author of the Abraham and Isaac episode. Abraham, he says, carried the knife and the fire-pot. Isaac carried the wood. A deft Anglo-Saxon poetic rendering of the scene, in the so-called Genesis A text, makes the connection swiftly and explicitly: *Wudu baer sunu* (2887B). "The son bore the wood," the poet says, calling attention to his line by the rhyme, most unusual in Anglo-Saxon composition. Or, since *wudu* and *sunu* possess identical forms in the nominative and the accusative cases, "The wood bore the son." Without dropping any other hint, the poet recalls to his audience a new field of significance, one unknown to Abraham and Isaac. The lad—from whom we hear not one word of protest against his father—foreshadows Christ, who carried the wood up another hill for a sacrifice, his own. Christ was Isaac, was the ram; Christ bore the wood to the altar, and *the wood bore him*. God spared the son of Abraham, but did not spare himself, so great was his love for the world.

To believe in a world governed by the all-wise and loving Father, who demands justice but whose very act of creation was a condescension, an act of mercy, is to know that divine providence is endlessly rich, embodied in the exploding galaxy and in the grain of sand on the shore. It is a world brimming with consequence: allusions shooting like weeds, wonderful and lush; paradoxes hidden like thrush's eggs in the tree-crotched nest; etymological parallels winking one to the other like the glaze of dewdrops on the first day. And as long as there are creatures like us, once naked in the garden, wise and innocent—now wise in our own minds, therefore foolish and half-blind and huddled up in disguises—the play of irony will thrive. We now experience irony mainly as that cold splash that wakes us, when we thought we knew what we did not; a child would experience it rather as that warm and sweet moment of wonder, when something whose meaning he did not know suddenly assumes its surprising and self-displaying place in the garden of knowledge and love and time, the created garden of God.

Part Two

The Irony of Time

6

The Play Beyond the Play

I used to enjoy plays that blurred the distinction between the actors and the audience, or between the actors and the director. Nowadays a critic would praise such a play for "transgressing boundaries," and raise himself a-tiptoe, as if the players were doing something new and brave. How brave it is, I can't figure, but it is not new. My favorite in the genre is a Renaissance play: Beaumont and Fletcher's *The Knight of the Burning Pestle*, a raucous send-up of bourgeois romances and the companies of boys who acted them. Just after the play begins in typically courtly fashion, a greengrocer in the audience gets up to complain. He wants something more to his own taste: a play extolling the chivalry of grocers. He barges onto the stage and, with the help of his wife (who interrupts from the audience) and his apprentice Rafe (dragooned into acting the lead in the new "play"), he compels the boys to weave into their play the adventures of that hero of grocers everywhere, the Knight of the Burning Pestle.

The result is a wild farce—yet it was not popular. Perhaps the burghers didn't want to be teased about their taste. But in their defense, people go to the playhouse to see plays about life (including that part of life called playing), and not plays about plays. And plays about plays fall back upon the assumption that "all the world's a stage, and all the men and women merely players"—to quote Shakespeare, who goes on to show how narrow and inadequate that point of view is.

Now if we are all actors, and if our drama isn't even a drama but an absurdist parody of one, waiting for a Godot who never arrives, searching for a play to play in and finding none, or if we are Tom Stoppard's Rosencrantz and Guildenstern bumbling across a stage of whose import we have not the foggiest notion, then life can be seen as fundamentally ironic. But the irony is timid and poor. It peters out. What more can you say, once you have said that there is nothing ultimately to say? Say that all the world's a stage, and you shy away from the heart of life. You miss the bravest ironies blooming in all their glory.

Let me explain. In the plays of Tom Stoppard, characters who think they know things are shown not only that they do not, but that there is nothing stable and objective to know. Their perceptions are circumscribed by their language. The dramatic irony works in two directions: the character experiences a crushing revelation of what we have known all along, namely that he is a character and his world a fiction. But then the author stands outside the frame and suggests that we ourselves are no better off. We are each of us the duped Birdboot searching for meaning and style in *The Real Inspector Hound*, trapped in our conventional critic's patois, only to find that we are part of that play ourselves, about to be murdered (in the play or out of the play, or is there no difference?) by our envious fellow critic Moon, who wants to steal our job.

That irony then must apply to the author himself, as authors who indulge in this self-referential playing will happily acknowledge. But then their analysis stops short. Stoppard is like the old skeptic Archelaus. Most skeptics would claim that they did not know anything for certain; Archelaus said he wasn't even certain about *that*. Thus pride and sloth masquerade as Socratic wisdom. Archelaus ducked and shuffled rather than face the fundamental flaw of all skepticisms, exposed later by Augustine: the skeptic claims that nothing can be known for certain, except one thing, that nothing can be known for certain. Thus he protects himself from the smiling scorn with which he regards everyone else.

It is special pleading. The skeptic maintains that no one can make any claim about the universe; yet that too is a claim about the universe. The postmodern writer denies the stability of human nature, yet asserts the absolute truth of that instability. He claims that human identity is as inconstant as the wind, but asserts that the inconstancy never changes. His irony dissolves its own container, and he will not see it. It is a tired dabbling with the impermanent, pretending that it has a meaning one believes it cannot have, enjoying the pretense, and enjoying the contrast between oneself and the less astute fellow who takes it seriously. Let us see how Shakespeare treats such a skeptic in *As You Like It*. He knew well that if the skeptic is correct, if time is a pointless succession of moments, then all drama is mere illusion.

Jaques, Who Wishes to Be a Fool and Is a Fool Already

PIECE OUT MY PALTRY words with your imagination. It is a forest in winter. No snow lies upon the ground, but the wind is stiff. Dressed in deerskin, a band of men wrap their arms round their chests or lean toward the low campfire. Their faces do not bear the creases of habitual poverty; these have had their poverty thrust upon them. They have followed their exiled leader, the Duke. Some are rankled and impatient; one, a sophisticate with the air of a man who thinks he is the center of attention, a Sir Oracle, picks raisins indifferently from a basket.

Suddenly they are interrupted by a youth, one Orlando, wielding a sword, demanding food. He too is an exile, thrust from his patrimony by the envy of an elder brother. He has wandered the trackless woods with a loyal old servant bearing the universal name: Adam. That brave heart, says the youth, now lies dying of hunger.

"You are welcome to it," says the exiled duke, adding that they too have known better days, and have learned by their suffering to pity misfortune. The youth hurries away to bring his old friend, and the duke turns to the sophisticate, a man so greedy for irony that he digs for the yellow metal at his feet and misses the golden sun. "See," he says, "we're not the only poor souls in this pageant of life."

The metaphor sets off a famous piece of wit. For Jaques, the sophisticate, replies:

> All the world's a stage,
> And all the men and women merely players.
> They have their exits and their entrances,
> And one man in his time plays many parts,
> His acts being seven ages. At first, the infant,
> Mewling and puking in the nurse's arms.
> Then the whining schoolboy, with his satchel
> And shining morning face, creeping like snail

Unwillingly to school. And then the lover,
Sighing like furnace, with a woeful ballad
Made to his mistress' eyebrow. Then a soldier,
Full of strange oaths and bearded like the pard,
Jealous in honor, sudden and quick in quarrel,
Seeking the bubble reputation
Even in the cannon's mouth. And then the justice,
In fair round belly with good capon lined,
With eyes severe and beard of formal cut,
Full of wise saws and modern instances;
And so he plays his part. The sixth age shifts
Into the lean and slippered pantaloon,
With spectacles on nose and pouch on side;
His youthful hose, well saved, a world too wide
For his shrunk shank, and his big manly voice,
Turning again toward childish treble, pipes
And whistles in his sound. Last scene of all,
That ends this strange eventful history,
Is second childishness and mere oblivion,
Sans teeth, sans eyes, sans taste, sans everything.
(*As You Like It*, 2.7. 138–65)

Jaques is too wise, he, to dally with *those* parts, but he does play at melancholy, and wishes to add "moralizing fool" to his repertoire. He looks down upon his fellows from his raisin-popping distance. They try to read in their hardships the lessons of divine providence; Jaques denies that there is anything to read but delusion and hypocrisy. They believe they act in a drama of great and mysterious significance. But the "play" Jaques sees is not a play at all, just a jumble of follies, ending in age and debility and death, defined by what we lose: eyes, teeth, voice, everything.

But what if Jaques were right, yet too foolish to understand how and why? What if the world *is* a stage—a battlefield for good and evil—whose script has been written? Then you might enjoy the rich irony of beholding an ironical fool like Jaques, prancing on his platform, claiming to have discovered what everybody knows better than he, and, in his arrogant assumption that the play ends in nothingness and absurdity, helping to illustrate for all but himself that the play has meaning and ends in glory. "'Tis the sport to see the enginer / Hoist with his own petard," as Hamlet says (*Hamlet*, 3.4.207–8). The bracketer would be bracketed; the satirist mocked; the skeptic gulled; the stylish "player" critiqued as a stammerer who misses his cues.

That is the irony that hoists the ironical Jaques. No sooner does he finish his keen harangue on man, revealing less about man than about himself, than Orlando reenters, bearing old Adam in his arms. It was he who followed Orlando from home, a fool for loyalty, using all his art of artless love to persuade the penniless lad that he could still serve him, for all his age:

> I have five hundred crowns,
> The thrifty hire I saved under your father,
> Which I did store to be my foster nurse
> When service should in my old limbs lie lame
> And unregarded age in corners thrown.
> Take that, and he that doth the ravens feed,
> Yea, providently caters for the sparrow,
> Be comfort to my age. Here is the gold;
> All this I give you. Let me be your servant;
> Though I look old, yet I am strong and lusty,
> For in my youth I never did apply
> Hot and rebellious liquors in my blood,
> Nor did not with unbashful forehead woo
> The means of weakness and debility;
> Therefore my age is as a lusty winter,
> Frosty, but kindly. (2.3.38–53)

What if his voice whistles? What if he comically tries to broaden his shoulders, begging Orlando the favor of companionship for his last few days? Is he the "lean and slippered pantaloon"? Is his a "second childishness"? Is his trust in providence mere ignorance of the passing days? Into the wilds he follows Orlando, and when he falls faint, his master leans above him, playing the part of a true man and friend by ironically pretending to be offended should Adam die before he returns with food. Adam understands the gentle game, and smiles weakly (2.6.13).

Now Orlando brings Adam before the others, aristocrats all, but men first, one in their suffering. While Adam feeds, the duke commands music to restore the soul: music to reflect the divine order that stands in judgment over man. The sad song is tinged with an irony that Jaques cannot reach:

> Blow, blow, thou winter wind,
> Thou art not so unkind
> As man's ingratitude:
> Thy tooth is not so keen,

> Because thou art not seen,
> Although thy breath be rude.
> Heigh-ho, sing heigh-ho, unto the green holly.
> Most friendship is faining, most loving mere folly:
> Then, heigh-ho, the holly.
> This life is most jolly.
>
> Freeze, freeze, thou bitter sky
> That dost not bite so nigh
> As benefits forgot:
> Though thou the waters warp,
> Thy sting is not so sharp
> As friend rememb'red not.
> Heigh-ho, sing, &c. (2.7. 173–89)

Jaques would have us believe that the duke's loyal men are fools, but the song proves otherwise. They see the folly of man, but unlike Jaques, they see more: they judge man's selfishness against God's free giving, and find that no winter in a fallen world can be as sharp as man's ingratitude. And as Adam regains a little strength, the good duke and Orlando speak aside, about better days long past, and the duties of friendship those days enjoin upon us:

> If that you were the good Sir Rowland's son,
> As you have whispered faithfully you were,
> And as mine eye doth his effigies witness
> Most truly limned and living in your face,
> Be truly welcome hither. I am the duke
> That loved your father. The residue of your fortune
> Go to my cave and tell me. Good old man,
> Thou art right welcome, as thy master is. (2.7.190–97)

No rebuke more final could be delivered, as Jaques is reduced to irrelevance.

The Christian will admit that human life is a drama. Admit it? He will proclaim it. As a man turns a corner or pushes open a door the next thing he does may have eternal consequences. It may gain for him, in the grace of God, eternal salvation; it may send him spinning to perdition; and he may lure along with him, either way, the souls of many others yet unknown to him. For God is the Creator of time, not bound by its chances and changes, but permitting what we call chance and change to unfold the glory of his changeless decrees.

7

Time Beyond Time: *Augustine's* Confessions

A Day of Business, A Moment of Peace

IN THE YEAR 387, a mother and her son, a highly regarded instructor of rhetoric, stood in a little house in the Roman port of Ostia, looking out of the window that faced the sea, and talking about the many strange events that led them there. The mother knew she had accomplished all she was meant to in life, and was awaiting with calm indifference the ship that was to take her back to her native town in north Africa. There she would live out her days and be buried beside the husband whom she had brought to the Christian faith by her patient obedience and love. But she never boarded that ship. She would fall ill of a fever and die a few days later, surrounded by her son, his natural son, and his friends, whom she had served as a daughter and cared for as a mother.

If you walk among the peaceful ruins of Ostia now you may find where that house stood, or so they say. A plaque commemorates the spot. No one then could have suspected the importance of the moment. Doubtless the street of the shipbuilders bustled with men boiling tar, twining ropes, patching sails, hawking chains and strongboxes and salt fish and other nautical necessaries.

The façades of the pagan temples gleamed in the sun, their handsome marble overlay embellishing crumbly piles of brick and stone. Now the riggers are dust, only the smoothed pavements of their shops remaining as fossils of what they were. The potholes in the counters of the delicatessens are empty. Much of the marble has cracked and fallen, or has been filched for use in churches and tombs. Packs of bony dogs straggle about, looking for scraps from the occasional tourist. And at that moment long ago, there stood beside his simple mother the man who would write about the inevitable end of this great city, this monument to human strength and its lust for domination. He would write about the time when it and all human cities would be no more: the time after time, when the truly eternal city shall have her mansions filled, and God shall be all in all.

Who could have guessed it? Yet, in the history of man, the journey of that man's soul outweighs all the commerce and industry of Rome. No question about it, since his journey is every man's, and mankind's journey too, the long meander of history leading to the choice between Christ or nothingness. So has it been ordained, by an Author most secret and profound.

What Does It Mean to Belong to a Story?

It is common, but incorrect, to say that Saint Augustine wrote the first autobiography. He wrote about the authorship of his life: how God had woven his grace into and around all his hopes (usually vain) and decisions (usually wrongheaded, and sometimes wicked) to bring him, despite his wilfulness and prodigious intellect, out of lofty error and into the humble fields of truth, to stand at his mother's side.

Augustine wrote not so much about his pursuit of God as about God's pursuit of him. For God is no abstract principle to discover by philosophical compass and straightedge. He is a God of love who resists the proud, and makes his abode in the humble heart. He is the selfsame, the Creator of time and of all the creatures of time, who became subject to time, that he might raise mortal man from death to eternity. He the Author is the first and the last, the guarantor of meaning in history, the world's and man's. That Author would endow Augustine with insight into what it means to dwell within a story: in particular, the story of the conflict between the city of man and the city of God.

It is a story that enfolds man's words, yet lifts man to a vision beyond words. Such ecstasy seized upon Augustine and Monica on that day long ago, "conversing together most tenderly, 'forgetting those things that are behind, and stretching forth to those that are before,'" seeking to slake their thirst at the fountain of the Almighty, yearning for a glimpse of the life beyond time:

> Raising ourselves up with a more ardent love to the Selfsame, we proceeded step by step through all bodily things up to that heaven whence shine the sun and the moon and the stars down upon the earth. We ascended higher yet by means of inward thought and discourse and admiration of your works, and we came up to our own minds. We transcended them, so that we attained to the region of abundance that never fails, in which you feed Israel forever upon the food of truth, and where life is that Wisdom by which all these things are made, both which have been and which are to be (*Confessions*, 9.10).

At a moment in time, in the fullness of time, they rise to a realm beyond time; from "the noise of our mouths, where a word both begins and ends," a word that must be spoken in time and must pass away to be spoken, to the timeless Word in whom all creatures, spoken by him into being, have their beginning and their end.

Manichean Time

MUCH OF CHRISTIAN LITERATURE is hard to understand unless one understands Augustine's view of time as an image of the eternal. Endings will appear sudden or forced—for example, the forgiveness scene at the end of Shakespeare's *Measure for Measure*—because the reader has not attended to the time, treating it as a neutral vehicle for the occurrence of material events, passing from moment to moment. Because he cannot see how time like a many-petaled rose may fold upon itself, he misses the flashes of the future in the past. He will be shocked by absurdity, where the Christian will be surprised by truth. He will find the art puzzling, even botched, where the believer will relish the irony of the revelation of order where order had been suspected but uncertainly, and where revelation had been glimpsed but dimly.

The young Augustine had fallen into the same trap. How could he understand how God works in time, when his Manichean heresy (and his sins) blinded him to the nature of God and time?

The self-styled prophet Mani was a mystagogue from the east who heated a smattering of the Christian scriptures together with ancient Persian dualism. He taught that there were two principles in the world, one good, one evil. The good was greater than the evil, sure enough. But the evil had been responsible for the world's ills, being the "darkness" or "hostility" present in raw matter. Good, meanwhile, was an animating spirit, but spirit also conceived as material, thin and ethereal though it was. The war between spirit and matter, good and evil, was waged on a universal stage and within the individual heart. The "perfect" attained to such spiritual heights that, as Augustine scornfully remarks, they claimed to transmute matter into angels by eating figs—so long as they had not sullied themselves by picking the figs with their own hands (3.10)! The imperfect were saved by the merits of the perfect. A fair deal, since they could then sin in the flesh and blame it on the evil principle that plagued them. So would Augustine, who as an adult took a woman companion, one whom his "wandering passion, empty of prudence, had picked up" (4.2).

The perfect were celibate. Why increase and multiply the number of embodied beings? That would be to multiply evil. To the imperfect was left the tawdry duty of propagating the race. Not that Augustine and his mistress wanted to propagate the race, either. Only later did he see that, unlike chaste wedlock, lust severs the act of sexual intercourse from time, freezing it in the present moment, to enjoy the pleasure and deny God's creative agency, the providence that, in the begetting of children, binds husband and wife to those who come before and after.

Ironically, it is a carnal imagination that denies the beauty and goodness of the flesh! For while the young Augustine considered it absurd that God could be born in the flesh, he yet attributed to God a thin corporeality that extended him, spatially and temporally, throughout the universe: "So gross of heart was I, and I had no clear idea even of my own self, that whatever was not extended over, or diffused throughout, or compacted into, or projected up into definite measures of space, or did not or could not receive something of this kind, I thought to be completely non-existent" (7.1) As with the body, so with time. Rejecting a God who transcends space and creates it and all things therein, the Manicheans could not conceive of a God who transcends time even while using time to effect his purposes. So they mocked the Mosaic Law, arguing that God was too great to be associated with its proscriptions and, especially, its material permissions. They sneer, "Are those to be judged just men who had many wives, killed other men, and made sacrifices of animals?" (3.7). They would limit God to their own vision of his limitlessness: a carnal infinitude, almost bodiless body, extending infinitely far in space, and perpetually backwards and forwards, never changing, into the past and future.

But God's infinity is not parceled out among creatures, with an elephant receiving more than an ant. He is entirely present everywhere, filling all things, yet contained by nothing (1.3). So too his immutability is not parceled out among times. He is the Lord of time. As the variety of creatures does not derogate from the beauty of the one God who made them, but reflects and expresses that beauty, so the variety of laws God commands from time to time reflects and expresses his immutable justice. The law is manifest in customs "adapted to times and places," while remaining "everywhere and always the same," "never one thing in one place and different in another" (3.7).

To illustrate, Augustine uses a fruitful analogy. In Latin poetry, syllables keep time by length, with two short syllables counting for one long syllable, and with each line's patterns of long and short, and permissible substitutions, precisely prescribed. The law of the poem does not change, though from line to line the patterns of the syllables do. In such a fashion does God, the author both of one's own history and of the history of man, express his unchanging intent in and through a variety of events. He punishes, yet that is his mercy; he forgives, yet that is his justice.

That does more than justify God's changing the rules once set for the Israelites. It affirms that one of the ways God teaches his people is to bring them up in history, by means of change: "In my blindness I blamed the holy fathers not only for using present things, as God ordered and inspired them to do, but even for foretelling future things, as God had revealed to them." The half-blind Manicheans see change and reject it, while God reveals through change his changeless will (3.7).

Trying to Redeem the Time Oneself

THE CONFESSIONS THEREFORE ILLUSTRATES two complementary ways of misunderstanding time. The first is to see no meaning in it, no direction. Time is an illusion, or a function of hostile matter rejected by the Manichean (or the Buddhist, or the poorly catechized Christian). The second, which may follow from the first, is to believe that man can manipulate time for his own purposes, even for salvation. Augustine labors to correct that error by stressing God's saving action in time and at all times. What seems a needless excursus on an infancy that Augustine could not remember is for the astute Christian one variation on the theme of God's gracious will. Though timeless, God condescends to us, showering us with timely mercies, even when we cannot say whence we have come or who we are. And indeed our infancy still exists only because it dwells within the memory, which is the perception, which is the providence, of God: "But see, my infancy is dead long ago, and I still live. Lord, you who live forever and in whom nothing dies . . . before the beginning of the ages, and before anything that can even be called 'before,' you are, and you are God and Lord of all that you have created, and with you stand the causes of all impermanent things and with you abide the unchanging sources of all changing things, and in you live the sempiternal reasons of all unreasoning and temporal things" (1.6).

Man who dwells within time recognizes extent, and imprecisely talks about past and future, though only the present truly exists, and that for an instant (11.15). Temporal, he attributes his limitations to God, asking, for instance, what God was doing before he created the universe (11.12). But because he is created in God's image, he too can grasp what it means to be past, present, and future, though not as God does in his eternal present. Man looks forward, considers, and remembers (11.28), as Augustine does when reciting a psalm by heart (11.27). So, limiting God and glorying in ourselves, we forget that we are characters in God's story, and that every moment of our lives is shot through with the graces of his unfolding but eternal providence. We make ourselves into the authors of our stories, as if *we* were lords of time.

These two poles of error—the belief that time flows apart from God's activity, like some neutral river, and the belief that we can craft our lives in time to suit ourselves, even to compel God to act as we wish—subject sinners in Christian literature to a most intricate irony. "I wasted time, and now doth time waste me," says Shakespeare's frivolous Richard II, still not seeing the hand of providence in his chastisement (*Richard II*, 5.5.29). Antonio in *The Tempest* treats time as a wheel of fortune, offering opportunities to those who have hands to snatch: to supplant your brother or kill a sleeping king (2.1.280–94). Yet while he discourses on opportunity, the powers, "delaying, not forgetting" (3.3.73), punish his first sin and prevent the murder he now devises. Chaucer's Pardoner is young in years, but decrepit of soul. He pitches his sham relics as wards against the mischance that one's next and perhaps last moment in time may bring: for if you are thrown from your horse you may rest assured of your salvation, having provided for it by a timely purchase (*Canterbury Tales*, 6.931–40). Yet when the Pardoner himself rounds the corner—when he points out mine Host, Harry Bailey, as the first man who ought to unbuckle his purse, he is thrown from *his* horse, so to speak, ridiculed in front of everyone, as Harry alludes to the relics the Pardoner would most like to keep secret. For the Pardoner is a "gelding or a mare" (cf. General Prologue, 691), lacking the testicles that link a man by procreation to the past and the future.

Such ironies would not have been lost on Augustine. He shows how in his youth his parents and teachers acted as if time were clay in their hands, not seeing themselves as clay, nor that other vessels were being fashioned than those they intended. For instance, they taught him the *Aeneid*, that tapestry of historical untruth, as preparation for a lucrative post in the bureaucracy of the empire. The *Aeneid* was a kind of holy scripture, affirming the divine foundation of Roman rule, though (as Augustine would have it) based on nothing but poetic fancy, and leading but to the frivolous affairs of worldly men. With shocking dismissal of that great poem, Augustine looks on his youth from the vantage of one who now knows what no one then saw. For he learned a glorious but false history, while ignoring the shame that lay before his eyes: "I was required to learn by heart I know not how many of Aeneas's wanderings, although forgetful of my own, and to weep over Dido's death, because she killed herself for love, when all the while amid such things, dying to you, O God my life, I most wretchedly bore myself about with dry eyes" (*Confessions*, 1.13). And if he spent his days playing instead of studying "the wanderings *of a certain Aeneas*," as the Latin reads with devastating nonchalance, the adults (who spent their own days playing) would punish him (1.10).

Augustine's father, Patricius, hardworking in the eyes of the world and provident, had fine dreams of the son he loved and admired. He put his estate in debt to give Augustine the "best" education he could afford, sending him in his sixteenth year to the great city of Carthage. Far richer citizens, says Augustine, would not do the same, but meanwhile "this same father took no pains as to how I was growing up before you, or as to how chaste I was, as long as I was cultivated in speech, even though I was left a desert, uncultivated for you, O God" (2.3). Patricius appreciates the "cultivated" speech—Augustine intends us to hear the metaphor of sowing and reaping—and expects it to bring forth a harvest of prestige and wealth. He does not see that the lush field is a desert.

Similarly, Patricius regards Augustine's youth and builds dreams of progeny: "When my father saw me at the baths, he noted how I was growing into manhood and was clothed with stirring youth. From this, as it were, he already took pride in his grandchildren, and found joy in telling it to my mother"

(2.3). He looks upon Augustine's nakedness and sees increase rather than the lust that would long enchain him, its sole fruit a son born out of wedlock (the good lad Adeodatus, who died young, without children). But God, planning athwart the purposes of the father, works within the heart of his wife Monica, laying "the foundation of your holy dwelling place" (2.3).

Patricius and Monica had long accepted the African custom of controlling one's time by delaying baptism. It was thought that if one were baptized too soon, "the guilt and defilement of sins committed after that cleansing would be greater and more dangerous" (1.11). Some people, no doubt, wished to manage their spiritual time so as to get their pleasurable sinning done in youth, and only with age to retreat and make things all right with God.

Such an attitude springs from weak faith or overweening pride. The believer implies that God's grace cannot safeguard the soul through the perils to come; man's plans would be more secure. Or he implies that God's favor can be purchased, in the nick of time, by the requisite ritual act; and that denies the gratuity of the gift of salvation. So Augustine's parents did not have their little boy baptized, not even when he contracted a dangerous infection and lay near death:

> You saw, my God, for you were already my keeper, with what effort of mind and with what faith I entreated the mercy of my own mother and of the Church, the mother of us all, for the baptism of your Christ, my God and Lord. The mother of my flesh was distraught—for she most lovingly was bringing forth my eternal salvation in her chaste heart and in faith in thee—and would have at once hastened to arrange that I be initiated into the sacraments of salvation and be washed in them, I first confessing you, Lord Jesus, for the remission of my sins. However, I immediately recovered from that illness. So my cleansing was delayed. (1.11)

Augustine cannot say it worked for the best that he had not been baptized. That would be blasphemous, implying that God required the evil that Augustine was going to commit, in order to wrest from it the great good of the repentant sinner, even the good of the book called *Confessions*. Still, God did bring good out of this bad custom, as he brought good out of the straying lad who suffered by it—one good thing in particular, as many Christians believe: it was Augustine who argued most persuasively for infant baptism.

Augustine was allowed to live; not so the closest friend of his youth. God, who fashions "sorrow into a lesson to us," who smites to heal, who slays that we might not die apart from him (2.2), touched with affliction a youth who had followed Augustine into the "superstitious and pernicious fables" of the Manicheans (4.4). Together the boys heaped scorn upon the scriptures. When he considers what happened to his friend, Augustine bursts into praise for the providence of God: "What was it that you did at that time, my God, and how unsearchable are the depths of your judgments? Tormented by fever, he lay for a long time in a deadly sweat, and when his life was despaired of, he was baptized while unconscious" (4.4). Not that the young Augustine thought anything of it. Like Patricius, he thought he was in control. His friend would recover, would learn that he had been baptized, would mock it, and would rejoin Augustine in their pursuits. How can it matter what happens to an unconscious body? But God is not bound by our consciousness, and may deign to work through such humble things as water and oil. So when the lad woke and Augustine tried to joke with him about the baptism, "he was horrified at me as if I were an enemy, and he warned me with a swift and admirable freedom that if I wished to remain his friend, I must stop saying such things to him" (4.4).

But Augustine refuses to understand. Things will be all right, he assures himself. His friend will heal, and his mind will change. "Then I would deal with him as I wished," he says. But God scourged the pride of Augustine even as he saved the friend from its perils: "He was snatched away from my madness, so that he might be kept with you for my consolation. After a few days, while I was absent, he was attacked again by the fever and died" (4.4).

For a long time Augustine could take no delight in life; all his haunts and pastimes reminded him of his friend. He could not distract his mind by "pleasant groves," "games and singing," "rich banquets," "the pleasures of the bedchamber," even books and poetry; all was "base and wearisome" (4.7). Time did eventually make the grief bearable, planting in him "other hopes and other memories" (4.8). But if Augustine no longer shed tears over the friend's death, the passage of time did cause him to meditate on why he had been so shaken with grief. The answer, he says, lies in our mistaking what it means to be a creature bound by time: "Why did that sorrow penetrate so easily into my deepest being, unless because I had poured out my soul upon the sand by loving a man soon to die as though he were one who would never die?" (4.8)

Note the sad irony. Man dwells in time. He knows he has had his dawn and will have his dusk. But he seizes a single moment and seeks to rest there, as if it would never pass away. Yet the Lord who created him slays him, killing his heart that it might live and enjoy the peace that passes understanding. God uses time to orient him towards eternity. And in ignorance the man cries out against his healer.

We love the beautiful things of this world justly, says Augustine, since they come from God. But such things do not possess their being all at once: "They rise and they set, and by rising, as it were, they begin to be" (4.10). So too our speech: words come into being by passing away. All these "words" of creation are partial goods, not the whole. What separates Christianity from philosophies that reject the world of time (Buddhism, for example) is its insistence upon their goodness, and on God's working in them and through them. For through Christ, who would take flesh of the Virgin, all things were made. Thus, the mystery of material creation is inseparable from the mystery of the Incarnation, an event in time, ordained beyond time, that occurs at the right time, and extends its meaning over all time:

> "For [Christ] did not delay, but he ran forth and cried by words and deeds, by death and life, by descent and ascension, crying out for us to return to him. And he departed from our eyes, so that we might return into our own hearts and find him there. He departed, but lo, he is here. He would not stay long with us, and yet he does not leave us. He departed from here, whence he has never departed, for 'the world was made by him' and 'he was in the world,' and 'he came into this world to save sinners'" (4.12).

Christ is the friend who died, and the friend who lives; made man in time, that man might be one with God in eternity.

A Fabric of Stories

PROVIDENCE IS A POWERFUL tenet of faith. For if God provides for all man's errant works and ways, then certainly he provides for the stories man tells about himself. Not only, then, do we live in a history that derives its meaning and direction from God, but the history we write is also part of that history. If the Lord can take on human flesh and be born in a feeding trough, against all the expectations of the Jews, yet by that humble act completing the meaning of their history, then he can surely, within history, play ironic changes upon man's tales. A camel and a comedy are equally subject to his governance.

In Augustine's time, Romans consulted their sacred book before making important decisions. It was called the *sortes Virgilianae*, the Virgilian drawing of lots. You open the *Aeneid* at random and act upon the first passage you see. For that poem was a holy narrative, prophesying for the Romans empire without end, and inventing and enshrining in immortal verse the beginnings of many a Roman tradition.

Now Augustine does more than question the historicity of the story of Aeneas. He sees in his own story the reversal of the *Aeneid*, or, more precisely, a true *Aeneid*, in that his wandering and homecoming are real. That is more than noting a few ironic coincidences between his life and the account of Aeneas. For Augustine asserts that they are *not* coincidences. Virgil never intended it, but the *Aeneid* plays its part in the story of salvation, as error that highlights the truth.

How so? When he was a boy, Augustine knew no better. He loved the *Aeneid*, especially the magnificent fourth book, recounting how Dido fell into a passion so consuming that she would slay herself rather than live without Aeneas. Virgil does not approve this passion: the "marriage" between Aeneas and Dido is celebrated with lightning and wailing nymphs as the two repair to a cave to escape a thunderstorm. It has been arranged, provided for, by the mutually suspicious goddesses Venus and Juno; and it will result in enmity between Rome and Carthage, and the deaths of hundreds of thousands of soldiers in war. Augustine now ignores the disapproval, remarking that in his love for the *Aeneid* he too was committing fornication, loving honor and praise more than he loved the Creator. And all those around him witnessed it and cried out, "Well done!" (1.13).

The boy was encouraged to enter imaginatively into the narrative of Aeneas, through dramatic recitation. He was to play the part of the fictitious Juno, clothing "with appropriate language" the anger of that implacable goddess (1.17), and striving to win a prize for the best dramatization. But as for remaining in one's own character and lifting up appropriate praises to God, that never occurred to Augustine's teachers. They looked for dross and missed the gold. They observed the proprieties of letters and syllables, but would "neglect everlasting covenants of eternal salvation" (1.18). Solecisms disturbed them more than sin: a man would be mortified to slip in public speech and pronounce *inter homines* ("among men"), but "he takes no care lest by his furious spirit he cause a man to be taken away from *inter homines*" (1.8).

So Virgil's poem about wandering Aeneas helped Augustine become what was considered a promising young man; yet it encouraged him in his own more perilous wanderings. And yet God would use the life of Augustine as a foil to the life of Aeneas; for, like Aeneas, Augustine too arrived at Carthage, beset by passions, where "a caldron of shameful loves" seethed about him on all sides. "I was not yet in love," he says, "but I was in love with love, and by a more hidden want I hated myself for wanting little" (3.1).

Like Aeneas, then, Augustine is a seeker, "for there was a hunger within me from a lack of that inner food, which is yourself, my God"(3.1). There at Carthage he first falls in with the Manicheans. But, suffering the insolence of the "wreckers," students who make a travesty of instruction by crashing courses they have not paid for and preventing the teacher from teaching, Augustine—like Aeneas before him—decides to leave. He sets out for Rome, and like Aeneas, he deceives a woman—his mother!—on the night before his departure. Dido, abandoned by Aeneas, curses him, invoking an avenger to come: the great Hannibal, who would exact in Roman blood the payment for her anguish. Monica, abandoned by Augustine, weeps and begs God to prevent him from sailing away. But God was working his timely miracles in both Monica and Augustine, perfecting her saintliness by patience, and steering him to the church in a way that far exceeded Monica's hopes. Monica, no doubt, would approve the irony, as God "had no care for what she then sought," that he might do for Augustine "what she forever sought" (5.8).

Rome would be, and not be, the terminus of Augustine's earthly journey. For he would soon leave Rome for Milan, in the company of fellow pilgrims journeying to the faith. There he met the man most responsible for his conversion, the bishop Ambrose. Ambrose *was* the Roman state in Milan, powerful enough to excommunicate the emperor Theodosius for a massacre of Arian heretics. He helped Augustine by his erudition *and humility* to read scripture aright. For the door to those truths is set low, that only the humble may enter; yet the mansion within is vast and profound. Aeneas founded a Rome that would die; Augustine left Rome behind, to come to Rome in the end, namely the Christian church whose head was the bishop of Rome.

A Picture of a Man Reading

ONE DAY AUGUSTINE AND his friends went to visit Ambrose at his house, full of questions regarding the Christian faith. Under the influence of this eloquent and virtuous man, Augustine had begun to see that in scripture what seemed difficult on the literal level might be explained by allegory (5.14), referring symbols in the Old Testament to what they foreshadowed in the New. For the God of time is not hemmed in by time, but may use one time to reflect another.

They found him within after the day's wearisome business, and were stunned by what they saw. Ambrose, perhaps to save his voice, had developed a unique habit: "When he read, his eyes moved down the pages and his heart sought out their meaning, while his voice and tongue remained silent. Often when we were present—for no one was forbidden to enter, and it was not his custom to have whoever came announced to him—we saw him reading to himself, and never otherwise. After sitting for a long time in silence—who would dare to annoy a man so occupied?—we would go away" (6.3). This is the first recorded instance of anyone reading silently. We should not be surprised: neither Greek nor Roman texts were easy to read. The space between words had not been invented, nor had lower-case letters. You had to declaim the sequence of syllables to help at deciphering the words.

Reading, then, was a physical act, something with a potential audience, requiring the pronunciation of words in time. But Ambrose read as if his "heart" divined the meaning; he did not need to "speak" the words to the ear of his mind. Any text has a beginning, a middle, and an end, but Ambrose read to lift the meaning out of time: to see, in an instant, what a sequence of words or ideas meant, and to see it as something changeless, not bound to the instant or to the sequence. He was silent so that he could hear; he read words as revealing the Word.

And that is exactly the sort of reading—in time, and out of time—that Augustine finally learns. We see him fascinated by astrologers, even casting horoscopes, yet not persuaded that his passion for time-telling is worth anything (4.3). As always, Augustine longed for something beyond the changes of a fallen world, something to excuse or make sense of evil, attributing one's sin to the positions of Venus or Saturn. Eventually, God would cure Augustine of this fascination by means of a story told him by a dabbler in astrology, one Firminus, heir of a rich estate, born at exactly the same hour, and therefore under the same planets, as was the son of a slave in his household, who remained a slave all his life (7.6). Yet God also used Augustine's astrology to expose the Manicheans. The latter pretended to know everything about the heavens and the earth, yet could not prescribe the motions of the heavenly bodies, whereas the "curious skill" of the natural philosophers could "measure the constellations, and plot the courses of the planets," predicting eclipses far in advance, according to principles explicitly set down and still in use (5.3). When

Augustine puts astronomical questions to the famous Manichean, Faustus, he finds to his disappointment but not to his surprise that the man knows nothing about the stars (5.7).

But even the natural philosophers miss the object of their desire. What they read is true, but not Truth himself. They then become the objects of irony. For by following the precise and orderly motions of stars and planets, they can foresee—with hard study and painstaking observation—the occultation of the sun or the moon. But the eyes of these same men are dazzled by pride: "Their own present eclipse they do not see, for they do not seek with a devout mind whence it is that they possess the skill by which they seek out these things" (5.3). The future they tell; that is, an insignificant piece of it. The present they miss. What is worse, if they attended to that same power of mind by which they tell that future, they would see that present: they would consider the God who endowed them with the power of reason. But pride intrudes, and they do not see.

God provided Augustine with a mind too restless to settle for questions about the sun and moon, and a heart too honest to slide over the absurdities and contradictions in the Manichean writings. He would be led to Neoplatonism, that time-transcending semimysticism claiming descent from Plato. Its principal exponent in the century before Augustine was Plotinus, who conceived of the universe as a series of overflowings of being, from what he called the One, to Mind, to the World-Soul (an animating principle instilled into an orderly world by the ordering Mind), to Matter. Following Plato, Plotinus asserted that the highest and timeless object of our reverence must be that which is most fully real, not subject to change. Plotinus argued that this object was the impersonal One.

What does the One do? Nothing. It overflows, yes; it is the source of all Being. But it does not will; it is not a person; indeed, if it could be said to have any characteristics at all, it would not be the One, but one of the Many. It is beyond naming or describing. Christianity would adapt and reject much of the Neoplatonic reasoning concerning a supreme being. For our purposes, it is important to note that in time, that is in the history of Augustine's life and therefore in the history of Christendom, the time-contemning philosophy of Plotinus played its crucial role. It showed Augustine the way to a God who, unlike the Manichean deity, transcended time and matter; but its rejection of time ironically prevented it from learning who this God was. The Neoplatonists soared beyond time; therefore they were bound to the age which produced them, and their names have fallen into oblivion. They saw much, and missed the meaning.

For when Augustine procured the works of the Neoplatonists—God used for this purpose "a certain man puffed up with most unnatural pride," whom Augustine notably does not name (7.9)—he reads, in so many words, that "in the beginning was the Word, and the Word was made flesh, and the Word was God," and that "the soul of man, although it gives testimony to the light, is not itself the light, but the Word, God Himself, is 'the true light'" (7.9). But he does *not* read that God would so love the world as to enter time in the flesh, that to men he would give power to be made sons of God, that he dwelt among us, that he emptied himself, taking the form of a servant. Missing from Neoplatonism is any activity in time, by means of time, by the deity—any love. The philosophers did not possess the intellectual vocabulary to understand that "according to the time," Christ "died for the ungodly" (7.9).

They had not learned that alphabet, Augustine suggests. Only the humble can learn it: "For 'you have hidden these things from the wise, and have revealed them to little ones,' so that they who labor and are burdened might come to him and he would refresh them." But those men "who are raised up on the heights of some toplofty teaching do not hear him as he says, 'Learn from me, for I am meek and humble of heart'" (7.9).

Return to that quiet room in Milan, where Augustine and his friends wait, not wanting to disturb the elder Ambrose as he reads in silence. What was he was reading? Perhaps a book to confound the Platonist at his own game: a book about a babe born in a manger, who was yet the *conditor siderum*, the maker of the stars, a book whose very words were ordained by the Word.

A Soldier Is Worth More than a Professor, Any Day

AN INTELLECTUAL PLOTS HIS autobiography around the uprisings and ambushes and campaigns of his mind: he persuades himself that he is as interesting as Napoleon, without, however, that ill-chosen foray into Russia. Not Augustine. For what is happening in Augustine's mind is God's work, bringing the man back to him. He who took flesh of the Virgin can enter the thoughts of man. Though Augustine does show how various intellectual errors were cleared away during his slow awakening into truth, it is never to glorify himself, but to assist the reader who may be struggling with some of the same, and to praise God, whence comes all light.

But the conversion does not occur once the intellectual problems are met. Our problem is not that we are ignorant, as Plato thought, but that we are fallen. We can do evil knowingly, and for its own sake, as Augustine did when he stole pears from a neighbor's garden, not intending to eat them or do anything with them other than to have stolen them (2.4). At the heart of sin is a vicious parody of God's omnipotence, as we claim the authority to do as we please, because we please (2.6). We must be converted by humility—even the humility of Christ, who assumes the burden of our sins, and whose grace grants us the power to be pleased in doing what God wills. For such a conversion it is fitting that God use not arguments but the stories of those who have come before us.

Therefore Augustine's autobiography is a story about the stories of other people, and how God wove their stories into one. In all these stories, he who turns to God turns away from something apparently important, and becomes what the world dismisses as a child. The case of the famous rhetor Victorinus is especially poignant, as his were the translations of the Neoplatonists that Augustine had been reading. When Augustine, then, accosted Simplicianus—the man who had baptized Ambrose—and asked him about those books, Simplicianus told him that he had been a friend of Victorinus for many years, and that Victorinus had often declared to him, secretly, "You should know that already I am a Christian" (8.2). Yet the old rhetor continued to make public sacrifices to the pagan gods, with who knows what mental acrobatics.

Victorinus was no hypocrite; just an intellectual. The intellectual can persuade himself that only ideas matter. He is beyond mere oil and water—or mangers, or crosses. Whenever Simplicianus objected that he would not believe it until he saw him in the church of Christ, Victorinus would parry with the reply of a man overestimating the human mind: "Is it walls, then, that make men Christians?" (8.2)

But secretly, Victorinus feared what people would say if, after a lifetime of incense for Minerva and Apollo and Jupiter, he were to renounce his past and his important office in the state. Then he read in scripture that whoever denies Christ before men, Christ will deny before his Father: "He saw himself as being guilty of a great crime by being ashamed of the mysteries of the humility of your Word" (8.2). Becoming "modest before the truth," he suddenly approaches his friend Simplicianus and says, "Let us go to the church. I wish to become a Christian" (8.2).

Note what Victorinus means. In saying, "I wish to become a Christian," after having insisted all along that he already was one, he concedes that you cannot become a Christian by making a vague decision about it in your mind.

Christ who humbled himself to be put to death on a cross asks us to humble ourselves too, that we may live. If that means we allow a baptized Christian to pour water upon our heads as he repeats the words given by Christ, "I baptize thee, in the name of the Father, and of the Son, and of the Holy Spirit," then so be it. Victorinus was placing himself under the authority of the Lord of time and of all men's stories: not a theory, not a philosophy, but that same One who appeared transfigured to Peter, James, and John.

Not already a Christian, but finally one! A new child was born that day. The priests offered to let Victorinus make his profession in private, but he humbly declined, saying that as in public he had taught rhetoric, in which there was no salvation, so now in public he should affirm the word of God. And so he did:

> Hence, when he arose to make his profession, all those who knew him uttered his name to one another with a murmur of congratulation. And who among them did not know him? A suppressed sound issued from the mouths of all those who rejoiced together, "Victorinus! Victorinus!" Suddenly, as they saw him, they gave voice to their joy, and just as suddenly they became silent in order to hear him. He pronounced the true faith with splendid confidence, and they all desired to clasp him to their hearts. By their love and joy they clasped him to themselves. Those were the hands by which they clasped him. (8.2)

Hearing the story of Victorinus, Augustine was all afire to imitate him, yet could not. He was "bound to the earth," burdened by his sins, particularly those of the flesh. He was even preparing to satisfy his lusts under the fiction of a legitimate marriage—to a girl who would not reach the age of consent for another two years (7.13). Nor would Augustine wait by remaining continent. When his longtime mistress was torn from him as a condition of the betrothal, she vowed she would remain celibate for the rest of her life, but he, "no imitator of a woman and impatient of delay," procured for his bed another woman to tide him over (7.15).

Now when Monica prayed to God for a sign that he was the moving power behind this marriage, "she saw certain vain and fantastic things, such as are wrought by the powers of the human spirit when concentrated on a matter like this," but she did not believe they came from the Lord (7.15). She who had long wanted Augustine to marry, to save him from his life of fornication, now received no clear answer. In the meantime, Augustine and his friends began to dream up projects for community life together, wherein "the whole would belong to each" individually (7.14), but when the question of wives arose—some of the men were married— the proposals fell apart. They could not see beyond their busy and transient thoughts the eternal counsel of God: "You derided our plans and you prepared your own, according to which you were to give us meat in due season, and to open your hand and fill our souls with blessing" (7.14).

Indeed, the same Augustine who pretends he can see his own future and hasten toward it can hardly wake himself to the present. As the truth grows clearer and the moment of his conversion approaches, he resists with the greater force, if sluggishness and fear can be called force: "When on all sides you showed me that your words were true, and I was overcome by your truth, I had no answer whatsoever to make, but only those slow and drowsy words, 'Right away. Yes, right away.' 'Let me be for a little while.' But 'right away— right away' was never right now, and 'Let me be for a little while' stretched out for a long time" (8.5).

If the example of Victorinus was insufficient, Augustine would hear more— and of braver and humbler men. One day a countryman of his, Ponticianus, came to visit. He picked up a book lying on Augustine's table, and noted with pleasure that it contained the letters of Saint Paul. When Augustine told him he was studying those letters, Ponticianus related to him and his friends the story of a man who never pored over books in his life. The man was Anthony, who walked into a church one day and took to heart the gospel account of the rich young man. He was what the world would call ignorant; but Ponticianus is rather amazed that Augustine had never heard of Anthony, one of the first fruits of the bountiful harvest that God raised up in the wilderness (8.6). Leave it to intellectuals to miss what is going on.

This story of Anthony, written by Saint Athanasius of Egypt, found its way into the hands of two members of the emperor's special agents, the pretorian guard. These men, said Ponticianus, were staying in the household of some Christians in Trier, and one day, while the emperor was idling the hours at the gladiatorial games, they happened upon that biography. They picked it up and read it. The reaction of the reader—a soldier, a man of action—is immediate. God allows him to see the vanity of the future he and his fellows had been banking upon, and grants him the grace to act at once:

> "Suddenly filled with holy love and by sober shame made angry with him-
> self, [he] turned his eyes upon his friend and said, 'Tell me, I ask you,

where will we get by all these labors of ours? What are we seeking for? To what purpose do we serve in office? What higher ambition can we have at court than to become friends of the emperor? In such a position what is there that is not fragile and full of peril? When will we get there? But to become God's friend, if I wish it, see, I become one here and now'" (8.6).

His friend agreed, as would their affianced brides. They gave up all they had, stripping themselves of the world to become monks and nuns in the service of God. Ponticianus himself witnessed it.

A Child Again

WHEN AUGUSTINE HEARS THIS story he is abashed. How long has it been since he picked up his first book of philosophy—twelve years? Yet still he delayed. Had he not sought chastity from God since the dawn of his youth? Always he would pray, "Give me chastity and continence, but not yet!" (8.7). How long had he pretended he was delaying his conversion because he saw nothing certain? Yet, he chastises himself, "Men who neither wore themselves out in search of truth, nor meditated for ten years and more on such things, win wings for their readier shoulders" (8.7).

He bursts into tears, crying out to his friend Alypius, blaming himself for his weakness despite all his learning, all his reading, while "the unlearned rise up and take heaven by storm!" (8.8). He rushes out into an adjoining garden, utterly ignorant of what was about to happen: "I was in a death agony that was to bring life: for I knew what a thing of evil I was, but I did not know the good that I would be after a little while" (8.8). Alypius follows quietly. Augustine longed for the change to come, was moving ever closer to his decision, yet did not decide, for "the nearer that moment in time when I was to become something different, the greater terror did it strike into me" (8.11). All at once the demons of his past rose before his eyes and cried that Augustine would be rejecting them forever—the pleasure of the bed, the pride of life, the vanity of power and glory. Boys and girls, widows and virgins, all could live in continence. Why could not the great rhetorician Augustine? But the answer comes to him that on their own they could do nothing. All depended on the grace of God. Then, whispers Holy Church, "Cast yourself on him. Have no fear. He will not draw back and let you fall" (8.11).

Augustine is pitched to the height of yearning prayer: he knocks, knocks with all his might, crying out, "How long, how long? Tomorrow and tomorrow? Why not now? Why not in this very hour an end to my uncleanness?" (8.12). And he hears a voice. The great Augustine hears a voice, a little girl or a little boy, he cannot tell. It does not advise him about the One and the Many; it is not adorned with rhetorical delicacies. It repeats, in singsong, one strange and simple sentence: *Tolle, lege! Tolle, lege!* "Pick it up and read it! Pick it up and read it!" That voice as of a child—whence could it be coming? Augustine could recall no such chant in any children's game he knew. He remembers the story of Anthony, and takes the chant for a command from God.

And he rushes back to where Alypius is sitting, and seizes the book, not the *Aeneid* of Virgil, but the letters of Paul. He opens it at random, and reads *in silence* this passage from Romans: "Not in rioting and drunkenness, not in chambering and impurities, not in strife and envying; but put you on the Lord Jesus Christ, and make not provision for the flesh in its concupiscences" (13:13–14). This is the moment in time provided for by God beyond time: "No further wished I to read, nor was there need to do so. Instantly, in truth, at the end of this sentence, as if before a peaceful light streaming into my heart, all the dark shadows of doubt fled away" (8.12).

When the same grace is granted to Alypius (who picks up the book and reads, "Now him that is weak in the faith take unto you"), the young men tell the news to Monica. She rejoices, seeing that God had long denied her what she wanted, so that he could give her what she wanted: "You turned her mourning into a joy far richer than that she had desired, far dearer and purer than that she had sought in grandchildren born of my flesh" (8.12).

The Eternal Sabbath

THE LAST FOUR BOOKS of the *Confessions* are an extended meditation upon time: what it means for man to remember, and what it must mean when scripture says that God remembers; what the first chapters of Genesis mean when they relate what God did "in the beginning"; how we are to understand God's creation of time, simultaneous with his creation of matter and his providing it with form; and what this beginning has to do with the end, including the end for man. The books place the life of Augustine, and any man's life, where that life belongs, within the context of the passage of all creation. By the grace of God we belong not only to the time when we live, but to the first day and the last, too. So Augustine can assert that the lives of redeemed Christians are signified by the command of God, "Let there be lights made in the firmament" (13.18). We ourselves are the lights that mark off the seasons, for the history of the world bears witness not to random or cyclical motion but to redemption: "For 'the old things have passed away, behold, they are made new,' and 'now our salvation is nearer than when we came to believe,' and 'the night is passed, but the day is at hand,' and 'you bless the crown of the year,' sending 'laborers into your harvest,' at the sowing of which 'others have labored,' sending them also to another sowing, the harvest whereof is the end" (13.18).

The irony is, in part, that we dwellers in time cannot, unless it is revealed to us, sense the connection between ourselves and Adam, or between ourselves and the crowd of saints shouting praise at the sound of the final trumpet; we do not fully know what is going on even in our own lives, nor how our own lives will touch those of countless others. The further irony is that we must regard this passing time as good, because it was made by God, and because in it we have been redeemed; but we also long for the time to pass away. We praise God for it, and we wish its consummation; the believer is to possess all things as if he possessed none at all. For it is now as it was in the beginning, and as it will be. We think that the seventh day of creation rose and set long ago, but behold, it is at hand. For this present day of ours, whether we see it or not, is the sixth day, the day of man, but the seventh day, to which scripture does not assign a setting, is made holy and will endure for all eternity. God works beyond time, always remaining at rest, and one of his works is to give us work, within time, that we may rest in God "on the sabbath of eternal life" (13.36).

We see things, says Augustine, because they exist, but the things exist because God sees them. We see them as beautiful and good, outside ourselves, but God sees them to be made, already made. We once followed our vain imaginations and did evil, and then finally we followed the promptings of the Spirit, and did good. But during all our trials, though we could not see it, God never ceased to do good. And the good we have done will pass away, but we hope in what we cannot see fully, the sanctification to come: the good that God will give us, his own life, forever in act, and forever at rest, "for your rest is yourself" (13.38).

This peace cannot be given by man or angel. Only God can grant it, and what does he require? At a moment, in a garden, in a slovenly garret, under a bridge, on the road to Michigan, in the dead of night, under the shifting clouds of a spring sky, when the doctor's hand moves to shut the eyelids, at no discoverable time and at any time, we must ask God. A humble thing to do, but our God once walked the earth in Galilee and broke bread with fishermen. We ask. So Augustine finally asked, and the meaning of time was revealed to him. He knocked, and the door was opened.

8

Time and the Body: Dante's Divine Comedy

Not a Hair Will Perish

AUGUSTINE'S IS THE STORY of every Christian, the story of sin, and grace, and redemption. But what happens to that story when it ends?

As we have seen, Augustine asserts that time comes into being only at the creation of the physical world. Yet he does not identify time with the motion of any of the heavenly bodies, or of any body at all. If that were so, he argues, then we could not speak of past or future, since past is past because it has ceased to be, and future is future because it has not yet come into being. Then if past and future exist, they must exist where they cannot suffer change. They exist in the mind of God.

The implications for the Christian life are profound. We are not bound to time; we seek, as Spenser put it in *The Faerie Queene*, the "time when no more time shall be" (7.8.2). Yet in that timeless "time," the works and days of our present time shall yet exist, for nothing can be lost from the memory of God. It is perilous to call it an afterlife, as if it were a smooth continuation of life on earth, without the cramps and corns. Such an existence would still be bound to time: it would have a duration parallel to ours, very long or infinite as the case might be, exactly as the souls in the underworld of Homer's *Odyssey* live on in their shadowy way, following events on earth by receiving accounts from the newly arrived. Neither is the time after time an obliteration of all we were and knew and loved: that would drown our personal identities in the Infinite. Nor could we make sense of the Resurrection, wherein we shall know even as we are known (1 Cor. 13:12).

The eternal mansion God has prepared for us, then, is neither an infinite extension of what we are now, nor its annihilation. It is the life that fulfills this life, the reality whereof this life is a shadow. Jesus implies as much when he shows that the kingdom to come is present germinally now: "The hour is coming, and is now here" (John 4:23). The doctrine requires a double temporal vision. We dwell in the body, and mark time's changes upon us, the years that "delve the parallels in beauty's brow" (Shakespeare, *Sonnets*, 60.10); but we look for a resurrection and glorification of that same body, not a preservation in everlasting amber (cf. 1 Cor. 15:42). If we are the young Dante, we fall in love with a beautiful woman, and in time the woman will die and the love will wane; but in time, and in the time after time, the woman lives still and the love is fulfilled. For God is the God of the living, not the dead (Matt. 22:32).

And there lies the irony: those who set their hearts upon the treasure that is not subject to change and decay, the heaven that robbers cannot rob nor moths consume (Luke 12:33), are those who most redeem the time (Eph. 5:16). They, like Saint Francis, best love Brother Sun and Sister Moon, and will find in the kingdom of God even that passing beauty restored unto them also. Because they are not "of the world," they are in it, deeply and lovingly. But those who trade eternity for the things of time will lose them also, since time must pass away. Such are of the world, and therefore do not know the world's life. They do not understand the earth upon which they set such store.

Let us now see how Dante weaves this irony into his comedy of salvation.

A Materialist in Hell

Two PATRIOTS STAND FACE to face in the graveyard of the heretics. The elder is imprisoned with his fellow misbelievers in a fiery tomb, though for the time being the stone lid lies to the side. He can raise his body up to look out. So he does now, naked, visible to the waist. He thrusts his square chest out and holds his head proudly, "surging as if he held all Hell in scorn" (*Inferno*, 10.36).

The younger is passing through, viewing the punishments of the damned, that by his long pilgrimage he might learn humility and be numbered among the blessed. It is no comfortable remedy for the soul, this descent into hell, nor did the pilgrim want to undertake it. Others have gone and returned, but as messengers of the time to come. One, the hero Aeneas, descended that he might tell of the future glory of Rome, both secular and spiritual:

> He learned of things which were the cause of both
> his triumph, and the mantle of the pope. (2.26–27)

The other, Saint Paul, was granted a vision of paradise (2 Cor. 12:1–5), that he might rouse in his hearers a surer faith and more ardent hope in the resurrection:

> Later, the Chosen Vessel also went
> > to bring back comfort, strengthening the faith
> > which is the first step on salvation's way. (2.28–30)

We will learn, as we proceed through the *Comedy*, that the poet too is a prophet, of time and eternity; he will reveal truths concerning both the empire founded by Aeneas (ordained by God, as Dante insisted) and the faith for which Paul fought and died. At first, though, all he knows is that he must go down to the dead because his own time is running out. As Virgil will later describe Dante's parlous state:

> This man has not
> Yet seen the final setting of his sun,
> > but by his folly it had drawn so near,
> > it left him very little time to turn. (*Purgatory*, 1.57–60)

Even Dante's beloved Beatrice, learning in heaven of the danger besetting him, worries that her begging Virgil to guide Dante through hell will have come too late (*Inf.*, 2.66)—and *she* is as prompt as grace (2.109–11).

Here surely is a contrast between the younger and the elder patriot. The younger was afraid to go down to hell; the elder was not. Do not attribute that fearlessness to wisdom. The elder, Farinata degli Uberti, had denied the existence of hell, or heaven, or anything else beyond death. He was (by Dante's report) a materialist. It is remarkable that despite all the Christological and Trinitarian heresies that beg for dramatic portrayal (one wonders what Dante would have done with the smug heresiarch Arius), the poet chooses the materialists, those who, following Epicurus, "put it that spirit dies when body dies" (10.15). His choice suggests that materialism is the fundamental, and fundamentally illogical, heresy. It collapses the mind—with its capacity to conceive of present and past and future, not to mention an eternal and infinite God—into transient matter, a body that will pass away and never be raised again. Materialists think they know much more than their neighbors do, and the main thing they "know" is that we can know very little, and only what is material.

The elder, lured by the language he knew in life, addresses the younger:

> "O Tuscan, you who speak with modest grace,
>   alive and traveling through this city of fire,
>   may it please you to pause here in this place.
> Your speech and accent make it clear to me
>   you were born in the noble fatherland
>   I may have punished once too bitterly." (10.22–27)

So sudden is the interruption that Dante shies away. He must be pushed to the fore by Virgil, who identifies the sinner and advises Dante that he had better use his short time to speak to good advantage.

This Farinata had been one of the strongmen in Florence in the generation before Dante was born. He was of the Ghibelline party: loosely speaking, the old-blood aristocrats who favored the interests of the Holy Roman Emperor. That was easy for them to do, because the Holy Roman Emperor tended to be a German living beyond the Alps or far down the peninsula in Calabria, and thus unable to meddle in the affairs of the Ghibellines. More important, the Ghibellines strove to thwart the interests of the pope, whose seat was a good deal closer to home, and of the rising middle class, among whom they had to live. Dante's family, by contrast, were Guelphs. Again speaking loosely, the Guelphs tended to play the papacy against the power of the emperor, not so much in devotion as for the leverage they could acquire against their natural rivals, the local aristocrats. Consider it a battle between an impostor Aeneas and an impostor Paul.

I should not stress too much the ideological basis of the party strife. Since the days of the Claudians and the Flavians, Italian politics had been primarily a contest of family loyalties. Further down in hell, Dante will suggest that the strife began as a family feud, occasioned when a girl from one family was jilted by a boy from another (28.103–12). Yet that strife was no small matter, as the blood of the Guelphs slain at the massacre of Montaperti (1260) could testify. And Farinata was the chief of the victors at that massacre.

So the first question Farinata asks means a great deal:

> At the foot of his tomb I stood, and he
> > looked at me for a little, till he asked,
> > with some disdain, "Who were your family?" (10.40–42)

Farinata here identifies family with party. He wants to place Dante, to fix him in the only time he knows. "At Montaperti," he seems to ask, though he refrains from mentioning a massacre that causes him some shame, "on which side did your forebears fight?" He is a John Calhoun among the damned, ever revisiting the one great aim of his life: for him, to establish his family as pre-eminent in Florence. Thus when Dante replies, Farinata responds as a man for whom the past alone, a severely circumscribed past, has any meaning:

> "They were bold enemies of mine,
> > fierce to my party and my ancestors,
> > for which twice over I sent them scattering." (10.46–48)

Note the irony of Farinata's question and reply. Farinata was endowed with a prodigious intellect. We see in this canto a glimmer of what should have been its grandeur. Yet what he believed about body and soul, Dante suggests, darkened his mind. For the materialist, time measures alteration in bodies, no more. Therefore the meaning of time is circumscribed by one's bodily experience of the time during which one lives. At best, the materialist can hope to transcend time—it is a delusive hope—by means of material perpetuation. For example, he can follow the fond recommendations of the usually confused and unreliable narrator of Shakespeare's sonnets: he can beget children and fight to make his family great; or he can fashion works of genius that will withstand the ravages of time. But works of genius fade into oblivion, and families decline and die. Farinata's family was ousted from power when the Guelphs reassembled and defeated the Ghibellines at Benevento (1264). They have yet to return from their exile. So Dante in measured voice flings Farinata's boast back in his teeth:

> "If they were twice cast out, they twice returned"—
> > I thus responded—"and from every side,
> > an art which yours, it seems, have not well learned." (10.49–51)

Time and the Poet in Love

IN THIS ENCOUNTER WE witness not a rerun of a past battle, but a clash between two ways of experiencing time and between two planes of knowledge
derived from the experience. One way is chained to time and to the devouring
grave; the other, duly thankful for the gifts of time, sees that time derives from
eternity both its source and its end. For before Farinata can respond again,
another spirit rises beside him in the tomb, a spirit not defiant but plaintive.
Like Farinata, he is a family man, but he expresses no interest in the city or in
parties; only in the glory of his son:

> Then next to him out of the lidless tomb
>   arose a shadow visible to the chin;
>   I think he must have risen to his knees.
> He looked around me, searched, as if he longed
>   to see if someone else was there with me,
>   and when his little hope was doused, he wept
> And said, "If through this dungeon of the blind
>   you go by means of genius at its height, ˙
>   where is my son? Why is he not with you?" (10.52–60)

The shade is Cavalcante de' Cavalcanti, father of Dante's friend and fellow poet, Guido Cavalcanti (1250–1300). Cavalcanti was a Guelph, but his
rumored Epicureanism lands him uncomfortably in the same tomb with Farinata, his son's father-in-law. The doting father gets everything wrong, and his
ignorance of the time is much to blame. Before we see why, let us complete
his conversation with Dante:

> And I: "I haven't come here on my own.
>   He who stands waiting leads me through this place
>   for one your Guido, maybe, held in scorn."
> I'd read his name already by his words
>   and by the manner of his punishment,
>   so I replied in full. But suddenly
> He drew upright and cried, "What do you mean?
>   You said 'he held'—isn't he still alive?
>   Has the sweet sunlight ceased to strike his eyes?"
> And when he noticed I was hesitant
>   and didn't answer him immediately,
>   he fell back, and did not come out again. (10.61–72)

Why does he long to see his son? It is natural in a father—unless that father happens to be in hell. He forgets his situation. What would it mean for Guido, if his father should see him here? But Cavalcante, who experiences in his own person proof to the contrary, still speaks as one who believes that the passing day is all there is.

Maybe Cavalcante senses that Dante is still alive, and, as a man who placed all his hope for posterity in the renown of his son, wonders with dismay why it is Dante taking the grand tour and not Guido. If so, he reveals still deeper ignorance. He assumes that Dante's presence is owing to "genius at its height." Set aside the question of the genius of Dante's poetry. The *character* Dante has told us why he is traveling through hell: his time for salvation was dwindling away when the grace of God intervened. Beatrice, the woman he loved when he was young, sent Virgil from the circle of the virtuous pagans to rescue Dante just in time. Cavalcante's mind conceives of perpetuity only, an endless continuation of earthly time. It never occurs to him to think of the irruption of eternity into that earthly time.

But if he thinks that Guido was a greater genius than Dante, he is also mistaken, and that has little to do with who possessed the more powerful intellect. It has rather to do with how Guido understood love and the soul of man. Guido helped create what came to be called the *dolce stil novo*, the "sweet new style" of Italian love poetry. This style merged the philosophical and theological language of the schools, expressed in the subtle metaphors of many a Provençal troubadour, with elegant and lyrical diction. Dante joined him enthusiastically in this enterprise; but for the elder poet there was no Beatrice to direct his attention to the heavens. Guido insists that love is a potent and irrational force, irresistible, as determined by nature as is the leaping of fire. Our intellects too are wholly determined. Guido seems to follow the Muslim philosopher Averroës, arguing that a man's mind is but one movement in an Agent Intellect that governs the cosmos. If so, then individual immortality makes no sense. Averroës argued that the soul is immortal only by its impersonal participation in the Agent Intellect. What makes us individual passes away with the passing of the body.

This is not Epicureanism, but it leads to the same grave. Dante says nothing definite about the state of his friend's soul; Guido died in the fall of 1300, a few months after the purported time of Dante's journey to the world beyond. Surely Dante held out a flash of hope that Guido might yet be saved—that he might yet turn to the one he "maybe held in scorn." That cannot be Virgil: no true Italian poet would despise the greatest master of the Latin tongue. It must be Beatrice, or rather the theology that Beatrice represents; it must be Christ, towards whom Beatrice always leads the mind and heart of her devotee.

The Stars That Move at the Urging of Love

WE FIRST HEAR OF the friendship of Dante and Cavalcanti in *La Vita Nuova*, Dante's allegorical account of his love for Beatrice, her early death, his partial falling away from devotion to her, and his resolution to return. It is not a story of "falling in love" as we would recognize it. Dante gives us almost no circumstances surrounding his few encounters with Beatrice; we do not even know what she looks like. But we are given, with excruciating care, the time of the love, as told by the clock of eternity: "Nine times already since my birth the heaven of light had circled back almost to the same point, when there appeared before my eyes the now glorious lady of my mind, who was called Beatrice even by those who did not know what her name was. She had been in this life long enough for the heaven of the fixed stars to be able to move a twelfth of a degree to the East in her time; that is, she appeared to me at about the beginning of her ninth year, and I first saw her near the end of my ninth year" (*La Vita Nuova*, II). Dante does not say, as we would, that he and she were about nine years old. Instead, he places the age of his lady within the context of a cosmic year, the time it takes for all the "spheres" of the planets and the fixed stars to return together to their original positions. The cycle of the cosmic year (about 38,800 solar years) was thought to correspond to the total age of the cosmos; the consummation of the world would occur when the year was complete. It is also important, as Dante reminds us, that the stars, fixed in place relative to one another, move slowly eastward, since from the East comes the rising sun of the world, Christ the daystar that never sets.

Before we know anything else about Beatrice we know that she has died and been raised to glory: she is "the now glorious lady of my mind" (II). Her salvation is implicit in her name, which Dante begs us to read allegorically, for *nomina sunt consequentia rerum*, names are consequent upon the things they name. Her name is Beatrice, the woman who blesses, and people who do not know her name, says Dante, by natural insight see that she is Beatrice.

To see Beatrice, then, is to be called to love, a call that has eternal consequences. The effect on Dante is instantaneous and draws responses, not all of them orderly, from the faculties of his body and soul:

At that very moment, and I speak the truth, the vital spirit, the one that dwells in the most secret chamber of the heart, began to tremble so violently that even the most minute veins of my body were strangely affected; and trembling, it spoke these words: *Ecce deus fortior me, qui veniens dominabitur michi* ["Behold, a god who is stronger than I am, who comes to be my lord"]. At that point the animal spirit, the one abiding in the high chamber to which all the senses bring their perceptions, was stricken with amazement and, speaking directly to the spirits of sight, said these words: *Apparuit iam beatitudo vestra* ["Now has your bliss appeared"]. At that point the natural spirit, the one dwelling in that part where our food is digested, began to weep, and weeping said these words: *Heu miser, quia frequenter impeditus ero deincepts!* "Poor me! For from now on I shall be thwarted again and again." (II)

These faculties—roughly the chest, the head, and the belly, to use C. S. Lewis's scheme in *The Abolition of Man*—greet the coming of love in strikingly different ways. The vital spirit, deep in the heart, senses that its life will never be the same; it trembles with fear and awe; it understands that it must now pay honor to the lordship of love; it respects the order, despite the fear. The animal spirit (or, we should translate, that which makes Dante a living soul) receives the sense impressions of Beatrice's beauty and interprets them for the sight, that sense closest to immateriality and thus noblest and most divine. "Your bliss *has* appeared," it says, using the perfect tense for something that has already happened, or for something whose consummation is implicit in what has happened. Obviously, the nine-year-old Dante has not been ravished into the heaven of heavens! That is yet to come; but the kingdom is already within him. "I have overcome the world," says Jesus *before* the Passion and Resurrection. Dante's bliss has appeared, is now appearing, and its fulfillment is to come. Already we sense that this mysterious Beatrice will be the means for Dante's enjoyment of "the good of the intellect," that *vision* of God, not through a glass, darkly, but face to face (1 Cor. 13:12).

Yet the belly worries. It too is a prophet, and it does not like what it sees. It moans that it will often be thwarted from now on. Evidently the love that summons Dante is all-consuming and passionate, yet not with such passions as to fill the rebellious desires of the belly. It is intensely erotic, yet virginal, and its aim is the summit of bliss. If such a love is not to the belly's liking, that must mean two things: that man is fallen, since his faculties suffer internecine strife; and that the belly—the appetite for material satisfaction—cannot be all there is.

If you are a materialist, then, you cannot understand Beatrice. You do not see her beauty. But then you cannot be raised to the summit of poetic excellence. You lack the knowledge. You are stuck in time, and cannot tell the hour.

Dante, however, says that upon his first sight of Beatrice he submitted to the authority of Love. It governed his soul, and his imagination granted it such lordship that, as the poet says, "I could only dedicate myself to fulfilling his every pleasure." This Love, as I read it, is none other than "the Love that moves the sun and the other stars," Christ manifest in the heart of a young lad smitten with the beauty of a young lady. Love is, Dante will say, the secret of his poetry. For when Dante is near the top of the mount of purgatory, he meets an older poet, Bonagiunta, one whom he had criticized for his earth-bound imagination, but who now praises Dante by quoting the first line of the most famous love lyric of the Middle Ages (the second canzone of *La Vita Nuova*):

> "But do I see the introducer of
> the new songs, and the verses which begin,
> '*Ladies who have intelligence of love*'?" (*Purgatory*, 24.49–51)

Those ladies who know love by intellect, that is, by direct and divine sight, will know the truth of Beatrice, "desired in highest heaven" (*VN* 19.29), says that canzone. Dante's reply to Bonagiunta shows that he now understands that his humble place as a poet is to accept what Love grants him to see:

> Said I to him, "I'm one who takes the pen
> when Love breathes wisdom into me, and go
> finding the signs for what he speaks within." (*Purgatory*, 24.52–54)

If poetry is the result of "genius at its height," as the materialist Cavalcante believes, what is the need for the in-breathed wisdom of Love? But without that Love, Dante would not now be passing through the lower world; Love made him a poet, and when he was in trouble, Love descended to send him on his long journey. It is beyond the capacity of the belly to understand. Not that the boy Dante fares much better. Youth is the season of passions, and the belly has a love of its own. Most of *La Vita Nuova* will examine, in ironic retrospect, the young lover's confusion, falling from the Love towards which Beatrice directs him to the self-indulgent infatuation wherein he wastes his time, weeping, brooding, and concealing the truth from himself and others.

What did Guido make of this Love? Dante, reading eternity back into the hours of his youth, notes that his vision appeared to him at exactly the ninth hour of the night. His young persona hardly seems to understand the significance of the hour (nine, he will note much later, is the square of trinity; and Christ died at the ninth hour; cf. *VN*, xxix). Still, he decides to write a poem about it, and sends it to the most famous poets of the day. Guido responds with a poem of his own, beginning with the cryptic phrase, "I think that you have beheld all worth" (iii). That day, says Dante, marked the beginning of their friendship.

What Guido meant by that line is hard to tell, but Dante uses it in *La Vita Nuova* as the first instance wherein Guido is seen as preparing the way for Dante, or rather wherein the love poetry that Guido wrote is superseded by a vision of Love that the young Dante does not yet fully understand. Later in *La Vita Nuova*, Love appears to Dante, saying, "See that you bless the day that I took you captive; it is your duty to do so" (xxiv). That "day" is placed immediately in the context of the history of man's redemption. When the poet looks up, he sees a woman coming his way—it is the beloved lady of his best friend, Guido:

> Her name was Giovanna, but because of her beauty (as many believed) she had been given the name Primavera, meaning Spring, and so she came to be called. And, looking behind her, I saw coming the miraculous Beatrice. These ladies passed close by me, one of them following the other, and it seemed that Love spoke in my heart and said, "The one in front is called Primavera only because of the way she comes today; for I inspired the giver of her name to call her Primavera, meaning 'she will come first' [*prima verrà*] on the day that Beatrice shows herself after the dream of her faithful one. And if you will also consider her real name, you will see that this too means 'she will come first,' since the name Joan [*Giovanna*] comes from the name of that John [*Giovanni*] who preceded the True Light, saying: *Ego vox clamantis in deserto: parate viam Domini* ["I am the voice of one crying out in the desert: prepare ye the way of the Lord"]. After this, Love seemed to speak again and say these words: "Anyone of subtle discernment would call Beatrice Love, because she so greatly resembles me." (xxiv)

Guido's "Joan" is as John the Baptist, crying out in a wilderness of dead poetry, as if to prepare the world for the coming of the true vision of Love. Thus, Dante's poetry depends upon that of his elder predecessor yet soars beyond it: not through Dante's powers, but because the Love that Dante is given to see is the fulfillment of that which Guido was given to see. Or, to put it more starkly, Guido's poetry is only important because it points the way to Beatrice.

Whether Guido agreed with that assessment is doubtful; hence Dante's hesitation about his friend's spiritual state in 1300, the year whose end Guido would not live to see. But Dante had no hesitation about his own spiritual state at that same time: he was on his way to perdition. Why? Beatrice will suggest that Dante betrayed her for the love of another woman. The sin is not sexual infidelity. After all, Dante was a married man, and Beatrice, shortly before she died, became a married woman. Rather, as Dante suggests in the *Convivio*, he fell in love with a lady called Philosophy—perhaps the same lady from whom, in *La Vita Nuova*, Dante derives some comfort after Beatrice's death (XXXV–XXXVIII). Philosophy is the handmaid of theology, says Thomas Aquinas, but the young Dante reverses the order. If that is the betrayal whereof Beatrice will accuse Dante so harshly (*Purgatory*, 30.112–38; 31.22–30), then the poet has provided us with a superb irony. To the extent that Guido understood his poetry of love as preparatory to a poetry celebrating the true and only Love, the Love that made and redeemed the universe, then Guido wrote well, and preceded Dante in more ways than one. His love was timely, and eternal. To the extent that Dante abandoned that same understanding, and chose the paths of philosophy (particularly Averroist philosophy) as superior to those of theology, then Dante fell astray. In that sense, which Guido's father does not understand, Dante does indeed go through hell because of "genius at its height," namely the same pride that damned Cavalcante and that threatens to damn his son.

Problems with Tenses, Problems with Time

AGAIN, A SIMPLE QUESTION, "Why are you here rather than my son? Why is my son not with you?" is not simple at all. Cavalcante knows only his hopes for his son's earthly career; but his question raises the meaning of Guido's poetry, the meaning of Dante's, the nature of Love, and the providential design of God, who Dante sees as intending that Guido should precede him, just as Primavera should precede Beatrice, the woman who blesses.

Dante's awkward and circumlocutory attempt to clear up the confusion for Cavalcante—for it would be prideful and flatly incorrect to agree that he is passing through hell under the power of his own genius—only makes matters worse for the poor sinner. Cavalcante does not hear the message. He asks nothing about the identity of the "One," nor does he wonder whether Guido really held that One in scorn. He does not pause to consider that if Guido *did* hold the One in scorn, he should only have been following in his father's footsteps! Instead he zeroes in on a single verb, or rather not the verb but its tense: "he *held*." That means only one thing to Cavalcante, who anticipates the answer (incorrectly), and will not wait for Dante's explanation. It means Guido is dead. The materialist, who by now ought to know better, still cannot imagine anything worse than death. "Has the sweet sunlight ceased to strike his eyes?" he asks plaintively, and with consummate illogic (*Inf.*, 10.68–69).

Dante fails to disabuse him of his error. He stands hesitant and puzzled, and we soon learn why. Meanwhile, Farinata resumes the conversation. It seems Dante has told *him* something unpleasant, too—though the greatheart-ed Farinata does not slump weeping back into his tomb. *He* stands as if impas-sive. But the news of his kinsmen's continuing exile cuts him to the heart:

> "If they have badly learned that art, that wrings
> more pain from me than does this bed of fire." (10.77–78)

He repays Dante with a prophesy of his own:

> "Yet fifty times the moon will not re-burn—
> that face of Hecate, the queen of Hell—
> before you find how hard that is to learn." (10.79–81)

Dante too will be exiled from Florence, nor, as it turns out, will he ever return. Though his words remain within the realm of time and change, Farinata tells the truth, and forges a connection between men who deserved better from their city. For after Montaperti, when the Ghibelline victors planned to level the city to the ground, Farinata stood against them, and saved Florence:

> "But when each man agreed to wipe away
> Florence from off the earth, I was alone,
> her sole defender in the sight of all." (10.91–93)

Strange, that the man who found nothing better to love than his city ended by nearly destroying it. Cavalcante and he are not so different after all.

This understanding between the exiles—and their shared love for the un-grateful city—offers the poet the chance to ask about something odd. He is still puzzling over his conversation with Cavalcante, and wonders why the old man did not know whether his son was alive or dead. Farinata has prophesied; so has Charon, the ferryman of the damned, foretelling another sort of ship for Dante's departed soul (3.91–93); and the Florentine Ciacco foretold the defeat of Dante's White Guelphs at the hands of the Black Guelphs, to which the Cavalcanti belonged (6.64–75). If souls in hell can see the future, why can't they see the present?

Dante puts the answer in the mouth of the man who would be most pained to confess it. Says Farinata:

> "As a man with bad vision," he replied,
>   "we dimly see things far away. So much
>   splendor the sovereign Lord still shines on us.
> When things draw near, or happen, emptiness
>   is all we see. If no one brings us news,
>   we can know nothing of your human state.
> Now you can understand that evermore
>   dead will be all our knowledge form the time
>   the future ends, and Judgment shuts the door." (10.100–108)

Hell reverses the natural mode of human knowledge. On earth, we see the present, we remember some of the past, and we dimly perceive what is to come. Our threefold experience of time, Augustine argued, suggests the immortality of our souls and reflects the Trinity. Farinata and his fellow materialists ignored the suggestion when they were alive, and now they are acutely aware of how they had turned time inside out. For now by the power of God they know what is to come, but they forget it as it draws near, leaving them only the past wherein to dwell, the now changeless past. To put it another way: the blessed dwell in eternity, where they enjoy all the flowers and fruit of time. But the damned, who ignored eternity, now dwell in time, but a dead time, an endless, wearisome time, wherein change serves only to remind the damned that nothing ever changes.

To mistake the nature of time as the materialists do is to deny hope, and that is to invite hell into one's house before hell's time. But man is made for hope, since he can apprehend what he cannot comprehend. As Browning puts it: "Ah, but a man's reach should exceed his grasp, / Or what's a heaven for?" ("Andrea del Sarto," 97–98). Why should we be made to conceive of the infinite, without being able to know it? To conceive of God, but never to see him? To know, and then to discover a blank wall that hems our knowledge in forever? No, Christians affirm that in this life man is made for hope, hope for an eternal flourishing of knowledge, for the vision of Truth that fulfills our love: "We see now through a mirror in an obscure manner, but then face to face. Now I know in part, but then I shall know even as I have been known. So there abide faith, hope, and charity, these three; but the greatest of these is charity" (1 Cor. 13:12–13). By contrast, the damned suffer a containment and constriction, and to use the words of Christ, "from him who does not have, even that which he thinks he has shall be taken away" (Luke 8:18). When the trump of doom sounds and the lids seal the tombs of the heretics, there will be no more future for them to see, nothing more to happen, nothing more to know.

Redeeming the Time

To FOLLOW THE TEACHINGS of Jesus, we must live for the morrow, and not for the morrow. We are to keep our lamps burning brightly, as we watch for the coming of the Bridegroom (Matt. 25:1–14); but we are to take no care about what we are going to eat or wear in the days to come (Matt. 6:25–34). We are to live in the present, for sufficient to the day are the troubles thereof (Matt. 6:34), and the kingdom of God is within us, and "this day is this Scripture fulfilled" in our hearing (Luke 4:21); yet we are also to know that "all flesh is as grass, and all the glory of man as the flower of grass" (1 Pet. 1:24), and that heaven and earth shall pass away (Matt. 24:35). We are to live in the past, as we recall the promises God made to Abraham, Isaac, and Jacob, and the witness of the prophets, and the Passover instituted by Moses; and we are to let the past be past, as the Lord could raise sons of Abraham from the very stones (Luke 3:8), and Moses fed our fathers manna in the desert, yet they died (John 6:49), and a greater man than Solomon is here (Matt. 12:42).

The question, then, is not which temporal direction we face, but whether the past and present and future we remember and perceive and foresee are infused with the grace of Christ. Outside of the Word, we are all old, and the clock ticks on towards our dread midnight. By grace, we play our part in the drama of our rejuvenation, wrought by God not despite our hours and days, but in them and through them.

Christians are not to imitate Marcus Aurelius, whose "salvation" depended upon his severe self-discipline, the removal of his affections from any transient object. The good but grim emperor left behind his elegant meditations of despair, and a son who agreed with him in at least one regard, that there was nothing really to live for—and that therefore one might as well be thoroughly debauched. Christians imitate Christ, whose life was full of dramatic entrances, of passionate friendship, of travel and toil, heartache and joy, celebrations in memory of the great works God had done for his people, and one celebration enacting a great work that God would do ever after.

The smallest gesture in Christ's life could mean salvation or loss. The rich young man asks what he must do to gain the kingdom of God; Jesus, with a rush of affection, invites him to surpass the observance of the commandments and to follow him. Whose heart should not leap at such an invitation from the lips of the Savior? And for a moment that young man might have sold all he had, and become one of the greatest of the saints. He chose otherwise (Mark 10:17–22). The old woman with the hemorrhage presses through the crowd and touches the hem of Jesus' garment (Mark 5:25–34). The men with the paralytic on the pallet cannot get into the house where Jesus is teaching, so they climb upon the thatched roof, tear a hole in it—a daring initiative, seeing that it is somebody else's house!—and lower him down into Jesus' midst (Mark 2:1–12). The Jews have left Jesus, scoffing at his telling them that they must eat his flesh and drink his blood; Jesus turns to his chosen twelve to ask them whether they will leave, too. There is an awkward silence; then Peter says, "Lord, to whom shall we go? thou hast the words of eternal life" (John 6:68). The jaded procurator asks him what his mission is. With unearthly calm, Jesus replies that he has come to witness to the truth, and that all who hear the truth, hear his voice. There is another uncomfortable pause; the procurator's life of bureaucratic climbing and strategic cruelty passes before his eyes. Here is a possibility of change, an invitation to hear—but the man shrugs, "What is truth?" And the door shuts (John 18:37–38).

One Moment, an Eternity

SHOULD WE EXPECT ANYTHING different from the Lord of time? Dante thought not.

The emperor rides forth from the great city, accompanied by his legions, their bronze shields and leather armor shining in the sun. He is a noble and patient man, this emperor, going off to war not to gain glory but to secure the border in far Dacia, that cold inhospitable land of mountains, west of the Black Sea.

> For there was told in sculpture the high glory
>   of the one Roman principate whose worth
>   moved Gregory to his greatest victory,
> I speak of Trajan, emperor of Rome;
>   and an old woman at his horse's rein
>   stood as one shedding tears and stooped with sorrow.
> Crowded about him pressed the cavalry,
>   and high above them stirring in the breeze
>   appeared the eagles in the field of gold.
> The poor old woman among all of these
>   seemed to say, "Justice, Lord! Avenge my son!
>   He's murdered, and the sorrow breaks my heart." (*Purgatory*, 10.73–84)

With a single hint—the "victory" of Pope Gregory the Great, occurring five centuries later—Dante places us in the audience of a drama whose actors are wholly unaware of the eternal significance of their actions. I shall have more to say about that victory. For now, consider the scene. Many an emperor had to leave Rome to fight on the frontier; and no doubt requests for justice, reaching beyond local corruption all the way to the emperor, wore away the man's time in the city. What should Trajan do now?

He has all the excuses on his side. He's in a hurry. The problems in Dacia are more important to the commonweal than is the case of one woman and her son. The cavalry are waiting. There are plenty of people who might see to the matter. It is unseemly for an emperor to get off his horse to investigate a crime, on the word of a raving old woman.

But if not for an old woman, then for whom? It may be the most terrible suffering in the world, that of a mother whose son has been slain unjustly. It is not a new thing; the reader may think of another woman who suffered the same. For the pilgrim Dante has just witnessed, on the walls of this first ring of purgatory, the living sculpture of the Annunciation:

> The angel who came down
>   with the decree that brought to earth the peace
>   for which men wept so many years, which freed
> The gates of Heaven long prohibited,
>   to us appeared so true, engraven there
>   in sweet and courteous pose, he did not seem
> A silent form. You'd swear you heard him say
>   "Hail!"—for the one who opened Heaven's high love
>   was there in image, she who turned the key,

> And in her pose was stamped the spoken word,
>> exactly as a seal in molten wax,
>> *"Behold, I am the handmaid of the Lord."* (10.34–45)

The humility of Mary, mother of sorrows, directs us to the humility of her son, conceived at this moment, to be born and to preach and to suffer and to die unjustly at the hands of those to whom he only sought to give life. Now everything changes; the Annunciation, not Christmas, marks the entry into time of the Incarnate Christ. This is the new year dawning: and, if we are to believe Dante, the stars are in precise position to shed their most benign influence upon the child conceived. Only once before had they held that position: at the creation of Adam. But Adam would sin—a mere six hours after his creation in Eden, says Dante (*Paradise*, 26.142). This new Adam would humble himself, even unto death upon a cross, to take away the sins of the world.

Between the sculptures of the Annunciation and Trajan, another sculpture stands as a bridge, giving us another account of a mysterious conception within the womb, and another king rendering justice. It tells of how King David brought the ark of the covenant into Jerusalem:

> Leading the way in dance and reveling,
>> his skirts tucked high, the humble psalmist came,
>> at once appearing more and less than king. (10.64–66)

Elaborately decorated though it was, that ark was a cedar box, no more. Yet it made manifest God's presence among his people. It bore the tables of the law given to Moses, Aaron's priestly staff, and a bit of the manna that fed the Israelites on their way through the Sinai. Naturally, Christians saw in that ark a foreshadowing of the womb of Mary: she would house the giver of the new Law, the sole high priest, and the Bread of Life. David's dancing, then, is a humble act of homage to God and to the Messiah to come; he is less than king because he descends to dance, and more than king, because his humility conforms him to his Creator and descendant, Christ the king. His wife Michal looks on in ignorance; she despises him for dancing with such abandon that his loincloth rises up over his shame, in full sight of the common women. For her contempt, the Lord punishes her with childlessness: *her* womb shall be closed (2 Sam. 6:23).

Those two sculptures compel us to see, mysteriously, the presence of God-with-us, *Emmanuel*, in the scene with Trajan, too, not that anyone in the scene would have understood it so. But we have a woman whose son was slain unjustly. We have a plea for justice, which kings were ordained by God to serve. We have a "field of gold" in the imperial flag, suggesting the changeless heavens. We have the eagle—symbol of the Roman Empire, and, as we shall see, the constellation formed in paradise by those saints who on earth loved justice. Christ is calling Trajan, though Trajan does not know it.

Unlike the rich young man, Trajan does not turn away:

> And he responded, "Wait till I return,"
>   and she, as one whom grief still hurries on,
>   "What if you never do return, my lord?"
> "The man who takes my place, he'll see it done."
>   And she: "What will his good deed do for you?
>   He performs his, and you neglect your own.
> Whence his reply, "Take comfort. I must do
>   my duty in this place before I move.
>   Justice demands it, pity holds me here." (10.85–93)

Trajan teeters on the brink of doing the reasonable thing. Had he done so, had he left the old woman in tears, he would not have moved Gregory to his greatest victory; he would have been shut out from eternal bliss. But he humbly admits that the old woman is right—*her* grief hurries her on, and justly so. Dacia can wait.

To believe in the goodness of the created world is to believe that what we do with our time matters. If God who created the world also sustains it now, not abandoning it but bringing it to its consummation by the ordering of his eternal providence, then no moment in our lives stands apart from the rest of time and its significance. In the scene with Trajan, it is providential, not coincidental, that an old woman should approach him; and even though he does the right thing, he does it with the necessary ignorance of someone within a story who, because he is within it and not beyond it, cannot know the full meaning of his actions. When he descends from his horse, the angels rejoice; yet Trajan will not hear those angels until many years have passed.

A Prayer in Time

FIVE CENTURIES AFTER THIS drama, as the legend goes, Pope Gregory thought about Trajan and the widow. So moved was he by the man's goodness, he prayed that the Lord would raise Trajan from the dead, that the emperor might hear the good news and die a believing Christian. From this pious legend Dante derives a lesson of tremendous power.

His pilgrim has accompanied Beatrice into paradise. They are in the sphere of Jupiter, the circle of the just rulers. There they see a constellation of blest souls spelling out the first words of the Book of Wisdom: DILIGITE IUSTITIAM QUI IUDICATIS TERRAM (Love justice, ye who rule the earth [Wisd. 1:1]). The souls thus not only propound the Word of God, but embody that Word in their persons—so deeply is the love of justice infused with the love of God, whose divine plan is the unfolding of righteousness in time.

The wicked, however, see how short man's life is, and, rejecting the immortality of the soul and the resurrection of the body, conclude that they ought to use that time while they can, practicing injustice: "The time of our life is short and tedious, and in the end of a man there is no remedy, and no man hath been known to have returned from hell" (Wisd. 2:1–2); "Come, therefore, and let us enjoy the good things that are present. . . . Let us oppress the poor just man, and not spare the widow, nor honor the ancient gray hairs of the aged. But let our strength be the law of justice, for that which is feeble, is found to be nothing worth" (2:6, 10–11). They see themselves as immersed in the present, but do not understand the time: in the end of man there *is* a remedy, and a man *will* come forth from the dead.

When Dante beholds the final "M" of the verse, the star-souls shift position slightly, transforming the M into the heraldic lily of France (the lily is the flower of the resurrection), and then into an imperial eagle, the same that graced the standards of Trajan's legions as they made their way to Dacia. It is this eagle, in a collective body, that speaks to Dante about justice. For Dante has been hungering for the answer to one question above all, a question that cries out for love of his old guide, Virgil, now returned to limbo, the first ring of hell, where dwell all those who were virtuous but who never heard the word of God. How can this be just?

The answer would involve us in a long discussion of the theological virtue of faith. Suffice it to say that the eagle's response is twofold. The first response is negative. The eagle reminds Dante of the limitations of human knowledge:

> "So in the justice of eternity
>> the vision of your world can plumb no more
>> than can the eye that stares into the sea,
> Seeing the bottom when you're near the shore
>> but not on the high main; and nonetheless,

> hidden in its profundity, the floor
> Lies there below." (*Paradise*, 19.58–64)

Not only should that limitation cause us, who "can't see any farther than a span" (19.81), to hesitate before we attribute injustice to God; it will provide plenty of nominally Christian rulers a terrible surprise when judgment comes:

> "Such Christians the Ethiopian will decry
>   at the division of the flocks that brings
>   man to eternal wealth or poverty." (19.109–11)

But the real irony is revealed when the eagle gives the second movement of his answer. It directs Dante's attention to the part of the constellation that forms the eye: for eagles were legendary for being able to gaze into the sun. The five souls that form the eyebrow, and the single soul who stands as the pupil, are those whom God has granted the ability to see most deeply into the nature of justice. In each case, the ruler is shown as one who did not understand something when he lived on earth, and now, with ironic justice, he does understand. The central soul is that of David, again presented as "the singer of the Holy Spirit, / the king who moved the Ark from house to house," who now understands that his humble songs, though inspired by God, yet win him merit, "insofar as they spring from his own will" (20.37–42)—though he could never have imagined that those songs could "earn" him the bliss he now enjoys! What we merit is still God's gift, because no one can merit the gift of himself that God showers upon those he blesses.

After David, just as around the mountainside of purgatory, comes Trajan:

> The spirit who stands nearest to my bill
>   of the five in the ring that forms the brow
>   consoled the widow with the murdered son;
> Now does he understand what debt you owe
>   not following Christ, by the experience
>   of this sweet life, and the opposite below. (19.43–48)

A pagan, in heaven? And, to add to Dante's astonishment, Trajan is not the only one. Here is the final soul named by the eagle:

> Who would believe, down in the world that errs,
>   that Ripheus the Trojan in this round
>   would be the fifth among the holy flares?

> Far more he understands of grace divine
>> than all the world can see, although his eye
>> can still not plumb the depth of the profound. (19.67–72)

When Dante expresses wonder and surprise, the eagle—glittering with the delight of blessed souls who enjoy watching someone learn what will delight him too—answers that no one can know the secret workings of God's grace in this life. Yet your next word as you turn the corner can mean life or death; such is the drama to which we are summoned. Heaven allows itself to be "won"; it prompts us to batter its walls, and that "loss" is its splendid victory. In that sense, the cases of Trajan and Ripheus are not exceptional at all. No one is saved without the extraordinary grace of God; what is really miraculous is not what happened to those two pagans, but what has happened to all of us pagans. The miracle is that God should have created us in the first place, and, having created us, should allow us, mere dust, to petition him for a bliss which we cannot merit, but which he wishes above all to give us. The miracle is that God made beings whose lives have eternal meaning—beings capable of love.

Then Trajan and Ripheus are saved by means of things that happen in their lives, no matter that in their cases the things were what we would call unusual. What could be more unusual than that God could provide dust with a tongue and then hear it crying out to him? Yet so he has done; and Trajan stands for all those unnamed multitudes who may be saved by the intercessory prayer of a man whom God in his mercy has made righteous. Says the eagle:

> To flesh and bone
>> the one returned from never-repenting Hell,
>> and that was the reward of living hope,
> Of living hope, with power to impel
>> prayers to God that he might rise once more,
>> and live, and so be moved to living well.
> Returned unto his flesh the briefest hour,
>> the glorious spirit I've been speaking of
>> believed in Him and sought His help and power,
> And in believing, kindled into love
>> so true, the second time he fell asleep
>> he merited his coming to this joy. (19.106–17)

A child will believe where the cramped materialist will rebel. Our lives are stories in time, as we are embodied beings, not equations. What would have happened had Trajan not descended from his horse? Gregory would not have fallen in love with Trajan's humility. He would not have been moved to pray his extraordinary prayer—or rather, simply to pray; for we have become accustomed to the idea of prayer, and fail to see the wonder of it. Then Trajan would not have been raised again. He would still be in the regions below. Will God do what God will do, regardless of my prayer? But he provides for my prayer; it is one of the causes he has foreseen. If we knock, says Jesus, it will be opened unto us. We may infer that if we fail to knock, it may not be opened; and if we persist in failing, Farinata and Cavalcante, those misconstruers of time, can tell us plenty about lost opportunities.

As for Ripheus the Trojan, he too is saved by a remarkable event, something that happened to him at a moment in his life. It was nothing so strange as being raised from the grave to hear a priest preaching the word; or perhaps it was stranger than that. It was a mysterious approach of God, whose name Ripheus did not know. It was a prompting of the soul, no less real than my being accosted by a friend on my way to work. It was more real, as it derived directly from the source of all Being:

> By grace that showers from a spring so deep
>   no creature's sight can penetrate into
>   its first upwelling wave, the other soul
> Placed all his love in righteousness below;
>   for which, grace upon grace, God raised his eye
>   and showed him our redemption yet to come,
> And he believed in it, and from that day
>   he could not bear the stink of paganism,
>   and he reproached the people gone awry.
> Those Ladies were his sponsors at baptism,
>   the three at the right wheel of the chariot,
>   a thousand years before the Baptist came. (19.118–29)

What vision Ripheus was granted, Dante does not say. All we know is that somehow Ripheus knew, just as somehow the mysterious Enoch long ago "walked with God" (Gen. 5:24), though as yet there was no clear prophecy of a Messiah, no covenant with Noah, no revelation to Abraham, no law given to Moses. Ripheus responded. He turned the corner, and his baptism really happened, with the noblest sponsors a newborn could have: the ladies named Faith, Hope, and Charity.

What joy it is, suggests the eagle, to live in such a world—a real drama, whose entirety we can never know! Knowledge is surely a gift of God, but so is the gracious withholding of knowledge, and the giving of knowledge that had been withheld for a time, now given at the right time, the fullness of time. The eagle's last words to Dante, and its last blissful gestures, are a hymn to the providence of God, wherein we find redeemed the hours of our lives, even the fleeting grace notes of a song:

> "O predestination, how remote
>> your root is from those sights that cannot see
>> the fullness of the primal cause! And you
> Mortals, withhold your judgment: even we
>> who see the face of God do not yet know
>> the number chosen from eternity—
> And it is sweet, this lack in what we know,
>> because in this good is our good made fine,
>> that what the Lord may will, we too will so."
> So was I given soothing medicine
>> to clear the haze from vision all too near,
>> by that bright icon, seal of the divine.
> And as an expert hand on the guitar
>> follows the singer with a trembling chord,
>> lending a greater pleasure to the air,
> So while the Eagle spoke I can recall
>> those two blest gleams of light, that I could see
>> flashing their happy flames at every word,
> Like eyes that blink in perfect harmony. (19.130–48)

For God who made time will allow nothing genuinely good to be lost forever: not the love of a young man for a beautiful girl named Beatrice; not his devotion to the city of his birth; not his admiration for the poetry of an old Roman master; not the songs of mamas at the cradle; not the affection of a proud father; not prayer; not the slenderest act of faith; not our flickerings of hope; not our rag-ends of charity. Farinata and Cavalcante, believing in the grave, were old before their time. But the One who sits on the throne, the Ancient of Days, has never aged. He is the wellspring of youth. "Behold," says he, "I make all things new" (Rev. 21:5).

9

The Fullness of Time: Shakespeare's Tempest

For centuries in Europe, the grandest festival of the year was celebrated on a day that has now largely fallen into oblivion.

Imagine that all the guildsmen in town have been busy preparing for the feast. Some are tightening the joints in the portable stages they used last year, and years before that. Others are stitching outlandish costumes; forked tails and masks with horns feature prominently. Others are rehearsing parts passed down from generation to generation—noisy and boisterous, as the players had to be heard above the fruit-hawkers and the children and the more raucous members of a delighted audience.

One guild might be in charge of the plays about Noah and the ark, and the rough time Noah had getting Mrs. Noah inside (so Chaucer recalls it, in "The Miller's Tale"); those would be the carpenters, naturally. Another guild (the goldsmiths?) might stage the play about when Moses received the Ten Commandments and came down the mountain to find the children of Israel dancing before the golden calf. Tanners, wheelwrights, tailors, fletchers, weavers, bakers, fullers, shoemakers: all took their assigned parts in a town-wide feast. Nor was it a play or two that they presented. From church to church, from one end of the village to the other, the worthy people of medieval Portugal and Spain and Germany and France and England would celebrate this feast in a series of plays that spanned human history, beginning with Creation and the Fall of man, and ending with the Final Judgment.

All of time was telescoped into a few days, and why not? There was no incongruity. For they believed that the beginning and the end of the story of man was already known, and was present in its entirety here and now: God created man; man fell by sin, then was redeemed by Christ, to be judged at the last. And the feast that gave birth to these cycles of plays—the West's first resurgence of popular drama in over a thousand years—was Corpus Christi, the feast of the Body and Blood of Christ, present in the sacrament of the Eucharist. Appropriately so, since the doctrine of the real presence of Christ suggests that this moment in time now can only be understood in light of the course of time from beginning to end. It asserts that the Word through whom the world was made in the beginning, and who became flesh at a certain time and place, and who would come again to judge the living and the dead, is present now, not symbolically but in reality.

Many of those popular plays are superb. *The Second Shepherds' Play* of the Wakefield Cycle is a masterpiece of deliberate anachronism: getting the time right by moving freely in and out of time. The shepherds speak about their troubles just as good English peasants would, and swear by Mary and the saints, and accuse a sheep-stealer of being in league with Judas, happily careless of the fact that English peasants did not live in Palestine at the birth of Christ, and that nobody watching over his fields on that holy night could possibly have heard of Judas Iscariot. No matter. The author understands that Christmas is now, too; not a memory of what was, but Christ still and always taking flesh of the Virgin and dwelling among us.

We may smile at the winning naïveté of the so-called mystery plays and their close descendants, the moral interludes, usually put on by traveling troupes of players. My favorite stage direction, in the fine *Castle of Perseverance*, calls for a devil to enter the stage "with fireworks in his arse"! No very dignified entry for the spirit so wicked, and so stupid, as to wage war against the Most High. But in England these popular plays endured from 1215, when Pope Innocent III proclaimed the new holiday, well into the sixteenth century, when they were frowned upon by the royal authorities; in Catholic countries they survived even longer. Cervantes mentions them in passing in *Don Quixote*, and Shakespeare saw them when he was a boy. Hamlet complains about raucous actors who don't know what they're doing, saying that they "out-Herod Herod" (*Hamlet*, 3.2.14), who was traditionally played as a blustering, bellowing tyrant and fool.

For all that Shakespeare distanced himself from the bombast and tomfoolery of the mystery plays, he inherited a great deal from them, too. His dramaturgy springs from the same conviction, often too deep to be expressed in words, that what happens now is related to what has happened and what will happen, that time curls back upon itself, revisits itself, includes the eternal in the passing hour. He too believed in "the fullness of time." That was no belief in some contrived happy ending for the universe, as if God could make everything better by pasting a smile upon the end of time. It was rather the belief that the kingdom of God is at hand, among us and within us, the same kingdom that will be revealed in its fullness at the end of time. Judgment and grace and redemption are all in act now, as they were in the beginning when Adam sinned.

To a materialist such talk is absurd. Time is the fourth dimension of a space-time continuum. If anyone talks about the "right" time for something to happen, he is only saying that it is the "right" time given his purposes. For instance, the "right" time to apply to a college might be when the pool of applicants is shallow. Or he might mean that the time is "right" because that's when something always happens, as determined by nature. You pick blueberries in August because that is when they are ripe. You can try to pick them in July, but you won't have much success.

The older view of time implies an order not only to creation but to all of men's purposes:

> To every thing there is a season, and a time to every purpose under heaven: A time to be born, and a time to die; a time to plant, and a time to pluck up that which has been planted; A time to kill, and a time to heal; a time to break down, and a time to build up; A time to weep, and a time to laugh; a time to mourn, and a time to dance; A time to cast away stones, and a time to gather stones together; a time to embrace, and a time to refrain from embracing; A time to get, and a time to lose; a time to keep, and a time to cast away; A time to rend, and a time to sew; a time to keep silence, and a time to speak; A time to love, and a time to hate; a time of war, and a time of peace. (Eccles. 3:1–8)

It should be easy to see which view of time presents the wider field of opportunity for irony. In the materialist vision, if I do something at the "wrong" time, my failure will quickly be evident. I should have known better than to try to pick blueberries in July. I should not have invaded Russia. I entered the Franco-Prussian War unprepared for Bismarck and his modern military tactics. I waited too long to publish my invention of the calculus, and by the time I got around to it that impostor Leibniz had already claimed the invention as his own.

Those mistakes can be ironic—can stress what someone is sure of, when all along he is mistaken. But imagine the irony of someone who sees that indeed the "right" time for his wicked deed is now, as the opportunity presents itself; but what he views as time, the neutral presenter of chances for shrewd power-seekers, is not time at all, or not time in its fullness. Then you may have the wonderful irony of people so attuned to the main chance (and feeling so superior to those who cannot see the "right" time to act) that they fail to see the real time passing them by, and the even more wonderful irony of people so apparently oblivious to the "right" time and so attuned to eternity that they always seem to do exactly what they ought to do, when they ought to do it. They who speak most vociferously about making the most of time cannot read the clock that ticks away their own last minutes, while they who order their days and weeks and years according to an eternal plan of salvation never seem to be in a hurry, and never arrive late at the shore.

Shakespearean Time

YOU CANNOT DELVE INTO the plays of Shakespeare without noticing his constant meditation upon time and man's works in time. Richard Plantagenet, duke of Gloucester, believes he knows better than duller wits exactly what the time calls for. Unlike Saint Paul, who becomes all things to all men to save some, Richard will be whatever he needs to be to amass power:

> Why, I can smile, and murder whiles I smile,
> And cry, "Content" to that which grieves my heart,
> And wet my cheek with artificial tears,
> And frame my face to all occasions.
> I'll drown more sailors than the mermaid shall;
> I'll slay more gazers than the basilisk;
> I'll play the orator as well as Nestor,
> Deceive more slily than Ulysses could,
> And, like a Sinon, take another Troy.
> I can add colors to the chameleon,
> Change shapes with Proteus for advantages,
> And set the murderous Machiavel to school.
> Can I do this, and cannot get a crown?
> Tut, were it further off, I'll pluck it down. (3 *Henry VI*, 3.2.182–95)

Yet Richard is strangely out of time, too. This awkwardness is one of the themes of the play that bears his name. "The glorious summer" enjoyed by the reign of Richard's brother, the newly crowned Edward IV, pleases everyone but Richard (*Richard III*, 1.1.2). So he works in secret, setting his "friends" against his enemies, only to destroy those allies when he no longer needs them. He knows that the chance he awaits will soon come: the death of the high-living Edward. When that happens, Edward's young son, Edward V, inherits the crown. That's an obstacle; in time, says one of the citizens, the lad might prove a just and wise king:

> In him there is a hope of government,
> Which in his nonage counsel under him,
> And in his full and ripened years, himself,
> No doubt shall then and till then govern well. (2.3.12–15)

But Richard will not allow time for ripening. When the new king boasts, boyishly yet bravely, that he intends to "win our ancient right in France again," recovering the land once won by Henry III and Henry V, Richard sneers aside, "Short summers lightly have a forward spring" (3.1.91–94)—precocious lads come soon to a bad end. Fine prophesy: for Richard already intends to have Edward and his brother trammeled up in the Tower of London for "protection," and then assassinated.

Richard sees himself as a manager and predictor of time, and yet in his own growing he was both precocious and sluggardly, too early and too late. A hunchback, he claims he was sent by nature into the world before his time, "scarce half made up" (1.1.18–21), yet provided with teeth to "gnaw a crust at two hours old" (2.4.28). His mother, though, says that "he was the wretched'st thing when he was young, / So long a-growing and so leisurely" (2.4.18–19). His disjunction from natural time is a sign of his disjunction from the moral order: so he makes the childish mistake of sending the scrivener an indictment of the Lord Hastings for treason, when Hastings would not even be *accused* until almost twenty-four hours *after* the scrivener saw the original draft. "Who is so gross," says the scrivener, "that cannot see this palpable device?" (3.6.10–11).

It will catch up with Richard in the end. When he alienates Buckingham, the ladder wherewithal he had ascended his throne, he finds himself pressed north and south by adversaries from the old Lancastrian families. He attempts to defuse this challenge by marrying the daughter of Edward's widow, Elizabeth, herself allied to Lancaster. That would forge an alliance between the two great clans of English noblemen—would forge it, in the service of a demon. But when Elizabeth demurs, Richard loses his temper and unwittingly prophesies his own destruction:

> As I intend to prosper and repent,
> So thrive I in my dangerous affairs
> Of hostile arms! Myself myself confound!
> Heaven and fortune bar me happy hours!
> Day, yield me not thy light, nor, night, thy rest! (4.4.397–401)

In fact, the man who has spent his days working evil will find himself deprived of the ease of night. On the eve of the battle at Bosworth Field, he will be visited by the spirits of all those he has murdered, calling upon him to despair and die. Our last words from the king will be those of a man alone on the field, on foot, needing and lacking the simplest thing to help him turn the battle: "A horse! A horse! My kingdom for a horse!" (5.4.13). The marriage to Elizabeth's daughter will take place, in the fullness of time, as ordained by God; only the groom will be Richard's opponent, the virtuous Earl of Richmond, now crowned Henry VII.

Seasons of Love

EVEN A GOOD MAN, if too full of his dreams, can mistake the time: so in *Love's Labor's Lost*, the youthful king of Navarre urges his courtiers to join him for three years in forswearing the company of women, as they shall turn the court into another academy of Plato, making themselves "heirs of all eternity" (1.1.7). But his most impish courtier, Berowne, finds such asceticism absurd, because it is ill-timed:

> At Christmas I no more desire a rose
> Than wish a snow in May's new-fangled shows,
> But like of each thing that in season grows. (1.1.105–7)

And indeed the king immediately learns that he must break his own edict, despite its penalty of public shame. Philosophers do forget themselves, and the king has forgotten that the French princess, "a maid of grace and complete majesty" (1.1.135), is even now arriving to settle a dispute between Navarre and France, and, though the king does not know it, to use her beauty to win him for a husband. Everyone in the audience can see it coming. The king will fall in love with the princess straightaway, as his three companions will fall in love with her maids-in-waiting, whom they have all known and esteemed before.

When the princess arrives she puts before the king the folly of his oath. She knows he has forsworn the company of women, but he does not know that she knows, and that gives the sprightly woman a fine chance to embarrass him. They meet outdoors, at some distance from one another, that the king might keep his word:

> KING: Fair princess, welcome to the court of Navarre.
> PRINCESS: "Fair" I give you back again; and "welcome" I have not yet.
>   The roof of this court is too high to be yours, and welcome to the wide
>   fields too base to be mine. (2.1.90–94)

The absurdity of wasting one's youth by playing the king's ascetic game is like the absurdity (or arrogance) of claiming the dome of heaven for the roof of one's court; and it is as ill-fitting as inviting a princess to bed down in the bare fields.

Of course the king must try to explain himself. But it will not do to bandy words with a woman. The princess plays ignorant, taking the king at his literal word in order to teach him his folly:

> KING: You shall be welcome, madam, to my court.
> PRINCESS: I will be welcome, then. Conduct me thither.
> KING: Hear me, dear lady—I have sworn an oath.
> PRINCESS: Our lady help my lord! He'll be forsworn.
> KING: Not for the world, fair madam, by my will.
> PRINCESS: Why, will shall break it, will, and nothing else.
> KING: Your ladyship is ignorant what it is.
> PRINCESS: Were my lord so, his ignorance were wise,
>   Where now his knowledge must prove ignorance. (2.1.95–103)

Here love is the corrector of a royal whim that had run counter to the season of youth; but often Shakespeare shows that a disorderly love runs to destruction because it will not wait for time. Such is the tragedy of *Romeo and Juliet*. Because of the irrational and city-dividing enmity between the Montagues and the Capulets, the love between Romeo and Juliet, a love perilously sudden and intense, can have no healthy time to ripen. It must be consummated now or never. So the lovers arrange a secret marriage just before the time when Juliet is to be given as wife to the young County Paris. Their spiritual counselor, Friar Lawrence, hopes eventually to reveal the marriage and to use it to bring peace to the warring families. But when Romeo kills Juliet's hasty-tempered cousin Tybalt in a street fight he had tried to avert, the young man must flee Verona and the friar must think of another expedient.

His plan is to give Juliet a drug to simulate death. She will die before she dies, will even be laid to rest in the family crypt. Meanwhile he will send a messenger to Romeo in Mantua to inform him of the plot and to tell him how to smuggle Juliet out of Verona. That will prevent the marriage to Paris and will win the young people some time. But the lovers are truly "star-crossed" (Prologue, *Romeo and Juliet*, 6). That is not, as is typically understood, because the fates have determined their demise, but because the time wherein they act is disjointed and disordered by the sins of their parents, whose strife erupts in violence, "where civil blood makes civil hands unclean" (Prologue, 4).

In such a state how could we expect Friar Lawrence's messenger to arrive in time? He is forestalled, and Romeo hears too soon, from someone else, that Juliet is dead. Quick in conceiving love, quick in plucking its early fruit, Romeo is now quick in concluding his own death. His words connect that death with the initial passion in a way he does not quite understand. Says he, using the words of a young man's longing, yet coldly and bitterly, "Well, Juliet, I will lie with thee tonight" (5.1.34). He buys a poison so potent that it is illegal to sell, and makes for Verona.

The unraveling is swift and terrible. Romeo happens to enter the crypt at night just when Paris arrives. Again, and without malice aforethought, Romeo kills a man; for Paris tries to arrest him as a felon, having no idea that Romeo was anything other than the slayer of Tybalt, or that Juliet died from anything other than grief over her cousin's death. When Romeo sees his beloved at last, it seems to him that she is alive yet, but he draws no conclusion from the blood in her cheeks. He compares the moment to "a lightning before death" (5.3.90). "O my love, my wife!" he cries in despair (5.3.91). All that remains for him is to shake off the "yoke of inauspicious stars" (5.3.112), the burden of time, to rest everlastingly beside Juliet, as a pilot in a storm, despairing of the port, will hasten his death by running his ship against the rocks (5.3.117–18). The last words Romeo utters before his final kiss give ironic praise to the druggist for at least one thing that manages to work in time: "O true apothecary! / Thy drugs are quick" (5.3.119–20).

As we should expect, Friar Lawrence arrives just after this dreadful deed, as Juliet wakes amid the shouts of the hurrying watchmen who have been roused by Paris's page-boy. The friar tries desperately to hustle Juliet out of the crypt, telling her of her husband's death, but she refuses, nor does he have the courage to stay. Kissing him to see if there remains upon his lips some poison—what she calls "a restorative" (166)—Juliet hears the watchmen coming. One moment is all she needs. She snatches Romeo's dagger and plunges it into the sheath of her heart:

> Yea, noise? Then I'll be brief. O happy dagger!
> This is thy sheath; there rest, and let me die. (5.3.170–71)

The dagger is "happy," she thinks, because it is at hand, in the nick of time. But the obvious and terrible sexual imagery (the Latin term for "sheath" is *vagina*) suggests that to love as hastily and unseasonably as she and Romeo loved is to court destruction.

The Fullness of Time

"Men are / As the time is," says the Machiavellian Edmund to his captain, promising him fine fortunes if he will kill Cordelia and her father, the infirm old King Lear, whom Edmund is holding prisoner in his cell. Not everything fits the occasion, says he: "To be tender-minded / Does not become a sword" (*King Lear*, 5.3.31–33). The captain, who sees it as "man's work" (5.3.40), agrees. He does hang Cordelia, but this muscle-bound opportunist never reckoned on the king, whose love gives him one last sudden surge of youth and vigor to send the villain to his death. Says Lear, leaning over the body of his beloved daughter, "I killed the slave that was a-hanging thee" (5.3.276).

Not that Edmund is alive to hear those words. He who waited his time to strike is snared in the meshes of his plots, at the apparent noon of his fortunes, when he is accused and mortally wounded by his banished brother Edgar. Edgar's own view of time is oriented toward the heavens, and though he is a pagan in pre-Christian England, he expresses a natural sense of man's duty to submit to the will of providence. We must await the fullness of time. Neither our birth nor our death lies in our hands. Says he to his blinded father Gloucester, who seeks to die:

> What, in ill thoughts again? Men must endure
> Their going hence, even as their coming hither:
> Ripeness is all. Come on. (5.2.9–11)

Men are as the time is. Ripeness is all. To accommodate oneself to the time, to wrest it to one's purposes, or to submit to the purposes of providence as they unfold in time: these are the positions of all those in Shakespeare who do not merely waste time. The positions are irreconcilable—with this qualification, that the wise man actually does seize the opportunity presented by providence, while the opportunist finds himself undone. The duke of Cornwall is crude and rash and ready to seize power in England, but when in a fury he puts out the eye of Gloucester for helping the king escape, a young retainer stands up to him to prevent him from putting out the other. Though in the scuffle the lad is stabbed in the back by Cornwall's wife Regan, he deals the duke his death wound. "Untimely comes this hurt," says Cornwall (3.7.100); they are his last words in the play.

Wholly unlike the hot-tempered Cornwall is the wise and patient servant Camillo, one of the laboring agents of providence in *The Winter's Tale*. When King Polixenes' son, Florizel, is revealed to have fallen in love with a girl everyone believes is only a shepherdess, Camillo seizes the opportunity to help the lovers and everyone else, including himself. Seeing after sixteen years a chance to return to his native land, and to restore the friendship of his current master Polixenes with his old master King Leontes (who had in a fit of jealousy wronged his friend), he advises the lad and the maiden to flee to Sicily:

> Methinks I see
> Leontes opening his free arms and weeping
> His welcomes forth; asks thee, the son, forgiveness,
> As 'twere i' th' father's person; kisses the hands
> Of your fresh princess; o'er and o'er divides him
> 'Twixt his unkindness and his kindness: th' one
> He chides to hell, and bids the other grow
> Faster than thought or time. (*The Winter's Tale*, 4.4.550–57)

And the end will prove more glorious than Camillo imagines. Leontes, long repentant, sorrowing for sixteen years, will not only be reconciled with his old friend but will be reunited with the daughter whose death he had decreed (it is in fact the shepherdess Perdita, "the lost girl" now found) and with the virtuous wife who had apparently died of grief.

A Storm in Time

IN ONE PLAY ESPECIALLY the ironic disjunction between man's time and God's time is the heart of the matter: *The Tempest.* It has long been considered Shakespeare's farewell to the stage, as if at the end of his work the playwright sought to reveal his most profound insights into youth and age and time and death. The title alludes to the temporal: a tempest is, literally, a storm that comes in season. Here it will be a storm sent in time to effect what extends beyond the edge of doom: everlasting love, and the regeneration of a sinful human soul.

Critics are fond of citing, as the inspiration for *The Tempest,* accounts of an English shipwreck off Bermuda, and what was hailed as the providential survival of the crew. No doubt Shakespeare had that shipwreck in mind. But far more important to the play are the allusions to scripture throughout. These allusions form a consistent and ironic pattern. In short, this farewell play is also a play of expectation—a play of Advent. The protagonist Prospero will say, at the end, that when he returns to Milan every third thought will be his grave (*The Tempest,* 5.1.312), but that is a meditation upon what lies *beyond* the grave. The characters suddenly castaway upon the island believe that their lives have ended, and in a sense that is true; but for at least two of them a new life is about to begin. The season of Advent refers both to Christ's coming in the flesh as a babe in Bethlehem and to his coming in glory at the end of time, at the beginning of the new heaven and new earth. At that time, says Jesus, it will be as in the days of Noah, when people were buying and selling, marrying and giving in marriage, as if they had all of time before them, when all along the floodwaters were about to break over their heads (Luke 17:26–30). Their eyes were wide for the right time to buy or sell or marry; yet when it came to God's time they were drowned in sleep. Hence Jesus' persistent warning: Be awake, watch (Matt. 25:13).

The Book of Common Prayer shows that among the readings Shakespeare would have heard at the obligatory services during Advent and the octave of Christmas were the entire book of Isaiah, the Letter of Jude, the letters of Peter, the gospel passages from Matthew that refer to the Second Coming, and the account in Acts of the travels and the shipwreck of Saint Paul. Every single important motif of *The Tempest* is to be found in these readings (particularly in Isaiah 29); there are no exceptions. All point to ends that are beginnings, and many comment ironically upon sinners who live amidst events and, as if they were sleepwalkers, cannot understand them.

Men Against the Time

MANY YEARS BEFORE THE events of the play, Prospero, the duke of Milan, cedes his authority to his younger brother Antonio. He wants to devote all his time to his library, reading in the liberal arts (including, it seems, books promising knowledge of the spirits of earth, air, water, and fire). But Prospero's abdication is unseasonable. It violates the providence of God, who placed him in that authority. And it has "awaked an evil nature" (1.2.93) in Antonio. He, unwilling to wait, desires not only the ducal power but the title. To gain it, he conspires with Alonso, the king of Naples, and Sebastian, Alonso's brother. Their pact: Antonio will subject his own people to the Neapolitans, levying a yearly tribute in exchange for Alsonso's help in getting rid of Prospero. Thus is power attained, says Prospero, who tells his daughter Miranda the story, by a "most ignoble stooping" (1.2.116).

Now Prospero is too dearly loved by the people to be murdered openly, so the conspirators give out that he is going on a voyage. They smuggle him and Miranda aboard a seaworthy ship "i' th' dead of darkness" (1.2.130). When the ship is no longer visible from shore, they transfer their victims to

> A rotten carcase of a butt, not rigged,
> Nor tackle, sail, nor mast; the very rats
> Instinctively hath quit it. (1.2.146–48)

The rats have left, and so the conspirators leave too. No ship, they think, can be worse: there is nothing aboard to give anyone a chance of controlling the ship's course. It is indeed the perfect ship, but not as they think. In *The Quest of the Holy Grail*, a ship that cannot be steered is an emblem of faith: Galahad and his companions enter and go where they are destined to go, not where they choose. Prospero and Miranda too will go somewhere—and not, in short time, to the bottom of the sea, as the conspirators trust.

For the Lord of time will not have it so. He stirs the heart of "the good old Lord Gonzalo" (5.1.15), a noble Neapolitan in the service of Alonso. Gonzalo stores the rotten hull with food, water, and, most important, Prospero's books. Bitterly does Prospero bemoan his fate and the wickedness of his brother, but the presence of his small child, smiling, "infused with a fortitude from heaven" (1.2.154), gives him strength to hope—indeed, to fulfill the meaning of his own name, "I look forward." They reach shore "by providence divine" (1.2.159).

There on a half-desert island—a place that is ironically both "uninhabit-able and inaccessible" yet at the same time, "of subtle, tender, and delicate temperance" (2.1.40, 44; cf. Is. 47:1)—they meet two creatures. One is the "freckled whelp, hag-born" Caliban (1.2.284), son of the late witch Sycorax. Caliban jabbers and would "gabble like / A thing most brutish" (1.2.358–59), until Prospero and Miranda teach him language: "How / To name the bigger light, and how the less, / That burn by day and night" (1.2.336–38). He repays their instruction by attempting to rape Miranda, and then he crows about it and is angry that Prospero came to Miranda's rescue in time:

> O, ho, O ho! Would't had been done!
> Thou didst prevent me; I had peopled else
> This isle with Calibans. (1.2.351–53)

Since that day he has been chained to a rock, though he is set free on occasion to gather firewood and other humble necessaries for his master. He does not suffer his punishment patiently.

The other creature is Ariel (in Hebrew, "lion of God"), a spirit visible only to Prospero. He had been penned in a cloven pine by the foul witch Sycorax for refusing to "act her earthy and abhorred commands" (1.2.274). Prospero freed Ariel and set the conditions for the spirit's service: Ariel would do his bidding for a certain time, and then be free absolutely.

As the play begins, the end of that time is fast approaching. Miranda is grown almost to womanhood, and the winds of providence have brought a Neapolitan ship near the isle. Aboard are Gonzalo, Antonio, Sebastian, Alonso, and Alonso's son, the prince Ferdinand. Prospero uses the auspicious time and, with the assistance of Ariel and other ministers of the elements, summons a storm that threatens to wreck the ship and kill every man aboard.

A Time to Obey

SUDDEN IT IS, THIS thunder and lightning that stun the audience into silence as the curtain sweeps aside. Yet it has been in preparation for years. And in the midst of this storm we find men who are also prepared, who obey authority, doing what they are called to do *at the right time*; we also find sinners, men of worldly power, reduced to impotence before the rage of the elements, ever in the wrong place at the wrong time. Shakespeare shows us the sailors first:

> MASTER: Boatswain!
> BOATSWAIN: Here, master. What cheer?
> MASTER: Good, speak to th' mariners! Fall to't yarely, or we run ourselves
>   aground. Bestir, bestir!
>
> *Enter* MARINERS
>
> BOATSWAIN: Heigh, my hearts! Cheerly, cheerly, my hearts! Yare, yare!
>   Take in the topsail! Tend to th' master's whistle! Blow till thou burst thy
>   wind, if room enough! (1.1.1–8)

Note the timely and manly delegation of authority. The ship's master
(whose duty is to preserve the vessel and the noblemen aboard) heeds the
wind and the rain, and calls to the boatswain, who appears on the spot. It is
no tyranny the master exercises: he calls the boatswain "good," short for "good
fellow," and begs him to relay his orders to the mariners in his charge. Their
relationship is like that which Ariel enjoys as the mediator between Prospero
and the lesser spirits, and is the means by which the mariners partake of the
authority of the master. They are to "fall to 't yarely," and the word "yare,"
repeated later, is critical, meaning "ready" or "in the nick of time"—for the
ship is speeding toward the rocky shore. The boatswain relays the command
with the master's same rough affection: the men are his "hearts," urged to
work "cheerly." The sails must come down before the buffeting winds catch
them—a tricky and highly coordinated maneuver. The boatswain cries to the
men to "tend to th' master's whistle," for in the howling storm the master simply cannot be everywhere at once to be heard by everyone. The master tries
to see to all things, but he is not God. Therefore he needs the men as much
as they need him, and he signals what they are to do by means of his shrill
whistle, heard above the winds.

Clearly, Shakespeare need not have included this interchange between
the boatswain and the master. It adds nothing to the plot; but it establishes
the pattern of prompt obedience and provident rule against which to judge
the other characters. For exactly at the wrong time the noblemen appear on
deck, with the king feebly trying to play a king's part:

> ALONSO: Good boatswain, have care. Where's the master? Play the
>   men.
> BOATSWAIN: I pray now, keep below. (1.1.9–11)

Alonso's advice is ill-timed. His command to "play the men" is unnecessary if directed to the sailors, who are bursting their hearts and sinews to do so. If directed to the men accompanying him, particularly to his brother Sebastian and Antonio, it is, as we soon see, ineffectual. More than natural courage is required here, and more than an opportunist of a king to arouse it. In either case, the king is the first to allude, unwittingly, to the time that ends all time, the day of judgment: his words echo Saint Paul, advising the Corinthians to arm themselves with faith. "Quit you like men," he urges them (1 Cor. 16:13), as they await the coming of Christ, or the persecution that will precede it.

With a crisp but polite command, the boatswain begs the noblemen to "keep below." They should be in the hold, not underfoot; the hierarchies are altered here, and for the common good, the king and his men should obey. They must humble themselves. It is ironic that had they known how to "keep below" in the first place, the climbing Antonio and Alonso would not now be here. But the king seems to want to overshoot the boatswain, and (again unwittingly) reveals how much he does not understand about authority:

> ALONSO: Where is the master, bos'n?
> BOATSWAIN: Do you not hear him? You mar our labor. Keep your cab-
> ins; you do assist the storm. (1.1.12–14)

"Do you not hear him?" cries the boatswain, incredulous. What should Alonso hear? The whistle—whose signals, he, since he is no seaman, does not understand; but also the thundering judgment of the Master above, rolling the storms. That is one Master whom Alonso long ignored. The Master is doing just what he intends, *that Alonso may come to hear him*; and indeed Alonso will later hear his sins roared back at him in the basso of the wind and the sea:

> O, it is monstrous, monstrous!
> Methought the billows spoke and told me of it;
> The winds did sing it to me; and the thunder,
> That deep and dreadful organ pipe, pronounced
> The name of Prosper; it did bass my trespass. (3.3.95–99)

In a sense that no one in the scene understands, then, the boatswain is right when he says that Alonso and his fellows "assist the storm." Of course, by their inopportune intrusion, born both of fear and pride, the aristocrats undermine the honest labor of the mariners and thus are "working" alongside the storm. But were it not for their sins of pride, there would have been no storm at all. To put it another way, they thought they could arrange their destinies as they desired, but the providence of God brings them where they never expected to be (cf. 3.3.53–58).

At this point Gonzalo interrupts to allay the boatswain's anger:

> GONZALO: Nay, good, be patient.
> BOATSWAIN: When the sea is. Hence! What cares these roarers for the
>   name of king? To cabin! Silence! Trouble us not!
> GONZALO: Good, yet remember whom thou hast aboard.
> BOATSWAIN: None that I love more than myself. You are a councilor;
>   if you can command these elements to silence and work the peace of the
>   present, we will not hand a rope more. Use your authority. If you cannot,
>   give thanks you have lived so long, and make yourself ready in your cabin
>   for the mischance of the hour, if it so hap. Cheerly, good hearts! Out of
>   our way, I say. (1.1.15–27)

The good old man recommends patience, a virtue required of every character in the play. Patience means more than forbearance, suffering the weakness of others (though it means at least that: here Gonzalo suffers the hot temper of the boatswain, and remarks, with ironical affection, that since such a man must be destined to hanging, the ship will surely find its way safely to shore!). We suffer their weakness because it is ours. We must wait with them for the fullness of time. So Saint Peter recommends patience to his followers who longed for the coming of Christ: God is patient with us, "delaying, not forgetting," as Ariel says (3.3.73), allowing sinners time to repent (2 Pet. 3:3–9).

When Gonzalo tentatively reminds the boatswain that there are noblemen aboard, the good sailor turns the point against him. What do the winds care? If you can stand on deck like a justice of the peace and calm the riot in the sea, then do it. Our hard labor might rest. The boatswain echoes the account of the storm on the Sea of Galilee: the disciples thought they were going to perish, but Jesus slept peacefully. When they woke him he chided them for their little faith, then rebuked and stilled the wind and the waves. The disciples were astonished by his authority: "What manner of man is this, that even the wind and the sea obey him?" (Mark 4:41).

He alone who has authority can calm the storm; and yet it is with a storm that he will come (Matt. 24:27–31). The proper duty of man in the meantime is to "hand a rope"—to work while it is yet day (John 9:4), and to prepare for the hour: Be yare; prepare ye the way of the Lord; keep your lamps burning; pray unceasingly. The mariners work hard, and that augurs well for their preparation; Gonzalo makes an affectionate jest at the boatswain's expense, and that augurs well for his. But the boatswain is again interrupted by Sebastian and Antonio. Like the monster Caliban (though Caliban exaggerates in his anger, cf. 1.2.365–66), they have no language but to curse:

> BOATSWAIN: Down with the topmast! Yare! Lower, lower! Bring her to
> try with main course! (*A cry within.*) A plague upon this howling! They are
> louder than the weather or our office.
>
> *Enter* SEBASTIAN, ANTONIO, *and* GONZALO
>
> Yet again? What do you here? Shall we give o'er and drown? Have you a
> mind to sink?
> SEBASTIAN: A pox o' your throat, you bawling, blasphemous, incharitable
> dog!
> BOATSWAIN: Work you, then.
> ANTONIO: Hang, cur! We are less afraid to be drowned than thou art.
>   (1.1.34–45)

The key word in the passage is *office*, denoting the duties of the mariners, but also suggestive of time. The daily Christian office comprises prayers said at specified hours of the day. The noblemen should be praying, but they reappear not only to shirk their own office but to thwart that of others. Antonio's speech — his first — is particularly churlish. The boatswain has suggested that the noblemen must be on the brink of despair, and in fact at several moments we will find them so (cf. 3.2.103–9, 5.1.11–14). It is as if God were thrusting them toward the cliff of doom that the very nearness of judgment might wake them from their moral torpor, just in time. But Antonio hears the Boatswain's words only as an accusation of cowardice, and flings the same accusation back at him. That mighty sailor will not deign to reply.

Sometimes God calls us to work when he knows we must fail:

> BOATSWAIN: Lay her ahold, ahold! Set her two courses! Off to sea again!
> Lay her off!
>
> *Enter* MARINERS *wet*
>
> MARINERS: All lost! To prayers, to prayers! All lost! [*Exeunt.*]
> BOATSWAIN: What, must our mouths be cold?

> GONZALO: The king and prince at prayers! Let's assist them,
>   For our case is as theirs.
> SEBASTIAN: I am out of patience.
> ANTONIO: We are merely cheated of our lives by drunkards.
>   This wide-chopped rascal—would thou mightst lie drowning
>   The washing of ten tides! (1.1.49–57)

When the mariners enter, having given up all hope in their work, they cry out that everyone must now turn to God. We will soon learn of the sailless and rudderless boat that the three men of sin long ago intended for Prospero's death; and while the boat in this scene does have a mast and sails, they can do no good. The sails must come down—the first hope for safety lies in just that nautical humility. When that fails, as in justice it should, the only hope lies in grace.

So how do Antonio and Sebastian reply? They say nothing. The boatswain turns to them with a grim sarcasm. Now, of all times, you have nothing to say? Now, your mouths are cold? As if shaking them from sleep, Gonzalo seizes upon the warning and urges them to join the king and the prince, who, note well, are *down below* at prayer. Though he does not yet know it, King Alonso is readying himself for punishment, and for redemption from his long-forgotten sin against Prospero and his child Miranda. *That* work of prayer needs to be done, and Gonzalo calls for their assistance. "Our case is as theirs," he says (1.1.54), meaning that they are all in the same boat; but is that not always so, with man? Are we not all sinners, in dread need of mercy? Again, Sebastian and Antonio cannot hear. Sebastian is "out of patience," disjointed from the duty of the hour. Antonio wishes upon the good boatswain a drowning unnaturally delayed, stretching out the moment of suffocation for ten days! He does not see that his own drowning has been unnaturally delayed that he might live. In fact, his last words in this scene show what he thinks of the work of prayer: "Let's all sink wi' th' king," says he (1.1.62).

Let Them Who Have Ears to Hear, Hear

I HAVE SPENT SOME time on that remarkable opening scene because it establishes the connection between preparing and obedience: between waiting for the right time and hearing the call of the Master. Conversely, it shows that the disobedient, the deaf, are constantly frustrated by what they perceive to be the untimeliness of what happens to them, and just when they think they sit atop fortune's wheel. They are cheated by drunkards, as Antonio says (1.1.55).

That pattern continues. The long scene that follows, wherein we meet the island dwellers, opens with a seemingly impatient Miranda begging her father Prospero to allay the storm. But it is wrong to call her impatient, a word that suggests an inability to suffer. For Miranda's heart conceives compassion at once:

> O, I have suffered
> With those that I saw suffer! A brave vessel
> (Who had no doubt some noble creature in her)
> Dashed all to pieces! O, the cry did knock
> Against my very heart! Poor souls, they perished! (1.2.5–9)

But Prospero assures her that no harm will come by this play he has staged:

> Wipe thou thine eyes; have comfort.
> The direful spectacle of the wrack, which touched
> The very virtue of compassion in thee,
> I have with such provision in mine art
> So safely ordered that there is no soul—
> No, not so much perdition as an hair
> Betid to any creature in the vessel
> Which thou heard'st cry, which thou saw'st sink. (1.2.25–32)

He echoes the New Testament, alerting us that the world of this play (like our own) is governed by a "provision," the foreseeing of the Almighty. For Jesus assures his disciples that they should never worry about what they are to eat or what they are to wear, as the Father has numbered the very hairs of their heads (Matt. 10:30). And when the ship taking Paul to Rome was battered and broken, the apostle assured the sailors, against all common sense, that not one hair of anyone aboard would perish (Acts 27:34).

Prospero's words suggest that this moment brings a crisis of grace: the old order must change, and a new order begin. Miranda heeds his command to be comforted, and hears that now is the time for her to learn who she and her father are. Prospero had long wanted to tell her, with what temptations of resentment and brooding hatred we can only imagine. But he too has been patient. He and she have obeyed the directives of time:

> MIRANDA: You have often
> Begun to tell me what I am; but stopped
> And left me to a bootless inquisition,

Concluding, "Stay; not yet."
PROSPERO: The hour's now come;
The very minute bids thee ope thine ear.
Obey, and be attentive. (1.2.33–38)

Now begins his revelation of the injury they suffered, for Miranda can remember nothing of the past, only a dim sense that she was once waited upon by some women. That is all; it has never stirred in Miranda any dreams of lost power, nor has Prospero encouraged them. She is shocked to hear that her father was the duke of Milan:

O the heavens!
What foul play had we that we came from thence?
Or blessed was't we did? (1.2.59–61)

Prospero's reply reminds us again that providence rules over the designs of wicked men, not simply to check them, but to bring forth unexpected good: "Both, both, my girl!" (1.2.61). And, as we shall see, the blessing is not simply that they arrived safely upon the island, but that at this moment a miracle is occurring that will change several lives forever.

Miranda begs Prospero to continue the story, which the old man interrupts with asides to her, as if he were worrying that, like his brother Antonio long ago, she might not have ears to hear: "I pray thee mark me" (1.2.67), "Dost thou attend me?" (1.2.78), "Thou attend'st not?" (1.2.87), "I pray thee mark me" (1.2.88), and finally "Dost thou hear?" (1.2.106). No trouble with Miranda's hearing, as she protests: "Your tale, sir, would cure deafness" (1.2.106). That is not because Prospero is speaking loudly and with animation, though surely he is, but because his is a tale that must be heard. Any human being with a soul would want to listen to it and learn from it. The inattention rather lies within the tale: Prospero tells us how unwise it was for him to abdicate, to overlook his brother's nature that could not bear virtuously the power of rule. That brother then grew impatient—"so dry he was for sway," says Prospero (1.2.112), comparing Antonio to a drunkard. So to seize as much power as he could, Antonio attended to the time—with great sobriety, as he no doubt judged it, and sent Prospero and Miranda to what ought to have been their deaths.

Tossed by the roaring seas, Prospero might have lost all strength to suffer more. He might have hastened his death in despair, but for the grace of God shining through his beloved child:

PROSPERO: There they hoist us,
  To cry to th' sea that roared to us; to sigh
  To th' winds, whose pity, sighing back again,
  Did us but loving wrong.
MIRANDA: Alack, what trouble
  Was I then to you!
PROSPERO: O, a cherubin
  ·Thou wast that did preserve me! Thou didst smile,
  Infused with a fortitude from heaven,
  When I have decked the sea with drops full salt,
  Under my burden groaned; which raised in me
  An undergoing stomach, to bear up
  Against what should ensue. (1.2.148–58)

Charming, that her first thought should be that she must have wailed and caused her father trouble. Again she shows that she can suffer with those she sees suffer; the contrast with the bawling noblemen is severe. A baby girl who can hardly speak is of greater assistance than two grown men. She cannot hand a rope, but she can brace her father to trust in the governance of God.

Mercy, Not the Letter

SUCH IS THE CONVERSATION between the father and his obedient, keen-hearing daughter. He concludes by telling her he must use the present hour diligently, as all his enemies now lie in his power. When his spell finally puts her to sleep, he summons the spirit Ariel, the principal executor of his designs. Ariel tells Prospero that the storm has shaken the wits of every man on the ship. Indeed everyone *except* the dutiful mariners has abandoned it in despair. Yet "not a hair perished" (1.2.217), and the men's garments are "fresher than before" (1.2.219). The prince Ferdinand has been separated from the rest, according to Prospero's instructions, suffering a tempest in his heart, "cooling of the air with sighs / In an odd angle of the isle" (1.2.222–23). The ship is harbored, all the seamen plunged in deep sleep by the combined power of their own hard labor and Ariel's charms.

All is going according to plan, as the minutes tick away, but much remains to do:

PROSPERO: Ariel, thy charge
  Exactly is performed; but there's more work.

> What is the time o' th' day?
> ARIEL: Past the mid season.
> PROSPERO: At least two glasses. The time 'twixt six and now
>   Must by us both be used most preciously. (1.2.237–41)

Yet at this moment Ariel chooses to delay. He tries to extort from Prospero, too soon, the freedom he understandably desires:

> ARIEL: Is there more toil? Since thou dost give me pains,
>   Let me remember thee what thou hast promised,
>   Which is not yet performed me.
> PROSPERO: How now? Moody?
>   What is't thou canst demand?
> ARIEL: My liberty.
> PROSPERO Before the time be out? No more!
> ARIEL: I prithee,
>   Remember I have done thee worthy service,
>   Told thee no lies, made thee no mistakings, served
>   Without or grudge or grumbling. Thou did promise
>   To bate me a full year. (1.2.242–50)

Ariel has done Prospero's bidding, and cheerfully, not under compulsion; yet much depends on his obedience for the next few hours. If he disobeys, not only will Prospero and Miranda never see their homeland again, but the salvation of Alonso and the marriage of Ferdinand and Miranda may well not come to pass; for at this moment the island is peopled with discontented sinners, harboring guilt and despair and murder in their hearts.

   Ariel will gain by obedience, though we do not now see it. He will enter into Prospero's designs not as a slave but as a fellow director, a lieutenant, calling him, with military affection, "my commander" (4.1.167). He comes to wish what Prospero wishes, as his master's ends become his own: "Thy thoughts I cleave to. What's thy pleasure?" (4.1.165); he will learn, though he is "but air" (5.1.21), to feel for the sorrows of the guilty noblemen and the good Gonzalo; he even desires what the slave Caliban has desired though basely—to be loved:

> ARIEL: Before you can say "Come" and "Go,"
>   And breathe twice and cry, "So, so,"
>   Each one, tripping on his toe,
>   Will be here with mop and mow.

Do you love me, master? No?
PROSPERO: Dearly, my delicate Ariel. (4.1.44–49)

For now, though, he drags his heels, demanding the letter of Prospero's promise. Prospero rejects the terms of the argument. For Ariel is attempting, legalistically, to hold Prospero to forgiveness of a debt, to compel mercy. But "the quality of mercy is not strained" (*Merchant of Venice*, 4.1.183); we grant mercy because we need it ourselves, or because we are grateful for having received it. Left to ourselves, we suffer as Ariel suffered, pent up in the pine by Sycorax, there, but for a Prospero, to wail till the end of time. The good Ariel was then free to refuse Sycorax's foul commands, as now he appears to be free to refuse Prospero. The old man does not want to compel him. He wants true service, born of gratitude—we may say, mercy in return for mercy. Prospero will threaten—idly, winkingly—to peg Ariel in an oak for twelve winters if he murmurs any more, but by then Ariel has thanked him and has undergone a change of heart. Ariel's contrition is forthright and noble, as Prospero's forgiveness is immediate:

ARIEL: Pardon, master.
 I will be correspondent to command
 And do my spriting gently.
PROSPERO: Do so; and after two days
 I will discharge thee.
ARIEL: That's my noble master!
 What shall I do? Say what? What shall I do? (1.2.297–301)

A Monster of Ingratitude

FROM THIS POINT ON we find only promptness and obedient love from Ariel. Not so from the next creature Prospero summons, the ill-shapen Caliban. All Prospero requires of him is that he wash dishes and gather firewood, two simple and humble tasks. But unlike Ariel, Caliban is slow and deaf:

PROSPERO: What, ho! Slave! Caliban!
 Thou earth, thou! Speak!
CALIBAN (*Within.*): There's wood enough within.
PROSPERO: Come forth, I say! There's other business for thee.
 Come, thou tortoise! When?

Enter ARIEL *like a water nymph*

> Fine apparition! My quaint Ariel,
> Hark in thine ear. [*Whispers.*]
>
> ARIEL: My lord, it shall be done. *Exit.*
> PROSPERO: Thou poisonous slave, got by the devil himself
> Upon thy wicked dam, come forth! (1.2.315–22)

When Caliban does finally drag his form on stage he levels a curse upon his master (we recall the foolish curses of Sebastian and Antonio) and grows lugubrious, remembering the time when Prospero arrived and distorting his memories to fit his hatred. Back then, says Caliban, he loved Prospero, and helped him find food, showing him "all the qualities o' th' isle, / The fresh springs, brine pits, barren place, and fertile" (1.2.339–40). That was because Prospero pretended—so Caliban interprets it—to love him, stroking him, giving him language, and lifting his gaze to the heavens, showing him those two great markers of time and teaching him "how to name the bigger light, and how the less" (1.2.337; cf. Gen. 1:16). All a ploy, says Caliban, a subterfuge, to win the island from him—power for which the "dry" Antonio and Sebastian might thirst.

But we learn from Prospero's reply that Caliban would have dwelt free to this day, a foster-child within Prospero's own cell, had he not tried to rape Miranda (1.2.348–50). Thus Caliban is not a "slave" because he must obey Prospero. Rather, in disobeying Prospero, he enslaves himself, groveling before his baser nature. This self-enslavement will soon be dramatized by his poignant longing to adore, even to lick the feet of, a new master, a drunken sot of a butler washed ashore on a cask of sherry (cf. 2.2.149–54; 3.2.24–25). Something must be done with a Caliban: the crime of rape deserves death, especially considering how vulnerable Miranda is, with only one man on the island to protect her. But Prospero has delayed. Why? Most readers assume that without Caliban, Prospero could not survive on the island, and at least to Miranda, the magician suggests as much (1.2.312–13); but it is hard to see how someone who can roil the seas can need a sluggish wretch to fetch firewood. Prospero gives the clue in his accusation of Caliban: "Thou most lying slave, / Whom stripes may move, not kindness!" (1.2.346–47). He echoes the Letter of Jude, who recommends that as the day of the Lord draws near, the faithful must use different means to save different sinners. Caliban wants his freedom (2.2.188–89), but that freedom can only be granted by grace. If so, then Caliban must be chained to the rock now that he may be set free in time; he is one to "save with fear, pulling them out of the fire; hating even the garment spotted by the flesh" (Jude 1:23).

That something like provident care still moves Prospero is evident from his desperate cry later in the play as he considers the monster's plot, with the ship's butler and his fool, to kill him:

> A devil, a born devil, on whose nature
> Nurture can never stick; on whom my pains,
> Humanely taken, all, all lost, quite lost! (4.1.188–90)

"This thing of darkness I acknowledge mine," says Prospero of the monster in the end (5.1.275–76), suggesting a personal and even paternal responsibility; and Prospero may be the readier to forgive Caliban a desire for vengeance since he himself has had to fight against it (cf. 5.1.25–32). His last order for Caliban will be another humble one, that the monster lead his conspirators to his cell to "trim it handsomely" (5.1.294), to which Caliban replies with refreshing and free humility, confident of pardon, and laughing at the baseness of the butler he had taken for his master:

> Ay, that I will; and I'll be wise hereafter,
> And seek for grace. What a thrice-double ass
> Was I to take this drunkard for a god
> And worship this dull fool! (5.1.295–98)

A Sea Change

LET US RETURN TO the opening of the play. Once Caliban has left for the firewood, murmuring, Shakespeare brings on stage the last character in this scene who must show patience. He is Ferdinand, the king's son. He is led by the strains of strange music, an air that rouses him from weeping over the death of his father. The music, played by Ariel and the spirits, allays his passions, as harmony is wont to do. Yet it does not, on the face of it, bring consolation:

> Full fathom five thy father lies;
> Of his bones are coral made;
> Those are pearls that were his eyes.
> Nothing of him that doth fade
> But doth suffer a sea change

Into something rich and strange.
Sea nymphs hourly ring his knell:

Burden. Ding-dong.

Hark! Now I hear them — ding-dong bell. (1.2.399–407)

The song is meant to make Ferdinand "heavenly comforts of despair" (*Measure for Measure*, 4.3.111), teaching him to hope even when hope seems folly, delaying his joy that it may be all the riper when it comes. Thus the song's despair is shot through with irony, as it describes not only the death that Ferdinand fears his father has suffered, but a transformation that neither he nor his father expects: "Of his bones are coral made; / Those are pearls that were his eyes." True it is that he fades, but nothing truly fades; everything about the king will suffer a change that only the might of the sea can enact.

Ferdinand does not know it, but his father is not the only one who will "die" and suffer a change "into something rich and strange." In fact, a sea change begins as soon as the song ends. That is when Ferdinand sets his eyes upon Miranda, and she upon him. So beautiful is man — though we are sinners and have dimmed the beauty, and familiarity blinds us to it — that Miranda at first thinks he must be a spirit:

I might call him
A thing divine; for nothing natural
I ever saw so noble. (1.2.420–22)

Ferdinand's astonishment is no less: "Most sure, the goddess / On whom these airs attend!" (1.2.424–25). In both, sight accompanies wonder, and wonder accompanies the desire to submit in love to a being superior to oneself. They see only because they have the capacity to admire (Miranda's name means "she who is to be admired," and she herself bursts often into admiration of others; see 5.1.181–84), just as only the obedient can hear the Master's whistle. Naturally they do what they ought to do, precisely at this moment, to the delight of the audience and of Prospero, who has hoped for it. They fall in love.

Should Prospero now applaud and welcome the young man to his home? Again he delays — for the sake of the lovers. He wants to put their patience to the test, that they may show themselves conquerors. Fallen man, after all, misprizes what comes to him too soon. Says Prospero, taking the audience into his confidence:

> They are both in either's powers. But this swift business
> I must uneasy make, lest too light winning
> Make the prize light. (1.2.453–55)

He will imprison Ferdinand, commanding the prince to suffer the indignity of moving logs—harder work than any we have seen Caliban do. Marriage is just such an imprisonment to those who do not understand love: full of labor, wearing out the day and night until death. But Ferdinand will be patient. He will cheerfully suffer, performing his unmerited labor willingly, out of love for Miranda. It is she who brings the dead to life:

> There be some sports are painful, and their labor
> Delight in them sets off; some kinds of baseness
> Are nobly undergone, and most poor matters
> Point to rich ends. This my mean task
> Would be as heavy to me as odious, but
> The mistress which I serve quickens what's dead
> And makes my labors pleasures. (3.1.1–7)

A wise young man is he, who can see that things simple and poor can "point to rich ends," and well-deserving of Miranda, who strives to outdo him in prompt and humble service. He is her "patient log-man" (3.1.67); she offers to bear the logs for him that he might rest (3.1.23); he wants to finish his task before the sun sets (3.1.23–24); as soon as he sees her his ready heart flees to her service (3.1.65). Miranda cannot wait a moment longer— nor should she. Her impatience is born of grace; she wants even now to be bound to Ferdinand forever, as wife or servant:

> Hence, bashful cunning,
> And prompt me, plain and holy innocence!
> I am your wife, if you will marry me;
> If not, I'll die your maid. To be your fellow
> You may deny me; but I'll be your servant,
> Whether you will or no. (3.1.81–86)

Ferdinand then kneels to *her:*

> FERDINAND: My mistress, dearest,
>   And I thus humble ever.
> MIRANDA: My husband, then?

FERDINAND: Ay, with a heart as willing
  As bondage e'er of freedom. Here's my hand.
MIRANDA: And mine, with my heart in't; and now farewell
  Till half an hour hence.
FERDINAND: A thousand thousand! (3.1.86–91)

How quickly they plight their troth—and how fully do they understand. They who redeem their time can jest that the half hour till they see one another again shall seem like "a thousand thousand." And how else should it seem?

Shepherds and Wolves

WHAT ARE THE NOBLEMEN doing meanwhile? We meet them again only *after* we witness Ferdinand and Miranda falling in love. But there is no deep fellowship among them. King Alonso is plunged in grief. He is sure (against the testimony of an eyewitness) that his son is dead; probably he is the surer of it because he secretly confesses that he deserves no better. Antonio and Sebastian are still grouching, despising the apparent barrenness of the island (though the barren island is also full of wonder and sustenance), and grumbling at Gonzalo and a young courtier, Adrian. Those two are chatting, trying to distract the king from his grief. Their conversation is not merely diversionary, however. Gonzalo plays the role of a priest visiting a grieving soul, providing what consolation he can, remarking on the strange freshness of their garments (that should stink of brine), the beauty of the isle (though only the innocent have eyes to see it), their miraculous escape (though they are in the hands of man's most terrible friend, the living God), and the hope that the king has not lost his son (though he *has* lost his son, to Miranda). Clearly, Gonzalo sees much, and there are glories in store that even he cannot now imagine. Alonso will hear none of it.

It is a group waiting to explode. Antonio and Sebastian are the tinder. All they do, while Gonzalo talks, is whisper snidely to themselves and interrupt him with what they think are timely barbs— for after all, what is Gonzalo, says Sebastian, but an old talker so predictable that one might as well use his wit as a watch to tell the time (2.1.14–15). For their part, they console the king by blaming him for the disaster, as if the wonder of the marriage feast they have just celebrated for the king's daughter in Tunis were the cause, and not their own long-ago sin upon the high seas. "Sir," says Sebastian with obvious desire to hurt, "you may thank yourself for this great loss" (2.1.128). Sebastian applies the wrong "cure" at the wrong time, suggests Gonzalo (2.1.141–44).

What should the courtiers do instead? If Sebastian is a bad surgeon, we should credit Gonzalo with desiring at least to be a good one, to heal the heart of the king. It is in this context that we must interpret his famous musings on how he would govern this island "T' excel the Golden Age" (2.1.173). His language is, as critics note, indebted to Montaigne's essay "On Cannibals," wherein that broadminded and inch-deep Frenchman discourses upon the relative innocence of the newfound natives of the Americas. No doubt the discovery of America prompted many literary utopias: if only men could sail far from Europe to a place where food was plentiful, they might start over and live like the harmless shepherds described in the old eclogues of Callimachus and Theocritus. But Gonzalo of all people should be aware of the problem. It walks beside him: sin. Antonio and Sebastian scoff at Gonzalo's vision, and are unwitting proof that it is vain to hark back to a time of supposed innocence:

> GONZALO: All things in common nature should produce
> Without sweat or endeavor. Treason, felony,
> Sword, pike, knife, gun, or need of any engine
> Would I not have; but nature should bring forth,
> Of its own kind, all foison, all abundance,
> To feed my innocent people.
> SEBASTIAN: No marrying 'mongst his subjects?
> ANTONIO: None, man, all idle—whores and knaves. (2.1.164–71)

Gonzalo does not really intend to be taken seriously, nor does Shakespeare want us to analyze the cultural customs of native Americans. They are not at issue. Innocence is. Gonzalo's speech springs from the longing to retreat from a world we have befouled, as if we could reverse the clock and return to a time before our sins, and be children again. But that would deny the providential course of time, imprisoning us in a dream of childhood. A naïve child may suppose that time does not go by, but we who have sinned are wiser:

> We were, fair queen,
> Two lads that thought there was no more behind
> But such a day tomorrow as today,
> And to be boy eternal. (*The Winter's Tale*, 1.1.62–65)

The classical poets were doomed to imagine that world *before* us, before the city, before war (see Lucretius, *De Rerum Natura*, 5.922–1452). Yet even in that world, man is a sinner and will die. *Et in Arcadia ego*, says the grinning skeleton of Death: "I too am a dweller in Arcadia."

No, we do not want to go back. The search for a Golden Age is no answer. Christ is. We want not our childhood again, but to be born anew, to suffer the sea change. The gold is yet to come; fittingly, it will be Gonzalo who will sing a hymn of wonder when he sees that the world redeemed is richer and stranger than anything he had dreamed before (5.1.205–13).

But now, weary of the conversation and weighted with grief, footsore and heartsore as he trudges over the barren isle, Alonso must lie down to rest, and Gonzalo and the others — all except Antonio and Sebastian — do likewise. The movement is strikingly symbolic. Alonso has gone *down* to the hold at the bidding of the boatswain; he has *fallen* to his knees in prayer; and at the end of the play he will *kneel* before Miranda to beg her forgiveness. This weariness is timely; Alonso ought to acknowledge his frailty and give way to sleep. Perchance during the sleep he will dream: that seems to happen later in the play, when he and his fellows fall into a trance before the vision of the vanishing banquet, while Ariel as a harpy accuses them of treachery against Prospero. Yet even in that fall there is an invitation to rise again. So Ariel cries out:

> Thee of thy son, Alonso,
> They have bereft; and do pronounce by me
> Ling'ring perdition (worse than any death
> Can be at once) shall step by step attend
> You and your ways; whose wraths to guard you from,
> Which here, in this most desolate isle, else falls
> Upon your heads, is nothing but heart's sorrow
> And a clear life ensuing. (3.3.75–82)

To persist as we are, sinners, time-servers, is to suffer lingering perdition, that drawn-out loss; it is Antonio's curse, sent down upon his own head, to be drowning and drowning not for ten days, but forevermore. Yet to go down to death — to take the sails down, to kneel, to obey — is to rise again, to possess one's child again, even to be a child. Forgiveness brings no Golden Age; only a foretaste of the time to come, incomparably greater.

Sleepwalkers in Charge

ANTONIO AND SEBASTIAN SEE none of it. While the others sleep, they remark that their own senses are wakeful and sharp, and they take it as a sign of their nimbleness and shrewdness, not their insensibility. For Antonio now sees *his* magical way to free Milan from its tribute to Naples. Why not make his friend Sebastian king?

> What might,
> Worthy Sebastian — O, what might? — no more!
> And yet methinks I see it in thy face,
> What thou shouldst be. Th' occasion speaks thee, and
> My strong imagination sees a crown
> Dropping upon thy head. (2.1.208–13)

Gonzalo imagines innocence, while the diseased mind of Antonio dreams of power. Yet in that dream he is plunged in ignorance. Sebastian suggests as much when he wonders whether Antonio is really awake:

> SEBASTIAN: What? Art thou waking?
> ANTONIO: Do you not hear me speak?
> SEBASTIAN: I do; and surely
>   It is a sleepy language, and thou speak'st
>   Out of thy sleep. What is it thou didst say?
>   This is a strange repose, to be asleep
>   With eyes wide open; standing, speaking, moving,
>   And yet so fast asleep. (2.1.213–19)

"Do you not hear him?" cries the Boatswain — and such as these two must answer no. For the schemer Antonio, Gonzalo is only a "lord of weak remembrance" (2.1.236) who will be forgotten soon after his death; Ferdinand surely is dead already (note the haste with which he and Sebastian assume what they secretly want to be true; see 2.1.236–48); most of their comrades have drowned too (see 2.1.255; of course not a hair has perished); and Antonio's own supplantation of Prospero should teach Sebastian what to do now. Just as conscience is only a sore on the heel, to be cured by a loose slipper, so the opportunist can use the time as he will (2.1.279–84). Antonio does not feel that deity, conscience, in his bosom; nor does he understand where he is and why, nor is he aware of what is happening around him.

We are our own providence, Antonio suggests, inviting Sebastian

> to perform an act
> Whereof what's past is prologue, what to come,
> In yours and my discharge. (2.1.256–58)

He means that the past—their plot against Prospero—is prologue for the play to come, meaning Sebastian's kingship. So he urges Sebastian to kill his brother the king while he sleeps, as Antonio will kill Gonzalo. Who in Naples will know? As for the other courtiers, they will fall in line with whatever Antonio and Sebastian say, because they will be opportunists too: "They'll tell the clock to any business that / We say befits the hour" (2.1.292–93).

But Antonio speaks truer than he knows. The past *is* prologue. Were it not for their past sin, they would not now be on the island. More: the sin of Alonso, who shared in their wickedness, is even now being purged. A great drama is unfolding around them, and they, in their self-importance, or rather their watching the clock for their chance to strike, have reduced themselves to the hacks and jesters that fill out the cast. They are strangely locked in time, about to repeat the past sin, as predictably as Milton's devils who cannot help but eat and eat the apples that turn to ashes in their mouths (*Paradise Lost*, 10.547–72). Yet they are unhitched from the time, too. They fail to see Ariel who, "with music and song"—ever in Shakespeare suggestive of order and harmony—enters the stage at exactly the moment foreseen by Prospero. Ariel wakes Gonzalo with a song that the conspirators cannot hear. Sleepers, wake:

> While you here do snoring lie,
> Open-eyed conspiracy
> His time doth take.
> If of life you have a care,
> Shake off slumber and beware.
> Awake, awake! (2.1.304–9)

"Let us both be sudden," says Antonio (2.1.309), but the sleepers, having fallen as by a thunderbolt, now as by a thunderbolt rise:

> GONZALO: Now good angels
>   Preserve the king!
> ALONSO: Why, how now? Ho, awake! Why are you drawn?
>
>   Wherefore this ghastly looking?
> GONZALO: What's the matter? (2.1.310–13)

Again the courtiers' mouths are cold. They heard no music, but confusion:

SEBASTIAN: Whiles we stood here securing your repose
  Even now, we heard a hollow burst of bellowing
  Like bulls, or rather lions. Did't not wake you?
  It struck mine ear most terribly.
ALONSO: I heard nothing.
ANTONIO: O, 'twas a din to fright a monster's ear,
  To make an earthquake! Sure it was the roar
  Of a whole herd of lions. (2.1.314–20)

The real baseness of this aristocratic plotting is revealed by a parallel plot dreamed up by Caliban: to kill Prospero and hand dominion of the isle to the butler Stephano (the Greek term *stephanos* means crown). Stephano and the jester Trinculo treat the monster with mingled fear and contempt, winning his allegiance by giving him "language," that is, by sticking a bottle of sherry in his mouth (see 2.2.84). Caliban has never tasted such wondrous liquor, and he who chafed to obey his teacher Prospero now abases himself before a sot. In gratitude (note that he *is* capable of gratitude) Caliban promises to deliver the island—*and Miranda.* He knows the right time to act: "I'll yield him thee asleep, / Where thou mayst knock a nail into his head" (3.2.63–64).

The plot fails, not only because Prospero is alerted by the ready Ariel, but because of the foolish delays of the rabble. Drunks always arrive too late. They can hardly be goaded by Caliban into action (see Sebastian, describing himself as "standing water," 2.1.225). They are always hanging back, diverted by an invisible drummer (Ariel, naturally) or by fancy-trashy clothing hung out on the line (by Prospero and Ariel). Poor Caliban, "tortoise" as Prospero called him, now is justly condemned to bear the sluggishness of his drunken god Stephano. Of course they use time unwisely: it lies in the very nature of wickedness to be too soon or too late. Caliban can complain all day as he tries to hurry his comrades: "We shall lose our time / And all be turned to barnacles" (4.1.247–48). They *must* lose their time; the more so, should they succeed. For if Caliban thought it was a burden to obey Prospero who took pains to raise him up, what will he think when Stephano is exposed as a fool?

A Wedding Song

THE DESTINY AWAITING ALL these belated wanderers, should they at last come in out of the rain, is suggested by the scene wherein Prospero welcomes Ferdinand as his son-in-law-to-be, revealing that that was his desire all along. No scene in the play is more perversely misunderstood.

Once he has apologized for his put-on severity and acclaimed Ferdinand for enduring those trials for love, Prospero gives Miranda to him "before heaven" (4.1.7), saying that her virtue will prove a greater gift than Ferdinand can now conceive. The youth accepts the truth of this prediction, even were it "against an oracle" (4.1.12).

But you cannot be worthy of Miranda unless you yield to the providence that has guarded her and to the heavenly grace she reflects. We have seen the untimeliness of sin, particularly when sinners seek occasion to sin. Why should there not also be a right time for the enjoyment of love? Rather, since the culmination of time is compared to a wedding feast, why should not married love of all things be the most profound revelation on earth of the timely grace of the eternal God?

Critics now say, with telling ugliness, that in this scene Prospero attempts to control Miranda's sexuality, as if her body were a territory to rule. Such critics assume that Antonio is fundamentally correct: power is all that counts. They dwell in Antonio's world, a duller, baser, narrower, and sleepier world than that of Caliban, who is made for obedience and wonder, regardless of how often he sins against his nature (see 3.2.138–46). They forget that Prospero has experienced the dreadful consequences of impatient sin, of violating the directives of providence. He urges the young people to obey an order that is both temporal and eternal, for only so will their love flourish. He makes no threat, but states the plain truth about the love-born sin that destroys love's hopes. If they sin, the rain of grace will not fall in season:

> No sweet aspersion shall the heavens let fall
> To make this contract grow; but barren hate,
> Sour-eyed disdain, and discord shall bestrew
> The union of your bed with weeds so loathly
> That you shall hate it both. Therefore take heed,
> As Hymen's lamps shall light you. (4.1.18–23)

They cannot play husband and wife before they marry—nor does Prospero wish again to awake by inattention an evil nature in someone he loves. Ferdinand understands the admonition, and couches his reply in terms of time:

> As I hope
> For quiet days, fair issue, and long life,
> With such love as 'tis now, the murkiest den,
> The most opportune place, the strong'st suggestion

Our worser genius can, shall never melt
Mine honor into lust, to take away
The edge of that day's celebration
When I shall think or Phoebus' steeds are foundered
Or Night kept chained below. (4.1.23–31)

How brave and manly is his jest—for neither father nor son-in-law is a prig, nor is the innocent Miranda! Ferdinand will wait—as he hopes for a peaceful marriage and for children to spring from their love. He will avoid opportunity, avoid the suggestions of the Antonios and Calibans of our nature. If for nothing else, he will not blunt the keen joy of the day itself, when the *justly* impatient bridegroom will look to the sky and cry out, with Spenser in his *Epithalamion*, "Ah when will this long weary day have end, / And lende me leave to come unto my love?" (*Epithalamion*, 288–89).

To solemnize their promises, Prospero reveals for Miranda and Ferdinand a work of his art, employing the ready spirits, directed by Ariel. It is a play that dramatizes the lessons of *The Tempest*: we are meant to see the abundance that man enjoys when he obeys time and its Master. Any farmer knows not to sow wheat in August or prune trees when the sap is running. For Christians the rhythm of the seasons reflects God's order: it is nature's prayerful office of the year. Thus it is as futile and foolish to seize one's inheritance before the death of the rightful owner, or to pluck the fruit of love before the minister of God has blessed it, as it is to try to glean corn in January.

Hence Prospero's masque invokes Ceres, goddess of the harvest (performed by Ariel), along with Juno, goddess of marriage and childbirth. Here is their timely song in honor of the virtuous lovers:

> Juno: Honor, riches, marriage blessing
>   Long continuance, and increasing,
>   Hourly joys be still upon you!
>
> Juno sings her blessings on you.
> [Ceres]: Earth's increase, foison plenty,
>   Barns and garners never empty,
>   Vines with clust'ring branches growing,
>   Plants with goodly burden bowing;
>   Spring come to you at the farthest
>   In the very end of harvest.
>   Scarcity and want shall shun you.
>   Ceres' blessing so is on you. (4.1.106–17)

Yet the images of time look forward to eternity: the full granaries, the abundant crop, the brimful wheat and wine, are all images of the kingdom of God, the wedding feast without end.

When he learns that the actors are spirits summoned by Prospero, Ferdinand says something else that rankles the modern critic:

> Let me live here ever!
> So rare a wond'red father and a wise
> Makes this place Paradise. (4.1.122–24)

It is a crucial moment. Ferdinand is not simply surprised by the presence of spirits on stage. He hears the message, as he has heard Prospero's warning. His praise of Prospero suggests that, regardless of the barren land and hard weather (and Ferdinand has seen little else from this isle), it is the father who makes this place a paradise. The magic may delight him, but it is wisdom he admires.

Prospero gently hushes the lad—it is not time to talk—and the spirits continue, concluding their masque with a harvest dance. We hear the echoes of scripture: the end of time, its fulfillment, is anticipated by earthquakes and lightning and storm, but is made manifest in the wedding feast, compared to the harvest, bringing in the sheaves (Ps. 126:6). The days of our labor point toward the holiday, the holy day:

> IRIS: You sunburned sicklemen, of August weary,
> Come hither from the furrow and be merry.
> Make holiday; your rye-straw hats put on,
> And these fresh nymphs encounter everyone
> In country footing. (4.1.134–38)

This feast here in Prospero's cell must end, however; the holiday is near, but not yet. Prospero dismisses the spirits suddenly, and they vanish "*to a strange, hollow, and confused noise*" (4.1.138). We are still in the world of sin, and must heed the time. "The minute of their plot," says Prospero, thinking unwillingly of Caliban and his comrades, "is almost come" (4.1.141–42).

A Time to Forgive, and Be Forgiven

WELL, PROSPERO WILL THWART their plot, as I have said; the drunkards linger over the "trumpery," and then all three are hustled away by Prospero and

Ariel, driving a pack of hounds after them (4.1.193–262). More important, he will lead to his cell all the courtiers, moping as in a trance. Ferdinand and Miranda remain within, unaware of what is going on. Slowly does Prospero reveal himself, and slowly do the spells of the island and the drugged sleep of sin clear away like fog from their minds. Alonso can hardly believe it is Prospero, but even before he is sure of his senses, he volunteers his repentance. The king, never more a king than now, is prompt to obey: "Thy dukedom I resign and do entreat / Thou pardon me my wrongs" (5.1.118–19). Sebastian and Antonio still stand outside the moment, extras that they are, misunderstanding. Sebastian even repeats the charge that the Pharisees leveled at Jesus, that "the devil speaks in him" (5.1.129; see Luke 11:15). Prospero denies it in one word, and repays them with delay—perhaps indefinite delay. "At this time," he says (5.1.128), he will not reveal their treachery to Alonso. Let repentance ensure that the time for exposure never comes. But Prospero's forgiveness is sincere and full, without glossing over the wickedness he must forgive:

> For you, most wicked sir, whom to call brother
> Would even infect my mouth, I do forgive
> Thy rankest fault—all of them; and require
> My dukedom of thee, which perforce I know
> Thou must restore. (5.1.130–34)

And again, Antonio's mouth is cold, not uttering a word for well over a hundred lines, till finally he jests upon the strange features of Caliban (5.1.265–66), whose monstrosity he sees, and whose nobility he misses.

We notice that Prospero has not yet reunited son and father. The time is growing ripe for it, but not quite yet. He delays, first telling Alonso that he himself has lost a daughter "in this last tempest" (5.1.153). Poor Alonso wishes—and unwittingly consents to what Prospero has arranged—that he were mudded in his son's oozy bed, if only Ferdinand and Miranda were alive in Naples as king and queen. At that, Prospero invites them into his cell, to show the king "a wonder to content ye / As much as me my dukedom" (5.1.170–71).

It is his last orchestration in the play. He draws a curtain. We see Ferdinand and Miranda within, oblivious of all around them, eyes for one another alone. They are playing chess, that opportunistic game of power. But they do not really care to win; it is all transformed by love. Perhaps Ferdinand impishly moves a pawn while giving Miranda a kiss:

> MIRANDA: Sweet lord, you play me false.
> FERDINAND: No, my dearest love,
> I would not for the world.
> MIRANDA: Yes, for a score of kingdoms you should wrangle,
> And I would call it fair play. (5.1.172–75)

On this marvelous island Alonso has heard strange noises and seen spirits vanishing into air; no wonder he can hardly believe the blessing he sees, the gift he is about to receive: "If this prove / A vision of the island, one dear son / I shall twice lose" (5.1.175–77). But God will not mock us with shows. Alonso does not deserve forgiveness, as he is well aware, having heard in the mysterious thunder of the isle that it was his sin that roused the tempest that killed his son, as he supposes (3.3.95–102). But mere repentance, mere gratitude for mercy, the merest movement of the heart, is enough in one moment to cancel all the mountained sins of time. For even the punishments of God are merciful, giving us time to mend. Thus, Ferdinand, stunned to see his beloved father, kneels to him and gives thanks to the timely storm: "Though the seas threaten, they are merciful. / I have cursed them without cause" (5.1.178–79).

I will not describe here the beautiful humility of Alonso, kneeling before a young girl to ask her forgiveness; or the boatswain, reverent in the noble company, telling of a ship intact and a master capering for joy to see her; or the reunion of the bosom friends Prospero and Gonzalo. The keynote throughout is wonder: but it is the wonder of a time to come when all who ask will find, all who turn back will be made welcome. "Ho, every one that thirsteth, come ye to the waters," exclaims Isaiah; come, eat, drink, enjoy the goodness of the king (Isa. 55:1). Prospero says he is old and must meditate upon his approaching death (5.1.312), but what that means is revealed in the epilogue he delivers.

There, Shakespeare invites all the audience into the feast. Prospero has no more magic; the playwright's art is finished; only the good will of the audience, by their applause, can hoist the sails of Prospero's ship, and only their cheers can raise the wind to billow them, wafting him from imprisonment on the island to freedom. We will grant Prospero the gift he asks if we remember that we are in need of the same gift. As we look to have God's forgiveness, so shall we forgive now, in love:

> Now my charms are all o'erthrown,
> And what strength I have's my own,

Which is most faint. Now 'tis true
I must be here confined by you,
Or sent to Naples. Let me not,
Since I have my dukedom got
And pardoned the deceiver, dwell
In this bare island by your spell;
But release me from my bands
With the help of your good hands.
Gentle breath of yours my sails
Must fill, or else my project fails,
Which was to please. Now I want
Spirits to enforce, art to enchant;
And my ending is despair
Unless I be relieved by prayer,
Which pierces so that it assaults
Mercy itself and frees all faults.
As you from crimes would pardoned be,
Let your indulgence set me free.

10

Time and the Neighbor:
J. R. R Tolkien's "Leaf, by Niggle"

If man is but an animal living on a bit of cosmic grit, we can say he "sees" spiritual truths only by draining the word "spiritual" of all meaning. The offense to the materialist, and to sensible people of all times, is that man is really meant to see certain truths about God and about eternity. As Tasso's Satan sneers:

> Man, man the vile, born of vile mud, He invites
> to rise instead to those celestial heights.
> (*Jerusalem Delivered*, 4.10.7–8)

That offense is doubled by Christianity's divorce of such vision from the unaided intellect. There is no reason, says the materialist, why anyone should see the meaning of this life (there is no meaning), but if anyone could do it, it must be the genius. Yet Jesus says the opposite. A child will see where the genius will stumble.

How can there be truths which only children, or those who become like unto them, can perceive? Consider the mind that accompanies the childlike heart. What world does the child dwell in? What is his experience of time? It is not the relentless ticking of a dying clock. No child would understand the speaker of Shakespeare's Sonnet 60, anxiously aware of coming death and of a life unfinished:

> Like as the waves move toward the pebbled shore,
> So do our minutes hasten to their end. (1–2)

Nor is time a dreary sameness, petering out to nothing:

> Tomorrow, and tomorrow, and tomorrow
> Creeps in this petty pace from day to day,
> To the last syllable of recorded time. (*Macbeth*, 5.5.19–21)

Shakespeare's King Polixenes can show us what it is, as he recalls the days when he and his old friend King Leontes were playfellows. They believed that there would be "such a day tomorrow as today" (*The Winter's Tale*, 1.1.64), trusting in their simplicity that goodness should never fade:

> We were as twinned lambs, that did frisk i' th' sun,
> And bleat the one at th' other; what we changed
> Was innocence for innocence; we knew not
> The doctrine of ill-doing, nor dreamed
> That any did; had we pursued that life,
> And our weak spirits ne'er been higher reared
> With stronger blood, we should have answered heaven
> Boldly, "Not guilty." (1.1.67–74)

Is that ignorance? Children, we think, are unaware of change and time and death; only as their minds develop do their notions of these things grow clear. But I suspect rather that as we grow to adulthood our sense of time ossifies; the possibilities narrow. Children are aware of the rhythms of day and night and of the seasons, while we listen to the whirr of the inexorable timepiece that tells us how little we have left to do the great things we have neglected. For a child, time is as alive and surprising, and as peaceful, as a branching tree. To see the world with an innocent heart is to dwell in time, to move with its ebbs and surges and whorls, as an easy swimmer plays happily and carelessly in the sea that bears him up.

Elven Time

SUCH TRUTHS ARE AT the heart of the work of many a Christian artist: consider the peasants in medieval Books of Hours, doing their seasonal work in the foreground while the spiritual time is shown in the heavens or in the great church feasts preparing on earth. Sin disrupts this harmony: so Chaucer's *Canterbury Tales* begins with a riotous awakening of nature as the year moves from March into April—yet the *meaning* of that awakening, the progress from Lent (and sin, and death) to Easter is lost on most of the pilgrims. So the aging Wife of Bath absurdly dolls herself up to snag a sixth husband, though she has been barren for her first five (three of whom she chose because they were "old bacon"); and old January of "The Merchant's Tale" foolishly marries a young woman who cuckolds him in a pear tree with his page boy; and the unnaturally young-old Pardoner, whose thin hair and bleating voice betray his being "a gelding or a mare," impotent and sterile (Gen. Prologue, 691), pretends that he is looking for a wife.

J. R. R. Tolkien too is a great chronicler of spiritual time. He provides his legends with their own histories, even with languages changing from century to century, that he may fulfill his calling as a "subcreator," an artist whose fictional world honors the orderly universe created by God. Tolkien's characters dwell in a time both natural and supernatural, a time whose artistic and moral end is alive at the beginning. Wise and patient, Frodo spares the life of the vile Gollum, hardly knowing why; yet Gollum is destined to "save" Middle-earth by biting the Ring of Power from Frodo's finger as they stand wrestling over the crater of Mordor. In that moment of ironic crisis they reenact the initial evil of the fall of Sauron, for Frodo suddenly wants to keep the ring, come what may.

Tolkien's short fairy tales are much the same. We may suppose that fairy tales spin themselves out in some timeless and placeless realm of the imagination. Tolkien gives us instead, in "Leaf, by Niggle," a tale that tells us who dwell in time and place what time and place are about. More, he tells us what time means in our lives from day to day, here in our humble villages, as we fall prey to our humble follies and strive to accomplish our grand and often silly dreams.

Elves are not really small—but hobbits are, and so is the little man who is the protagonist of this wonderful story. Niggle is, as his name suggests, a niggler, "a very ordinary and rather silly little man" (*The Tolkien Reader*, 102). Yet the first thing we hear about him places him in time—the faraway time of fairy tales, and the all-too-fleeting time that we adults know well. Here is the opening sentence: "There once was a little man called Niggle, who had a long journey to make." "Once upon a time," the story begins, lulling us into the comfort of the timeless, only to remind us that the journey is our own. It is as if Tolkien had said, "Once upon a time there was a man who was going where you, reader, will also go."

The Wonder of the Ordinary

IN HIS LITTLENESS, NIGGLE is not unusual. Each of us is invited, in the fairy world of the story, to put himself in Niggle's place, to consider himself a niggler, too. Our Niggle has all the marks of a wondrous ordinariness about him. It is not faceless, this being ordinary, for in Niggle we recognize the feelings, trivial and profound, that move us from day to day. So we have Niggle's mostly forgivable ambition, his castle-building for his future, all the more forgivable because it is mingled with excuse-making, a bit of ineptitude, a warm love, and—we will discuss this shortly—a transforming touch of true vision. That vision, happily, is not strictly dependent upon Niggle's intelligence: "Niggle was a painter. Not a very successful one, partly because he had many other things to do" (100). Ironically, Niggle does most of these other things fairly well, illustrating our sad and laughable inability to recognize what we are really made for. But other things got in Niggle's way. For one, he had too much time: "Sometimes he was just idle" (100). For another, the time he had would never suffice: "He had a number of pictures on hand; most of them were too large and ambitious for his skill" (100).

Niggle's painting reflects his personality. He is like most of us: his "goodness" is rather the absence of a remarkable vice than the vigor of a remarkable virtue. He is not strong enough to refuse his neighbors when they ask him to do what he really is good at (mending things, for example). He does not respond to their needs with genuine concern: "He could not get rid of his kind heart. 'I wish I was more strong-minded!' he sometimes said to himself, meaning that he wished other people's troubles did not make him feel uncomfortable" (101). In particular, Niggle must put up with the troubles of his only real neighbor, Mr. Parish. Parish has no concern for paintings, but he does remark on the weeds in Niggle's garden. These men are like two half-lame wayfarers on the road from Jerusalem to Jericho, neighbors to one another whether they like it or not. They are typical specimens of man, about whom Jesus delivered his ironical judgment: "How wilt thou say to thy brother, Let me pull out the mote out of thine eye; and, behold, a beam is in thine own eye?" (Matt. 7:3).

Yet there is something that distinguishes Niggle. There is not anything to suggest that, deep inside, Niggle is extraordinary, nor any nonsense from Tolkien about genius being equally distributed. The wondrous is alive all around us, and most of us do not see it—a far more poignant irony than that of the professor and the banana peel. But Niggle *does* see it. He does not see much, mind you; after all, his garden is a horror. But there's one picture that Niggle cannot get out of his mind, the one great work he must perform before he goes on his "troublesome journey." This picture, or such flashes of it as come to Niggle, is a gift, a grace, a thing with its own life, apart from the painter: "It had begun with a leaf caught in the wind, and it became a tree; and the tree grew, sending out innumerable branches, and thrusting out the most fantastic roots. Strange birds came and settled on the twigs and had to be attended to. Then all round the Tree, and behind it, through the gaps in the leaves and boughs, a country began to open out; and there were glimpses of a forest marching over the land, and of mountains tipped with snow" (101).

As Tolkien shows us in his sad tale *Smith of Wootton Major*, some people are chosen to visit the dangerous Land of Faery, and they return to our oblivious and ungrateful world a touch of the magic they find there. For all his smallness, or perhaps *in* all his smallness, Niggle enters that land with his vision of this picture. Or rather the picture enters and envelops Niggle. It has a secret life of its own, this picture. It bears its own time. It is always growing, not in length and breadth but in infinitely receding depth, revealing vistas behind vistas of mysterious reality. The picture as a whole is a fine analogue of the ramifying tree, with its labyrinth of branches and roots. Tolkien is thinking of the Yggdrasil, the World Tree of Norse mythology; but to say so is to engage in the sort of trivializing archaeology which Tolkien rejects in his companion essay to this tale. We want to know where this tree came from before it was made manifest in that Norse imagination. We want to know what it is.

Recall Christ's beautiful and ironic parable of the kingdom: "It is like a grain of mustard seed, which, when it is sown in the earth, is less than all the seeds that be in the earth: But when it is sown, it groweth up, and becometh greater than all herbs, and shooteth out great branches; so that the fowls of the air may lodge under the shadow of it" (Mark 4:31–32). The kingdom of God is as ordinary as a bush—yet nothing is more surprising. Its origins are too tiny to see, and its fulfillment too great to be fathomed. Rome had its wolf-suckling twins Romulus and Remus, and her citizens enjoyed contemplating her humble beginnings and comparing them with her glorious conquests.

Not that Romulus remained humble: by the time he had sent his rival brother packing to the shades below, and had ravished a village of its young ladies, he was recognizably a Roman commander and had little of the underdog about him. But a carpenter's son, nailed to a cross like a common thief? That was too minuscule a mustard seed for the ordinary-sighted pagan of Rome; nor are the pagans of our day, Christian and otherwise, possessed of keener vision. As for the fulfillment of that kingdom, not the most patriotic adorer of the state will confuse the swarming streets of Augustan Rome, with its grandeur of marble and convenience of sewers, with the golden streets of the New Jerusalem. What Niggle sees in his picture is the cosmos: for to the Christian the cosmos is none other than the unfolding of the kingdom of God in time and place.

To Be a Leaf

THE PICTURE BEGINS AS a "leaf caught in the wind," a small thing, tossed apparently at random by an unseen force. Why a leaf? Why not a root, or a seed? Recall another of Christ's parables: "I am the vine, ye are the branches" (John 15:5). Christ is not speaking ironically here, but there is a special irony in how his words apply to Niggle. That is because the whole of Niggle's vision of branch and trunk and root and forest and mountain arises from his care and reverence for one small leaf. The pagan myth of Romulus leaves its smallness behind; the Christian vision is to cultivate smallness—even, when smallness is born a child in Bethlehem, to adore it. Niggle wanted "to paint a whole tree, with all its leaves in the same style, and all of them different." That task is beyond any artist's power, for what it describes is no less artful than the portrayal of the human race, not as an abstraction, but as a fully recognized type, with all of its individual instances precisely and uniquely realized. We too have all been made in the same style, and all of us different.

Niggle's attention to the tiny leaf, then, is laudable, even saintly. So too would be his attention to his hobbling neighbor Parish, with all of Parish's small-lobed problems, if Niggle could come around to paying that attention. Poor Niggle, tugged this way by his desire to paint the grand vision of his heart (which painting, apart from the single leaf here or there, he executes rather poorly), and tugged that way by his duty to help his neighbor, one small leaf beside another (duties which, to his chagrin, he executes rather well). He was made to be a small man. Let not the pagans sneer. In his smallness consists a perfection which no prodigy of human talent, will, and fortune can achieve.

Tolkien once said that he wanted to farm exactly three square feet of earth, and tend to everything perfectly. Others may be impressed by arid size; the Christian, granted a glimpse into the womb of Mary as she says, "Be it done unto me according to thy word," should know better.

Alas, Niggle doesn't understand that he is meant to paint leaves, not the vine with all its branches—the universe. So he gets caught up in bigness, and forgets the small charities of every day: "Soon the canvas became so large that he had to get up a ladder, and he ran up and down it, putting in a touch here, and rubbing out a patch there," and "when people came to call, he seemed polite enough, though he fiddled a little with the pencils on his desk. He listened to what they said, but underneath he was thinking all the time about his big canvas, in the tall shed that had been built for it out in his garden (on a plot where he had once grown potatoes)" (101).

We see that as Niggle becomes more preoccupied with the *vastness* of his undertaking, he loses all proper sense of time. He is always running late. Had he more time, no doubt, he would not take a friend's visit for an intrusion. How ironic, but how true, that the quickest way to shorten one's life—in one's telescoping perception, if not in years—is to make oneself out to be greater than one was meant to be. The dimensions do not fit. Time ill-used is tragically short; the wicked man dying in his bed feels just what the man in the cart used to feel, as he rounded the last corner to the scaffold and noose. Time well-used partakes of eternity; thus we read that the saints were not only prepared to die, but felt that they were dying just when they were meant to, no matter how early.

Fighting Against Time

So, ABSORBED IN HIS busyness, Niggle suffers time rather than uses it: "He rolled up his sleeves and began to concentrate. He tried for several days not to bother about other things. But there came a tremendous crop of interruptions" (102). These interruptions are all *leaves*, as it were, "interrupting" the portrait of the tree. Niggle thus ignores the substance of his vision for the accident. He wants to paint a tree, but turns away from that same tree. The interruptions are revelations, but he cannot see them so. For one cannot enjoy a vision of the kingdom of God by ignoring its citizens, "the least of these my brethren" (Matt. 25:40). And all along, that journey looms: "At length Niggle's time became really precious. His acquaintances in the distant town began to remember that the little man had got to make a troublesome journey, and some began to calculate how long at the latest he could put off starting" (102–3).

This journey—an allegory for death—is "troublesome" for the same reason why it is difficult for Niggle to paint those leaves, and why he feels compelled to help his neighbors despite his desire to ignore them. Time is at the heart of the matter. Christians believe that this world is to be loved dearly. So Augustine learned, meditating upon what it meant that God declared the world he created to be good. Yet at the same time, that world is to be scorned as dust by comparison with God, who alone is lovely. The careful cultivation of proper love for the world—implying, ironically, a proper contempt for the world—is among our duties in the world. If this world were trash, then Niggle's journey would be a joy or a relief. If it were the fulfillment of beauty, then Niggle's journey would be a catastrophe. In neither case could the journey be described as troublesome; just as, if there were only individual leaves and no tree, or only a tree and no leaves, there would be no cosmic vision to disturb Niggle's days. But the journey is troublesome because the world really is to be loved, correctly, and because we will be judged according to whether we believed in the Creator and embraced his world with a shadow of the love by which he brought it into being.

Neither Niggle nor Parish possesses faith and its consequent love so abundantly. Absorbed in his own concerns, each man seems always put out, harried, behind time. Autumn has come, and the urgency of Niggle's situation has been pressing upon his mind, even as he tries to deny it or to bargain with his vision: "He knew that he would have to be leaving soon: perhaps early next year. He could only just get the picture finished, and only so so, at that: there were some corners where he would not have time to do more than hint at what he wanted" (103). The "perhaps early next year" reads as a self-delusion: Niggle wishes to appear levelheaded, not giving himself an absurd length of time remaining; yet all along he has been leaving his garden, and his friends and neighbors, in neglect.

Thus, whenever Parish and Niggle meet, a silent third commentator walks beside them, Time, preventing them from behaving "naturally," that is to say, with our habit of ignoring the truth: "There was a knock on the door. 'Come in!' he said sharply, and climbed down the ladder. He stood on the floor, twiddling his brush. It was his neighbor, Parish" (103). The confrontation between the painter who doesn't want to understand gardening and the gardener who doesn't want to understand painting is a study in nervously concealed rudeness:

"Well, Parish, what is it?" said Niggle.

"I oughtn't to interrupt you, I know," said Parish (without a glance at the picture). "You are very busy, I'm sure."

Niggle had meant to say something like that himself, but he had missed his chance. All he said was, "Yes" (103).

When Parish describes his problem—the wind has blown not leaves off a tree, but tiles off his roof, and the rain is pouring in, and Mrs. Parish is ill—it is with mock consideration for Niggle, and with reckless haste. First, he is worried for no reason: his wife, it turns out, has only a cold. But the fretful Parish will help ruin his neighbor's health over it. Second, he needs canvas to cover the hole in his roof, but his obliviousness to Niggle's painting makes it awkward for him to ask for that, of all things. So Parish does what we all do. We ask for it anyway, gracelessly, and with a pretense that it is only borrowing: "'I think I ought to get to the doctor. And to the builders, too, only they take so long to come. I was wondering if you had any wood and canvas you could spare, just to patch me up and see me through for a day or two.' Now he did look at the picture" (104).

Thy Will Be Done

HERE WE SENSE THE ironic "cruelty" of the Lord—that kindness we neither expect nor want, but need desperately. Surely Parish would not be so hard-hearted to ask that Niggle's precious canvas be torn so that he could patch a hole in his roof! Well, Parish would *like* to ask—but in his pride he keeps up the pretense that he isn't asking for much, and that he is thus vaguely ill-used: "'But I see you are busy,'" he says curtly, when Niggle offers to move Mrs. Parish downstairs and pointedly does *not* offer to go to the builders or to the doctor. "'I had rather hoped you might have been able to spare the time to go for the doctor, seeing how I'm placed: and the builder, too, *if you really have no canvas you can spare*'" (104; emphasis added).

The irony of being Christian! They who place their hope in spiritualism see their delusive visions as the only reality, and to the devil with missing tiles and leaky roofs. They who assert that only matter exists may see the neighbor's missing tiles and the leaky roof, but to the devil with the vision—and with the command that they ought to do something about the tiles. Christians must understand both spirit and matter, and in their proper relation. True spiritual vision is incomparably great: yet it also shows the greatness inhering in small and unprepossessing things. The universe is greater than one man, but it is that one man, not the universe, that is made in the image and likeness of God. Parish should never ask for Niggle's canvas, because Niggle's heart is in that painting; and Niggle should offer that piece of canvas, because such an affirmation of the small and homely is of the very essence of his painting. He will learn later that something of Parish is in those leaves. If he knew what his painting was about, he would give it away. Can the Lord require such a sacrifice? The Lord who was crucified can and may.

Nevertheless, Niggle does, in a sense, offer the painting, because he offers *time*. He does not offer it out of sentimentality, or out of the fire of charity. At the moment he decides to make the bicycle trip to the doctor's and the builder's, his heart "was merely soft without feeling at all kind." Yet offer he does, suspecting that he is throwing away the last little time he has for his picture: "Of course, Niggle had a picture and barely time to finish it. But it seemed that this was a thing that Parish had to reckon with and not Niggle. Parish, however, did not reckon with pictures; and Niggle could not alter that. 'Curse it!' he said to himself, as he got out his bicycle" (104–5). Niggle rides furiously, racing against his allotted time, unaware that he is, ironically, even *now* completing one of the works for which he was made: not a picture, but a bicycle trip, or the picture as made manifest in the bicycle trip. As we will see, Niggle's time becomes his own only when it is at the disposal of a higher authority.

The Solely Punctual

UNFORTUNATELY, NIGGLE FINDS NEITHER the doctor nor the builder at home, but he does manage to soak himself to the skin and fall ill. The tardy doctor "arrived next day, which was quite convenient for him, as by that time there were two patients to deal with, in neighboring houses" (105). Indeed, everyone in Niggle's land seems out of joint with time. The storm continues, but "the builder did not come" (105). Nor did the Parishes. Mrs. Parish now spends her time mopping the floor and accusing "that Mr. Niggle" of having forgotten to call at the builder's. A Councillor will even suggest that Niggle should have been sent on his journey *ahead of time*, because Niggle was of no use to society — meaning, of no economic utility. Niggle and his picture will soon fade from everyone's memory. These disjointed people are much like us: our time eroded by overorganization, leaving us neither the wisdom to perceive nor the love to preserve what is worth our while.

But there is one being who always comes at the appointed time. That is because he derives his orientation from beyond time. He is the Driver of the carriage sent to take Niggle on his troublesome journey.

Just when Niggle feels a little better and is about to resume painting, he is *interrupted* again—it will be the last interruption—by an Inspector of Houses, who blandly notes that Niggle's neighbor's house should have been patched up by Niggle's picture:

> "There is plenty of material here: canvas, wood, waterproof paint."
> "Where?" asked Niggle indignantly.
> "There!" said the Inspector, pointing to the picture.
> "My picture!" exclaimed Niggle.
> "I daresay it is," said the Inspector. "But homes come first. That is the law." (106–7)

As the Inspector is politely firm about the relative importance of houses and pictures, so his double the Driver will allow no bargaining, no *niggling* over the time to leave:

> "Driver? Driver?" he chattered. "Driver of what?"
> "You and your carriage," said the man. "The carriage was ordered long ago. It has come at last. It's waiting. You start today on your journey, you know."
> "There now!" said the Inspector. "You'll have to go; but it's a bad way to start on your journey, leaving your jobs undone. Still, we can at least make some use of the canvas now."
> "Oh, dear!" said poor Niggle, beginning to weep. "And it's not even finished!"
> "Not finished?" said the Driver. "Well, it's finished with, as far as you're concerned, at any rate. Come along!" (107)

The Driver drops him off at a train without a timetable: the terminus is unique to each person. "Niggle!" shouts the Porter, and Niggle stumbles out of the train unprepared, without luggage, and is sent to a Workhouse Infirmary. Time is objective in this sense: it is independent of anyone's perception of it. But it is subjective, even personal, in this sense: it is the medium through which the appointed experiences come to the appointed people. It is the fiber in the fabric of the story.

Here two sorts of readers may balk. One will find all talk about time, after Niggle has "died," beside the point. "First, I do not believe in an afterlife," I hear him say. "But even if I did, by the testimony of your own philosophers I am told that Niggle should enter eternity, a timeless realm. I understand that to continue the allegory we need to continue the story line, in which events have a beginning, a middle, and an end. But that necessity is literary and fictional. Discuss salvation or justification if you like, but not time, which for Niggle has ceased to exist."

But so sharp a severance between time and eternity forms no part of Christian dogma; else how could we understand the "new earth" we are to inhabit (Rev. 21:1)? And as the finger of God may be seen in the veining of every leaf of time, so in us temporal creatures, the eternal is present too. "The kingdom of God is within you," says Jesus, not claiming that it is a subjective experience, but recalling us to a personal contact with the Lord, meeting him now, to bring about in ourselves now, and in all the world, his kingdom. Time is pregnant with eternity. No one knows what Paul saw when he was carried into the heaven of heavens—but Christians may suppose that if we have been made for eternity, then somehow eternity will be fit for us, for our mode of being. Things may happen to us—as they do to the blessed in Dante's *Paradise*. In one sense that will mean no change, no instability, for "neither height, nor depth, nor any other creature, shall be able to separate us from the love of God, which is in Christ Jesus our Lord" (Rom. 8:39). Yet in another sense there will be change: development, deepening, grace upon grace, a neverending adventure into the heart of love.

The second sort objects, "But Niggle must either be saved or damned, and at once." Now we are told by Paul that we will be transformed "in the twinkling of an eye" (1 Cor. 15:52), but we also know that "one day is with the Lord as a thousand years" (2 Pet. 3:8). It may be that our purgation will consist of one clear look from our just judge, before whom we will join in Job's cry, repenting "in dust and ashes" (Job 42:6), suffering in that instant a world of mortification. But once it is conceded that real purifying must take place, then it hardly matters whether we experience this purifying as of infinitesimally short or of very long duration. In either case, it is one of those things that will happen to us: we are saved by Christ's merits, then scoured clean by the medical action of the Trinity. That this scouring should take time, and should involve some response from us, imparts no limit to the majesty of God, but merely indicates the sort of creatures we are.

Cleansed As by Fire

IN ANY CASE, NIGGLE undergoes a medical treatment, which is not to his liking. How could it be, since Niggle is not yet to the liking of the "very severe
doctor" who treats him? "It was more like being in a prison than in a hospital,"
says Tolkien. Niggle is made to work hard, in two ways. First, in the body,
and at tasks which employ real but humble abilities, while mortifying the
one ability upon which he founded his pride. So he does "digging, carpentry,
and painting bare boards all one plain color." Then his mind must work hard:
"They kept him in the dark for hours at a stretch, 'to do some thinking,' they
said" (108). Under such circumstances—he is not allowed outside—Niggle
loses track of time.

This loss is appropriate and merciful. For Niggle, time is now marked by
the improvement, glacially slow, in his spiritual health. He is spared worrying
about the present and the future. Since he doesn't know the time, he cannot,
even if he wished, violate Christ's command that we take no care for the morrow. But he can still engage in one of man's more futile follies. He can fret
about the past. Ironically, as this new "eternal" time continues and his health
improves, Niggle loses those frets too. It is as if he were shifting from a lower
mode of time to a higher:

> At first, during the first century or so (I am merely giving his impressions),
> he used to worry aimlessly about the past. One thing he kept on repeating
> to himself, as he lay in the dark: "I wish I had called on Parish the first
> morning after the high winds began. I meant to. The first loose tiles would
> have been easy to fix. Then Mrs. Parish might never have caught cold.
> Then I should not have caught cold either. Then I should have had a week
> longer." But in time he forgot what it was that he had wanted a week longer
> for. If he worried at all after that, it was about his jobs in the hospital. He
> planned them out, thinking how quickly he could stop that board creaking,
> or rehang that door. (108)

In this new mode of being, Niggle experiences time, though he has none
of it to himself, as his servant; "he began to know just what he could do with
it" (109).

Compelled to Give in Evidence

AFTER A CHANGE IN discipline—digging, day after day, which was the one thing Niggle liked least to do—and after being left in the dark "for hours or for years, as far as he could tell" (109), Niggle hears two voices, as of "a Medical Board, or perhaps a Court of Inquiry," discussing his medical—or is it legal?—case. The First Voice, one of command and justice, is severe, more severe than the Doctor's. The Second Voice, one of mercy and hope, was gentle, "though it was not soft."

Their judgment upon Niggle is searching and just, wholly unlike Niggle's judgment of himself, probably and embarrassingly more acute than the reader's judgment of Niggle, and, as we shall see, a devastatingly ironic commentary upon the world and its criteria for judgment.

The first thing to notice is that Niggle's smallness, not his greatness, is cause for mercy. When the First Voice puts the case against him—his heart didn't function properly, he hardly ever thought, he wasted time, he failed even to amuse himself, his journey found him unprepared, he made poor use of the "talents" given him—we can only hope that our record will be no worse! The Second Voice, however, appeals to Niggle's *unimportance*: "'But, of course, he is only a little man. He was never meant to be anything very much; and he was never very strong'" (110). Sad state of human merit, when among the best or most exculpatory things that can be said of us is that we were never meant to be much. But in that smallness dwells a grace. Reviewing the records of Niggle's life, the Second Voice begins by noticing Niggle's affection for the small, and tallies it in the man's favor: "'He was a painter by nature. In a minor way, of course; still, a Leaf by Niggle has a charm of its own. He took a great deal of pains with leaves, just for their own sake. But he never thought that that made him important'" (110).

Fortunate Niggle. We are rather taught nowadays to view every pittance of a talent as making us quite important indeed. In many ways the reader, at first encouraged to smile and look down upon Niggle, now sees the little painter rise above him, in the very words with which the voices are discussing his worthlessness. For Niggle *could never* have become important by lavishing attention upon leaves. In doing so, he stepped, now and then, into the child's world of play, into love of beauty for its own sake. Whenever he squandered his hours gazing upon the beads of dew strung upon a leaf, losing all sense of making his way in life, he truly lived and used his time well.

In another sense, too, Niggle used time well, according to the Second Voice. He answered many "Calls." The Voices discuss what calls he answered and why, with the First asserting that Niggle called them "'Interruptions,'" and the Second excusing the "'poor little man's'" lack of perception. What we have here, as the voices examine the chronicles of Niggle, is a time parallel to the time we perceive. In our own chronicles we mark time by great deeds, wars, and masterpieces. But in heaven's time—in real time—who knows where the critical moments fall?

C. S. Lewis makes the same point in *The Great Divorce*. The narrator sees a woman so grand that angels, men, and beasts follow reverently in her train. He supposes she was some queen on earth. But she was only an ordinary country woman—ordinary in the world's terms, extraordinary in her love. So warm was her charity that she changed many of the lives that touched hers; like Monica, she was a mother to many. Who knows how many ages of providential design had been preparing to bring this saint upon earth? Who knows the history of the gifts of the Holy Spirit? We do not know the import of the time we inhabit. That may well be a good definition of what the Middle Ages called "the World": that state in which no one really knows what is going on.

Did Niggle know what was going on? The Second Voice suggests that in his last call, the one that resulted in the wet bicycle ride, Niggle did guess that his end was near, "that he was throwing away his last chance with his picture" (111). It is this final adjustment of priorities that settles the discussion: "'I think you put it too strongly,'" says the First Voice, "'but it is your task, of course, to put the best interpretation on the facts'" (111).

A New Timetable for the Train

WHAT GENTLE TREATMENT DOES Niggle now receive? A more natural time; Niggle's time, as it should have been, had Niggle not been a fallen man. The sun rises, filling Niggle's cell with light. The Doctor—the ministering Spirit—gives him gifts to fortify him for the journey: salve for his sore hands, good advice, a bottle of tonic. Best of all, he gives him a last eucharistic meal—a biscuit and a glass of wine. Niggle leaves for the train station, whose only timetable is set to Niggle himself. Thus, the cars appear newly painted. "Even the track that lay in front of the engine looked new," for this is the first time this train has run, and its destination has not existed until now, or has always existed in its Maker's design, but in the fullness of time is only now being made manifest. This train is going to *Niggle*.

It is the land of Niggle's dreams, as he disembarks and bicycles along toward it; it is the reality whereof Niggle's fitful glimpses of beauty were but the shadow: "Before him stood the Tree, his Tree, finished. If you could say that of a Tree that was alive, its leaves opening, its branches growing and bending in the wind that Niggle had so often felt or guessed, and had so often failed to catch" (113). This tree "redeems the time." If Niggle did not always work, now at least this task is lovingly completed for him: "All the leaves he had ever laboured at were there, as he had imagined them rather than as he had made them; and there were many others that had only budded in his mind, and many that might have budded, if he had only had time. Nothing was written on them, they were just exquisite leaves, yet they were dated as clear as a calendar" (113). It is the living record of Niggle's insight, the truest and finest statement of the artist Niggle ought to have been, inextricably intertwined with what Niggle in his charity sometimes was, in spite of himself.

Something else about this tree suggests the wedding of time and eternity: one can walk into the scene it frames without losing a sense of the whole. The distant draws near, but remains "distant," as if distance measured not length but depth of perception, or of wonder. In life we finish nothing, because our vision is weak and our wills rebel; then death finishes us. Here in eternity everything is finished, everything is as it should be; but nothing is "finished with," meaning that we delve more and more deeply into what is already there. Better still: there are regions about the tree, in the forest, that by grace have been left "inconclusive," for Niggle to continue, as it is Niggle's love and his work:

> He sat down under a very beautiful distant tree . . . and he considered where to begin work, and where to end it, and how much time was required. He could not quite work out his scheme. "Of course!" he said. "What I need is Parish." (115)

No Joy without the Neighbor

Is THAT A VISION to enjoy alone? Is eternity given to man for solitude, each soul packed away in its own ice? If not, if we have not been made for loneliness, then what can we mean when we say we have no time for other people? What is time for, if not love? How can the day be holy, without celebration?

So Niggle can never be fully healed without a companion for his time. That companion must be Parish. Their years of "interrupting" each other become lives of shared time and of exchanged gifts: "As they worked together, it became plain that Niggle was now the better of the two at ordering his time and getting things done. Oddly enough, it was Niggle who became most absorbed in building and gardening, while Parish often wandered about looking at trees, and especially at the Tree" (115). Niggle's more efficient use of time indicates his further progress towards spiritual health. But we are not to suppose that Parish uses his time foolishly. Instead, he is now doing what *he* neglected to do in life. *He wastes time.* I don't mean that the time is really wasted; one could hardly be better employed, unless there is some pressing matter to attend to, than in "messing around in boats," to use Kenneth Grahame's fine phrase, or wandering about, looking at trees. We are not made for work, merely: we are made for praise, whereof beholding wonder is the first and necessary verse. "'This is grand!'" (115) Parish exclaims. That would have been a good way for him to dally in that wondrously odd corner of the old world called England.

Eventually, after the two have ceased to disagree—for they did occasionally disagree—and have ceased to feel weary—for the Doctor's tonic, mixed with water from a spring, has seen to that, and has even healed Parish's bad leg— "Niggle found that he was now beginning to turn his eyes, more and more often, towards the Mountains" (116). "I will lift up mine eyes unto the hills, from whence cometh my help," says the Psalmist (121:1), and Tolkien, the lover of Norse myth, has the good sense to take him at his word. There is a land within this picture, yet beyond it, as one realm may lead to the threshold of a wider, more comprehensive realm. When Niggle and Parish walk towards that threshold, Niggle knows what time it is. Just as the train stop read "Niggle," so now the dial reads, "The time for Niggle to climb the mountains." A man "like a shepherd" appears, volunteering himself for a guide (117).

But the time for Niggle is not the time for Parish. "'I must wait for my wife'" (117), the gardener says. He hopes to show her the house and the gardens which he and Niggle have made as beautiful as they could, so that she (daughter of Eve!) could make it better, "more homely." The place is given to them, and they give themselves and each other to the place, that it may become, in both the active and the passive sense, *their gift.* So when Parish asks the shepherd what the name of that land is, the reply shows both men what they failed to see in their time on earth:

"Don't you know?" said the man. "It is Niggle's Country. It is Niggle's Picture, or most of it: a little of it is now Parish's Garden."

"Niggle's Picture!" said Parish in astonishment. "Did you think of all this, Niggle? I never knew you were so clever. Why didn't you tell me?" (117)

Well, on earth Niggle and Parish were too busy missing the wonder in one another: "Old Earthgrubber" is what Niggle called his neighbor then. But now they shake hands, hoping to meet and work together again; and Niggle ascends the mountains.

What Time Is It Now?

THERE THE TALE MIGHT end. But Tolkien brings us back, startlingly, to the world of Inspectors and laws. We become aware of the irony of parallel times, of very different things going on at once, or, better, of people in a shadow world unaware of what is going on in the real world, yet all the while taking themselves for the only reality.

Three men discuss the passing of Niggle, and whether he amounted to anything. Their names are all diminutives: Tompkins (son of little Tom), Atkins (son of little Andrew), and Perkins (son of little Peter). Councillor Tompkins—important, he—asserts that Niggle was "'a silly little man'" (118), which we already know. But what Tompkins means by "silly" we (and the lowly schoolmaster Atkins) would call wise. For Tompkins, the only worthy use of Niggle's time would have been his "'washing dishes in a communal kitchen or something'" (118). As for those who spend their time looking at trees, his judgment is merciless. Says the Councillor: "'I should have put him away long ago.'" "'Put him away?'" asks the Schoolmaster. "'You mean you'd have made him start on his journey before his time?'" (118). But the Councillor laughs at the notion that time is not some dead thing we employ at will. Painting, too, is dead for him; propagandistically useful, perhaps, but never to be an expression of wonder for mere beauty.

Atkins, however, has saved a scrap of Niggle's picture—"a mountain peak and a spray of leaves," and has it framed and placed in the town museum, where it stands with the placard "Leaf: by Niggle," a dim, poor, tiny glimpse of Niggle's vision granted a temporary and distant memorial. The picture is hardly noticed; the museum burns down, and the earth knows the name of Niggle no more.

But that name endures elsewhere. For time on earth cannot escape the clasp of eternity. With a few strokes Tolkien brings into harmony all the joyful ironies of this tale. Tolkien gives the last words not to Niggle, nor even to the sympathetic Atkins, but to the voices of the Lord of Time. Niggle's picture may not be hanging in the museum; there may not even be a museum; but the life of his vision is now a place more real than any place he ever loved. As once he was healed by that vision of the tree and mountains, so now the "doctors" send other souls there, to that particular place, for a certain length of time — to strengthen them for the time that is eternity:

> "It is proving very useful indeed," said the Second Voice. "As a holiday, and a refreshment. It is splendid for convalescence; and not only for that, for many it is the best introduction to the Mountains. It works wonders in some cases. I am sending more and more there. They seldom have to come back."
>
> "No, that is so," said the First Voice. "I think that we shall have to give the region a name. What do you propose?"
>
> "The Porter settled that some time ago," said the Second Voice. *"Train for Niggle's Parish in the bay*: he has shouted that for a long time now. Niggle's Parish. I sent a message to both of them to tell them."
>
> "What did they say?"
>
> "They both laughed. Laughed — the Mountains rang with it!" (120)

Part Three

The Irony of Power

11

The Stone Rejected

Niggle was a small man. But love, let us be true to one another. In comparison with the maker of heaven and earth, or even with the least of the angelic hosts, where are the giants among us?

With Christianity a new idea enters the heart of man. It may have lain dormant before, or distorted, tricked out in glories until it could no longer be recognized for the humble thing it was. Christianity asserts that the powerful are not so great after all. The pagans saw that—sort of. Sophocles' half-mad Antigone rails against the tyranny of Thebes, as she disobeys King Creon's law and gives her brother, the instigator of a civil war, his due burial rites. That lone woman, does defy the state, but only to champion the old earth-religions and the traditions of aristocrats, nor does she show any interest in what happens to anybody else at Thebes. She would not understand the corollary to the Christian assertion above: that it is in the weak and the poor that power truly resides.

The heroine in Christianity is not Antigone, with her passionate speeches and her courtship of death, but a simple village woman who says little, who does not accost the great power that has subjugated her country, yet who gives birth to the One who has conquered the world. That carpenter himself never wrote a word, and his mission ended with what seemed to be complete failure.

Jesus of Nazareth, King of the Jews

THE HISTORICAL IRONY OF Jesus is that he should never have been who and what he was: for Christians, the Messiah; for all others, surely the most influential man who ever lived. Yet the theological irony is that only such a man as Jesus could have been the Messiah. No one would have predicted it, yet Christians believe it had been predicted for centuries.

The Jews of Jesus' time had been expecting the Christ to enter Jerusalem as the anointed king of glory, to free the nation and reestablish the throne of David. That was common sense. Predict a king, expect a king. Yet their vision was constricted in place and time. What was happening then in far Britain, let alone what would happen there centuries later, never entered their consciousness.

A king for here, now: that was what Simon the zealot sought, and what put the Romans on their guard. So the Jews who wished to destroy Jesus (possibly because he seemed to be a blasphemer, possibly because his teachings would destroy Jewish political hopes, or would, conversely, undermine the tenuous privileges which the leading Jews had won from the Romans for the whole people) called him an insurrectionist, a traitor to Rome. Too clever, they accused him of playing the Messiah they expected, so that the Romans would execute him—while they remained sure he was *not* the Messiah they expected. Ironically, as Christians believe, he was the Messiah they *did not expect*, but might have expected, had they attended to their own messianic scriptures and to the irony of their history.

For Jesus is in himself the story of the Jews, the unconsidered people, the servant in whom nothing beautiful was seen, the sufferer, the stone the builders rejected. Quite aside from his fulfilling various prophecies, his life can be seen as the culmination and fulfillment of those ironic reversals that make up the history of the chosen people:

> Abel, the younger son, was the just son, slain by the elder Cain
> God promises to make Abraham, without descendants and stricken in years, the father of a mighty race.
> God favors the younger Jacob, not the elder, warlike Esau.
> The second youngest son of Jacob, Joseph (son of Rachel, long despised for her barrenness, but best loved by Jacob) is sold into slavery, beginning one of the greatest and most ironic "underdog" stories of all time. The infant Moses is hidden among the reeds and

is taken up by the Pharaoh's sister. This foundling will overcome the mighty army of Egypt.

Gideon defeats the Midianites with the tag-end of an army, as commanded by the Lord.

David, youngest son of Jesse, is presented last to the prophet Samuel, almost as an afterthought. Samuel anoints him king. David's battle with Goliath, a sling and pebbles for his weapons, is an emblem of the history of outmatched Israelite armies fighting against oppressors from Assyria, Babylon, and Egypt.

The prophets were revered after they had died, but were outcasts while alive: lonely, despised, and hunted, often at the edge of mental and physical collapse, yet a threat to the politicians of the day. They were not delightful to behold or to hear. Elijah went to Mount Hebron to die, pursued by the politician-queen Jezebel, and crushed by the fear that all his preaching had been in vain.

Jeremiah was thrown into a cistern to die for his prophecy that Jerusalem would be overrun by the Babylonians. Had he preached in our own foolish century, Ezekiel would have been confined to an asylum. How else to curb those bizarre, physical prophecies of his: lying in the desert upon one side for three weeks, or eating over a dung-fire.

Those prophets and the Psalmist speak of a Messiah despised of men: "Yet it was our infirmities he bore."

Not the Jewish nation, but Sion (for the glory of God's name) shall draw all nations together in worship. This union shall be accomplished by a remnant of the race, as in the days of Noah the world was repopulated by one just man and his family.

This history of the unimpressive and the rejected rising up in ironic triumph continues in the New Testament. Leaving aside the life of Jesus of Nazareth ("Can there anything good come out of Nazareth?" snorts Nathanael upon hearing of him [John 1:46]), we have in Acts the incipient battle between the weakling Christians and mighty Rome, the astonishing irony of various fishermen and a voluble tentmaker daring to preach the new faith from the shores of India to Spain; the small and weak-voiced Paul, erstwhile persecutor of Christians and now least of the apostles, surviving arrests and stonings and shipwrecks, to become the great evangelist to the Gentile world. The world thinks it has Peter in chains—has often thought so, and will think so again—but the angel appears at the darkest hour to set him free.

In this vision, Jesus is the sum of both Jewish history and Christian history to come. Thus, in the lives of the saints he appears as the appropriate but unexpected One. He is the child carried on the back of the ogreish Christopher, a child who grows oppressively heavy, carrying the weight of the world's sins. He is the tattered beggar accosting Martin of Tours, prompting the soldier first to divide his coat, and then to give up his way of life altogether. He is the leper to Francis, overcoming in that most amiable of saints a revulsion against the ugly, filling him with such grace that the young man races back down the road to give him a kiss. The message of Christianity, preached by Jesus and revealed by the life of Christianity itself, is that the lame shall enter first. The publicans, the whores, the off-scourings of the world will enter the kingdom of God. It is the mighty who will have to sweat.

A Redeemer All Wrong: François Mauriac's *A Kiss for the Leper*

CHRISTIAN WRITERS HAVE NEVER ceased to explore this marvelous irony. In Tolkien's *Lord of the Rings*, Sauron ignores the hobbits because they are small; that proves his undoing. The courtly mouse Reepicheep in Lewis's *Chronicles of Narnia* is a parlous enemy of evil. The hunted "whisky priest" in Graham Greene's *The Power and the Glory* is a martyr in the making, though he thinks he is worthless and on his way to damnation. His death, so desired by the communist lieutenant, will help sweep that government from the earth. The little knight Pan Michael, of Henryk Sienkiewicz's novel by that name, defends a key garrison against a Turkish onslaught, saving it by sweat, cunning, and audacity, only to watch in dismay as the "powerful," the leaders of his own government, betray him by surrender. Fulfilling his vow to God, Michael leaves his bones and blood on the heights of Kamenyetz; and that defeat of one small man brings down upon the Turks the vengeance of the savior of Europe, John Sobieski.

The redeemers and the redeemed are not whom we expect. This irony is the motive for François Mauriac's gemlike novella, *A Kiss for the Leper*. Its hero is Jean Peloueyre, the young heir to a large estate in southern France, and thus potentially a very important man, at least in his cranny of the world. But Mauriac is keenly sensitive to the "wrongness" of Christ. Thus Jean is like a miscarriage that survived: "He was so short that the low dressing mirror reflected his pinched little face, with its hollow cheeks and long, pointed nose. It was red in color, and seemed to have been worn away like a stick of barley-sugar as the result of prolonged sucking. His cropped hair grew to a point low on his prematurely wrinkled forehead. When he grinned he showed his gums and a set of decayed teeth" (3). It is as if Jean's temporal plane were tilted or cracked. He should have died *in utero* but did not; his form has never grown to adulthood, yet seems precociously aged, falling apart. He is no more appealing in his personal habits or in his rare conversation. He loves the heat of summer afternoon for the escape it affords him from the health and vigor of others, especially of females. His is an asceticism born of self-loathing and shame: "He could slip down the street, keeping to the thin line of shade cast by the houses, safe from the giggling mockery of young girls seated with their sewing in the open doorways. The sight of him miserably slinking past was sure to provoke an outburst of feminine laughter, but at two o'clock in the afternoon the women were still asleep, sweating with the heat and complaining of the flies" (4).

A "loathsome cricket," unfit for society, Jean is at home in the woods and the swamps, where he loves to spend hours shooting wildfowl. He is unmistakably male despite his misshaped body, and accordingly he enjoys this innocent pleasure, a gunsmoke-tarred and muddy aftertaste of paradise. Imprisoned in his shell of a body, deformed by it, but, as we shall see, *formed* by that body too, formed for holiness, is a masculine spirit longing for the raptures of love. The contradiction is pathetic. The presence of other human beings who look upon his body twists Jean's thoughts and hopes into the absurdity of a cartoon: "Thinking, with him, was accompanied always by much frowning, gesticulation, bursts of laughter, odds and ends of poetry spoken aloud—in short, a complete pantomime productive of constant mirth to the people of the town" (4). But this odd, sad, ugly little man will marry a beautiful young woman, and they will become for each other, in and through their mutual revulsion, the call to sanctity. In Jean the holy and the unclean are one.

The Song of the Blond Beast

MAURIAC CASTS HIS TALE as an assault on Friedrich Nietzsche's views of power. In *On the Genealogy of Morals* Nietzsche celebrates the moral code of strong, free aristocrats, at enmity with the skulking envy of priests and their weak followers:

> The knightly-aristocratic value judgments presupposed a powerful physicality, a flourishing, abundant, even overflowing health, together with that which serves to preserve it: war, adventure, hunting, dancing, war games, and in general all that involves vigorous, free, joyful activity. The priestly-

> noble mode of valuation presupposes, as we have seen, other things: it is
> ·disadvantageous for it when it comes to war! As is well known, the priests are
> the *most evil enemies* — but why? Because they are the most impotent. It is
> because of their impotence that in them hatred grows to monstrous and un-
> canny proportions, to the most spiritual and poisonous kind of hatred. (1.7)

Against the shiftless sentimentality of the modern age, our greatest and truest
critic, aside from heroic Christianity properly understood, is Nietzsche. Mauriac knew it well, and peoples his novellas with just such weak and strength-
sapping parasites as Nietzsche's priests: the appalling mother in *Genetrix* who
allows her daughter-in-law and rival to die of puerperal fever after a stillbirth;
the priggish churchgoing children in *The Knot of Vipers* who spy on their
atheist father, seeking to protect their inheritance; the heroine of *The Woman
of the Pharisees*, who uses her vision of the will of God to crush the hearts of
all who oppose her.

Now that Christianity has largely been diluted to social niceties, it is brac-
ing to read Nietzsche's unapologetic insistence on the naturalness of raw power: "To demand of strength that it should *not* express itself as strength, that it
should *not* be a desire to overcome, a desire to throw down, a desire to become
master, a thirst for enemies and resistances and triumphs, is just as absurd as
to demand of weakness that it should express itself as strength" (1.13). The revenge of the weak consists in hating the strong for their strength, and then to
redefine as good the humiliations they could not prevent. They are eunuchs,
preaching chastity!

Nietzsche relishes the savage irony of an aristocratic class, conscious of
its superiority, willing to fling life away in a gay gesture of defiance. The old
Germans, living by herding and pillage in a land of long winters, developed a
keen sense of the swiftness and suddenness of death, and met it neither with
hope nor with faith, but with the dark laughter of understatement. So marked
was this penchant that it survived well into the Christian era. A few examples
will illustrate the point.

In the Anglo-Saxon epic *Beowulf*, the monster Grendel has invaded Heo-
rot, has slaughtered and eaten dozens of King Hrothgar's men, leaving the hall
splashed with blood. He has returned several times for more. When one night
he seizes Beowulf — who has watched with cold patience as Grendel slit one
of his men from the throat to the chops and gobbled him down — he finds, as
the poet says, that the strength of this warrior was rather more than he had expected. And when, in their struggle, Beowulf twists Grendel's arm behind his

back till it is tearing clean off, the poet pauses to note, at coolly ironic length, pretending that we do not know what is plainly obvious, that this was not a good day for Grendel.

Or consider this episode in the Icelandic *Njal's Saga*. Gizur and his men surround the home of their enemy Gunnar. They intend to burn it down with him in it, but need to make sure he is home. The house is a thatched dugout, with at most only one or two windows; it is not easy of approach. So Gizur orders one of his men, Thorgrim, to scramble over the roof and peer through the window. He returns a few minutes later, his belly split straight down the middle:

> Gizur looked up at him and asked, "Is Gunnar at home?"
> "That's for you to find out," replied Thorgrim. "But I know that his halberd certainly is."
> And with that he fell down dead. (169)

Such humor is dark with the high cheer of despair. What can the Christian reply to a culture so brave in the face of destruction? How do we respond to Nietzsche?

But We Do Worship Power

IT BECOMES CLEAR EARLY in *A Kiss for the Leper* that Mauriac will engage Nietzsche on the philosopher's own ground. Jean Peloueyre is the slinking dog Nietzsche despises. The task is to grant the philosopher all the truth he speaks, including the truth against Christians, and then, without any absurd sentimentality, to defeat him anyway in the person of the leper. For Christians misspeak when they say the weak are most powerful. What they really mean is that the world, and that includes the fitfully blind and perspicacious Nietzsche, cannot see strength where it stands.

One summer afternoon, Jean visits the home of his friend Robert, the son of the district physician, Dr. Pieuchon. This Robert is all that Jean would like to be: handsome, sociable, well on his way to making a mark in the world. He has the ease of aristocratic grace so admired by Nietzsche. His room is a gaily decked, masculine ballad to Dionysus: there is "holiday reading" of pornography, with a curdled classical air: *Aphrodite, The Latin Orgy,* and so forth, mingled with scraps of a decadent aristocracy: *The Garden of the Suppliants, The Journal of a Chambermaid.* These lie scattered among tickets for students' balls, and a "skull with a cutty stuck mockingly between its teeth" (5). The impression is of a vigorous animal, wedded to a fair but not breathtaking intellect, in the joy of its youth, yet dabbling with death, as if the skull grinned to have the student's life in its ironical chaps. We do not actually meet Robert in the novella, for this young lover and time-destroyer is to contract consumption and die. *Pace* Nietzsche, but strong young men who frequent certain establishments have been known to do that.

Nevertheless, as he rummages through Robert's books, Jean finds one marked at a certain page. It isn't a letter by Saint Paul, and Jean is not Augustine, but the Lord works in ironical ways. The passage will set Jean, who in his walking death is more alive than Robert in his banal sexuality, on his path to a tragic holiness. Jean opens a volume of Nietzsche and reads a passage that applies to him in a way that Nietzsche himself would not have understood:

> From an open trunk came the stale smell of the young man's summer clothes which have been stuffed away just as he took them off.
>   This is what Peloueyre read:
>   "What is the meaning of *good*?—All that enlarges the sense of power in a man, the will to power, and power itself. What is the meaning of 'bad'?— Whatever is rooted in weakness. Let the weak and the failures perish: it is for us to see that they perish. What is more harmful than any vice? —Active pity for the feeble and the underdog: in fact, Christianity." (6)

The Christian ought to be grateful to Nietzsche. With him there is no rigging of a half-warmed corpse pieced out of the joints and organs of a discarded faith. Nietzsche sees that between Christianity and the world there is contradiction and enmity. Rather than make might bow to goodness, he defines goodness in terms of might, and centers all morality in man's will to achieve this might. His notable misogyny follows from this apotheosized masculinity. Wherever the highest virtue is *virtus* indeed—unapologetic aggression and strength—women, the physically weaker sex and the bearers of infants, must lose. "Let the weak . . . perish." If vices corrupt, the most corrupting of all is Christian mercy for the weak: charity for women and for such contemptible males as Jean Peloueyre.

Now the irony of this "appalling passage" is that it applies, surprisingly, as well to the healthy young doctor's son as it does to Jean. Who is the weak who should perish? Robert, as I have mentioned, will die of consumption, and Jean will contract the disease *from him,* just as he has here contracted the disease of Nietzschean will-to-power. Yet the joke is on Nietzsche too. For Mauriac's Christian vision of power does not merely invert the Nietzschean vision. The irony of that would be quickly noted—not very interesting. Rather, Mauriac accepts what Nietzsche says, and then shows that the philosopher spoke truer than he knew. Goodness shall in fact "enlarge the sense of power" in, of all people, the *heroine* of this story. Evil shall in fact be seen as rooted in weakness—though we will have to discern what kind of weakness it is, and where it is to be found. Nietzsche will play the same role that Caiaphas once played, priest and political schemer that he was. Knowing that Jesus was innocent, in his very condemnation he unwittingly became a prophet of the atonement: "Ye know nothing at all," he said to his slower-witted comrades, "nor consider that it is expedient for us, that one man should die for the people, and that the whole nation should perish not" (John 11:49–50).

The immediate effect of this passage upon Jean is "like the blaze of noon when the shutters of a room are thrown open" (6). The blaze of truth (Mauriac does not deny the truth of what Nietzsche says) shows Jean what he and his religion are. The sight is not pretty. As he regards himself in the mirror, he considers "what a wretched little ferrety face he had, a country face . . . with a miserable, undeveloped body, untouched by the normal miracle of puberty" (6). When he glances at Nietzsche's *Beyond Good and Evil*, concerning the "Morality of the Masters and the Morality of the Slaves," it seems that his faith lies "like a stricken oak at his feet" (7). In a moment, faith returns, but with the saddening awareness that "religion, for him, meant refuge," escape, consolation, a Virgin mother to care for his stunted body. The conclusion is inevitable: "He could discern in himself the distinguishing mark of servitude. . . . His whole being was made to be trampled underfoot" (6). He resembles his father, who makes much of religion, cerebrally. "Where would I be now if I had not had Faith?" old Peloueyre is wont to exclaim (8). Yet that faith is insufficient to send the selfish valetudinarian to Mass when he has a cold. Jean's father too is a weakling, using his philosophical and theological reading for a crutch.

In his first confrontation with the world, the naïve Christian is tempted to wrestle it on its own terms, with its own weapons. For a while, as he walks home, Jean pretends "that the burden of his faith had fallen from him" (8); he feels inebriated with freedom. Mauriac surely is thinking of Jesus' invitation to the weary: "Come unto me, all ye that labor and are heavy laden, and I will give you rest. Take my yoke upon you, and learn of me; for I am meek and lowly of heart: and ye shall find rest unto your souls. For my yoke is easy, and my burden is light" (Matt. 11:28–30). In *Pilgrim's Progress*, sin and its guilt make the burden that Christian cannot shuck off until he sees a vision of the crucifixion. All men are sinners, but the Christian yoke is easy; all are as slaves or oxen, but in Christianity men will find rest and freedom. Yet for a while Jean feels the loss of an admittedly selfish faith as the loss of a burden, not as the weighing down with an even heavier burden of sin and folly. Along with this mistake, he tries to revive his faith by redefining or justifying it in Nietzschean terms: "He set himself to prove to an audience consisting of trees, piles of stones and blank walls that there have been Masters even among Christian men, that the Saints, the great Orders, the whole fabric of the universal Church, have offered a sublime example of the Will to Power" (8). If Mauriac is out to show that Christianity is more Nietzschean than Nietzsche, the partially understanding Jean is out to show that Christians can boast their Nietzschean heroes *too*, esteeming his faith by how well its proponents live up to Nietzsche's ideals. He would save his faith by losing it.

This revaluation of Christianity coincides with Jean's misunderstanding himself and those about him. Accepting Nietzsche's division of the race into masters and slaves, he looks upon the well-built grandson of their housekeeper with more than his usual shy envy. This grandson is the picture of barnyard animal health, and has a way with the girls, as all such boys do: "Would it not have been more fitting that he, the weakling, should serve this young and glorious God of the garden?" (9). We must take care in answering this rhetorical question. For in a way which Jean cannot now grasp, it would be fitting: "Whoever will be chief among you, let him be your servant" (Matt. 20:27). And even in Jean's longing, there is a real appreciation for the boy's masculine beauty, an appreciation that shows that Jean is not so self-absorbed as at first appears. He has a heart made for friendship and beauty, but it is locked in a body that frustrates its desires.

Still, Jean does err. He would now see the "God of the garden"—the erectile Priapus, buffoon and god of good luck—as rightfully a master, to command his cringing servant. Jean's humility is so tainted with self-loathing that it becomes but the diseased obverse of the will-to-power: a hardly distinguishable will-to-weakness. Ironically, the grandson knows better. When Jean falls ill, he makes it his business to carry his master out to the veranda and show him the game birds he has shot, for gaming had been one of the few pleasures in Jean's life.

And He Shall Have Dominion over You

THUS SHAKEN OUT OF his religion-as-refuge and introduced to the religion of power, Jean is vulnerable to the suggestion by the local curé that he take a wife. The curé is neither insane nor stupid. He wishes to protect the pretty girls of the parish from being ruined, and to keep the Peloueyre estate out of the hands of the family's church-hating, power-hungry kinsmen. The woman he has in mind is Noemie, long admired by Jean from a terrified distance, a girl with a face such as Raphael would have painted for the Virgin, attached to a plump, strong, peasant body: "She roused the best and the worst in Jean, stimulating him to noble thoughts and to grossly voluptuous dreams" (12). She is a peasant, and always will be, as Mauriac frankly declares: "Gifted with a strong sense of duty, submissive to God's ordinances and to her husband's will, she would develop into one of those mothers who are still to be found, women whose fundamental ignorance of life is proof against any number of pregnancies" (16). Intellectually, then, she is hardly more admirable than Jean is physically, although her ignorance will constitute her strength. How absurd that in his present state Jean should consider her worthy of one of Nietzsche's heroes: "Here, surely, was an opportunity at last to escape from the herd of slave-men, and to act like a Master? This unique moment had been given him that he might break his chains and become a man" (17). Poor Jean now strides through the town without his neural tics, even tipping his hat to the townsfolk, who fall silent in astonishment. Escaping to the woods, he cries, with silly glee, "I am one of the Master Race, the Master Race, the Race!" (17).

If we are quick to smile at Jean's incongruous pride—and Mauriac is merciless with him—we miss the point. Since the grave awaits both Jean and his robust friend Robert, is it really so much less incongruous for the handsome and gifted man to strut as if he were almighty? "All flesh is grass," cries the prophet (Isa. 40:6). Mauriac fools the reader into believing there is something special about Jean, when in fact Jean is our Everyman, illustrating our smallness and transience with more than usual clarity. Jean's awkward courtship meetings with Noemie reveal the fatuities of our pride. He is not one of the clear-singing cocks that mark the hours, but "a frightened cricket cowering in the darkest corner available" (19). Yet while the venal kinsmen spread indecent rumors concerning certain inadequacies rendering Jean unfit for marriage, Jean, "looking at himself in the glass, decided he was not so ill-favored after all" (21)! He even holds forth, for the benefit of the stunned Noemie, on the virtues of reading Nietzsche, "whose influence well might force him to alter his whole attitude to the problem of moral obligation" (21).

Judge him not too harshly. What can return foolish man to his senses? Little, if he is blessed by nature with the small gifts that veil his yawning insufficiencies. Some people, "vain in their imaginations," "professing themselves to be wise" (Rom. 2:21, 22), lapse into comfort and self-satisfaction, as a fish swims easily and stupidly into a trap. Such ones are so full of all-important ephemera that they miss the miracle before them.

It is a commonplace of medieval romance that only the faithful will have "adventures," literally "comings," for they alone are prepared for the unexpected. If Jean meets an adventure, it is his weakness that provides for it, not his strength. Jean does not behave as do his more gifted peers, believing themselves masters by the tedious millions. "Untouched by the normal miracle of puberty"—a mine of Christian incarnational truth dwells in that phrase—Jean is more than usually susceptible to beauty, as by compensation. In the presence of beauty he is overawed. The Nietzschean daydream falls like scales from his eyes, and he knows himself for the leper he is. That is how the Old Testament prophets experienced God: "Woe is me! for I am undone," cries Isaiah, "for mine eyes have seen the King, the Lord of hosts" (Isa. 6:5). "I have heard of thee by the hearing of the ear: but now mine eye seeth thee," says Job, "wherefore I abhor myself, and repent in dust and ashes" (Job 42:5–6). For poets of the Middle Ages, beauty provided an analogous experience: the lover felt unworthy, unclean, in the presence of something *sanctus*, set apart, untouchable, yet able to exert a terrifying spiritual and physical effect upon the beholder. "*Ego dominus tuus*," says the magisterial Love, holding in his arms the sleeping form of Beatrice, as Dante looks on in his dream, forever changed (*La Vita Nuova*, 2). Those who deride beauty as mere social construct not only practice absurd anthropology, they deface our most immediate means of apprehending the transcendent. One might as noxiously prate about "mere joy" or "mere truth" as about "mere beauty."

So on that day of terror, his wedding day, before the priest and the incredulous congregation, Jean "could feel the mystery of a woman's body trembling at his side, though he did not turn to look at her" (24). If the day is dreadful, the night is worse. In a shabby old hotel, walls blotched by crushed mosquitoes, angel statues hiding their faces for shame, the master of the race, in an epic combat, impregnates the body of his bride with death: "Long was the battle waged by Jean Peloueyre, at first with his own ice-bound senses, and then with the woman who was as one dead. As day was dawning a stifled groan marked the end of a struggle that had lasted six long hours. Soaked with sweat, Jean Peloueyre dared not make a movement. He lay there, looking more hideous than a worm beside the corpse it has at last abandoned" (25). Poor Noemie must endure the endless ministrations of her entomological hero, and know in her young flesh that her life is over before it has begun.

Wherever You Go, I Will Go

HOW DOES THE HAPLESS bride manage her life? She does so with the outward form of a married woman. She will do much rather than let Jean know how repulsive he is to her, and her well-meant but tactless sacrifice makes his life all the more painful. Mauriac indulges no easy sentiment. Noemie will never come to love Jean's form. She "went through all the movements of a wife who is made happy by the return of her best-beloved" (27). But her name reveals what she is meant to be: Noemie, or *Naomi*, the widow in the Book of Ruth. At the close of this novella, she will, against the promptings of heart and flesh, embrace a lasting widowhood, just as, in her role as Mary, she has already been pierced in the heart. There is nothing so brave, so virginal, and so femininely humane as what this peasant girl does when she lies in the dark with her husband: "Now and again Noemie, stretching a hand to touch the face which now, because she could not see it, seemed less odious, would find it warm and moist with tears. At such times, filled with remorse and pity, she would strain the unhappy creature to her, as, in the Roman amphitheatre, a Christian virgin might, with closed eyes and teeth fast clenched, have leapt forward to throw herself before the waiting beast" (27).

Her strength lies in what the world would consider shocking stupidity. She has submitted to the wishes of the curé and of her mother, and might as well have said with Mary, "Be it done unto me according to thy word" (Luke 1:38). She submits to a husband she cannot love, and feels shame for her failure. As recompense, and as a way also of keeping out of her husband's path, she ministers to his selfish father's needs: "Nothing disgusted her, not even having to help him when he visited the lavatory" (29). Note that she prefers this noisome duty to making love to her husband. And when, after Jean's death, she denies herself the love of the handsome, young, strong, ineffectual iodine-prescribing doctor who has helped both Jean and Robert on their way to the grave, it is her ignorance that comes to her aid, as neither bad gossips nor cheap novels have ever taught her the meaning of her desires.

But the rewards of Noemie's un-Nietzschean strength begin to appear. Renouncing this life for something beyond, she finds joys the worldly cannot apprehend—even if we grant that the worldly really desire the terror of true joy. Her marriage is, as it happens, more than an impossible welding of bodies. Though they are pained in each other's presence, "they decided to say their prayers side by side. Enemies in the flesh, they found union in their nightly supplications. Their voices at least could mingle. Kneeling there together, each in a world apart, they met in the infinite" (30). And this marriage is fertile in charity: "One morning they met, entirely by accident, at the bedside of a sick old man. They jumped at this new pretext of proximity, and, therefore, once each month, paid regular visits to all the sick of the neighborhood, each giving to the other credit for this act of charity" (30). Her physical feelings do not change: "On all other occasions Noemie carefully avoided Jean, or, rather, her body avoided his, while he was for ever in flight from her disgust of him" (30). She is genuinely happy when, under the curé's instigation, Jean goes to Paris ostensibly to research the history of their parish. Her health improves while he is away! Yet the same woman can say of Jean as his body lies in state, and say it without illogic, pretense, or patronizing sentiment, "'He was beautiful . . .'" (57).

And, in all his blighted dreams and his horribly blessed body, Jean Peloueyre is beautiful. Perhaps it is the gift of the outcast to see more clearly than the rest of us, who are aware of being seen. Once you have passed a certain degree of decrepitude, it hardly matters who sees you; and then you are free to see others. In Paris, Jean observes the washed-out faces in the crowds, the petty whores, the slobbering johns: "Hungrily he sought one single face that might bear the distinguishing mark of a ruler, of a master of men" (38). He sees none; but even had there been one, death still looms over all—death, not merely the cessation of life, but that realm to pronounce judgment upon life's meaning, or, for some, upon its vanity. Thus Jean bursts out madly, as he might have done on the dirt roads of his village, quoting Pascal: "'When the game is done, one is always the loser. Bear witness to that, O Nietzsche of the softened brain—one is always the loser'" (38). But, as in the midst of life we are in death, so in this life and death there is a fount of strength. Says Jean, "'There are no Masters. We are all of us slaves and we grow into the freedom of the Lord'" (38).

A Germinal Freedom

WHAT, FOR JEAN, is "the freedom of the Lord"? I do not think Mauriac meant what Paul meant by it in Galatians, the freedom from outward forms of the law. Or perhaps he did mean it, in this way: having committed the supreme sin of his life, his "Master Race" marriage to Noemie, Jean spends the rest of his few days repenting of that sin by refusing to hold her to the legalistic bonds of their marriage. His "freedom of the Lord" is a sacrificial attempt to set her free, by keeping away from her in the daytime, by staying on his own side of the bed at night, by keeping his grief to himself, by taking himself off to Paris, and, finally, by putting himself, already sickly (he hardly eats in Paris, and is so frail when he returns that he cannot carry his suitcase), in the way of contracting tuberculosis from young Pieuchon, if he has not already contracted it in the streets of the capital. But if he gains his freedom by setting Noemie free, she gains her freedom by binding herself the more irrevocably to him.

How this freedom works out shows the vanity, the weakness of what the world considers strength. In his son's illness, Dr. Pieuchon calls in a young expert from the outside, from "the county town" (41). There is something risible about this provenance. What is the great difference between such a town and the village of the Pieuchons, or, really, between it and Paris? Mauriac describes this young doctor's practice matter-of-factly, with biting irony: "He treated tuberculosis with strong doses of tincture of iodine, of which medicine the patient had to take several hundred drops diluted with water" (41). He treats a degenerative lung disease with poison for the digestive tract. So ignorance masquerades as expertise. The young doctor is a man of the world; why, he has a cure for consumption! The invalid Peloueyre senior sees through it: "Monsieur Jerome expressed doubts whether the Pieuchon boy's stomach could tolerate such a mixture" (41).

Arriving at the village, this virile doctor meets Noemie and asks her the way to the Pieuchon house. After that, every time he passes by her window he bows in her direction, with his open silk shirt. And it is this doctor for whom, against Noemie's wishes, Jerome sends to minister to Jean, since "Pieuchon never left his son's germ-infected pillow" (44). Given Jerome's doubts about the young doctor's methods, we can guess at the indifference lying beneath this solicitude. This doctor does come, less for Jean than for Noemie, as she thinks: "It was, after all, rather an extraordinary thing to make a doctor drive six miles on a dark night just to listen to the chest of an exhausted man" (46). He fails to diagnose tuberculosis in Jean—and excuses his failure to help young Pieuchon on the grounds that the boy's case had advanced too far. Likewise he weasels out of trying to do anything real for Jean: "He is not," he says, "so much tubercular as *potentially* tubercular" (46)—a slothful diagnosis that might apply to anyone with a cold.

Whatever that evasion means, Jean is listening closely to both the matter and the tone of the conversation: "The medical talk came strangely from lips better suited to dispense kisses than scientific comments" (46). It does not say much for the doctor's acumen. He is a larger, less clumsy version of the housekeeper's hayseed grandson: "His drawling, rustic voice filled the room with the sense of something massive, something masculine" (46). His whole visit is a tryst: "He asked whether Monsieur Peloueyre would like him to come again, if only for the purpose of giving him his injections" (46). Initially, Jean leaves it up to Noemie, testing her; she refuses with so vehement a protest that Jean must amend things by leaving it up to the doctor, which worthy scientist immediately, as Jean must have foreseen, agrees to come.

And so Jean puts Noemie in the way of love, as he puts himself in the way of death. Who now is the strong man, the sturdy doctor or the wraith who sees through him and uses him to achieve a noble end? In the meantime, as her disgust for Jean's proximity remains unabated, and as her amorous instincts have been awakened by the doctor, Noemie fights all the harder to keep her faith: "Often she would call out in the night, begging [Jean] to come to her. When he pretended to be asleep she would get up, go over to his bed, and kiss him—as saints, once upon a time, were in the habit of kissing lepers. No one can tell us whether the stricken wretches rejoiced to feel upon their sores the warm breath of the Blessed" (47). Jean does not rejoice—he "cried aloud in tones of horror, 'Leave me alone!'" (48). Why this *noli me tangere*? Jean has never treated Noemie so brusquely. But her kisses tempt him to re-enter an illusion he has bravely abandoned forever. It is an illusion as absurd, perhaps, as the one that enrolled him in the master race: that Noemie can love him. Noemie cannot know it, but in her sacrifice she tempts Jean back towards selfishness and a false sense of strength. There is no time to lose. Unbeknownst to his wife, who thinks he is going on long walks in the woods, Jean begins to make daily visits to the Pieuchon boy, "now *in extremis*." One night he returns with his quarry. Hearing him cough, Noemie lights a candle and looks upon her husband as he lies in bed. He is confident in a providence now alive within him in the form of lowly bacilli: "His eyes were closed, and his mind seemed concentrated upon the mysterious working of something deep within him. He smiled at his wife, and she was tormented by the spectacle of so much gentleness and calm" (48). For now, perhaps, it is Noemie's turn to be destroyed by the breath of the blessed. Says the contented Jean, echoing the words of Christ on the cross, "'I'm thirsty'" (48).

And there is peace for Jean. In a terrible irony, his worst suffering has been his witnessing the terror at the side of his now dead friend: "Rest! Rest after those horrible afternoons at young Pieuchon's bedside, listening to the dying man's despairing outbursts as he thought of all that he was leaving" (50). What was he leaving, then, this brave and prodigious reader of Nietzsche? How great and how paltry it seems, this list of vanities, with its youth and vigor and its exhaustion and facelessness: "Riotous nights in Bordeaux, dancing to a mechanical piano in roadside cabarets; bicycle expeditions, with the dust clinging to his thin, hairy legs, and that feeling of being all-in; above all, the kisses of young women" (50). Empty promises, empty glamor; the frantic cries of unbelievers trying to imitate joy, calling out, "Eat, drink, and be merry, for tomorrow we die."

But the weak Jean Peloueyre has come to know something better than kisses: "[He] would not let her kiss him . . . but liked to feel her cool hand on his forehead. Did he believe now that she loved him? Assuredly he did, for he was heard to murmur, 'Be thy Name for ever blessed, O Lord, for thou hast let me know the love of a woman before I die'" (50–51). Jean's words echo the *nunc dimittis* of the old prophet Simeon, seeing the baby Jesus brought to the temple: "Lord, now lettest thou thy servant depart in peace, according to thy word: For mine eyes have seen thy salvation" (Luke 2:29–30). He speaks a line of his favorite poetry, "My Polyeucte arrives at his last hour," from Corneille's play *Polyeucte*, uttered by the hero's beloved (51). In so doing, Jean speaks the part of Noemie, who he now trusts does love him. No such quiet courage is shown by Jean's Nietzschean friend.

Is Jean one of those oppressive people who derive joy only from hating and rejecting life? Certainly he has always thought of himself as a contemptible wretch, and as he looks back upon his life he cannot doubt it now. Yet a martyr is one who suffers to testify to the truth, and Jean has so testified all his life, unwittingly and for the most part patiently. He has testified by his example, and now he testifies by parting with the only person he has ever really loved, in order to set her free. Pieuchon has died, but Jean is entering upon life: "What stagnation! But under that sleeping surface had stirred a life-giving freshet, and now, having passed through life like a corpse, he was, on his death-bed, as a man reborn" (51). Then he *is* a member of the only master race: the brave martyrs, saints all, whose exits from this world have come in all manner of ways, some grandly epic, some sudden, some torturous, and, at least one, slowly and quietly, with nothing in his past to show that he might prove a martyr save his faith, his hope, and his love. But those three will suffice.

While this weak man lies dying, the muscular doctor is reduced to a beast, a dog—for the weakest of martyrs is more powerful than the strongest hero; or perhaps we should say that it is not always apparent which is the hero and which is the dog. The doctor is unaware of the drama occurring before him: "The young man, wrapped in his goatskin and shirt away in a small world smelling of fog and tobacco smoke, knew nothing of the stars that twinkle above the tree-tops" (52). He is like those self-important college bureaucrats in C. S. Lewis's *That Hideous Strength*, who, in the midst of a climactic battle as good and evil fight to claim the earth, think that the matter at hand has to do with which college faction wins in the next election. The self-styled powerful of the world are seldom perceptive. The doctor's, not Jean's, is the cramped, constricted, muffled world: "He kept his nose to the earth, like a dog on the scent. When he was not thinking of the kitchen fire in front of which he would soon be drying himself, or of the soup laced with wine that was awaiting him, his mind was busy with Noemie" (52–53). He too is a hunter. What should it imply, then, if he loses to such as Jean? But he hardly suspects the truth: "'I've winged her,'" he thinks to himself, as if he were out shooting woodcock, "'she's wounded'" (53). Later, when Jean—the "discarded bit of rubbish" near death, as he is considered by the devoted physician—watches quietly and invisibly as Noemie places the iron bedstead between herself and the doctor, the dying man says, in loving triumph, stressing the caesura at the end of the second word, "'Mon Peloueyre touche à son heure dernier'" (55)—My Peloueyre arrives at his last hour.

We Are More than Conquerors

JEAN WILL NOT SEE the close of the drama before him, and as he dies, his passions one by one are replaced by peace and charity, for Noemie, for the doctor, for the gentle grandson of the housemaid, for the "crowing of cocks, the jolting of waggon wheels" (57), and for all the small things that made this life, in this place, a thing to be loved. He is so insignificant that the townspeople, who make no such mistake with the terrible passing of young Pieuchon, "confused his passing-bell with the ringing of the morning Angelus" (57). In their confusion they allow Jean's death to merge with the Incarnation, the event which Christians believe has sanctified, now and forever, all this physical creation, including that loveliest of things, the human body. Appropriately, the words of the priest giving Jean the viaticum, the strength for the wayfaring soul, end on a note of complete victory: "*Go forth, Christian soul, into life everlasting, in the name of the Father who made thee, in the name of the Son who redeemed thee, and of the Holy Ghost who sanctified thee, and in the name of Angels and Archangels, of Thrones and Dominations, of Principalities and Powers . . .*" (57).

And Jean's triumph over his rival is complete. The denouement of Mauriac's tale, swift and ruthless, sees the young doctor "convert" to Christianity, attending church to be near Noemie (for he, not she, has been "winged"). Yet when, one year after Jean's death, she decides to wear the widow's garb for the rest of her life, the doctor's apparent strength collapses: "[His] Christian feelings broke down. He avoided not only the church but his patients as well. Old Dr. Pieuchon heard a rumor that his young colleague was drinking heavily, and that he even got up during the night to take a swig of the bottle" (58). But Noemie has yet the ardent longings of her youth. What is a sacrifice worth, if one is half dead? One last time she sees the axle caps of the carriage of the young doctor, a gleaming sight able to waken more of love in her than could the very stars. But before he can see her—she overhears him prescribing the ever-ineffectual mighty dose of iodine—she retreats, plunging into the heather to hide. Why? Mauriac dismisses all commonplace explanations: that the town would have thought it indecent of her to marry the doctor, that being a widow was respectable, or that she risked losing her portion of the Peloueyre inheritance: "Small she might be as a human being, but she was condemned to greatness" (60). Self-styled members of the master race jockey for power and wealth; people like Noemie are condemned to a grander and more arduous fate. Why should greatness be so severe a trial, even a condemnation, if not that it really is different from what the world suspects? Noemie too manifests the truth that Jean proclaimed on the streets of Paris: "Born a slave, she had been called to a throne and must exercise regal powers. Do what she might, this rather fat, middle-class woman could not avoid a destiny that had made her greater than herself" (60). Who desires the "greatness" of crucifixion? But God wants royalty from Noemie, whether she likes it or not: "Every path but the path of renunciation was closed to her" (60). In her half-ignorant, half-blind loyalty, she embraces a fate that exalts her—as the Son of man was lifted up, folly to the Greeks and a stumbling stone to the Jews, but to those who have the courage to believe, the wisdom of God, and the power of God: "Across the dry heath she ran until, at last, worn out, her shoes filled with sand, she flung her arms about a stunted oak whose brown leaves were still unshed, and quivered in the hot breeze—a black oak which had about it something of the look of Jean Peloueyre" (60).

12

The Power of Obedience

Machiavelli at the Lectern

IF THERE ARE NO masters in this world, as Mauriac's hero says, what do we make of structures of authority?

One of the delights of being a professor of literature is the sight of small-ish specimens of either sex, members of the professoriate, tamely ensconced in a great swindle of modern America, to wit, higher education, discoursing sagely about *power*—political power, sexual power, power in verse, power in academe—ever with a smug awareness of how much power they wield, and a tinge of resentment for their not wielding more. Thus, studies of power are produced like automobiles on an assembly line, with metronomic originality.

What is that "power"? Generally one meets the definition assumed by Machiavelli in *The Prince*: power is the ability to make someone do what you want him to do, or the ability to prevent him from doing what you do not want him to do. Despite all modifications and qualifications, this view of power is a zero-sum game. If I can make you do what I want, and what you do not really want, then I have power, and you do not. If you could refuse me, that would limit my power. Always there will be those who can impose their will, by arms, persuasion, money, or threats, and those who suffer the imposition. They will follow along, pay up, or be cowed into surrender. Thus, the Machiavellian view of power is essentially competitive: one gains power by defeating the other claimants, and one keeps it by ensuring that they stay defeated.

I admit that this analysis does not do justice to Machiavelli. I share his republican ideals, and note with approval that in the *Discourses on Livy* he praises not the strong man who can scramble up as much power as he can, but a prudent and courageous *people* who know when to obey, when to compromise, when to fight their enemies, when to set up kings, and when to do away with kings forever. Still, all in all, Machiavellian power is finite and coercive. And that, on the whole, is the vision of power preached from the college lectern, if it even rises so high; for the "empowerment" recommended to the individual—the legal right to pursue your "dreams," whatever vanity may flit and float therein—is so detached from any concern for the common weal that Machiavelli would deride it as effeminate and debased.

Now Machiavelli also sets forth a slightly different and more interesting vision of power. It is suggested by his amoral use of the word *virtu*, Latin *virtus*, meaning not virtue properly understood, but virility, manhood, the ability to get important things done, against opposition. He wrote *The Prince* with the unification of Italy—and the repulse of invaders from other nations, particularly France—in mind. Men may fight to attain it, but power is most visibly manifest not in the fight, but in accomplishments for one's people. A man might want to be king not to unify the peninsula, but merely to be king. But if he truly is powerful, if he wields *virtu*, he will solidify his power by doing something great and noble with it. Thus, the "power" of Queen Elizabeth of England consisted not only in her ability to ward off rivals to the throne, but in using her authority and such charms as she possessed to unite the English people and to take England's first toddling steps towards empire.

Power and Obedience

ABSENT FROM THESE DEFINITIONS of power is any notion that, by nature, some people should be deferred to, or that authority inheres in anyone for any other reason than that he can use his ingenuity or force to gain it. So Machiavelli praises the lowborn Agathocles, who employed treachery and cruelty to usurp the throne of Syracuse, and who then ruled with a measure of justice and good sense [*The Prince*, ch. 8]. But, any suggestion that the father (or grandfather, or maternal uncle) is the *natural* head of the household (an uncontroversial suggestion for every known human society until our own, and enshrined in political philosophy as late as John Locke) would be ridiculed by the modern critic as "essentialist" or "reactionary" or "patriarchal," or whatever the abusive adjective of choice happens to be.

But how can we discuss power in *mere* political terms when the writers we are studying did not view it that way, and therefore did not always write or do what we might have written or done? To be fair to them, we must imagine what it might be like to believe that certain people, by the nature of their relations to us, or by the nature of some character imprinted upon them by God, justly wield authority over us.

I have said nothing so far that would embarrass a good pagan. Aristotle asserted that some men were meant by nature to rule, and others to be ruled. Therefore it was right to let the natural rulers achieve the perfection of their nature by ruling, and the natural subjects to achieve theirs by being ruled. In practical terms, the doctrine justified slavery, that institution whereby the privileged few in Greece and Rome (and, later, the American South) enjoyed the leisure to produce works of art and high culture, while being fed and clothed and housed and bathed by the many.

Henryk Sienkiewicz understood what that meant for Roman slaves: not just brutal work, or being sent for trifling "offenses" to the horrible prisons in the country. It meant being regarded as less than human. So the aristocratic Romans let themselves be massaged and bathed and scraped by bevies of male and female servants, without any more embarrassment than if they were naked before dogs; or they could enjoin girls and pretty boys to appear before them naked, like living statues, for the weary delight of their eyes, without any sense that the slaves might feel embarrassed in front of them or in front of one another. In one terrible scene from *Quo Vadis?* the tribune Vinicius orders his slaves to bring the woman he loves, the Christian Lygia, from Nero's palace to his own home, where he intends to seduce her or compel her submission. When Lygia is intercepted by Christians along the way, the slaves must report the disaster to Vinicius. They are bloodied, and a few even died in the fight. But despite their valiant service in a bad cause, they are terrified to give Vinicius the news. They choose as their messenger an old man, Gulo, who nursed Vinicius when he was a child. To no avail:

"See our blood, lord! We fought! See our blood! See our blood!"

But he had not finished when Vinicius seized a bronze lamp, and with one blow shattered the skull of the slave; then, seizing his own head with both hands, he drove his fingers into his hair, repeating hoarsely,

"Me miserum! me miserum!" (70)

If Vinicius must abandon the idea that he has power merely because he was born to have it, and if Christians reject the idea that power is what we attain to impose our will on others, then what is power and where does it lie? Christians do believe that power is a good thing, and they do believe that some people are ordained by God to be obeyed, but they do not agree with Machiavelli and they do not agree with the slave-states of Greece and Rome. What, then, does Christianity change?

Rank upon Rank of the Blest

FIRST, CHRISTIANITY DOES NOT obliterate hierarchies. It transforms them, and the transformation gleams with the irony of the unexpected and appropriate.

Jesus says that "the first shall be last and the last shall be first" (cf. Matt. 19:30, 20:16; Mark 10:31; Luke 13:30). That may invert the world's hierarchies, but it preserves hierarchy nonetheless. There will be a first and a last in the kingdom of God. We are warned not to take the best seat at a banquet, not because in the kingdom of God there will be no best seats, but because if we do, we may be asked to move lower down, while the humble will be asked to move forward. For "whosoever exalteth himself shall be abased; and he that humbleth himself shall be exalted" (Luke 14:8–11). Some fields produce a bigger bumper crop than others; one good servant was given five talents, and the other was given ten; from him who has been given much, much shall be expected; harlots and publicans will enter the kingdom before those who think they are righteous.

Paul preaches the Body of Christ, refuting the notion of equality that a superficial understanding of Christianity might encourage. Although all members of the Body are equally members of the Body, and although all are worthy and necessary, they are not equivalent; and they observe a hierarchy. Not all are apostles, and not all are called to be elders (1 Cor. 12).

Compare Paul's symbol with a famous fable told by Livy. The plebeians had threatened to leave Rome, taking with them the bulk of the population and the labor, not to mention a lot of money. Their aim was to gain political power, long withheld from them by the old patrician families. At a critical moment in the uprising, an aristocrat named Menenius Agrippa appears before them and tells them a story. Once upon a time, he says, the members of the body rebelled against the belly, calling it good for nothing, and insisting that they could do as well without it. But the belly protested that in digesting food it spread nourishment to all the other members. The implicit lesson justifies patrician ease and consumption; it is good for the state that the patricians hire laborers, eat costly foods, and employ slaves. What Menenius says may or may not make economic sense; the point is that the good of the state happens as a by-product of what the belly does for itself. Not so in the Body of Christ, wherein each member is to act *for the good of all the other members.* And the ruler of this Body is not the belly, but the head, Christ, who gave his life for the church, to sanctify it, and make it his bride without blemish (Eph. 5:25–27).

Paul's teaching on the Body of Christ is consistent with his emphasis on decorum, proper order, and submission to legitimate authority. That, after all, is how a body works. Legitimate authority implies dutiful submission, but in the Body of Christ it is a submission that entails a gain and no loss of dignity. The idea that one might become great by submission is foreign to neopagan modern man, certainly foreign to the Machiavellians behind the lecterns, and explains why modern readers find certain passages in Colossians, Ephesians, and 1 Peter so objectionable.

We could go on in this vein for quite some time. Jesus submits to the Father and sends the Spirit: a mystery of power and obedience. Jesus is the king whom angels obey; he may command legions lest he dash his foot against a stone (Matt. 4:6); the winds and the waters defer to his command (Matt. 8:23–27); he comes in power and glory to judge the living and the dead (Matt. 25:31–46). They who believe in him share in his kingship, becoming a royal priesthood (1 Pet. 2:9), destined to sit in judgment upon men and angels (1 Cor. 6:3). Obedience is how the Christian expresses his love, "for if you love me," says Jesus, "you will keep my commandments" (John 14:15). If God fashioned the universe in love, then in love man freely gives thanks to God and wields the dominion God has lovingly granted to him. He wields that dominion *by obeying.* Obedience reverses the sin of Adam.

Even among the apostles we find a hierarchy of grace, or of rule. Jesus singles out Peter, James, and John: they are the apostles present at the Mount of Transfiguration, and in the Garden of Gethsemane. Peter is the head of the apostles, first in every list of their names, highlighted as the one who calls Jesus the Messiah, the Son of the living God, or who tries to walk on water to come to Jesus, or who answers for the rest when they have heard in dismay the discourse on eating his flesh and drinking his blood, or who confesses his sins and begs Jesus to depart from him, or who steps out upon the portico on Pentecost to preach to the throngs of Jews below. Jesus commissions him to feed his sheep; Jesus predicts Peter's death; Jesus prays that Peter might strengthen his brothers. Paul, the "least of the apostles," submits to the judgment of Peter and James at the Council of Jerusalem. Yet Paul also rebukes Peter for heeding what people might think of him if he were seen breaking the Mosaic dietary laws. The least can rebuke the greatest; and the greatest is great only because he can be rebuked by the least. Why, Jesus himself submitted to Joseph, obeying the father who was his own creature.

Blessed Are the Meek

WHAT ABOUT THE QUEST to attain power? The Beatitudes, rife with irony, turn our Machiavellian assumptions upside down. "Blessed are the meek," says Jesus, "for they shall inherit the earth" (Matt. 5:5). He does not say they shall inherit heaven after the proud have had their way with the earth. In fact, Jesus issues not simply a prophecy but a piercing analysis of how even this sinful world works. For as pride goeth before a fall, so they who submit to what is truly great will share in that greatness.

But sinners hate to submit. Jesus rebukes James and John for jockeying for position in the kingdom of heaven, as if they were courtiers elbowing their fellows out of the way. The moral is that of many of Jesus' parables: those who think they deserve the highest seat of honor may be in for a surprise on the day of judgment. The parable of the good Samaritan hinges upon an ironic reversal: Levites, priests, and Pharisees walk past the suffering man and fail to fulfill the commandment of love. They do not get off the road to descend into the ditch. Instead, a member of a detested group—a half-pagan, a Samaritan—fulfills the commandment. And he fulfills it in a humble and bodily way: he does descend from the road into the ditch. His hands touch the sufferer, cleansing his wounds with wine and oil. He hoists the poor man onto his mule and takes him to an inn. He clothes him in fresh linen. He pays the innkeeper and instructs him to continue the care, for which he will reimburse him when he returns. In all these ways he is like Jesus; and to be like Jesus is to be like the almighty Father.

When Jesus washes the feet of his disciples, he tells them that "if any among you would be first, he must serve the others," establishing a hierarchy based not on might but on love. When Peter protests that Jesus must not descend so low as to wash *his* feet, Jesus replies, "Thou hast no part with me." "Not my feet only," says Peter then, "but also my hands and my head" (John 13:8–9). Peter's initial refusal was an act of false humility. Others, he implies, will be blind enough to let you kneel before them and wash their feet, but I love and esteem you too much for that. Of course, the Jesus he says he loves is the Savior who came into the world precisely to wash us clean. Peter must be led back into true humility, which will grant him true authority.

Indeed, Jesus scoffs at the "benefactors" of mankind (Luke 22:25), rulers who impose their will on others and then call their despotism benevolence. His disciples, by contrast, are to practice humility: he sends them forth to rule the world *by means of sacrificing themselves for it.* What else should we expect from the suffering servant?

And that is the starkest reversal of all: a slain Lamb rules on the throne.

The Wisdom That Appears to Be Folly

CHRISTIAN POETS, THEN, HAD to interpret simultaneously Christ's insistence upon hierarchy and his dissolution of typical hierarchies, the one in light of the other. They could not be egalitarians; they could not be Machiavellians. The Christian vision of power is neither worldly politicism nor otherworldly lawlessness nor enlightened compromise. It is, like the Incarnation, an in-forming of the earthly by the heavenly. No area of human life may escape the transforming power of grace. If there is kingship in the world, there will be Christian kingship, too; in the world, but not of it.

One way to understand this vision is to consider God's two primary acts of power: Creation and Incarnation. If power is to be seized from others, then the God who creates the world in Genesis is an arrant fool. The result of his creation is to produce human creatures who themselves have power, and by God's own command: "Be fruitful, and multiply, and replenish the earth, and subdue it" (Gen. 1:28). God's power shows itself most fully when he creates— when he deigns to descend and make what is not God. And unlike the gods of the neighboring Mesopotamians, who create slaves to burn incense for them and to do work they do not want to do, God creates men in his image and likeness, to be powerful and good and wise, as he is. He grants them dominion over creation, not to abuse it (as the Mesopotamian gods abuse men), but to cherish it and foster it. So he allows Adam to name the animals, exercising a godlike authority.

In an act of generous power, God gives his power away; it is an act of almighty humility to create the universe, not fashioning it from idle matter but speaking it into being from nothing. His power is inseparable from his love, as befits a Father who insists upon obedience not for his sake (God needs nothing from us, not the smoke of holocausts, nor the work of our hands) but for the dignity and the training of his sons, that they might prove worthy of the power and responsibility he gives them.

If the creation brings forth splendor from nothing, so does the Incarnation: for we may deem it more glorious to redeem a world by suffering than to create a world by speaking. For now God does not make, but remakes, and not the body, but the spirit. To refashion man and man's world he does more than condescend to speak. He descends as man, not in appearance but in reality, true flesh to redeem flesh. The God who powdered the heavens with stars is born as a child and laid to rest in a manger. God becomes man, a mighty laying aside of his might, that sinful man may become like God again. It is a power that longs with all the yearning of love to make its object worthy of love. So the hero of Graham Greene's *The Heart of the Matter* considers the willing weakness of God, putting himself at the mercy of men who hardly know the meaning of love: "How desperately God must love, he thought with shame" (228). But the Lord, says Paul, wants sons, not slaves. How else can we share in the power of a God who humbles himself, unless by obeying him? That is worlds away from Machiavellian politics.

The Blind Man in Prison: Milton's *Paradise Lost*

JOHN MILTON HAD LONG combined a Christian belief in the God-given dignity of man with a fearless rejection of all human institutions that set themselves up as arbiters of the conscience. As a Christian he believed in the church, the mystical Body of Christ; but he never joined a church on earth, preferring to remain in communion with his fellow believers by remaining alone. He was deeply suspicious of democracy, as were all the great writers and philosophers of the Renaissance, yet he hated monarchy, too, throwing his support to the leveling forces in Cromwell's New Model Army. And when Cromwell and his allies in Parliament had King Charles I beheaded for high treason, he chose

Milton to be his Latin secretary, asking him to write letters to the monarchs of Europe and treatises justifying the deed.

Cromwell did not prove to be the saving hero Milton hoped for; and, what with the strain from all his reading and writing, the once promising young poet, now a prematurely aged man, went blind. His enemies called it a judgment of God for his having helped to overthrow a divinely anointed king. He had long broken with the Presbyterians, who comported themselves with as much arrogance as the ousted Anglican bishops had; the protectorate did not survive Cromwell's death; and at the restoration of the monarchy under Charles II, Milton was sent to prison for treason. Only the pleas of his astute friend and fellow poet, Andrew Marvell, saved him from the chopping block.

This lonely and blind man knew that the polity to which he had sacrificed his genius—for he had written almost no poetry during those years of political strife—was no more. A king was on the throne again. Milton was disgraced, outcast. But now, finally, he determined to write the epic he had longed to write since he was young, an epic whose subject would be grander than anything imagined by Homer and Virgil of old. He would write of that blind and lonely Satan, cast out of heaven for trying to dethrone heaven's king. He would write *Paradise Lost.*

Milton's political situation is so obviously analogous to Satan's that it has led many a critic to catch *that* irony and miss the rest. Milton "was of the Devil's party, without knowing it," says the poet William Blake (*The Marriage of Heaven and Hell*, plates 5–6). Our sympathies, we are told, are stirred by Satan's courage in adversity, his standing alone against the wrong. But Milton was too clever and too faithful a Christian to have played so easy a game. *Paradise Lost* indicts us for our propensity to play the king and the bishop—as Milton sees it, to claim power that belongs to God alone. Satan, not God, plays the haughty monarch. Man, not God, is the despot. Sin, not obedience, leaves the soul in bondage. To be free, even to exercise a just authority in the world, is to obey the commands of God, and thus to become like God, a God who glories in the good of his creatures.

In Wanton Ringlets Wav'd

HERE I WILL FOCUS the discussion of power in *Paradise Lost* by addressing what may seem but a charming bit of descriptive poetry. Specifically, I wish to ask, "Why is Adam's forehead broad?" and "Why is Eve's hair long?"

Let us set the scene. By the permissive will of God, Satan has escaped from the "dungeon horrible," the "mournful gloom," the "livid flames" of hell, to make his way half-flying and half-thrashing through chaos and night,

> Directly towards the new created World,
> And Man there plac't, with purpose to assay
> If him by force he can destroy, or worse,
> By some false guile pervert. (3.89–92)

He has looked on the universe hanging like a pendant by a golden chain from heaven, and has seen the splendor of the sun. Has seen it, and been moved to despair:

> O thou that with surpassing Glory crown'd,
> Look'st from thy sole Dominion like the God
> Of this new World; at whose sight all the Stars
> Hide thir diminisht heads; to thee I call,
> But with no friendly voice, and add thy name
> O Sun, to tell thee how I hate thy beams
> That bring to my remembrance from what height
> I fell, how glorious once above thy Sphere;
> Till Pride and worse Ambition threw me down
> Warring in Heav'n against Heav'n's matchless King. (4.32–41)

Satan has pretended that sin worked no essential change, only a tarnishing of his "outward luster" (1.97), but he knows he is lying. He was once beautiful and bright, and hates what is beautiful and bright. So he will look with envy and frustrated yearning upon the youthful beauty of the stripling angels Ithuriel and Zephon, and will smolder in shame at the thought that they no longer recognize him:

> Abasht the Devil stood,
> And felt how awful goodness is, and saw
> Virtue in her shape how lovely, saw, and pin'd
> His loss; but chiefly to find here observ'd
> His lustre visibly impair'd. (4.846–50)

One would think that leaving the sun for the earth would provide a respite for Satan's despair; after all, the sun is more glorious than the earth, is it not? But if we say so we do not reckon on the bounty of the Lord, who has made the sun to serve the earth and man therein. That is clear when we see what kind of earth God has created: lush and beautiful, bursting into a wildness of happy growth. No art could tell, says Milton,

> How from that Sapphire Fount the crisped Brooks,
> Rolling on Orient Pearl and sands of Gold,
> With mazy error under pendant shades
> Ran Nectar, visiting each plant, and fed
> Flow'rs worthy of Paradise which not nice Art
> In Beds and curious Knots, but Nature boon
> Pour'd forth profuse on Hill and Dale and Plain. (4.237–43)

Grapevines, flowers, fruit, grasses, branching trees, shady grots, cliffs, meadows, the lithe beauty of the animals, and they not hemmed in but as free as the splashing and wandering streams: it is all horrible to the creature who must recognize their beauty but who recoils in contempt for their lowliness, their being mere clay.

It is a bad day for Satan, but the worst is to come. For finally he sees the most achingly beautiful wonder of the universe, to which all the spiraling galaxies are but the pretty striations of a stone on a beach. Let me quote the passage in full:

> The Fiend
> Saw undelighted all delight, all kind
> Of living Creatures new to sight and strange:
> Two of far nobler shape, erect and tall,
> Godlike erect, with native Honor clad
> In naked Majesty seem'd Lords of all,
> And worthy seem'd, for in thir looks divine
> The image of their glorious Maker shone,
> Truth, Wisdom, Sanctitude severe and pure,
> Severe, but in true filial freedom plac't;
> Whence true autority in men; though both
> Not equal, as thir sex not equal seemed;
> For contemplation hee and valor form'd,
> For softness shee and sweet attractive Grace,
> Hee for God only, shee for God in him:
> His fair large Front and Eye sublime declar'd
> Absolute rule; and Hyacinthine Locks
> Round from his parted forelock manly hung
> Clust'ring, but not beneath his shoulders broad:

> Shee as a veil down to the slender waist
> Her unadorned golden tresses wore
> Dishevell'd, but in wanton ringlets wav'd
> As the Vine curls her tendrils, which impli'd
> Subjection, but requir'd with gentle sway,
> And by her yielded, by him best receiv'd,
> Yielded with coy submission, modest pride,
> And sweet reluctant amorous delay. (4.285–311)

For this stunning moment, when Satan and the reader are taken aback by the glory of naked innocence, Milton chose his words most precisely. Let us now, phrase by phrase, examine those words. They affirm the Christian ironies of power.

Two of Far Nobler Shape, Erect and Tall

EVIDENTLY THERE IS A hierarchy among the creatures on earth. It is noble to be a deer or a lion, but the human shape is "far nobler," expressing in bodily form the spiritual dignity that God has conferred upon man.

The first thing Milton says about that shape is that man stands "erect and tall," indeed "Godlike erect." It is a critical point. A king for whom power is the enforcement of his despotic will wants his noblemen weak, unless he needs them for war. But God makes man tall. What can tallness mean, in the context of an infinite universe—and among oak trees and the giraffe? For one, it is a sign of relative strength. These are, physically, intellectually, and morally, not the weaklings so mocked by Beelzebub when Satan first offered the plan to tempt man to his fall. Indeed, being immortal, Adam and Eve can suffer no lasting physical injury from the self-styled lord of hell, as Satan well knows. Hence the suggestion that the devils will "drive as we were driven, / The puny habitants" (2.366–67), is a face-saving lie, meant to soften the shame of having to settle for seduction and corruption. The same angel who would be almighty is cowed by Adam's stature and is reduced to ruining him by deceiving his wife.

Satan is not now inhabiting the body of the serpent, but to hide he must infuse himself into a tiger, a cormorant, and, notably, a toad squatting "close at the ear of Eve" while she sleeps (4.800). The comparison is striking. Satan pretends to be the great liberator of his fallen angels, but he is compelled to skulk, to duck, to slink. Nor are his troops any better. Approving of Satan's plan, those brave angels show the difference between the power one gains by obeying God and the abject weakness one suffers by disobedience:

> Towards him they bend
> With awful reverence prone; and as a God
> Extol him equal to the highest in Heav'n. (2.477–79)

Flat on their faces they give their misleader hosannas, while Adam and Eve will stand hand in hand as evening falls, raising their eyes and their voices to the heavens, and praising their Creator in a hymn at once humble and exalted:

> Thou also mad'st the Night,
> Maker Omnipotent, and thou the Day,
> Which we in our appointed work imploy'd
> Have finisht happy in our mutual help
> And mutual love, the Crown of all our bliss
> Ordain'd by thee, and this delicious place
> For us too large, where thy abundance wants
> Partakers, and uncropt falls to the ground.
> But thou hast promis'd from us two a Race
> To fill the Earth, who shall with us extol
> Thy goodness infinite, both when we wake,
> And when we seek, as now, thy gift of sleep. (4.724–35)

Adam and Eve are "Godlike erect" not because God stands straight in some manlike shape. There is neither up nor down nor right nor left with God; Milton is careful to describe only the splendor of God, his eye, his smile, his voice. What can the phrase mean, then? Adam and Eve stand erect for the same reason Dante ends each of the three canticles of the *Commedia* with the word *stelle*, "stars." To be erect is to face one's destination and perfection, the heavens—whence Satan has been thrust because of his pride. The beasts do not stand erect, and "of thir doings God takes no account" (4.622), says Adam. But to turn away from one's perfection, as the devils have done, is to become depraved, distorted, "bent," as C. S. Lewis puts it in *Out of the Silent Planet*, taking his cue from Milton and Dante ("Guai a voi, anime *prave*!" cries Charon to the damned awaiting their passage across the Acheron to hell—"Woe to you, *crooked* souls!" [*Inf.*, 3.84]). So when Adam and Eve stand erect, they signify the power they enjoy by virtue of their submission to the heavens that stir their yearning. If for God power is inseparable from love and grace, in us creatures it is inseparable from love and obedience.

In Native Honor Clad in Naked Majesty

THE WORD "CLAD" IS ambiguously placed: it can be construed either with "Honor" or with "Majesty" without straining the syntax. What does it mean for Adam and Eve to be "clad in native honor"? In the world of political materialism, the words "native Honor" are meaningless. How can one be born with what must be seized, to use Satan's words, by "force or guile" (1.121), or, to use Machiavelli's words, by the ways of the lion or the fox? Yet Milton wants us to view Adam and Eve—creatures such as we were meant to be—as so noble that others must naturally honor them. They *are honored*, even as they *honor* God. To be deserving of honor, and to grant honor that is deserved, are natural to them. Even Satan is struck by this native honor, and in flattering Eve will call her, with deceitful exaggeration, "Queen of this universe" (9.684). The lowly animals, too, will not enter the private bower of Adam and Eve, the chamber of their love, their church, their royal palace, "such was thir awe of Man" (4.705).

It is another delightful irony that the first couple are "clad" in honor, since they are not clad in anything at all. Until they sin, they have no need to cloak themselves with "these troublesome disguises which wee wear" (4.740). Indeed, when the angel Raphael descends to earth to warn Adam and Eve of the approach of their demonic foe, Adam strides forth to meet him, unashamed, stately, yet submissive. He needs no robes, no glitter, no attendants:

> [Adam] walks forth, without more train
> Accompanied than with his own complete
> Perfections; in himself was all his state,
> More solemn than the tedious pomp that waits
> On Princes. (5.351–55)

Stateliness and pomposity are all the rage in hell, whose capitol, Pandemonium, is a baroque cathedral of bitumen and gold. But there is no one in Eden to overawe with the trappings of power; and in their innocence Adam and Eve would prefer to follow the example of their God, and elevate their people, their children, to proper authority. Instead the signs Adam and Eve "wear" are intelligible symbols of an inward truth. We are what we wear; they wear what they are.

Thus to be *clad in naked majesty*—a breathtaking phrase—is to be clad not *as* a king, but with kingliness itself. Such "clothing" cannot be put on and taken off. It is part of the person, and can only be destroyed by disobedience, by refusing to honor the source of one's kingliness. And the force of that line compels us to compare how we dress our souls with how we dress our bodies. Adam and Eve are most powerful when most obedient, and most clad when naked. Milton presses the point to reveal to us the nakedness, the moral shame, that we wish to conceal from ourselves and others. We are the ones who wear disguises. We grow comfortable with a willed ignorance, coming to believe that the rags we throw upon our souls to hide our motives are robes of virtue.

But there really is a majesty about Adam and Eve, an air that moves lesser beings to approach with reverence. Such majesty, embodied in the loveliest forms ever to grace man and woman on earth, must be the more majestic for its nakedness, more dazzling to the eye than if it were clothed. It is less that nakedness is majestic, than that true majesty is naked, frank, innocent, free. And Adam and Eve are "Lords of all": except for the single pledge of their obedience, the tree of knowledge of good and evil, they are "Lords of the World besides" (1.32). The reader must never forget that until the Fall he is in the presence of the king and queen of Eden, beings incomparably superior to himself and to the one creature *he* most resembles: Satan.

And Worthy Seemed, for in Their Looks Divine / the Image of Their Glorious Maker Shone / Truth, Wisdom, Sanctitude Severe and Pure

WHEN, IN THE PROEM to Book 3, the blind poet recounts the beautiful things now dark to him, he ends with the loveliest thing in all the physical universe: the "human face divine" (3.44). Not all the stars in their spangled constellations show forth the glory of God as complexly and as engagingly as does one innocent human face. The "looks" of the Son are described as "mild" or "serene," but that is as far as Milton will go in describing the face of God; and the Father's countenance seems to be beyond feature. Yet those spiritual faculties which bind Adam and Eve to God shine most clearly in their countenances. It is the image of God, made manifest differently in the two, as it is made manifest in a unique way in every human being. So Gerard Manley Hopkins understood this unity in the diversity of countenances and spiritual gifts, as we are led "to the Father through the features of men's faces" ("As Kingfishers Catch Fire," 14).

That this image should be *glorious* is also an occasion for dramatic irony, as the naked and obedient Adam and Eve are glorious by participation in the superabundant glory of God. By contrast, Satan who watches them (and we are in Satan's position) has sought his glory from himself, with dire result. As Beelzebub puts it, shocked into a fleet moment of honesty, they now dwell with all their "glory extinct, and happy state / Here swallow'd up in endless misery" (1.141–42). Those words give the lie to the devils' slander against God, for no tyrant would have granted them glory in heaven, not to mention a happy "state," that is, a happy reign.

The list of nouns here specifies what it means to bear the image of God shining through one's face. These two naked human beings, who apparently do not yet know how to build a fire ("No fear lest Dinner cool," says Milton of their nectarous repast [5.396]), are oriented wholly towards the Truth, who is God. They are, to be sure, quick-witted, and God has blessed them with a charming curiosity about their world, leaving them the fine joy of discovery. They are meant to revel in the wonders of the world, including the stars above, which God has created for their love and their dominion. Their eagerness to learn is another of the gifts of God, who would withhold nothing from them, not even the direct vision of heaven.

In the temptation, Satan will suggest to Eve first that God wants them to remain stupid (and who would obey a God like that?), and then, without Eve's noticing the contradiction, that God would praise her for daring to learn what was forbidden (for, after all, why should man not try what has already profited the snake?). But the curiosity Satan arouses and disorders cannot make man wise. That is because curiosity knows no end other than the immediate. Misused, allowed to govern, it makes us fools. For now, the minds and hearts of Adam and Eve are turned toward the source of truth, not in curiosity, but in love and obedience. This humility exalts them, for "the fear of the Lord is the beginning of knowledge" (Prov. 1:7).

If the wise couple know and revere the holy, that reverence or "fear" makes *them* holy. They are endowed with "sanctitude," and that means more than blessedness: "But you are a priestly people, a royal nation, a people set apart" (1 Pet. 2:9). To sanctify something means to set it aside, to designate it as untouchable, to choose it as special, endowed with favor. The word increases their attractiveness to the reader and (despite himself) to Satan, and their distance from us. But in their turning to the Truth they are set apart, really made holy—for the Lord they revere delights to see them deserving of reverence.

This sanctitude, however, is "severe," as Milton wishes to stress, repeating the word as the sentence continues: "Severe, but in true filial freedom plac't, / Whence true autority in men" (4. 294–95). Somehow the word "severe" might lead to wrong conclusions, so Milton qualifies it, explaining that theirs is a severity compatible with "filial freedom." What does he mean by "severe"?

Filial Freedom

FIRST, IT SHOULD BE noted that for Milton "severe" is a word of high praise. Thus he describes the angels who catch the Satan-toad trying to give Eve foul dreams:

> So spake the Cherub, and his grave rebuke,
> Severe in youthful beauty, added grace
> Invincible. (4.844–46)

Here is the severity of the high-hearted soldier, a severity of brave young men and chaste young women, rare in our slouching age. It is severe not because it adheres to a stern enforcement of arbitrary rules. That is precisely the misconception Milton wishes to quell. Rather, the Latin etymology suggests that this severity is to be revered or feared. It instills awe; it causes the beholder to yield. It is the attribute of naked majesty. Even the devil is momentarily in awe.

Thus, the severity of Adam and Eve, like the active, youthful, happy severity of their guardian cherubs, may restrain others (for their own good), but they themselves are not restrained by it, for they enjoy "true filial freedom." This phrase encapsulates the irony of a God who fairly commands that his subjects be free—I say it is ironic because we sinners find the idea absurd. We never "command" freedom of those who must obey us. But Adam and Eve do obey and are free. Milton is thinking of Saint Paul: "And because ye are sons, God hath sent forth the Spirit of his Son into your hearts, crying, Abba, Father. Wherefore thou art no more a servant, but a son; and if a son, then an heir of God through Jesus Christ" (Gal. 4:6–7). To be free is to acknowledge God as Father; to be enslaved is to suffer him only as judge and ruler. There is no third possibility. The freedom is "filial," proper to a mature and obedient son; yet it confers authority upon those who obey it, for it is a filial "freedom."

Consequently, "filial freedom," embracing both obedience and dignity, is the source of "true autority in Men" (4.295). Because Milton goes on to discuss differences between the sexes, it is natural to misread the passage thus:

"Whence men derive their true authority over women." That reading miscon-strues the theology. Milton is saying that whatever authority human beings claim over others—or whatever power or "authorship" they have in creating a decent human society—they derive it from this free obedience. They do not derive it, as many in Milton's day insisted, from birthright (cf. the Father praising the Son, "by Merit more than Birthright Son of God" [3.309]). They do not derive it from priestly anointing, nor from political wrangling (the devils are always playing at political maneuvers, even in so small a matter as bearing the infernal banners: "That proud honor claim'd / Azazel as his right, a Cherub tall" [1.533–34]). The logic of the Christian position is simple, though the ambitious miss it: only by obedience will you be found worthy to be obeyed.

Seeing power as only instrumental, not arising from love, Satan unwit-tingly reveals the truth by means of his reductive blindness. Even when he envies God, he envies only his own projection of himself, for to him joy and power are intensely selfish. He vows to remain

> Irreconcilable to our grand Foe,
> Who now triumphs, and in th' excess of joy
> Sole reigning holds the Tyranny of Heav'n. (1.122–24)

As far as he can imagine, a god commands to be obeyed, to exalt himself, and that is that. It cannot pierce his darkened heart that God commands that those who obey him may then command in turn, in a train of loving and creative authority.

Here it is interesting to ask how God *can* delegate authority without dero-gating from divine providence. Milton laughs at the devils who, while Satan is away on his petty enterprise, discourse on free will, fate, and providence, and lose themselves in labyrinths of minutiae, "in wand'ring mazes lost" (2.561). The point is not that we should refrain from attempting to understand the harmony between free will and providence, but that the sinful devils secretly wish they had had no choice but to sin. Satan will, privately, confess the self-delusion:

> Hadst thou the same free Will and Power to stand?
> Thou hadst: whom hast thou then or what to accuse,
> But Heav'n's free Love dealt equally to all? (4.66–68)

Our choices matter; such power has God granted his creatures. It is not that God exerts a slack macro-providence within which our micro-choices can tweak insignificant moments this way or that, without affecting the whole. That would be to understand God as a large version of ourselves, with too much to do to attend to details. Rather our free will in the multiplicity of choices we might make is embraced by providence. This is how we can explain God's sending the angels down to protect Adam and Eve. From any point of view besides the divine, those guardian angels really would have helped to avert the Fall of man, had man remained faithful, as he was free to do.

Note too that when God grants the angels rule, he necessarily grants them hierarchy. It is another ironic motif of the poem. The devil stands publicly for egalitarianism, liberty, and fraternity—"patron of liberty," says Gabriel in scorn (4.958), but he is a Machiavellian tyrant imposing upon his "peers," rather his flunkies. When it comes to acts of glory, even delusive glory, Satan will brook no partner: "This enterprise," says he of the temptation, "none shall partake with me" (2.465–66). By contrast, part of the charm of the young cherubs who seize him in Eden is that they submit their considerable initiative and high spirits to the direction of their leader, Gabriel, who is a greater angel than they, but no more angel than they, exactly as in the Body of Christ the foot and the head, though not equal, are equally members of the Body.

As Their Sex Not Equal Seemed

THIS EQUALITY WITHIN HIERARCHY is granted also to the human race, again as a gift, in the division of the sexes: Adam, says Milton, is formed for contemplation and valor; Eve, for softness and sweet attractive grace. Only a misogynist, for whom the feminine is to be trodden underfoot, can fail to appreciate the beauty of the gifts granted to Eve. For the innocent (which we are not—as Milton would have us confess), a gift given to another is not a gift withheld from oneself, but a source of joy; and what devilish pride and ingratitude would it be to acknowledge only God as one's superior? Or what shame is it to acknowledge a superior, when even the angels do not disdain to descend to earth to minister to flesh?

Moreover, the gifts granted to Adam and Eve are complementary, and claim a due deference the one from the other. Adam and Eve are each sufficiently graced to live in holiness, but their joy is made perfect by means of their weakness—their insufficiency, if you will. Again this is a point that Milton expects his readers at first to misunderstand, that he may place them in the ironic position of implicitly agreeing with the would-be monarch, Satan. God himself is a community of three persons, a community reflected in the union of man and woman in marriage. Adam and Eve are thus more perfect, more God-like, in their need for one another, than they would have been had God created a single sex (as the fallen Adam will bitterly wish God had done [10.888–908]), for the "one flesh" they create is a higher and holier thing than is the individual alone.

But the most problematic line in the passage is that which asserts that Adam was created for God only, Eve for God in Adam. I concede that Milton's expression is unfortunate, though there is scriptural warrant for it. Eve was created to be Adam's helpmeet, not the other way around, although certainly Adam is also called upon to help Eve. She is "for him" in a way in which he is not "for her"; the difference is precisely what causes all cultures to consider a woman to be a type of man, and never a man a type of woman. In addition, if we construe the line closely with those which precede it, we see that the contemplation and valor for which Adam has been formed have their sole object in God, while Eve's softness and grace have their object in God indirectly, through their effects upon others, especially upon the only other human being now alive, Adam. Thus, the marriage would be analogous to the classical distinction between the contemplative and the active life, or between theoretical and practical philosophy.

Is the lower position an affront to Eve? One might as well ask, "Is it an affront to man that angels exist?" For the Christian, all position, any position, is a gift. Those who scorn the lower misunderstand the creation, turn the Incarnation of Christ into a tactical error, and set themselves firmly on the side of the straitlaced devil, who confesses that he had hoped that

> one step higher
> Would set me highest, and in a moment quit
> The debt immense of endless gratitude. (4.50–52)

Having fallen by ambition, he blames God for not having created him "some inferior Angel" (4.59). Having spurned the "bright eminence" (4.44) God bestowed upon him, wishing for even greater, mistaking the source of his greatness for a rival to it, Satan now wishes he had been the lowest of all the angels, not that he might have rejoiced in the superiority of those above him, but that he might have lain low, unaspiring. Here he is no different from the vile Belial, who hopes that if the devils in hell do not actively provoke God, he will "not mind us not offending" (2.212). That is craven abasement, not humility.

But Eve is grateful for Adam's superiority. Her gratitude must embarrass us sinners, who would not be grateful for such a thing. She sees it as God's gift to her to enjoy. She has reaped greater blessings than has Adam, she says, lovingly exaggerating the glory of her husband. She enjoys him, after all, "preeminent by so much odds" (4.447).

Eve will not always feel that way. After the Fall she becomes one of us, and we hear our worldly wisdom applied in most disgraceful fashion: she thinks at first that she will *not* give the god-making apple to Adam but keep it to herself, "for inferior who is free?" (9.825). She does not see that God had already made her like unto the divine, and does not remember what the angel Raphael had offered as God's intention, to raise Adam and Eve by their obedience that they too might enjoy the delights of heaven in the flesh (5.493–503). In one sentence she denies freedom to all creatures who are not God, and refashions God to her own limited and sinful understanding. For it is clear now that if Eve were God, *she* would not grant freedom to her inferior creatures.

She has even unwittingly denied freedom to the Son of God, who most wondrously expresses his freedom in his willingness to save mankind. The scene deserves attention. In the council at Pandemonium, Beelzebub had painted in terrible words the dangers of a voyage alone from hell to the created universe, through darkness and chaos. Who would undertake it? None of the demons steps forward: none of those "Heav'n-warring Champions," Milton sneers, can overcome his fear of the dark unknown (2.423–26). That is just what Beelzebub is banking on, or rather Satan, since Beelzebub is his mouthpiece. When silence falls upon the assembled demons, Satan offers to do the job—for the sake of his fellows, of course. He rises "by transcendent glory" above his peers, "with Monarchal pride / Conscious of highest worth" (2.427–29). He ends his offer abruptly by commanding that no one but he shall go, lest another of the devils pretend to offer, knowing that he would be refused and thus "winning cheap the high repute / Which he through hazard huge must earn" (2.472–73). Such is the freedom of the rigged politics of hell.

But when the Father foresees that Satan will tempt man to his Fall, he offers to all the angels the opportunity to sacrifice themselves for man, to die the death that is due to justice: "Die hee or justice must" (3.210). It is a genuine offer, yet silence falls upon the angels in heaven, as silence fell upon the demons in hell. At this point, says Milton, man would have been utterly lost, had not the Son of God offered himself in love:

> Behold mee then, mee for him, life for life
> I offer, on mee let thine anger fall;
> Account mee man; I for his sake will leave
> Thy bosom, and this glory next to thee
> Freely put off, and for him lastly die
> Well pleas'd, on mee let Death wreck all his rage. (3.236–41)

"Inferior, who is free?" is the motto of pride and ambition and selfishness. It cannot survive logical scrutiny, since it binds its adherents to lives of ceaseless climbing and suppression of others. But the Son shows here that he is greater than all the angels, incomparably greater, precisely because of love so great that it would accept death not for a friend but even for an enemy.

Here is how the Father, who Satan says holds "the Tyranny of Heav'n" (1.124), responds:

> Because thou hast, though Thron'd in highest bliss
> Equal to God, and equally enjoying
> God-like fruition, quitted all to save
> A world from utter loss, and hast been found
> By Merit more than Birthright Son of God,
> Found worthiest to be so by being Good,
> Far more than Great or High; because in thee
> Love hath abounded more than Glory abounds,
> Therefore thy Humiliation shall exalt
> With thee thy Manhood also to this Throne;
> Here shalt thou sit incarnate, here shalt Reign
> Both God and Man, Son both of God and Man,
> Anointed universal King. (3.305–17)

One of the rewards of the Son's free descent is that, with generosity that over-leaps the bounds of retributive logic, the Father will raise man to the throne of God. Man wished to become as God, and the final judgment is that God shall become man, and the God-man shall govern man whom he has saved. Christ's manhood—the inferiority—is not temporarily assumed and then discarded, but eternally exalted. The Only-Begotten sits at the right hand of the Father by "birthright" (a right the fallen angels rejected in peevish envy), but more by "merit," by quitting his lofty throne, his glory next to the Father. In other words, he most merits being glorified as the Son by his willingness not to be glorified as the Son.

Even man unredeemed understands something of this deep truth about humiliation and glory. The Roman patrician Cincinnatus was revered precisely because he was poor: when the senate called upon him to become "dictator" (an office with extraordinary powers, granted to a trustworthy man in cases of emergency, and limited to a certain term) to repel the Aequians, they found him plowing his fields, clad in a rough tunic. He assumed the dictatorship, defeated the enemy, resigned the office after a few days, and returned to the poverty of his farm. Yet sin curdles even such apparent acts of humility. Satan thus speaks truer than he knows when, on the morning of the fall, he comments on the disgusting necessity to inhabit the form of a snake:

> O foul descent! that I who erst contended
> With Gods to sit the highest, am now constrain'd
> Into a Beast, and mixt with bestial slime,
> This essence to incarnate and imbrute,
> That to the highth of Deity aspir'd;
> But what will not Ambition and Revenge
> Descend to? who aspires must down as low
> As high he soar'd, obnoxious first or last
> To basest things. (9.163–71)

What he means is that the avenue to glory lies through bootlicking, flattery, and petty and repulsive deeds, as part of one's strategy for obtaining power. So the great Monarch of Hell, always stooping, even to flatter the duped angels whose ambition he secretly fears.

His Fair Large Front and Eye Sublime Declared Absolute Rule

LOVE IS LOVE PRECISELY because it can be rejected, says Mauriac, and Milton agrees. God's aim is, in love, to create loving and thus free creatures, for there is no love without the freedom not to love. Says the Father:

> Not free, what proof could they have giv'n sincere
> Of true allegiance, constant Faith or Love,
> Where only what they needs must do, appear'd,
> Not what they would? what praise could they receive? (3.103–6)

This freedom is manifest in Adam's royal looks: the capacious forehead suggesting intellect and judgment, the eye suggesting insight and deliberation. Adam is kingly. But what is he the king of? Here it is easy for the modern reader to misconstrue Adam's "absolute rule." In a few lines we will see what is amply borne out by the rest of the text, that Adam may never so rule as to violate the dignity of Eve. Rather, Milton uses the phrase in a contemporary sense: one enjoys absolute rule when one is "absolved of," or "freed from," the unruly direction of the passions (the inward storms, for example, that batter Adam and Eve after the Fall [cf. 9.1121–26]). This definition of "absolute rule" implies that Eve possesses it too, although rule is not marked on her body as prominently as it is upon Adam's. It is proper to man as man, not to man as male.

Such absolute rule is an earnest of the fuller gift to come. For after the Final Judgment, God will create a new heaven and a new earth, at which point rule will no longer be necessary, as God will so have exalted all creation unto himself. Then, says the Father to the Son,

> Thou thy regal Sceptre shalt lay by,
> For regal Sceptre then no more shall need;
> God shall be all in all. (3.339–41)

The breathtaking freedom of love is an ironic contrast to the fetters of pride. Satan, who would have absolute rule as we understand it, as he sits upon the "bad eminence" of his throne in hell (2.6), does sense the irony. The devils think they would like to steal his rule, but that would only forge bonds worse than those they suffer now:

> While they adore me on the Throne of Hell,
> With Diadem and Sceptre high advanc'd
> The lower still I fall, only supreme
> In misery; such joy Ambition finds. (4.89–92)

Milton understands that the reader will assume that freedom means being able to do as you please, but Adam is *absolutely free* to do as he ought. His freedom is ineradicable from his obedience. The devils, however, have a strictly functional, even childish view of freedom. You are free when you can get away with disobedience, as, for instance, when you are far away from your despotic Father:

> Here at least
> We shall be free; th' Almighty hath not built
> Here for his envy, will not drive us hence:
> Here we may reign secure. (1.258–61)

That notion of freedom is belied by the fixity of will that Satan insists upon as his mark of defiant courage, for, as he idly boasts, nothing will ever change "that fixt mind / And high disdain, from sense of injur'd merit" (1.97–98). But no real choice is left for Satan, as his henchman Beelzebub admits: "War hath determin'd us" (2.330). He freely chooses evil—God does not compel him to do so; but he is now utterly self-compelled to choose evil, and cannot choose otherwise. Milton illustrates this bathetic fixity when, after hearing Satan's report on the "success" of the temptation, all the devils in hell, including Satan himself, suddenly are transformed into snakes, compelled from within to eat the apples of hell, apples that allure them with their aroma but taste of ashes and death. They thus repeat (and will repeat, year after year), the sin of the Fall, wanting to repeat it, and hating it when they have done so (10.538–72).

If the absolutely free Adam and Eve seem beyond the reach of our imagination, that is but Milton's point. Since we are sinners, we cannot know what it is like not to be, so we attribute to Adam and Eve the motives we would have if we were in their place. But sin makes us less human, not more, for God created us to be like him. When we sin, we descend into what is unworthy of our dignity. Satan reveals the truth, as he desperately tries to persuade himself that hell will not be so bad a place after all:

> What matter where, if I be still the same,
> And what I should be, all but less than hee
> Whom Thunder hath made greater? (1.256–58)

"If" here is the operative word. Satan speaks as if his nature were a function of his absolute will and not of his willed actions; as if he could will the deeds that make him a devil, yet will not to be a devil! But he does know better, and when on the fateful day he prepares to seduce Eve, he allows himself the "imbrutation" that is the diseased parody of the Incarnation and an outward sign of the venality to which he has stooped (9.163–66). Note that Satan does not actually assume the flesh of the serpent—it is not a true incarnation. He merely infuses himself into the serpent's body. That alone is enough to disgust him.

The Hair of Adam and Eve

GODLINESS AND OBEDIENCE ARE marked together on the bodies of our first parents. We see it in their hair! First Adam:

> And Hyacinthine locks
> Round from his parted forelock manly hung
> Clust'ring, but not beneath his shoulders broad. (4.301–3)

We know why his hair must not fall below his broad shoulders: it is unbecoming in a man, as Paul says (1 Cor. 11:14). The breadth of those shoulders should be left prominent, as a sign of strength and protection. But why "hyacinthine"? The curly hair (as in Michelangelo's *David*) associates Adam with the Greek and Roman ideals of male beauty, as evident in classical nude statues of gods and heroes. Milton has appropriated for Adam all that the Greeks honored in Apollo and Zeus. Those were cheats and fables, says Milton; but the most classically excellent man who ever lived dwelt in obedience to the God whom the Greeks were too proud to acknowledge.

Adam's hair is curly, as is Eve's; yet the length of her hair marks her difference from Adam and her subjection to him:

> Shee as a veil down to the slender waist
> Her unadorned golden tresses wore
> Dishevell'd. (4.304–6)

She wears her hair as a veil, in accordance also with Pauline directives. This veil is a sign that she is subject to her head (her husband), but it is also a sign of her feminine innocence, since she, unlike the women whom Paul advises, needs no veil for her hair. Her hair is her veil and her glory: it both conceals and reveals the holiness of body and soul. Thus is Eve exalted in the queenly sign of her submission to her husband. And as Adam's naked innocence is his most royal robe, so Eve's most lovely adornments are her simplicity and carelessness of adornment. Milton has in mind Tasso's Sophronia, the pure virgin who goes forth in modesty and courage before the pagan king to take upon herself the punishment he has decreed for her fellow Christians:

> If chance or art has touched her lovely face,
> if she neglects or adorns herself, who knows—

of nature, of Love, and of all the heavens impart,
her artlessness is but the noblest art. (*Jerusalem Delivered*, 2.18.5–8)

Yet Eve's hair partakes of the artistry of God: it is

Dishevell'd, but in wanton ringlets wav'd
As the Vine curls her tendrils, which impli'd
Subjection. (4.306–8)

God is no bald "realist," as is, according to Lewis's Screwtape, "Our Father
Below." In Eden the "rule" is unruliness, luxuriance, abundance, playfulness.
Such exuberant growth and glory is to be found everywhere Satan turns. Like
Eden, like the boundlessly creative God, Eve's hair is "wanton," and given her
perfect innocence, why should it not be? Merriment is no sin. The animals,
too, sport innocently before Adam and Eve (4.340–47).

Yet Milton implies that this wantonness, this apparent directionlessness,
must be subordinate to something higher. Not that it must be kept in check—
that it may be wanton so far, but no further! It means that without a principle
of order, wantonness degenerates into chaos, and thus loses itself; whereas
order makes it the more luxuriant, exactly as pruning the branches in Eden
causes them to grow all the wilder and more lush (2.623–32). Milton puns on
the word "implied," intending the Latin meaning "folded into." Enfolded in
the curls of Eve is the straight and the orderly: the curls "imply" subjection to
it. So too, we may assert, the curls of Adam.

Eve's subjection is also expressed here by the classical symbolism of the
vine and the elm. Without the grapevine, the elm is sterile and gives no nourishment; without the strong elm, the vine has nothing to cling to. Together
they create something far greater than either would be alone. The allegory is
easy to adapt to the Pauline doctrine on marriage, and was popular among
Christian authors: the elm cherishes and protects the vine, and the vine clings
to and honors the elm. Milton had this partnership in mind when Adam reminds Eve of the mutual assistance and the proper order of marriage:

The Wife, where danger or dishonor lurks,
Safeliest and seemliest by her Husband stays,
Who guards her, or with her the worst endures. (9.267–69)

Subjection, but Requir'd with Gentle Sway

HOW IS ADAM TO exercise his authority over Eve? Milton's models are the Father's primacy (in equality) over the Son, and God's rule over the angels. That rule is one of love; God desires to have the angels as free and as highly honored as they can be. Therefore he offers to them, as I have mentioned, the glorious opportunity to sacrifice themselves for mankind: "Dwells in all Heaven charity so dear?" (3.216). The devils will flatten themselves to the floor of hell to praise their deceiver; but when the angels hear of the Son's offer and of the Father's abundant favor, they praise Father and Son while standing erect, laying down their crowns while singing the glory of him who made them princes. When they are done, they reassume those crowns, to God's delight.

Except for Satan, we never see the other devils out of their prison; Satan will not yet allow it, lest his authority be questioned. But the angels may come and go as they please, whenever they have not been given an express command by God or by their superiors. When they do not have the joy of obedience, they have the joy of their own will—but their obedience is what they are honored to perform, and their will is always in concord with the will of God. Satan depends upon this freedom when he deceives Uriel, the angel of the sun. On his way to earth he pretends to be, in the first of his many humiliating disguises, a "stripling Cherub" drawn by curiosity to see the earth and to praise its glorious Maker (3.636ff.). Far from finding the impulse suspicious, Uriel praises the lad and directs him the way to go. The angels dwell happily in this freedom, which is a participation in God's essence. In that sense they are, as the Father is happy to call them, "Gods" (3.341).

So if Adam is to rule like the Father, he must exalt Eve and give her authority next to, sharing in, and proceeding from his own. He must rule by love. Modern man, reversing Paul's hymn to love, too often believes in nothing, hopes in nothing, and endures nothing, seeing in all love the machinations of power. But Christianity sees in true power the heart of love; for love, not power, is the defining ultimate for God: "God is love" (1 John, 4:8).

That is why Eve's subjection to Adam is placed in the context of amorous desire. It is

> requir'd with gentle sway,
> And by her yielded, by him best receiv'd,
> Yielded with coy submission, modest pride,
> And sweet reluctant amorous delay. (4.308–11)

The sexual submission is queenly. Eve "requires" no less, and Adam is the better pleased for it, as any true king would be.

But why does Eve not submit to Adam immediately and frankly? Is she a seductress? That, again, is to interpret innocence in the light of sin. Eve's power over Adam is not that of feigned unwillingness, but of joyful expectancy. The key word—an intensely erotic word—is *delay*. In a world of sin and ignorance, delay breeds impatience and worry and despair. In Eden, it breeds the greater love of wonders to come. For the all-seeing God has given his creatures both the gift of knowledge, that they might see, and the gift of time, that they might come to see what they now cannot. The tension between *already* and *not yet* reflects the pattern of sacred scripture, as Augustine shows: for the word of God is a delightful and thought-stirring interplay of the clear and the obscure, between the already-here and the still unrevealed. Could God be God, if all his wonders could be grasped in an instant? Would we want it that way? Adam then is Godlike in his request, and Eve, Godlike in her granting it in time. But to refuse to wait, to deny God the government of time, is to turn creation into a rapacious quest for power or pleasure: "Let our strength be our norm of justice," say the wicked, "for weakness proves itself useless" (Wisdom 2:11).

The paradox that strength should express itself in weakness, or that weakness should be exalted, is inscribed upon the physical universe. Perhaps those most tempted by the Manichean heresy can best appreciate how strange it is that God who is spirit (John 4:24) should create what is not spirit, and find all of it, all material creation, very good. The easier and in some ways more sensible point of view is to consider matter a hindrance to the ascent of the spiritual heights. But true Christianity, as opposed to Gnostic, Docetist, and feminist heresies, is scandalous in this regard. Christ asked for a fish to eat after he had risen (John 21:12–13)! In *That Hideous Strength*, C. S. Lewis has the devilish and vague spiritualist Wither avoid any contact with the grime and wetness of the physical world. In *Out of the Silent Planet*, the perverted lovers on Sulva (the moon) are so fastidious—the Spenserian word for it is "dainty" (cf. *Faerie Queene*, 1.2.27.9)—that brides and grooms sleep not with each other but with cunningly fashioned mental images. In *Perelandra*, Lewis praises the uncombined smallest material particles of the universe, the dust of creation, for its luminous closeness to the direct hand of God. For God brought forth that dust from what it remains so near to: nothing.

But from "things which are not," God has chosen "to bring to nought things that are" (1 Cor. 1:28). The devils are scandalized by corporeality. They hate it; they think it beneath them. One thinks of Lewis's Screwtape, who describes, with mingled yearning and disgust, the salvation of a "thing of earth and slime": "By Hell, it is misery enough to see them in their mortal days taking off dirtied and uncomfortable clothes and splashing in hot water and giving little grunts of pleasure—stretching their eased limbs. What, then, of this final stripping, this complete cleansing?" (*The Screwtape Letters*, 157).

The devils consider that God, in dabbling with such low creatures, is doing something obscene. "This animal," moans Screwtape, "this thing begotten in a bed, could look on Him" (159), Yet, ironically, it is devils who, in Christian poetry, suffer the indignity of punishments upon the body. Typical are Tasso's devils of many and variegated forms, snake and lion and man and angel and other things incongruously and hideously melded, in ridiculous parodies of marriage and the Trinity: "a rabble of discordances in one" (*Jerusalem Delivered*, 4.5.8).

But if we love God we must love the world he has made. So we must love the body; that too is a part of human love: "So ought men to love their wives as their own bodies" (Eph. 5:28). Therefore Satan will tempt Eve not only to "usurp authority over the man" (1 Tim. 2:12), but to scorn all creatures beneath her and, subtly, to scorn the physical basis of her union with Adam. For though Satan can see, as from the outside, the beauty of the bodily things in Eden, he cannot feel it within him. He is like Lewis's Weston in *Perelandra*, who idles his hours pulling apart the limbs of small animals because for the moment he has nothing better to do. Adam is right when he says there is probably nothing the enemy envies so much as the conjugal love that he and Eve share; and that hatred extends to the smallest particle of creation. Satan hates the animals, the plants, the rivers, the very dust he will be compelled to lick. He hates food; he hates sex. The devils never sleep and never eat (except the ashen apples they detest). They are racked by desire, "among our other torments not the least" (4.510), forever unfulfilled.

Satan aims to have Eve despise such things too. It is the snobbish and prissy side of ambition. In his first serpentine speech to Eve, after exalting her to deity—

> Wonder not, sovran Mistress, if perhaps
> Thou canst, who art sole Wonder . . . (9.532–33)

and subverting the hierarchical status of both the angels and Adam, if not of the Son himself by addressing the woman as "Fairest resemblance of thy

Maker faire" (538), Satan dismisses with scorn all the animals, and the particularity of Eve's marriage to one man, Adam:

> But here
> In this enclosure wild, these Beasts among,
> Beholders rude, and shallow to discern
> Half what in thee is fair, one man except,
> Who sees thee? (and what is one?) who should'st be seen
> A Goddess among Gods, ador'd and serv'd
> By Angels numberless, thy daily Train. (4: 542–48)

Yet it is only by relying on Eve's love for the animals that Satan, gamboling before her in his voluminous snaky folds, can approach unsuspected.

I have long believed there is something antiseptic and sterilizing about feminism. The modern feminist critic, preoccupied with raw power, misses Satan's contempt for the corporeal. So Satan describes what life was like, as a serpent, before he ate the apple. His thoughts, he says, were low (if we write "humble" here, we catch his prideful fastidiousness immediately), fixed upon food and sex. The first question Eve should ask is, "What is wrong with thoughts of food and sex?" What else *should* you be thinking about, if you are a serpent? For a snake, for any animal, those thoughts are what God has willed: they are innocent and blessed. How else should the animals be fruitful and multiply?

Take the matter of food first. In a sense, food is a mystery. Why did God create men—and, as Milton claims, even angels—to need such lowly stuff? The reason, Milton suggests, has to do with the goodness of all creation and its hierarchies of love. Hunger is a sign of one's creatureliness. Some creatures need plants for food, yet there is humility in that need, and real pleasure in its fulfillment.

Food is granted a participation in higher things—or the hierarchies of God are expressions of generous, self-humbling love. Nowhere in *Paradise Lost* is this clearer than in the dinner scene between the human couple and the affable angel Raphael. If an angel comes to dinner, what do you serve him? Milton's scandalous answer is that angels eat the sorts of things we too might eat, and not in appearance only, but "with real hunger" (5.437). Raphael enjoys a repast of delicious fruits he has never tasted before, and gives thanks to God for the variety of his bounty. When Adam marvels at it, Raphael replies by placing the need for food within a hierarchy of being:

> O *Adam*, one Almighty is, from whom
> All things proceed, and up to him return,
> If not deprav'd from good, created all
> Such to perfection, one first matter all,
> Indu'd with various forms, various degrees
> Of substance, and in things that live, of life;
> But more refin'd, more spiritous, and pure,
> As nearer to him plac't or nearer tending
> Each in thir several active Spheres assign'd,
> Till body up to spirit work, in bounds
> Proportion'd to each kind. (5.469–79)

Again, though Satan would never deign to eat—he sits unwittingly upon the tree of life, and does not taste its fruit—he depends upon that lowly need in Eve, and leads her to the forbidden tree at noon, when her appetite has begun to quicken.

As for sex, Milton's view can be summed up in his brilliant defense of its holiness in paradise:

> Our Maker bids increase, who bids abstain
> But our Destroyer, foe to God and man? (4.748–49)

Milton is following an ancient Christian belief, expressed by Ambrose and Thomas Aquinas, that sexual intercourse was commanded by God and was, or would have been, more pleasurable in paradise than it is now. Like eating, sex is a lowly thing we have in common with the beasts, required for the perpetuation of our race; but like eating it also participates in the generative power of God. Thus, without contradiction Milton gives us scenes that are at once tenderly human, ravishingly erotic, and profoundly spiritual. Adam and Eve, going to sleep, do not immediately go to sleep:

> Nor turn'd I ween
> *Adam* from his fair spouse; nor *Eve* the rites
> Mysterious of connubial Love refus'd. (4.741–43)

After their lovemaking, petals fall gently upon their naked innocence; and the narrator closes by reminding the reader of the all-generous power of God. If we trust in God, we will have all we need, and infinitely more than we could claim for ourselves:

Sleep on,
Blest pair; and O yet happiest if ye seek
No happier state, and know to know no more. (4.773–75)

Delay and the Child

THEY WHO DISMISS THE created order of sex inevitably hate the smallness, weakness, messiness, and inconvenience of children. For a Christian, sex must mean more than it means for the beast, as indeed eating means more: but it can never fail to mean *at least* what it means for the beast. Paradoxically, lust is the sin we commit when we despise our bodies, which are meant, are built, for procreation. We think ourselves too good for that mire—and leap into the mud of disordered and unnatural desires. We insist that our "spiritual needs," by which we chiefly mean our appetitive egos, must be served; so we use sex to engender lovely little ideas about ourselves, our youth, our sufficiency, our potency. With sinful man, such is the case all too often, even when these lovely little ideas can toddle about and talk.

Children defer until far in the future the fulfillment of our lovemaking now; they reveal a love and a glory for which we must wait in humility. Therefore the devils hate them. Properly first in Milton's catalogue of demons is the hideous Moloch, "horrid King besmear'd with blood / Of human sacrifice, and parents' tears" (1.392–93). He is a "fertility" god who demands, as his price for good harvests, the death of babies; his parent-worshipers, then as now, must stoke themselves into a frenzy to blind and deafen themselves to the truth:

Though for the noise of Drums and Timbrels loud
Their children's cries unheard, that pass'd through fire
To his grim Idol. (1.394–96)

But Adam and Eve, before retiring for the night, pray for children, as they pray for the blessings of hands to help their creative tending of the garden, and souls to increase their joy (4.732–35).

The devil is right to hate children. These most powerless of the human race are held up by Christ as examples to which the faithful must aspire. So the foul witches who tempt Macbeth to his destruction toss into their cauldron the "finger of birth-strangled babe / Ditch-delivered by a drab" (4.1.30–31); so Macbeth is given the terrible vision of a crowned babe (4.1.86–89); so Lewis in *That Hideous Strength* has his nature-hating "progressives" desire to wipe out organic life; so his Merlin calls the young and once pagan heroine "the falsest lady of any at this time alive" for conspiring with her husband to thwart a conception that had been centuries in the preparing (278).

Sterility, a weakness that extends into the future without end, is the just consequence of sin. Tolkien's Sauron wanted to amass all power in himself; the result is that he cannot create, but only fashion ugly parodies of what has already been created. After the Fall, Eve will suggest to Adam that they avert the curse from passing to their progeny: they should abstain from sexual intercourse, or, if that proves too difficult, they should attain the goal of that willful abstinence by committing suicide. After praising her courage, Adam, resuming his role as rightful head of the household, redirects Eve's attention to the promise hidden in God's punishment of their sin: that one day her seed, a child, shall bruise the head of the serpent (10.1028–46). That child would be Christ the Messiah, at whose newborn cry, as Milton celebrates it in his hymn *On the Morning of Christ's Nativity*, all the jabbering, shrieking, riddling charlatans from Delphi to Cumae would fall silent, now and forever, world without end.

13

The Power of the Weak:
Manzoni's I Promessi Sposi

Liberté, Egalité, Fraternité

IT IS ALL WELL and good to theologize about how power is made manifest in
obedience. But what about the corrupted currents of this world? How, when
the wicked and ignorant sit upon thrones or swagger down the halls of justice,
can the poor Christian find strength not only to endure but to prevail?

That question occupied the mind of Alessandro Manzoni (1785–1873),
whose masterpiece *I Promessi Sposi* (The Betrothed) is the first great Italian
novel. Manzoni was not brought up a Christian. His family frequented the
Parisian salons where the skepticism of the Enlightenment was in vogue. As
a youth he witnessed both the secular jubilance and the terror of the French
Revolution; that experience instilled in him a commitment to human liberty
and to the unification of his own country. Yet his political idealism was always
balanced by a remarkable moral realism. Manzoni observed men too closely,
and with too sympathetic an imagination, to be fooled by a political slogan
or a fashionable philosophy. His conversion to Christ—he became an ardent
Roman Catholic—allowed him to see a portion of the solution that eluded
revolutionaries such as Marat and Robespierre. If man is made for God, then

no politics that ignores man's soul can succeed. Injustice, as Manzoni saw, cannot be fought on the political level alone, because its site is the sinful heart of man. The only power, then, that can break the hold of the mighty is the same that can break the hold of sin within both mighty and weak. The power is God's, and is made manifest in what the world ignores as weak and contemptible. It is the power of love.

From the very beginning of *I Promessi Sposi*, Manzoni shows us that in our world injustice is the rule. The mountains north of Milan are in the control of Spanish dukes, constantly jockeying for authority against the Venetians and the French, not to mention the local Italian population. Lecco, the principal town near the village where the story opens, has the "advantage" of a Spanish garrison, whose soldiers "taught modesty to the damsels and matrons of the country; bestowed from time to time marks of their favour on the shoulder of a husband or a father; and never failed, in autumn, to disperse themselves in the vineyards, to thin the grapes, and lighten for the peasant the labours of the vintage" (*I Promessi Sposi*, 8). The savage irony is worthy of Voltaire, but unlike Voltaire, Manzoni will not lapse into the lazy and foolish demand that men *écrasez l'infame*, raze to the ground the notorious church that curbs their freedom. You can send to the galleys all the lords and bishops in the world, and sin would still remain.

Nor is it clear that those in nominal authority have the power to quell injustice in any case. The Italian villages are infested with *bravi*, bandits in the hire of local lords, usually Spanish, who make their lords' power felt by various means, from gentle threats to thrusts of a dagger. To give the Spanish rulers some credit, Manzoni lists at length the decrees outlawing such *bravi*, stipulating severe punishments from Their Excellencies the Duke of here and the Count of there, but the sheer abundance of the decrees proves how ineffective they were. The Captain of Milan, de Acevedo, did succeed in "contriving cabals and exciting enemies against his great enemy, Henry IV [of France]," and he did manage to steal a city from Savoy, "but as to this pernicious plant of bravoes, certain it is that it continued to blossom" (12).

One day the local curate is accosted by two such flowers of manhood and is threatened, on peril of his life, lest he go through with the announced marriage of Lorenzo Tramaglino, a barely literate silk-weaver, and Lucia Mondella, a beautiful and simple peasant girl. The marriage is to take place this very day, but the ruler of these bravoes, the Spanish-named Don Rodrigo, has cast a wager with his cousin that he can steal and win the girl for his own use. The curate, Don Abbondio, is a weak man, and trusts rather in his own prudence than in the Lord. He caves in: he *wishes* he could remain faithful to his office, but he replies to the bravoes, stuttering that they should report him "disposed . . . always disposed to obedience" (15).

Don Abbondio makes up for his moral weakness by bullying people who are subject to him: when we cannot avenge ourselves on our superiors, we holler at the housekeeper. So when Renzo comes to see him, the curate invents all kinds of impediments against the poor lad, tossing in a phrase or two of Latin to intimidate him. The priest finally blurts out the name of his oppressor, but only after Renzo issues a veiled threat of his own:

> "Do you wish me to be killed?"
> "I wish to know what I have a right to know."
> "But if I speak, I'm a dead man! Surely I'm not to trample on my own life?"
> "*Then* speak." (32)

A young man in love is not the most levelheaded creature in the world, and Manzoni leads us to believe, for a while, that his story will chronicle the romantic gallantry of Renzo as, against all odds, he wrests justice from Don Rodrigo by his own hands. No such thing. For not only is the vengeance that Renzo seeks impossible to obtain, it is *wrong*; it would render him weaker, not stronger, and unworthy to marry the girl in whose cause he seeks the vengeance. He had been a peaceful young man, says Manzoni, and now for the first time in his life he walks home contemplating murder: "The unjust and oppressive, all those, in fact, who wrong others, are guilty, not only of the evil they do, but also of the perversion of mind they cause in those whom they offend" (34). Renzo mulls over the impregnable garrison from which Don Rodrigo rules with all his bravoes; then he thinks of Lucia, and the promise he made to his parents when they died. His love for Lucia makes him want to kill; but it also raises his mind: "The thought of God, of the Blessed Virgin, and of the saints, returned upon him; he remembered the consolation he had so often experienced from the recollection that he was free from crimes; he remembered the horror with which he had so often received the news of a murder; and he awoke from this dream of blood with fear, with remorse, and yet with a sort of joy that he had but imagined it" (35).

Indeed we are shown that whenever Renzo relies on his own strength, apart from prayer and innocence, he goes wrong, even when his motives are understandable and just. He does try the appropriate avenues of justice first, seeking a lawyer who proves to be in the pay of Don Rodrigo, and begging the intervention of the saintly Capuchin friar Cristoforo, about whom I will say more below. When these measures fail, Renzo loses patience with man and God and decides to take matters into his own hands. Against the better judgment of Lucia, who cannot tell why she thinks it is wrong but simply knows that it is, he tries to engineer an illicit but valid marriage by sneaking into the curate's house with Lucia and two witnesses and pronouncing the appropriate words in his presence. The plan is thwarted when Don Abbondio springs from his chair with a cloth and binds Lucia's mouth before she can speak, while raising the town with a cry for help. By the grace of God, Renzo and Lucia and her mother Agnese had left their homes just when the bravoes of Don Rodrigo had broken in to kidnap the girl. In the uproar they manage to flee, and are conducted to safety by Father Cristoforo.

"There must be justice at last, even in this world," grumbles Renzo (52), to which Manzoni comments that "a man overwhelmed with sorrows knows not what he is saying" (52). There is justice at last, but not the justice we expect, and it does not come from whence we expect it. Renzo has tried to scramble up some "friends," when Father Cristoforo pulls him up short: "'What! you went in search of friends . . . and such friends! . . . who could not have helped you, had they been willing, and you forgot to seek the only One who can and will assist you! Do you not know that God is the friend of the afflicted who put their trust in Him? Do you not know that threatening and contention gain nothing for the weak?'" (70)

The Strength of a Man Who Owns Nothing

THAT IS NO SENTIMENTALITY from Father Cristoforo. As the friar is the novel's moral touchstone, Manzoni interrupts the narrative to tell us his story. It reveals the weakness of the power by which the world overcomes, and the power of the weakness that overcomes the world. This Cristoforo, baptized Ludovico, was a keeper of bravoes in his youth, back when he yearned to be accepted by the very noblemen he hated. He used his power to protect the weak, not because he loved them, but because it pleased his pride and his hatred: "He had a natural and sincere horror of fraud and oppression—a horror rendered still more vivid by the rank of those whom he saw daily committing them—exactly the persons he hated. To appease or to excite all these passions at once, he readily took the part of the weak and oppressed, assumed the office of arbitrator, and intermeddling in one dispute, drew himself into others; so that by degrees he established his character as a protector of the oppressed, and a vindicator of injuries" (56). But such a career made him hated in turn, and rendered him subject to the bravoes he was compelled to employ to effect his wishes: he had "to live with villains for the sake of justice" (56).

Disgusted with his life, he often thought of renouncing his riches and becoming a friar. The local Capuchins begged their daily bread from house to house, owned nothing but the clothes on their backs and a basket for begging, and spent their days in prayer and works of mercy for the poor. So admired were they, and such influence they wielded because of their weakness, that a man who turned friar was considered a paragon of holiness, yet lost to the world, just as if he had been sentenced to the darkest of prisons.

Finally, one terrible incident decides the issue. Ludovico was walking alongside a wall when "an arrogant and overbearing man, whom he had never spoken to in his life, but his cordial enemy" (57), approached on the other side. How strange, in the world of power, that one can make enemies of people one has never met! And Manzoni shows how powerless are those who worship power: they are caught in the meshes of their own importance. For as the power brokers grow near, it is clear that one or the other must yield the wall, but neither will do so:

> The Signor, eyeing Ludovico with a haughty air and imperious frown, said, in a corresponding tone of voice, "Go to the outside."
> "You go yourself," replied Ludovico; "the path is mine."
> "With men of your rank the path is always mine."
> "Yes, if the arrogance of men of your rank were a law for men of mine."
> (57)

How powerful can one be when one's reputation depends on whether one walks next to a wall? And is that the power for which men of lesser rank should strive? Here the petty argument erupts into violence, with drawn swords, and in the scuffle Ludovico's loyal steward, a kindly man with a family to support, is stabbed to death trying to save his master. When Ludovico sees that, in a fury he does just what Renzo now wishes he could do to Don Rodrigo: he buries his sword in the body of his provoker.

What justice here? Ludovico flees to a Capuchin monastery, sick of his empty life in the world, and seeing in his victim the man he could not see before: "Yet the impression made on his mind by the sight of one man murdered *for* him, and another *by* him, was new and indescribable;—a disclosure of sentiments before unknown. The fall of his enemy, the sudden alteration of his features, passing in a moment from a threatening and furious expression to the calm and solemn stillness of death, was a sight that instantly changed the feelings of the murderer" (59). So changed is he that when the Capuchins accept him as a monk, to make atonement for his sin, he adopts the name of his steward Cristoforo, that he might never forget the suffering his pride once caused.

"To oblige a man to relinquish his property," says Manzoni, "shave his head, and walk barefoot, to sleep on straw, and to live upon alms, was surely a punishment fully equivalent to the most heinous offense" (61). Still, the pride of the family must be satisfied; the offender must submit to them publicly, that it may appear to all the world (for worldly power consists largely of appearance) that it is the family that has delivered the sentence. The family's Signor thus demands that the monk be expelled from the city and sent to another house. The Capuchin superior agrees, and Ludovico accepts the humiliation as a way to suffer for and partly expiate his sin.

As the day for his removal approaches, he makes a surprising request of the father superior. He is thinking not only of himself but of the evil that his sin has introduced into the heart of the murdered man's brother: "'Allow me, Father,' said he, 'before I quit the city where I have shed the blood of a fellow-creature, and leave a family justly offended with me, to make what satisfaction I can by at least confessing my sorrow, begging forgiveness of the brother of the deceased, and so removing, please God, the enmity he feels towards me'" (62). When the signor hears of it, he sets the hour for the morrow, staging a scene to redound to the glory of his family. His relatives will all come to his house "for the purpose of receiving a common satisfaction" (63). The courtyard bustles with people of high rank, with all their attendants, pages and maids and bravoes, to witness the humiliation of Friar Cristoforo. The signor stands alone in the center of his great hall, looking like a portrait of importance, "grasping in his left hand the hilt of his sword, while with the right he folded the collar of his cloak over his breast" (63).

At such a moment the least reservation of power for oneself, the least suggestion that one *knows* that one is superior to the being to whom one is about to bow, would destroy everything. Cristoforo must not only behave as if he were unfit to touch the hem of the signor's garment—he must *know* he is unfit to do so; only thus will both he and the signor be healed. As Father Zossima recommends to his young monks in *The Brothers Karamazov*, one must bow to the earth and confess one's responsibility for one's sins and for all the sins of men, for each of us is guilty of the whole, sharing the common sin of Adam. One must know this guilt. One cannot rely on a tattered scrap of virtue here.

When Friar Cristoforo appears, his penitence appears so marked upon his bearing and his face that it takes the onlookers by surprise, disarming them. He sees the signor, moves directly for him, crosses his hands over his breast, bows his shaved head, and falls to his knees, saying: "'I am the murderer of your brother. God knows how gladly I would restore him to you at the price of my own blood, but it cannot be: I can only make inefficacious and tardy excuses, and implore you to accept them for God's sake'" (64). The signor is struck to the quick. After all, he well knows that his brother was no easy man; all along it has been his dignity that was hurt, not simply his brotherly love. He bends towards the kneeling friar: "'Rise,' said he in an altered tone. 'The offence—the act certainly—but the habit you bear—not only so, but also yourself—Rise, Father—My brother—I cannot deny it—was a cavalier—was rather a—precipitate man—rather hasty. But all happens by God's appointment. Speak of it no more. . . . But, Father, you must not remain in this posture.' And taking him by the arm, he compelled him to rise" (64). Cristoforo obtains the Signor's pardon, to the cheers of all present, and, again moved by the friar's deep remorse for the evil that forgiveness could not undo, the signor "threw his arms around Cristoforo's neck, and gave and received the kiss of peace" (64).

The signor goes so far as to respond in love: he invites the friar to stay for dinner. But Cristoforo will not stay; sumptuous meals are no longer for him. In gratitude he will accept a loaf, he says, "'that I may be able to say I have shared your charity, eaten of your bread, and received a token of forgiveness'" (65). From this loaf, Cristoforo will save one crust, placing it in a small box he carries on his person, as a reminder of the sin and the moment of unexpected grace and forgiveness. As for the signor and his family, they spend the rest of the day reveling in a very different pleasure than what they had intended. That evening, the signor mutters between his teeth, angry and pleased and puzzled at once, "'The devil of a friar!—if he had knelt there a few moments longer, I should almost have begged *his* pardon for his having murdered my brother'" (66). Manzoni's final comment on the scene shows that the day the signor had intended as a celebration of glory really does strengthen the man, but by making him gentler and more human: "From that day forward he became a little less impetuous and a little more tractable" (66).

An Ambassador without an Army

IT IS THIS CRISTOFORO who undertakes to intercede with Don Rodrigo on behalf of Renzo and Lucia. The very lie of the land shows how daunting the task is. Rodrigo's palace stands atop a cliff overlooking the town, with a smattering of cottages roundabout, inhabited by the families of his servants and the farmers of his manor. These people, raised in the shadow of the great man's power, inherit also the family's arrogance and violence: "The very children, playing in the road, displayed in their countenances and behaviour a certain air of provocation and defiance" (71).

When Cristoforo enters the palace hall, Don Rodrigo and his friends — among whom are the corrupt lawyer who refused Renzo, and the Podesta charged with restraining the noblemen from abusing the poor — are embroiled in a debate over whether, according to the strict laws of chivalry, it is permissible to beat an ambassador who brings a challenge to a duel. Most of the men present are too cowed to answer, fearing to offend one power or another. Rodrigo turns to Father Cristoforo to settle the dispute — turns to him with a sly desire to embarrass him, because he knows on what errand Cristoforo has come, and wishes to make a show of his authority. But Cristoforo refuses; he claims to know nothing of the rules of chivalry; and when he is pressed, he resolutely declines to judge the world according to the world's terms: "My humble opinion is that there should be neither challenges, bearers, nor blows" (77).

Such an answer, in such company, is bound to produce gasps of astonishment and even laughter. It would turn the world upside down, the diners cry! No, the pulpit is one thing, and it may be a good thing, but the world is another. Everything in its place. So the friar listens in silence, as the world puts forth "reasonings deduced from a wisdom so ancient, yet so new" (78).

When the dinner is over and Father Cristoforo finally has a chance to speak with Don Rodrigo in private, the petty lord tries to overwhelm him with his power and authority. He uses polite and even Christian language as a veil for command: "'How can I obey you?' said Don Rodrigo, standing in the middle of the room. His words were these; but the tone in which they were pronounced, clearly meant to say, remember before whom you are standing, take heed to your words, and be expeditious" (83). The effect rather upon Father Cristoforo is to inspire him with courage. He begins by giving Rodrigo a way to save face, suggesting that men have employed the lord's name in effecting a wicked design against two innocent persons. Rodrigo, he says, need only say the word to confound their wickedness and restore order. But the lord interrupts him repeatedly, always placing upon the friar's words the most sinister construction he can, even accusing him of the baseness of entering his home as a spy. To the friar's pleas that Rodrigo listen, lest he have to repent someday, the lord mockingly suggests that Cristoforo is assigning him a rank beyond what he possesses, because after all only real princes are wealthy enough to keep a preacher in their homes! He pretends not to know what Cristoforo is talking about, and says with a dismissive sneer: "'I can only suppose there must be some young girl you are concerned about. Make confidants of whom you please, but don't have the assurance to annoy a gentleman any longer'" (85).

Don Rodrigo does not understand this friar, and I daresay the reader does not understand him, either. We think the friar is Rodrigo's opponent, but *he loves* the man, meaning that he intends for Rodrigo all the blessedness he hopes for himself. Thus he replies to Rodrigo's assertion that he is concerned for the girl: "'I am concerned for her, it is true, but not more than for yourself: there are two persons who concern me more than my own life. Don Rodrigo! I can only pray for you; but this I will do with my whole heart. Do not say 'no' to me; do not keep a poor innocent in anguish and terror. One word from you will do all.'" (85). But Rodrigo replies, with consummate snideness, that in that case the friar should place the girl under his protection, where she shall want for nothing—and where, as both the friar and Rodrigo understand, she will be the lord's mistress, to serve his whims. That taxes the friar's patience beyond endurance, and he bursts out in an impassioned reproach and admonition. No longer does Rodrigo have the power to cause Cristoforo the slightest hesitation or unease; his very wickedness has made Cristoforo strong:

> "I speak as to one who is forsaken by God, and who can no longer excite fear. I knew that this innocent was under God's protection; but you, you have now made me feel it with so much certainty, that I have no longer need to ask protection of you. Lucia, I say—see how I pronounce the name with a bold face and unmoved expression."
>
> "What! in this house!"
>
> "I pity this house; a curse is suspended over it. You will see whether the

justice of God can be resisted by four walls, and four bravoes at your gates. Thought you that God had made a creature in his image, to give you the delight of tormenting her? Thought you that he would not defend her? You have despised His counsel, and you will be judged for it! The heart of Pharaoh was hardened like yours, but God knew how to break it. Lucia is safe from you; I do not hesitate to say so, though a poor friar: and as to you, listen what I predict to you. A day will come . . ." (85–86)

Rodrigo will not allow the friar to continue. Nor will we continue with Don Rodrigo; the novel is too long and complex for a thorough analysis of all its many dramatic confrontations between apparent power and apparent weakness. We will beg the reader to wait until the next part to learn what happens to Rodrigo. Let it suffice here to note that God knew how to break the heart of Pharaoh, who had hardened it against the Israelites (cf. Ex. 8:32). Perhaps God allows the wicked man so to harden his heart that only God himself can break it, as George Herbert says:

> The heart alone
> Is such a stone
> As nothing but
> Thy power doth cut. ("The Altar," 5–8)

We think the friar predicts the destruction of Rodrigo's house and the lord's downfall, and we may be right. But within the prediction dwells a promise and a prayer, too. For in the balance hangs nothing less than the salvation of Rodrigo's immortal soul.

The Power Too Terrible to Name

RENZO AND LUCIA ARE driven from town and must take separate paths: Renzo, to Milan; Lucia and her mother, to a convent in the nearby city of Monza. Both the lad and the girl will suffer greatly from the sins of others, particularly from the human habit of judging everyone else according to our own standards of behavior. So Renzo will be accused of insurrection in famine-ridden Milan, and will have to flee for his life; Lucia will be betrayed by the very nun—La Signora they call her, "The Lady," for her high rank and imperious ways—who at the bidding of the Capuchins takes her under her protection. Of all the adventures in *I Promessi Sposi*, what happens to the betrayed Lucia shows most clearly how powerful a thing it is to have no power but one's innocence and one's trust in God. To this I devote the rest of this essay.

Lucia is, as I have said, an ordinary peasant girl, ordinary, yet possessed of a surprising courage, a deep modesty, and holiness. All these are intimated by her dress and her manner when we meet her, as her mother and her friends prepare her for the happy wedding: "Her friends were stealing glances at the bride, and forcing her to show herself; while she, with the somewhat warlike modesty of the rustic, was endeavouring to escape, using her arms as a shield for her face, and holding her head downwards, her black pencilled eyebrows seeming to frown, while her lips were smiling. Her dark and luxuriant hair, divided on her forehead with a white and narrow parting, was united behind in many-circled plaitings, pierced with long silver pins, disposed around, so as to look like an aureola, or saintly glory, a fashion still in use among the Milanese peasant-girls" (36). There is, in fact, nothing rich about her, nothing that an aristocrat ought to notice — unless it is a feminine beauty (not to be distinguished from feminine virtue) so powerful that the walls of the hardest heart might not prevail against it.

Indeed, Don Rodrigo cannot put Lucia out of his mind, partly because when she flees he suffers the indignity of having been bested by a friar and a couple of peasants, and partly for the beauty he cannot help but desire. With all his bravoes and his wealth, he finds himself powerless, and turns to the assistance of a man more powerful than he, whose "friendship" he has bought, by doing him a few unmentioned services, probably at the cost of other people's blood.

The lord whom Rodrigo seeks is of such dread power that Manzoni merely calls him the Unnamed. He has loved power for its own sake: "To do what was forbidden by the public laws, or rendered difficult by an opposing power; to be the arbiter, the judge in other people's affairs, without further interest in them than the love of command; to be feared by all, and to have the upper hand among those who were accustomed to hold the same station over others: such had ever been the principal objects of this man" (313). His habits launch him on a long career of bold undertakings that no other man would dare, until he is at last bound by that power, straitjacketed by the knowledge that should he ever withdraw from his audacity he would lose his reputation. Thus he is self-ensnared, the instrument of weaker lords who seek his assistance.

The Unnamed is not exactly attached to wickedness. Only the exercise of power stirs his blood. Often he would take the part of the weak and the oppressed, not for their sakes to be sure, but for the pleasure of bending a fellow tyrant to his will. More frequently, however, "his power and authority ministered to iniquitous desires, atrocious revenge, or outrageous caprice" (316). His name was whispered whenever a body was found dead in an alley; he became the subject of dark and fabulous legends in the country roundabout.

When Rodrigo relates the "wrong" done to him by Father Cristoforo, and tells the Unnamed that Lucia is now in the custody of La Signora at the convent in Monza, the Unnamed cuts him short and replies that he will take the enterprise. For one, he had always hated Cristoforo as "the open enemy of tyrants, not only in word, but, when possible, in deed also" (321). Also, the Unnamed has a henchman well-placed for the purpose, one Egidio, who has united in lust with the Signora and who has helped her murder at least one of her fellow sisters who found out about it. Thus, the Signora's power is beholden to a ruffian, and the ruffian must answer to the Unnamed, and the Unnamed, to preserve his reputation, must answer to the helpless Don Rodrigo.

Lucia is kidnapped by Egidio and his thugs, with the grudging connivance of La Signora, and taken away up the long mountain track that leads to the castle of the terrible man. But while she is gagged and bound, looking with wide-eyed horror at her captors, the Unnamed broods alone in his castle, prey to thoughts that will not let him rest. For no sooner has Rodrigo left him, than the Unnamed feels a battering at his mind, a slow and fearful revelation of his essential weakness: "For some time past he had experienced, not exactly remorse, but a kind of weariness of his wicked course of life. These feelings, which had accumulated rather in his memory than in his conscience, were renewed each time any new crime was committed, and each time they seemed more multiplied and intolerable: it was like constantly adding and adding to an already incommodious weight'" (321). When he was young, the Unnamed was fooled by the vagueness and the distance of the future to fall back into a "supine and presumptuous confidence" (321). A brilliant adjective, that—the Unnamed, whose body is full of vigor and whose courage seems unshakeable, is supine, contemptibly submissive to the ruling passion of his life.

Now things have changed. The Unnamed would ever be roused to courage at the prospect of being overcome by another man; he does not fear a dagger or a sword. But what arms can he take against the inexorable enemy who makes his quiet presence felt "in the solemn stillness of the night, and in the security of his own castle"? (322). Death approaches, and with death, judgment. What had once elevated him in power beyond all other tyrants now leaves him in solitude. Yet the solitude is not complete; always the Unnamed hears a quiet knocking, or the battering of a ram, against the door of his heart: "That God, of whom he had once heard, but whom he had long ceased either to deny or acknowledge, solely occupied as he was in acting as though he existed not, now, at certain moments of depression without cause, and terror without danger, he imagined he heard repeating within him, 'Nevertheless, I am'" (322). Against that knocking the Unnamed struggles all the more to reaffirm the man he once was, by engaging in deeds as pitiless as ever. So he gives his orders to Egidio.

Lucia's fate rests in the hands of God, true—but God gives her the strength to fight against her oppressors. Had she opposed them with kicks and curses, as justified as these might have been, they would have laughed her to scorn, and would have reported the matter to the Unnamed, who no doubt would also have smiled bitterly and immediately ordered the peasant girl's removal to the house of Don Rodrigo. She does what the henchmen least expect: she reminds them of women they might once have loved; she prays for them; she forgives them: "'Oh!' cried she, 'for the love of God and the most holy Virgin, let me go! What harm have I done? I am an innocent creature, and have done nobody any harm. I forgive you the wrongs you have done me, from the bottom of my heart, and will pray God for you. If any of you have a daughter, a wife, a mother, think what they would suffer, if they were in this state. Remember that we all must die, and that you will one day want God to be merciful towards you. Let me go; leave me here; the Lord will teach me to find my way'" (328–29). The men's reply is a frank confession of weakness: "'We cannot'" (329). Winning no mercy from them, Lucia turned to "Him who holds the hearts of men in His hand, and can, when it pleaseth Him, soften the most obdurate" (329). She prays her rosary more earnestly than ever before.

Lucia does not know it, but God is even now answering her prayer. The Unnamed watches from his turret as the carriage makes its slow way up his fearful mountain. He is uneasy in his mind, feels a revulsion, even "alarm, at the authority he was exercising over this Lucia—a stranger, a poor peasant-girl!" (329). His heart begins to pound— the great tyrant fears. When anticipation proves too much for him, he commands an old housemaid to descend the hill to meet the carriage and take Lucia away from the men, settling her in her own room. And he orders the woman to do what at first she does not fathom, so strange is the command: "'Try to encourage her'" (331).

When his ruffian finally arrives at the castle, the Unnamed asks him how the kidnapping went. Everything was all right, says he, except, well, something the strong man could not reckon with, that reduced his false manhood to weakness:

> "But . . . I will tell the truth; I would rather have been commanded to shoot her in the back, without hearing her speak—without seeing her face."
> "What? . . . what? . . . what do you mean?" (331)

The Unnamed may feel a flicker of hope that Lucia will prove a harridan, and thus the easier to dispose of. The hope vanishes:

> "I mean that all this time . . . all this time . . . I have felt too much compassion for her."
> "Compassion! What do you know of compassion? What is compassion?"
> "I never understood so well what it was as this time; it is something that rather resembles fear; let it once take possession of you, and you are no longer a man." (334–35)

It "resembles fear," says this vulture, and he is right, it does. It is akin to the fear of God, because it recognizes the weakness of man in God's sight: we have compassion for one another, because we know what we are, and we know what God is.

The Unnamed is deeply troubled. He asks the henchman what Lucia has done to excite this compassion, and the answer makes matters worse: "'O, most noble Signor! such a time! . . . weeping, praying, and looking at one with such eyes! and becoming pale as death! and then sobbing, and praying again, and certain words . . .'" (335). How can the Unnamed escape? He must confront those eyes, having been forewarned, and hear those pleas, and if the innocence in the eyes and the earnestness of the pleas had been powerful before, now they will be all the more powerful for having worked in his imagination. The Unnamed reacts hastily, in terror. He must not see her. He must get rid of her. He must send her to Don Rodrigo at once. So he is about to give the command, when something—a wall-crushing intervention by the direct might of God, yet as quiet as a whisper in the heart—gives *him* a command: *no*.

He struggles against the command; longs to be weak again, that is, submissive to what must be, his destiny of wickedness, the fulfillment of his promise to Don Rodrigo. He will not see her in the morning—he will see her—he must see her. When he knocks at their chamber and the old woman opens, he sees that Lucia has not slept in the bed, but has cowered on the floor, crouching in the corner farthest from the entrance. She is too terrified to get up when he bids her, and when he loses his patience and thunders, saying that he will do her no harm, she rises to her knees and resigns herself to be slain: "Here I am, kill me if you will'" (337). The response takes him aback, and he repeats that he will do her no harm. But why then, adds Lucia, has he made her suffer the agonies of hell? "'Why—why have they seized me? Why am I here? Where am I? I am a poor harmless girl. What have I done to you? In the name of God . . .'" (337).

At that the Unnamed storms in. Is Lucia threatening to overmaster him with a power greater than his own? Is God a word by which the weak terrify the strong? Is that what she can expect from this God? Lucia, however, knows nothing of what is going on in the man's soul, nor is there a trace of guile in her calling upon God. In fact, it is not Lucia alone whom God will assist:

> "O Signor, expect! What can a poor girl like me expect, except that you should have mercy upon me? God pardons so many sins for one deed of mercy. Let me go; for charity's sake, let me go. It will do no good to one who must die, to make a poor creature suffer thus. Oh! you who can give the command, bid them let me go! They brought me here by force. Bid them send me again with this woman, and take me to—where my mother is. Oh! most holy Virgin! My mother! my mother!—for pity's sake, my mother. Perhaps she is not far from here . . . I saw my mountains. Why do you give me all this suffering? Bid them take me to a church; I will pray for you all my life. What will it cost you to say one word? Oh, see! you are moved to pity: say one word, oh say it! God pardons so many sins for one deed of mercy!" (337)

The Unnamed will complete this one deed of mercy—and many more. Not immediately; he defers Lucia's liberation to the morrow. He desperately wants an excuse not to set her free. He tries to drive the "fooleries" of remorse from his head. He thinks of new and desperate projects; tries to imagine how to employ his ruffians therein, all in vain. When the image of Don Rodrigo appears before his mind, it arrives with a strange question—an obvious question, but one he had never asked before. Why on earth should he, the Unnamed, do the will of such as Rodrigo? No worthy answer comes; it has all been the craven willingness of "a mind obedient to its old and habitual feelings, the consequence of a thousand antecedent actions; and to account for this one deed, the unhappy self-examiner found himself involved in an examination of his whole life" (345). What he finds is vanity, all his wickedness presented to him frankly, without the excitement or the lust for authority that had spurred him and that had prevented him from perceiving the simple monstrousness of his soul. He reaches for a pistol.

And there in the night, alone and unloved, he continues "alternately snapping and unsnapping the cock of his pistol with a convulsive movement of his thumb" (345), imagining what it will be like in the morning when his people find him dead . . . the rumors, the rejoicing of his enemies . . . and then the possibility that the life beyond this life will not have been merely an invention of priests. If there is no such life, then "'what matters all that I have done? what matters it? It is an absurdity . . .'" (346). But if there is another life, then what? The reader may think that is enough to move the Unnamed, for prudence, to submit to live another day. Not so: "At such a doubt, at such a risk, he was seized with a blacker and deeper despair, from which even death afforded no escape. He dropped the pistol, and lay with his fingers twined among his hair, his teeth chattering, and trembling in every limb" (346). In other words, the Unnamed is not cowed into submission by a power like his own but greater. It is not as if the priests held an invisible weapon to his head. Rather, the weapon is weakness, so to speak; it is the mercy of God, now speaking to his heart with authority: "Suddenly the words he had heard repeated a few hours before rose to his remembrance:—God pardons so many sins for one deed of mercy!—They did not come to him with that tone of humble supplication in which they had been pronounced; they came with a voice of authority, which at the same time excited a distant glimmering of hope" (346). In that hope he tries to concentrate his wavering mind upon the image of Lucia: "She seemed to him no longer like his prisoner and suppliant, but in the posture of one who dispenses mercy and consolation. He anxiously awaited the dawn of day, that he might fly to liberate her, and to hear from her lips other words of alleviation and life" (346).

But man is weak; his resolutions fail, and the Unnamed knows it. He fears that after this morning there will come another day, and another. What he needs is a bulwark of strength, an authority to obey—a father. That is what God provides. When the day breaks, the Unnamed hears bells ringing in the distance. He rushes to the window and sees the people of the mountain villages, in holiday dress, filling the roads, hastening right past his mighty castle. "He looked and looked, till he felt more than common curiosity to know what could communicate so unanimous a will, so general a festivity, to so many different people" (347).

He Was Lost, and Now Is Found

IT IS THE ARRIVAL in town of Cardinal Federigo Borromeo, a great and holy man. What difference between the weak and the strong! The Unnamed has long garrisoned himself with ruffians and lives in a fearful loneliness; but at the news that the good cardinal is visiting, whole villages of people who scrape from meal to meal leave their work and come thronging. The Unnamed too will come: he determines to see the man for himself, and walks down his mountain approach, alone, without a word of command to the bravoes who look to him in expectation and incomprehension. Ignoring the astonished people whispering his name, he finds the curate's house where the cardinal is visiting. Manzoni devotes an entire chapter to a biography of Federigo Borromeo; let us but mention here that because the cardinal is a man of great talent who has never sought authority, he is just the man to understand what true authority is all about. When he was young, everyone had predicted ecclesiastical dignities for him, but he,

> persuaded in heart of what no one who professes Christianity can deny with his lips, that there is no real superiority of a man over his fellowmen, excepting in so far as he devotes himself to their service, both dreaded exaltation, and sought to avoid it; not, indeed, that he might shrink from serving others—for few lives have been more devoted to this object than his own—but because he considered himself neither worthy enough of so high and perilous a service, nor sufficiently competent for it. For these reasons, the Archbishopric of Milan being offered to him in 1595 by Clement VIII, he seemed much disturbed and refused the charge without hesitation. He yielded afterwards, however, to the express command of the Pope. (353)

To this cardinal, then, who lives off scanty fare and wears somewhat shabby vestments, that the poor of his diocese may have the more to eat—and who endows the Ambrosian Library with priceless volumes bought with funds from his own inheritance; to this benefactor of scholars and this simple lover of poor illiterate children, to this kind *father* the Unnamed now comes.

Here again a soul hangs in the balance. Should Federigo stand on his dignity and demand that the Unnamed wait outside, should he do anything to suggest his power, that might rouse in the Unnamed an answering resentment. But like Lucia, Federigo is direct and unassuming. As soon as he hears that the Unnamed wants to see him, he shuts the book he has been reading and cries out—to the consternation of many of the priests around him—"'Let him come in!—let him come in directly!'" (361).

Their meeting shows the master hand of Manzoni, who knows the strange corners of the human heart. The Unnamed does not entirely know why he is there. Desire and hope for relief from his torment fight with shame and embarrassment. He can say nothing, nor does he try. But when he raises his eyes and looks at the cardinal, he himself is raised up too, not in pride, but in submission which affirms his dignity as a man: "He became gradually filled with a feeling of veneration, authoritative, and at the same time soothing; which, while it increased his confidence, gently subdued his haughtiness, and, without offending his pride, compelled it to give way, and imposed silence"(362–63). Federigo, whose bearing is "involuntarily commanding" (363), peers with his benevolent and peaceful eyes into the countenance of the Unnamed. He is searching for something, and finds it. The cardinal is the first to speak—is the first to ask pardon! "Imagining he discovered, under that dark and troubled mien, something every moment more corresponding with the hope he had conceived on the first announcement of such a visit, 'Oh!' cried he, in an animated voice, 'what a welcome visit this is! and how thankful I ought to be to you for taking such a step, although it may convey to me a little reproof!'" (363) The Unnamed is both surprised and set at ease by Federigo's words. He cannot understand what reproof the cardinal could mean, nor why the cardinal rebukes himself for not coming to the Unnamed first. "'You come to me!' he exclaims. "Do you know who I am? Did they deliver my name in rightly?'" (363), asks the Unnamed.

The cardinal's reply is more astounding still. Consider how disarming it must be to learn not only that the man who should be your enemy will return your evil with good, but has been doing good for you for years, though you did not know it:

> "And the happiness I feel, and which must surely be evident in my countenance, do you think I should feel it at the announcement and visit of a stranger? It is you who make me experience it; you, I say, whom I ought to have sought; you whom I have, at least, loved and wept over, and for whom I have so often prayed; you, among all my children, for each one I love from the bottom of my heart, whom I should most have desired to

receive and embrace, if I had thought I might hope for such a thing. But God alone knows how to work wonders, and supplies the weakness and the tardiness of His unworthy servants." (363–64)

The weakness of Federigo—his daring not to hope for the salvation of the Unnamed—is compensated by the strength of God. And it may be that only to those who acknowledge their weakness is the strength supplied.

What good news has the Unnamed come to bring him? he asks. But the poor nobleman knows none; he is tormented; he cannot find God; but if he could only see him! And what would God want with such a man anyway? Federigo does not, in reply, make light of the sins the Unnamed has committed. But in love, even honesty is possible:

> "What can God do with you? What would He wish to make of you? A token of His power and goodness: He would acquire through you a glory, such as others could not give Him. The world has long cried out against you, hundreds and thousands of voices have declared their detestation of your deeds . . ." (The Unnamed shuddered, and felt for a moment surprised at hearing such unusual language addressed to him, and still more surprised that he felt no anger, but rather, almost a relief.) "What glory," pursued Federigo, "will thus redound to God! *They* may be voices of alarm, of self-interest; of justice, perhaps—a justice so easy! so natural! Some perhaps, yea, too many, may be voices of envy of your wretched power, of your hitherto deplorable security of heart." (364–65)

Not for a moment has Federigo been deluded into thinking that the Unnamed is strong. The nobleman's will and perseverance, when God invigorates them with love, shall be strong—and then, who knows what marvelous works God may bring forth from him? "'Who are you, weak man,'" cries the cardinal, "'that you should imagine yourself capable of devising and executing greater deeds of evil, than God can make you will and accomplish in the cause of good?'" (365). The only reply the Unnamed can muster is to yield. He covers his face with his hands, and weeps.

Nor will Federigo allow him to hang back, to dwell alone in his remorse; love is too powerful for that. He offers to take the man's hand, begging him for the favor to take the hand that will not only redress so many wrongs, but "be extended, disarmed, peacefully, and humbly, to so many enemies" (366). In the end, the Unnamed is overcome neither by force nor by persuasion, but by the sword of love: "[Federigo] threw his arms round the neck of the

Unnamed, who, after attempting to disengage himself, and making a momentary resistance, yielded, completely overcome by this vehement expression of affection, embraced the Cardinal in his turn, and buried in his shoulder his trembling and altered face. His burning tears dropped upon the stainless purple of Federigo, while the guiltless hands of the holy bishop affectionately pressed those members, and touched that garment, which had been accustomed to hold the weapons of violence and treachery" (366).

What happens then? The reader must open *I Promessi Sposi* and learn for himself. The world may be surprised that an old man with no weapons and no bravoes can defeat the hardened tyrant. Or is it that God defeats the human heart, battering it with love? So we must imagine the thief at the side of Jesus, who had joined his fellow in jeering, now moved by the innocent man who returned love for hatred, forgiving his enemies almost with the last breath he could take. That thief had shed blood, was a man who used cunning and brute strength to take what he wanted. But the dying Savior beside him uses his strength to take what *he* wants: the soul of the thief, to raise it to glory. Be not afraid, says our Shepherd, when all the arms of the world are aimed to destroy the good and just and holy. Love's a man of war. So says the Truth: "I have overcome the world."

Part Four

The Irony of Love

14

Not in the Garden of Epicurus

Within the vast rectangular walls of the Lazzaretto lie more than ten thousand souls, in various states of squalor, debility, and misery. Dull-eyed children toddle about in rags, usually barefoot, sometimes wearing nothing but a shirt. She-goats have been brought in by the hundreds to suckle the babies whose mothers are dead or so wasted by hunger and disease that their lank bodies can no longer provide sustenance. Whole families have been wiped out. Noblemen, accustomed to command at ease, stoop their shoulders to beggary. Raucous and obscene body-bearers, bells on their heels to warn of their approach, bring the sick into the Lazzaretto in wheelbarrows, and take them thence to the burial pits by the same conveyance, several at a time. Immune to the plague that will slay three-quarters of the population of Milan, these *monatti* make hay of their good luck, rifling the treasures of the sick. They toss infected rags broadside in the streets, crying out, *Viva la malanna!* Long live the plague!

It is ever thus with man; but in this scene there is also something new. I say new, though it is now two thousand years old: I mean a love that does not refer principally to oneself, or even one's clan or nation.

In the middle of the enclosure stands an octagonal chapel, with open colonnades on all sides but the east. At the altar, visible to the multitudes gathered in the courtyard, stands a Capuchin friar whose name at this unlikely moment suggests happiness: Father Felice. And among the faithful is a poor man from the mountains, searching in fear and hope and despair for his beloved Lucia, who should have been his bride had it not been for the violence of the local nobleman, Don Rodrigo. Now Rodrigo too lies dying in the Lazzaretto, no better than the meanest beggar, all his wealth seized by his chief henchman—who died the next day of the contagion.

Father Felice sounds the new note, speaking to the survivors, admonishing them, "corrected by affliction," to give their hearts to God in gratitude and to employ their lives in works of goodness. Why else do they live, if not that their sufferings should instruct them in compassion toward others? In the meanwhile, he says, let those among whom they have suffered and hoped, brethren all, be edified by their behavior:

> "God forbid that they should behold in us a clamorous festivity, a carnal joy, at having escaped that death against which they are still struggling. Let them see that we depart in thanksgiving for ourselves and prayers for them; and let them be able to say, 'Even beyond these walls they will not forget us, they will continue to pray for us poor creatures!' Let us begin from this time, from the first steps we are about to take, a life wholly made up of love. Let those who have regained their former vigor lend a brotherly arm to the feeble; young men, sustain the aged; you who are left without children, look around you how many children are left without parents! be such to them! And this charity, covering the multitude of sins, will also alleviate your own sorrows." (Alessandro Manzoni, *I Promessi Sposi*, 593–94)

And the good father concludes by begging forgiveness from the crowds, if he or his fellows had sometimes grown weary, or impatient, or proud, or if human frailty had led them to sin against charity in any way.

So Manzoni imagines the scene, reconstructing it from the copious historical records available to him. Here the chronicler and not the novelist testifies. The Capuchin friars provided the only effective assistance during that outbreak of the plague. Sent to Milan in force by their provincial, who himself took charge of the Lazzaretto, the Capuchins tended to the sick and the dying, tirelessly ministering to their corporal and spiritual welfare, helping them sip a little wine when they could no longer eat, anointing their heads with oil when they were soon to depart. They did these things with the cheer of Christians, not the grim duty of Stoics—who, let it be noted, would never have condescended to change the dressings or wash the limbs of the plague-stricken. Those friars then worked without hospital masks or rubber gloves or antiseptics, and so eight of every nine Capuchins in the province died. The archbishop himself, Federigo Borromeo, cousin of the elder Charles, was spared as by a miracle, for no one was more tireless than he to visit the sick and bring them every scrap of food or clothing at his disposal.

The ancient world knew nothing of such love. Their best advice to the sufferers: die like men, and leave us alone. Indeed, the world today knows nothing of such love, except in such countries whose cultures have been formed by the teaching of Christ, and even there it is rapidly being forgotten it. Pagans long ago testified to it in puzzlement and wonder: Julian the Apostate lamented that in the midst of misfortune the Christians would take better care of the pagans than would the pagans themselves.

I do not deny the rapes, murders, and slaughters that can be laid to the charge of people professing to be Christians. But the world has always known rapes, murders, and slaughters. The Holocaust, the Cultural Revolution, the starving of the Ukraine, the genocidal wars of the Turks in Armenia—these evils are not new. But a Father Damien of Molokai, a Belgian priest who *connives* for the opportunity to minister among lepers in Hawaii, in a place so ridden with disease and crime and the immorality of the hopeless that no sensible person would want to go near; a David Livingstone, making his way to the heart of the Congo, alone, to bring the natives the word of God; a Mother Teresa, loving and tending the destitute of Calcutta, even the pariahs whom a good Hindu of higher caste was forbidden to touch—these are new to the world.

The Old Dance

IF THERE'S ONE THING the world thinks it knows, it is love. Songs of love abound in the ancient world: of that desire to possess another as one's own. It is part admiration, part violent appetite. In the *Metamorphoses*, Ovid spins dazzling fables of the loves of gods and men, but in all his myths of Jove stooping to assume the form of a bull to sweep Europa away, or Apollo racing after the terrified Daphne with a barrage of plausible lines, is there a single instance of a love that desires to lay down its life for the beloved? Orpheus ventures down to the underworld to fetch Eurydice. He survives; she does not.

The message of Christ presses further—is madder still. The world knows that sometimes one hates the person one loves: *Odi et amo*, says Catullus, with cheerful frankness, "I hate and I love." And that contradictoriness can deliver moments of great dramatic irony: consider the lovelorn Dido, dreaming of Aeneas as a huntsman pursuing her, as in the form of a deer bleeding from an arrow she tries to escape. She loves Aeneas and fears him, is being destroyed by him, though he does not know it. And when he does not return her mad love, she will hate him and curse him. Dido herself is ignorant of the hatred ready to crest over the banks—she whom Aeneas could mollify by a single word of capitulation. She does not know her own heart.

The madness of Dido makes sense to the world; not so the madness of Christ. When does the world ever preach that one must love the person one hates? Renzo, the youth who hears Father Felice's sermon, is struck to the heart. He has thought he knew what love was: his tender feelings for Lucia. Nor is he entirely wrong. But to become worthy of Lucia's love, he must enter deeper into love's mystery. He must turn to Christ, whose love will judge the world. He had been meditating a just revenge against Don Rodrigo. But now he sees that miserable sinner near death, and hears the example of Christ. Still not knowing whether Lucia is alive or dead, Renzo does what he had never dreamed of doing. For a greater danger threatens him than the plague he has survived. Says his advisor, the holy Father Cristoforo: "'Perhaps the salvation of this man and your own depend at this moment upon yourself, upon the disposition of your mind to forgiveness, to compassion . . . to love'" (590).

Renzo is not asked to toss away a little forgiveness as you would toss a coin to a beggar; he too is a beggar, though no one but the wise Cristoforo might see it. So the young man prays for himself and Lucia and the wicked man who wronged them, using a language only God can understand: "On reaching the foot of the little temple, he went and knelt down upon the lowest step, and there poured forth a prayer to God, or rather a crowd of unconnected expressions, broken sentences, ejaculations, entreaties, complaints, and promises; one of those addresses which are never made to men, because they have not sufficient quickness to understand them, nor patience to listen to them; they are not great enough to feel compassion without contempt" (596).

So different is Christian love from fallen man's hobbled parody of it, that that difference alone must lend ample opportunity for irony. Christian authors often show their lovers failing, like Dido, to understand their own hearts; but, unlike Dido, they are judged by a love that does not also hate. Often, like Sidney's Astrophil, they think they love and do not; sometimes, like Greene's whisky priest (*The Power and the Glory*), or his British policeman Scobie (*The Heart of the Matter*), or the birthmarked rationalist (*The End of the Affair*), they think they do not love, when they do. And sometimes, in the grace of God, when all hope has vanished, a hater may learn to love in truth. But even had Adam never fallen, there would have been irony in our experience of love. That is because God's love soars beyond our comprehension, and is the foundation and the aim of all our loves. We would inevitably have had much to learn.

The Insignificant Center

> What is man, that thou art mindful of him? and the son of man, that
> thou visitest him?
> For thou hast made him a little lower than the angels. . . . (Ps. 8:4–5)

Christians celebrate a truth at once humbling and exalting: that the redemption of man should be the motive behind the history of the world. The audacity staggers the mind. All the wars, migrations, inventions, bustlings of trade, all the famines and plagues, all the bright flowerings of prosperity, are at most instrumental in the accomplishment of what history really is for, the salvation of souls.

But man is not the center of God's plan because man is important. Christians can cite plenty of Scripture to trounce the notion that man, in himself, deserves to be waited on by the Creator. Rather, man is important because he is at the center of God's plan, and he is so, not because he merits it, but because God in his love has willed it. The universe turns about God's love, and that love happens to be aimed at sinful, undeserving man. That includes the ceaseless activity of the ministering angels, beings of intellectual power unimaginably superior to man's. Thus, as Christians see it, to remove us from the center of the story of the world is to reject the heart of it all: God's love. It is to take the pale defendant from the witness box, where he was the target of perhaps more judgment and more mercy than he could bear.

Thus the inverted irony of the Christian message. It is wholly inappropriate that we created beings, mere dust, and sinful dust at that, should be the center of anything, let alone the history of salvation. Yet for that very reason, sinners show forth the love and mercy of God. The angels, fallen or steadfast, are but peripheral to this drama of ashes and glory. We are most fittingly at the center of things precisely because we have no reason to be. That irony is at the heart of the poetry of George Herbert, to whom we turn.

Reasonable Damnation, Unreasonable Love: Herbert's *The Temple*

LET US BEGIN WITH the final poem of Herbert's volume *The Temple*, as it will show us most clearly the love for which we have been made. In "Love (III)," the soul is the "reasonable" party, and Love—Christ—is the gentle but firm ironist. The poem is a dramatic dialogue between the mere man, who is right about everything, and Christ, who makes everything right. Here is the poem in its entirety. (Here and throughout, I have modernized Herbert's orthography.)

> Love bade me welcome, but my soul drew back,
>   Guilty of dust and sin.
> But quick-eyed Love, observing me grow slack
>   From my first entrance in,
> Drew nearer to me, sweetly questioning
>   If I lacked anything.
>
> "A guest," I answered, "worthy to be here."
>   Love said, "You shall be he."
> "I, the unkind, ungrateful? Ah my dear,
>   I cannot look on thee."
> Love took my hand, and smiling made reply,
>   "Who made the eyes, but I?"
>
> "Truth, Lord, but I have marred them: let my shame
>   Go where it doth deserve."
> "And know you not," says Love, "who bore the blame?"
>   "My dear, then I will serve."
> "You must sit down," says Love, "and taste my meat."
>   So I did sit and eat.

"Love bade me welcome," says the speaker, and we should not be too hasty to personify this love. Christ bids him welcome, but as an act of love, because there is no reason why the soul should be welcome. In truth, he is not "well come," and he knows it: "Yet my soul drew back, / Guilty of dust and sin." That soul may be timid, but its timidity is rational. It fears the center, as a poorly dressed man would fear the spotlight. It is afraid to be loved, and knows it should not be loved. How much more fitting it would be if the soul could slink away to the justice it deserves.

Fitting indeed, for this soul flatly cites Scripture to its own damnation: it is "guilty of dust and sin." Into this one strange phrase (how is one guilty of "dust"?), Herbert compacts a theology of justice. He alludes to Christ's parable comparing the kingdom of God to a wedding feast that a king gave for his son. When one of the guests arrived unsuitably dressed for the occasion, the king ordered him bound hand and foot and cast into the outer darkness, where there was wailing and gnashing of teeth (Matt. 22:11–13). To be "guilty of dust" is to be mortal, to suffer death, the wages of sin. The "dust" lies on the clothing of the arriving soul—but it is also what the body is made of, and what the body must return to as a consequence of sin. No sin, no offending dust; but there is sin, and so there is death, and so there is also the dust of a deeper mortality that soils the garments we bring when we meet our Maker. We cannot fit ourselves for the wedding feast, just as we cannot bring ourselves to life. We are all that poor man in the parable.

The soul in Herbert's poem would courteously spare the king the trouble. It sees itself in that shameful light, and is eager to fall away from Love and embrace the darkness. The love of God is more terrifying than his justice: for in love his essence shines forth more radiantly. That love exalts dust. It raises the tattered mortality we are robed with, and it forgives sin when there is no reason in our natures or in the world why it should do either. The trans-logic of God's forgiveness is celebrated by Herbert's daring reversal of the parable from Scripture. The soul flings Christ's own words back at him, to prove why he should not show mercy! But, in seeming to violate his own just law, Love fulfills his just mercy, giving us what we cannot have expected, and thus, from Love, what is above all to be hoped.

Love is "quick-eyed"—as a solicitous bridegroom orchestrating the celebration, careful to observe any hesitation or discomfort among his guests. The lord of the universe, who spies the secrets of man's inmost heart, is here a cheerful, tactful young man, the prime servant for the feast held in his honor. That homely reduction is part of the message of the Incarnation and the Atonement: who would have thought that God could or would become man? The rational soul resists the invitation. No surprise: our rational souls, in action, are but bundles of pride laced up with a thread or two of logic. We do not deserve the invitation, we say, when secretly we feel that the invitation offends the high sense of our tragic insignificance. But if the soul will not move to the center, the center will move to it. So the young groom, the host of the feast, the Creator of life and light, asks the stunningly understated question: "Do you lack anything?"

How can such a question be answered? Love asks it, as if he were asking the newly arrived guest whether he needed a trifle, like a place to leave his coat, or a drink, or a chair. Yet, as with the phrase "guilty of dust and sin," the question implies a theology. In the presence of its redeemer the soul lacks *everything*. Christ's question is both invitation and gentle accusation. The speaker understands it so. What does he lack? Knowing that he falls infinitely short of the glory of God, and infinitely short of the love he owes to the Lord who has loved him, he fashions a reply which he thinks leaves no room for exception: "'A guest . . . worthy to be here.'"

The lack is not in what the speaker has, but in what he is. That lack is total. He himself, what God meant him to be, is lacking, is absent; all that remains is for the sinner he has become to make himself absent too. The speaker knows he lacks the slightest quality to merit the host's attention. But this host is called Love, and that literally *makes* a difference: "Love said, 'You shall be he.'" The sentence is not to be construed rhetorically. The soul will not simply be *considered* or *named* a worthy guest, but will actually *be* one, by the creative fiat of Love. What in an earthly host would be a polite pretense ("You are worthy after all") or a jocular exercise of authority ("You are worthy, because it's my day, and I say you are") is here a command and an act. Love supplies the lack, by making the speaker a worthy guest, drawing good not only out of evil, but out of nothingness.

Still the soul holds to its view of the fitness of things: "'I the unkind, ungrateful? Ah my dear, / I cannot look on thee.'" Why should it be loved? It is not natural, for the soul has been "unkind," a perversion of its "kind" or "nature," a frustration of its innate purpose. It is not just, for the soul has scorned or misused the free gifts of God, ungratefully returning evil for good. The last thing ingratitude merits is another free gift, another grace; the last thing unkindness can arouse is the warmth of natural affection.

Yet the soul, overcome with shame and love, utters its truest and least calculated phrase: "'Ah my dear.'" In this phrase the speaker acknowledges the transcendent worth of Christ: he is "dear" or "priceless," the one whose precious blood redeemed or bought us back from the bondage of sin. He also confesses that he longs for Christ as the only object of his deepest and truest love. Yet he uses the phrase as a way of excusing himself from love! One endearing irony of Christian love is that it should be at once so modest and so bold, as the bride in the Song of Songs who, drunk with love, dares to ask her Creator and Redeemer for a kiss. With the exclamation "ah my dear" the soul wavers in its small rationality. It moves uncertainly between the shy bravery of true love and the proud diffidence of rejection. The soul is that of a sinner, caught between desire and disdain; wanting much to be loved, and wanting much not to be loved. On its own it can do nothing. All is up to Love, who takes the speaker's hand. The gesture is firmly paternal and gently respectful of the poor sinner's dignity. Then Love fixes the speaker's gaze with a smile, and, not scorning to use the lowly pun as an instrument of grace, asserts his sovereignty over all things material and spiritual: "'Who made the eyes but I?'"

At this, the speaker's last hold upon his paltry dignity slips away. A note of desperation enters his abrupt reply: "'Truth, Lord, but I have marred them: let my shame / Go where it doth deserve.'" Herbert touches upon a psychological profundity that only the strongest believers or the strongest resisters perceive: most souls would find it more comfortable not to be saved. The speaker does not plead justice, though that is the logical content of his plea. He begs for mercy, the mercy of mere justice! He argues for justice as a strange form of compassion. "Look at how filthy I am," says the embarrassed beloved. "Please, please let me leave this place. I deserve no better." But the soul leans upon a straw, in calling the name of justice for mercy's sake, and instead is reminded that the claims of justice have already been mercifully fulfilled: "'And know you not,' says Love, 'who bore the blame?'"

Of course the soul knows, to its anguish. Beaten from his last ward, the speaker capitulates, but upon condition: "'My dear, then I will serve.'" I will agree to my salvation, so long as I retain the appropriate judgment attendant upon my sin. Since I do not deserve to be here, if I must be here, let me be saved only somewhat. Let me, in a dainty reserve that looks like humility, serve the others, and thus not be so searing a focus of Love. Yet even that will not do. For Love is jealous, and will have all. "'You must sit down,' says Love, 'and taste my meat.'" You must submit to your exaltation. Emptying yourself of all self-centered judgments of worthiness or unworthiness, you must allow yourself to be the center of Love's attention. You, Simon Peter, must have your feet washed. You must be served by Love.

It is fitting that Herbert should recall that moment at the Last Supper. In "Love" we have the servant, Christ, present at his wedding feast, at which he himself, the Paschal sacrifice, is served. As Love by his own power supplies the worthy guest, so Love himself is the feast he serves. Christ's giving of himself is not figurative. When Love insists that the soul taste "his meat," he means not the food that belongs to him, but the food he is: "For my flesh is meat indeed, and my blood is drink indeed" (John 6:55). Love invites the soul to taste of Love, to be nourished by it, to be refreshed and re-created by it. So it is both true and misleading to say that the salvation of an individual soul is the center of Herbert's Christian universe. The soul attains that honored rank, or rather is granted that honored rank, by emptying itself, rejecting the decisiveness of its sin, and accepting Christ, who is center and circumference both. The human is subsumed in Incarnation: in sharing this great communion, it is not the man who assimilates the food to himself, but the food that assimilates the man to itself. Of all the mysteries of God's love for his people, this is the most improbable. There is nothing left to say. The poem and Herbert's volume end on a note of submission and sublime simplicity: "'So I did sit and eat.'"

Why should God so love the human soul? I do not know. If I thought I knew, I would not be Christian.

A Crisis of Love

THE EUCHARISTIC CELEBRATION THAT crowns Herbert's *The Temple* is a re-enactment of his long dramatic poem, "The Sacrifice." Presented near the beginning of *The Temple*, "The Sacrifice" provides a thematic and emotional bass against which the other lyrics may be heard. This poem recounts, from Christ's both human and divine view, the act of self-sacrificial love that makes the assemblage in "Love (III)" a feast and not merely a judgment.

For our purposes, what is remarkable about "The Sacrifice" is the extent to which Herbert takes advantage, for bitterly ironic purposes, of the chasm between what Christ knows about his agony and what his tormentors and accusers think they know about it. He turns the ancient litany of the Improperia—the "impropers," the reproaches Christ delivers to his misbelieving people—and hammers and twists them into intellectual and theological barbs. For man has repaid God's love with evil, and God repays man's evil with love. The irony works a double-reverse: man derives his very life from God, yet repays him by killing the Son. In return for this ingratitude, and even by means of the ingratitude, the God-made-man suffers to bring man life again. Man gives God what God does not deserve—evil. So God gives man what man does not deserve—good. It is propriety in impropriety. And all the while, strutting in his gaudy rags upon a stage of sticks and rubble, man thinks himself the world's wise and just ruler. But that is the way of men, as the Lord shrewdly observed (see Luke 22:25). We flatter our oppressors, and curse the One who would do us well.

Such harsh ironies require a harsh and cunning meter, and Herbert's choice is perfect. Each of the stanzas of this poem is a rhyming triplet in iambic pentameter, followed by the unrhymed refrain "Was ever grief like mine?" taken from the Lamentations of Jeremiah (1:12), the traditional reading for Good Friday services. The third line of a triplet is ideal for ironic reversal, surprising commentary, or dramatic climax, while the short austere stanza, with its ritual refrain, strikes with the oppressive power and monotony of a litany. The effect is like that achieved by a similar hymn in thundering triplets, the *Dies Irae*. What keeps the poem from lapsing into stasis or fruitless repetition is its inexorable march—interrupted by meditation, outcry, and judgment—from Gethsemane to the cross. Thus the small climaxes themselves surge towards the only moment that gives them meaning.

Condemned by His Own Creatures

"THE SACRIFICE" IS TOO long a poem to treat in full, but a few examples will show how the stanzas work and the ironies they cast before the guilty reader. Here Jesus recalls how the Jews accused him before the high priest Caiaphas:

> Some said, that I the Temple to the floor
> In three days raz'd, and raised as before.
> Why, he that built the world can do much more:
> Was ever grief like mine? (65–68)

The first two lines, a complete couplet, present the accusation. It is a piece of misunderstanding by the Jews. Jesus had said, "Destroy this temple, and in three days I will raise it up," referring, as the evangelist John glosses, to "the temple of his body" (John 2:19, 21). But the Jews assume that Jesus is speaking of the Temple of Solomon, the house of God among His people, which had taken thousands of men forty-six years to build. The irony in John's gospel is that, as often, the Jews and Jesus are talking at cross-purposes. But that is not exactly the irony of Herbert's stanza. There, Christ does not admit he was speaking metaphorically. Quite the contrary, the *razed/raised* pun suggests that the Jews were not far off the mark. When Christ *raised* the Temple (of his body) after three days, he *razed* the Temple (of Old Testament worship) to the floor, to be rebuilt under the New Covenant. And this *razing* and *raising* occur through the punishment insisted upon by the Temple-defenders themselves.

The new Temple recalls the name of Herbert's volume, *The Temple*, and suggests not only a church which the believer must enter, but a sacrifice and a body, a part of which it is the believer's privilege to become. The Temple is the resurrected Body of Christ.

Thus, the third line, "Why, he that built the world can do much more," concedes nothing. To build a Temple in three days is impossible, practically, but it is still commensurable with building a Temple in three weeks, or three years, or forty-six years. All such periods of time are nothing to Christ, whose amen raised his body from the grave and razed temple worship as well, forever. That act is akin to the command that began the world; it is a new *fiat lux*. He that built the physical world (whoever he may be, says Jesus, with mock ignorance) can trifle with the two or three grains of sand that make up Solomon's Temple. He can, in fact, wholly alter what that Temple is and what it is for. The world itself, his own building, he can tear down and recreate in three days, if he should wish.

In effect, Christ pleads guilty to the charge which, rightly understood, is a promise of redemption. But the Jews treat it as blasphemy:

> Then they condemn me all with that same breath,
> Which I do give them daily, unto death.
> Thus Adam my first breathing rendereth:
>   Was ever grief like mine? (69–72)

Man cannot even reject and despise his Savior without the strength, the life, and the breath that the Savior gives him. Without that mercy, we could not rail against the Merciful. Thus, much of the irony of this stanza is clear. Yet when we examine the first sentence closely, we detect a strange ambiguity, one that makes the allusion to Adam in the third line most appropriate. Herbert means either, "Then they condemn me all unto death, with that same breath which I do give them daily" (the sense most people will make of the sentence upon a first reading), or "Then they condemn me all—with that same breath which I do give them daily, until *they die*" (the more provocative sense, but no less plausible than the other). The tension between these two readings is resolved by the figure of Adam.

When Adam disobeyed, he did not die immediately, for the curse of death was mitigated by mercy. He was allowed to live for many years, sustained each day by his Savior, who had instilled in him his first breath: "And the Lord God formed man of the dust of the ground, and breathed into his nostrils the breath of life; and man became a living soul" (Gen. 2:7). Had Adam not sinned, the breath of life would never have failed him in the body; but because he sinned, the breath is given to him, as to all men, "unto death," only for a determinate time. When the breath fails, Adam must return to the dust (Gen. 3:19). All Adam's sons are in like condition. In justice, the dread punishment for sin should fall at once, and we should die. The Savior's merciful will alone keeps breath in our bodies. It is as if Herbert were punning on the humble prayer the Lord instructed us to pray: "Give us this day our daily *breath*"!

To summarize: Christ breathes the breath of life into Adam, and he becomes a living soul. Adam repays God by disobeying him. Pronouncing sentence, God yet allows Adam and his descendants to live, though subject to sin and death. To redeem man from sin and death, the Savior enters the world as a man. Men use their "daily" breath, or "render" God's gift of life back to him, by condemning the Savior to die. Specifically, the Jews, instructed by Jesus to "render to Caesar the things that are Caesar's, and to God the things that are God's," shamefully display their supposed loyalty to their Roman overlords, rendering to Caesar their own Messiah. But through that same death, against man's consummate sin, the Savior performs his work, and gives man life again.

Stories of Love

IF ALL THIS SOUNDS straightforward, it is only because the story is familiar. Once again, to recapture the startling ironies of the Christian story of salvation, we almost have to forget what we know—for it is a story, and ironies abound.

The Jews understood that their religion was the story of God's dealings with them: "We will [show] to the generation to come the praises of the LORD, and his strength, and his wonderful works that he hath done." (Ps. 78:4). The ancient Christians understood it, too. As I have noted, they read the Scriptures *typologically*, trusting that the histories composing the Bible were all parts of one grand history, and thus were meant to shed light upon one another. In particular, events and figures in the Old Testament represented shadowy *types*, anticipations, imperfect symbols, intimations of events and figures in the New Testament. Thus, the church fathers were not engaging in fanciful, arbitrary exegesis when they saw in Noah's flood a type or prefiguring of baptism and of the Last Judgment, or when they saw in the swallowing of Jonah by the whale a prefiguring of Christ's death and resurrection. It is exactly what we ourselves do as readers when we assume that the author knows what he is doing. The Bible blesses such reading. Christ practices it (see Luke 17:26–32), and he, as Christians must believe, is the Son of God, the Author who has woven the interconnections from the beginning.

Nowadays, typological reading is dismissed as childish by the professional Bible interpreter, who prides himself on what he calls, in a stunning bit of question-begging, his more accurate "history." What can the bronze serpent in the desert (Num. 21:9) really, which is to say *historically*, which is to say *according to a naturalistic interpretation of causes and effects*, have to do with the death of Christ on the cross? But the typological reader is more historical than the historicist, because he sees the *story* in the *history*, while the historicist rules the story out from the start.

So when, in "The Sacrifice," Herbert relies upon typology, he is not merely playing clever games with his text, as poets of the seventeenth century were wont to do. Rather, his keen eye for dramatic irony has caught a real truth in the story, an illuminating twist in the plot. Consider the lovely stanza linking the cross with the tree of life, but this time with a surprising shift of focus from ambitious man to disappointed Savior:

> O all ye who pass by, behold and see;
> Man stole the fruit, but I must climb the tree;
> The tree of life to all, but only me:
> Was ever grief like mine?

Once again, the ironies build upon each other until they reach the accusatory climax. Man sinned by eating the fruit of the tree of knowledge. God punished man with death, driving him out of Eden and preventing him from sealing his sin by eating also of the tree of life. To atone for that sin, Christ—God-made-man to stand in man's place—must climb the gallows tree. But that tree, the cross, is the true tree of life to all. To all, that is, except to the only One who does not need to partake of it. To him alone that tree means death. Herbert means to jolt us into a grievous awareness of our guilt, forcing us to view the theology of the crucifixion as flowing from, and subordinate to, the terrible fact, the terrible *story* of the crucifixion. It is to reverse the comfortable direction of interpretation. We like to think that Christ's death means our salvation. It is rather more disconcerting to think that our salvation meant Christ's death.

But Herbert will not ease up on us. He continues with the Genesis typology, all the more to plunge us in the agony of the re-creating Christ:

> Lo, here I hang, charg'd with a world of sin,
> The greater world o' th' two; for that came in
> By words, but this by sorrow I must win:
>   Was ever grief like mine?

A "world of sin" weighs upon the shoulders of Christ, who takes it up as his load, his charge. That world is heavier than the physical universe, says Herbert; and it is a greater and more grievous thing to redeem that world than to have created the other. If we think those words were great at whose sound the stars and the sun and the earth leapt into being, then how much greater must be the grief that makes a new creation of the world of sin, "the greater world o' th' two"? When Love suffers to redeem the world, we lack the mind to conceive or the tongue to utter the grandeur.

Herbert answers this question with an image of the final annihilation:

> Such sorrow, as if sinful man could feel,
> Or feel his part, he would not cease to kneel
> Till all were melted, though he were all steel:
>   Was ever grief like mine?

If we could know not the sorrow, but our own part in causing it, we would kneel till the dissolution of the world, or, what in one sense is the same thing, till the melting of our hard hearts. Thus, in these two stanzas, creation and original sin look forward, through the sacrifice of Christ, to the last day and, we hope, to repentance. Of those two, Herbert leaves unclear which is the more tremendous.

Before we leave "The Sacrifice," the reader might be interested to see the stanza that immediately follows the previous one. It is the climax of Christ's grief, so unspeakable that Herbert would sooner break the pattern of his stanzas than record Christ's words:

> But, *O my God, my God!* why leav'st thou me,
> The son, in whom thou dost delight to be?
> *My God, my God—*
>   Never was grief like mine.

At such a moment it is best to bow with Herbert and say nothing.

Beware, Lest Love Answer Your Call

IT WAS ONE OF C. S. Lewis's great insights that goodness is more terrifying than we imagine. "After all, he's wild. Not like a *tame* lion, you know," says Mr. Beaver of Aslan (*The Lion, the Witch, and the Wardrobe*, 182). Much the same can be said about love. If John's assertion that "God is Love" does not strike us as a fearful mystery, it is probably because we have tamed the Lion of love. We know what the tame lion will do: he will do what we want. But if we call to mind the tremendous other-ness of God, we see that to love him and to be loved by him is to involve ourselves in a story over which we have no control. The gap between our power and God's power, and between our knowledge and God's knowledge, would make it madness in us to court him, were it not for the inconvenient fact that he has created us just for that dangerous madness. We were made to love the *wild* Lion.

So when it comes to this greatest of love stories, there must be a curious disjunction between what we think we will find when we fall in love with God, and what God gives us. That disjunction is the subject of Herbert's blunt poem "Affliction (I)." It is the story of a love affair turned bitter. The speaker sees himself as duped by the Lord, who lured him with joys and then delivered him over to cross upon cross. Thus, there are two narratives at odds in the poem: the story of the speaker's life as it should have unfolded had God only followed the simplest rules of poetic, not to say moral, justice; and the story of the speaker's life as it is. The ironic contrast is so stark that any reasonably worldly person must agree that the affair must be broken off. But that is impossible. The speaker is loved by God, and must love God in return, whether he likes it or not.

In the beginning all was bright and hopeful:

> When first thou didst entice to thee my heart,
>   I thought the service brave:
> So many joys I writ down for my part,
>   Besides what I might have
> Out of my stock of natural delights,
> Augmented with thy gracious benefits. (1–6)

Notice that the object of *entice* is not me but "my heart." From the first, the poem presents itself as a lesson in disappointed love. Yet there could be no disappointment unless there remained some love, too; for if God enticed the speaker's heart to fall in love with him, the word "first" suggests that he did not stop there. But the speaker took the lure, half in love with vanity, with his vision of himself beloved by a generous, predictable, and appreciative deity. He "writ down" those joys, as if he had been his own providence.

Devastating ironist that he is, God plays along with the speaker's plot, for that, at first, is the best way to nourish his newborn love. It is also appropriate for God's larger purposes. To convict the speaker of sin, and thereby to win him utterly, God allows the man to know what a keen pleasure it is to have one's will in all things:

> At first thou gav'st me milk and sweetnesses;
> I had my wish and way;
> My days were straw'd with flowers and happiness;
> There was no month but May.
> But with my years sorrow did twist and grow,
> And made a party unawares for woe. (7–12)

The "milk and sweetnesses" refer to the instructional methods of Saint Paul. New believers are given easily digestible truths, like pablum for babies: "I have yet fed you with milk, and not with meat: for hitherto ye were not able to bear it, neither yet now are ye able. For ye are yet carnal" (1 Cor. 3:2–3). Thus, the early good fortune the speaker enjoyed was, as he now sees, but a temporary stage in his education. God gives the speaker what the speaker *thinks* is most appropriate for a believer, "milk and sweetnesses," but what is really only appropriate for a neophyte. God wishes his beloved to grow past May; the speaker thinks May is all there is.

But had there been "no month but May," the speaker could not be redeemed. For quietly sprouting up alongside his youth are the tares of sorrow. Herbert recalls the parable of the farmer whose enemy sowed weeds in his field. His servants ask, should the tares be pulled up? "Nay; lest while ye gather up the tares, ye root up also the wheat with them. Let both grow together until the harvest: and in the time of harvest I will say to the reapers, Gather ye together first the tares, and bind them in bundles to burn them: but gather the wheat into my barn" (Matt. 13:29–30). The Lord allows these sorrows, sown by the enemy, to spring up beside the wheat. Strong remedies await; it is not yet time for such love. But even in May there are things the speaker does not see. And the year will go on.

Affliction and Love

THIS, THEN, IS HERBERT'S answer to the question, "Why am I afflicted?": "Because God loves you." Don't call the answer flippant or glib. It means more than "God knows what is best for you, so afflictions must be blessings." It is precisely the crux of the matter that the speaker and the infinite Creator do not yet agree on what that "best" is. The speaker wants more than his wish: he wants his way. And that, were it the holiest way in the world, is exactly what God who loves him cannot allow. From the speaker's point of view, God has withheld all the promises of love. From God's point of view, the speaker has withheld from him his whole heart. Disillusionment is the speaker's; but the rage of unrequited love, that is the Lord's.

Yet it is a steady, wise anger, this of the Lord. He does not simply plunge the speaker into grief. No, he betrays him with prospects of ease or respite or unanticipated praise, luring him back to "the service" as he once lured him with the knickknacks of the ministry. Then he takes those gifts away again:

> Thus doth thy power cross-bias me, not making
> Thy own gift good, but me from my ways taking.

"As many as I love, I rebuke and chasten," says the Lord (Rev. 3:19). Because of the example of Christ, the converse must also be true: "Whom I do not cross, whom I do not make conform to me in my suffering, I do not love." At every step, God uses mercy and chastisement to "cross-bias" the speaker, to run athwart his way, and make that way finally the way of the cross. That love of God re-makes the speaker, taking him out of his own will. God loves the speaker even as he is, and that is why he will move heaven and earth lest he remain so.

How should the heart respond to so destructive a love? I use the word "destructive" advisedly, since there can be no building the new without burning, razing, leveling, and burying the old. The speaker sees the unreasonableness of his complaints, and knows he must thank God for what he suffers. Still, he is only human, and he chafes. If this is love, it makes no sense to love. One had better bestow one's heart elsewhere:

> Yet, though thou troublest me, I must be meek;
> In weakness must be stout.
> Well, I will change the service, and go seek
> Some other master out.

The first two lines are an exasperated repetition of well-known doctrine, and a protest. Well and good that the Christian must be "stout" in "weakness," but how? Herbert gives no answers here. The speaker seeks not answers but ease. So he indulges the same error with which he began his love affair: the illusion that it is he who has chosen God, not God who has chosen him. It is not a matter of breaking a business partnership, or even of running away from a harsh master—and there is, ominously enough, only one "other master" he can run to. The speaker knows all this, and is as far from wanting release as the Lord is from granting it:

> Ah my dear God! though I be clean forgot,
> Let me not love thee, if I love thee not.

That final line of the poem is no tautology. Herbert equivocates on the word "love," exactly as his model Sir Philip Sidney had done in *Astrophil and Stella*:

> O Doctor Cupid, thou for me reply,
> Driv'n else to grant by Angel's sophistry,
> That I love not, without I leave to love. (61.12–14)

Let me explain the allusion, to help illustrate what Herbert is doing. Sidney's narrator Astrophil has received a troubling lesson from Stella, the chaste married woman whom he woos to no avail. It is simply that if Astrophil truly *loved* Stella, his soul and his senses would be captive to her, and then, rather than seek to impose his desires upon her, he would learn from her what those desires were to be. Astrophil understands the lesson perfectly well, which is why he scorns it as "Angel's sophistry." He has no reply, but hopes, with humorous pathos, that that renowned doctor of philosophy, Cupid, will know what to say. As he characterizes the scene, Stella's angelic beauty is so great that, without the wisdom of Cupid to assist him, he would be compelled to accept wordplay as truth. How, after all, can you only begin to love when you have left off loving? But the implied question is foolish. It is itself a piece of childish sophistry. The very point that Stella is trying to make is that the word "love" does not always mean the same thing. She equivocates in order to teach Astrophil that what he calls love is not the truest love. The play on the word is meant to highlight the distinction.

It Is One Thing to Love, and Another Thing to Love

IF HUMAN AFFAIRS ADMIT of such equivocation, much more so must the love between God and man. I refer not only to the linguistic difficulty in using finite words to describe a transcendent, infinite God. Rather I mean that, although the love of man for God may be distantly analogous to the love of God for man, yet for all practical purposes man's *experiences* of those loves are terribly unlike. If God loves with a consuming, destructive, purgative, creative, jealous love, then if that love is at all analogous to our love it demands to be answered by a self-annihilating, utterly obedient and surrendering love. Yet that kind of love is hardly what we typically feel when we love; we even shrink from it with a kind of disgust. We want to have what we love. We do not want to be had by what loves us.

Something of this disjunction is preserved in Herbert's final line, which avoids tautology precisely because of the incommensurability of God's love and man's love. To ruin the epigram by paraphrasing it, this is what Herbert means, as I read him: "My dear God, please, if I find it not in my heart to surrender myself wholly to you (if I love thee not), then take away this longing that I feel for you (let me not love thee), so that with a free conscience I may forget myself and you in my search for a better master." But the exclamation undermines itself. It is addressed to the "dear God" as a plea from the beloved to the implacable and inscrutable lover. It is God alone, then, who can "let" the speaker not love him; yet the form of the speaker's plea affirms that love. The grand irony is that the speaker, who knows that his affliction would be eased immediately if he did not love God, cannot cease loving God, nor does he really desire to cease loving him.

There is another possibility. Perhaps the tense of the verbs is equivocal. The speaker does love God, and curses himself should it ever turn out otherwise. And that worst affliction, the worst imaginable, would be this: the failure to love God! Thus the sentence would read: "Ah, my dear God, even though I have completely forgotten myself in my complaining against your treatment of me, I do still love you. And if I do not love you *now*, do your worst, and that is, let me not love you *hereafter*." The riddle is clear, and reveals the gulf between God and man. There is nothing better, and nothing worse, than to be loved by God; so there is no longing so piercing, no joy so rapturous, as to love God in return. Affliction is but to be expected from a love so painful. Says the apostle: "It is a fearful thing to fall into the hands of the living God" (Heb. 10:31). Fearful it may be; but hope cries out:

> Call to remembrance the former days, in which, after ye were illuminated, ye endured a great fight of afflictions;
>
> Partly, whilst ye were made a gazingstock both by reproaches and afflictions; and partly, whilst ye became companions of them that were so used.
>
> For ye had compassion of me in my bonds, and took joyfully the spoiling of your goods, knowing in yourselves that ye have in heaven a better and an enduring substance.
>
> Cast not away therefore your confidence, which hath great recompense of reward.
>
> For ye have need of patience, that, after ye have done the will of God, ye might receive the promise.
>
> For yet a little while, and he that shall come will come, and will not tarry. (Heb. 10:32–37)

As the speaker began the poem, his greatest disappointment was that his love affair with the Lord did not end at the beginning. Now, as he accepts his afflictions, his greatest hope is that it will truly begin only at the end.

Love on a Starry Night

IT IS AN ADVENTURE to be loved by God—to be racked from dust to infinity, as Herbert puts it. But God has also huddled himself from the infinite into a tiny enclosure of dust. What Love has in store for man, then, is shown in reverse by that wondrous moment when God made himself capable of incapacity, when he who uttered the words that created the universe became, for love of man, a little child that could not speak. Such tenderness is a new thing in this old hard world. And Herbert understands its healing balm in a life full of loves that disappoint. Here is his poem "Christmas," made up of a sonnet and a song to follow:

> All after pleasures as I rid one day,
>> My horse and I, both tir'd, body and mind,
>> With full cry of affections, quite astray;
> I took up in the next inn I could find.
> There when I came, whom found I but my dear,

My dearest Lord, expecting till the grief
    Of pleasures brought me to him, ready there
To be all passengers' most sweet relief?

O Thou, whose glorious, yet contracted light,
    Wrapt in night's mantle, stole into a manger;
    Since my dark soul and brutish is thy right,
To Man of all beasts be thou not a stranger:

    Furnish and deck my soul, that thou mayst have
    A better lodging than a rack, or grave.

The shepherds sing; and shall I silent be?
    My God, no hymn for thee?
My soul's a shepherd too; a flock it feeds
    Of thoughts, and words, and deeds.
The pasture is thy word: the streams, thy grace
    Enriching all the place.
Shepherd and flock shall sing, and all my powers
    Outsing the day-light hours.
Then we will chide the sun for letting night
    Take up his place and right:
We sing one common Lord; wherefore he should
    Himself the candle hold.
I will go searching, till I find a sun
    Shall stay, till we have done;
A willing shiner, that shall shine as gladly,
    As frost-nipt suns look sadly.
Then we will sing, and shine all our own day,
    And one another pay:
His beams shall cheer my breast, and both so twine,
Till ev'n his beams sing, and my music shine.

The speaker is a man in love, spurring his horse hard, and what does it bring him? Weariness of body and mind, and worse. To give the horse free rein, in "the full cry of affections," is to go astray, to come to grief. "The grief of pleasures" the speaker calls it, having felt how compulsively and desperately we can love what we do not love, and pursue what holds us in its unbreakable and static clutch. He rides after pleasures, and the ride takes him into the middle of nowhere.

Thank God for grief. It has cleared the mind of many a prodigal son. We lose ourselves, and in that loss we may be found. Here the speaker, benighted and lost, manages to find somewhere to stay: "I took up in the next inn I could find." Herbert recalls the account of the Nativity: Bethlehem was thronged with travelers coming to register for the census, so when Joseph and Mary arrived in the evening they had to rest in a stable, for there was no room for them in the inn (Luke 2:7). Here in the poem, the Christ child already waits at the inn, the place of the man's disappointment. So says the speaker, with fine tenderness: "There when I came, whom found I but my dear, / My dearest Lord?" It is Christ and him alone whom the speaker has loved all along; as Christ has known, and the speaker has not. Indeed Christ is *himself* the inn for all of us weary wanderers by the way.

But in the last six lines of the sonnet, Herbert turns the metaphor about. We are lost, he has said, and Jesus is the next inn we can find. Yet Christ once "stole into a manger," wrapt not only in swaddling clothes but in the mantle of night, contracting his light and his glory. There in that manger he lay, born into the world, and, as the pious legend has it, the ox and the ass knelt to behold him. If Christ can steal into such a mean lodging, perhaps he might steal into the soul of man? It too is dark. The old stable was a place to house the innocent cattle; man's stable is brutish in its own right. Of all the poor beasts on earth, the speaker pleads, be not a stranger to man, be not a stranger to me!

For *man himself* is to be the inn where Christ will dwell; nor can man furnish it. The work is Christ's. In the final couplet of the sonnet we are shown that the quiet love now sleeping upon the hayrack, later to give himself to death to heal us his enemies, is meant also to dwell within us. The speaker has begun his poem by stopping at any way station, the first he can find, in the whirl of a life whose pleasures skirt the marches of death. He ends the sonnet by praying that he may be remade within, to give his Lord a fitter dwelling than Bethlehem (and Jerusalem) once afforded him. So will the Lord furnish them who ask: "Abide in me, and I in you" (John 15:4).

In the song that follows—a song that could never be sung without the pasture of God's word and the nourishing streams of grace—the joyful speaker will not rest content with the short, "frost-nipt" sun of late winter. His joy will sing forever, crowding out the night, calling upon the sun to hold its candle steady before the glorious light of the Lord. But if the sun cannot do that, he says, he will search out another, punning on "son": he will find a *sun* that shall "stay, till we have done." How can one have done in praising God? That day, "all our own day," is the everlasting day of joy that never sets. On that day Love is made perfect in us: not that we are filled with God as from without, but that we will be one with God, loving and loved. Then will our loves be harmonized all, one with another. Then, says the singing shepherd, my music will shine, and the beams of the Lord will sing. We go to the dwelling place of the infinite Lord, who makes his dwelling place within us.

15

The True Eros

The Kisses of His Mouth

IS EROTIC DESIRE MERELY a convenient vehicle for expressing the love with which God pursues the human heart, or with which the heart longs for God? Or does it suggest something essential about God as he has revealed himself? God loves. This is the clear message of the Old and New Testament: "For I am persuaded that neither death, nor life, nor angels, nor principalities, nor powers, nor things present, nor things to come, nor height, nor depth, nor any other creature, shall be able to separate us from the love of God, which is in Christ Jesus our Lord" (Rom. 8:39). It is an ardent love that desires union: "[I pray] that they all may be one; as thou, Father, art in me, and I in thee, that they also may be one in us" (John 17:21).

If marriage is a symbol of the church, then the sexual love that expresses itself within marriage is an appropriate symbol for Christ's love for the church. Further, if each marriage is an image of the union of Christ with the church, then love in marriage must in itself be holy. Christian charity exalts and perfects eros. It does not obliterate it.

When, for example, Bernard of Clairvaux wrote his *Commentary on the Song of Songs*, he read that sensuous poem as an allegory of the soul's longing for her lover, Christ. But his reading heightened the sensuousness. Far from taming the Song of Songs, he read it with such theological eros that by comparison any merely bawdy tale would seem tame. Here, from Sermon 7, is his exegesis of the first line:

> She loves most chastely who seeks him whom she loves and not some other thing which belongs to him. She loves in a holy way, because she does not love in fleshly desire but in purity of spirit. She loves ardently, because she is drunk with love so that she cannot see his majesty. What? He it is "who looks on the earth and causes it to tremble" [Ps. 103:32]. And she asks him for a kiss? Is she drunk? Indeed she is! And perhaps then when she burst forth thus she had come out of the wine-cellar [Sg. 1:3, 2:4]. She said afterward that she had been there, glorying in it. For David, too, said to God concerning such, "They shall be intoxicated with the plenty of your house, and you will give them the torrents of your pleasure to drink" [Ps. 35:9]. Oh, what force of love! What great confidence of spirit! What freedom! (3.3)

We might add, what shamelessness! Bernard is well aware of what separates the sinful soul from the majesty of God. Only love so ardent that it supersedes prudence and logic could presume to ask for a kiss. Logic must yield in humility. The seraphim burn in love, the cherubim burn in wisdom; and the seraphim are closer to the divine vision than the cherubim. The wedding feast of the Lamb will be no meek affair.

Notice that Bernard's ardent bride is described as free. What does that mean? Doubtless, she is "free" with her speech and her desires. She tosses caution to the wind. She loves and demands love in return. If she were hungering after a man rather than after the Lord of hosts, we should call her a little too free! But such freedom as she claims is all to her credit. She makes free with her speech because the Lord she loves wants her to be free. As he is not prim, so does he not want primness in return. Her freedom sets her free.

Bernard was no lone oddity in the Middle Ages. We could fill hundreds of pages with poetry and devotional writing from those years, all aflame with love for Christ, and joyously using the most sensuous imagery of eros to describe that love. Francis of Assisi, Bonaventure, Julian of Norwich, the great Dante, and even that most careful of logicians Thomas Aquinas all use such imagery, often with abandon. But sometimes one little devotional song, written by no one knows whom, reveals more about the lived faith of a people than will the poetry and philosophy of the learned few. Consider this by no means unique poem from fourteenth-century England:

> When I see blosmes spring
> And here foules song,
> A swete love-longing
> Min herte thourghout stong,
> All for a love newe,
> That is so swete and trewe,
> That gladieth all my song;
> Ich wot all mid iwisse
> My joye and eke my blisse
> On him is all ilong.
>
> When I miselve stonde
> And with min eyen seo
> Thurled fot and honde
> With grete nailes threo—
> Blody wes his heved;
> On him nes nout bileved,
> That wes of peines freo—
> Well well oghte min herte
> For his love to smerte
> And sike and sory beo. (*Middle English Lyrics*, 107)

My transcription:

> When I see blossoms spring
> And hear the birds' song too,
> A sweet love-longing
> Pierces my heart through,
> All for a love so new,
> That is so sweet and true,
> It gladdens all my song.
> Certainly I know this,
> My joy and my bliss,
> All in him belong.
>
> When by myself I stand
> And with my eyes I see
> Him pierced both foot and hand
> With great nails three—
> His head was covered with blood,
> In him was thought no good,
> Who was in pain so free—

> Well ought my heart
> For his love to smart
> And sigh and sorry be.

These are the first two stanzas of a lovely little poem which needs no interpretation, only thanks for the heart that composed it. Notice how naturally the poet moves from springtime to love to the sorrows of Christ. It is as if it were only to be expected, when the first crocuses poke through the loosening soil, for the young soul to think of its beloved, its true love, "sweet Jesus." The same religion whose Christ is warrior and judge can also portray him as "Jesu, milde and swete." That is not surprising. Think of Bethlehem.

It can also, without embarrassment, portray Jesus as a handsome young knight proving his love in the world's tournament. So, in the thirteenth-century *Rule for Anchoresses*, Jesus woos the soul:

> "Your love," he says, "is either to be given wholly, or to sell, or to be ravished and seized by force. If it is to give, where can you bestow it better than upon me? Am I not of all things the fairest? Am I not of all kings the richest? Am I not of the highest lineage? Am I not the wisest of all wealthy men? Am I not among men the courtliest? Am I not with all things the noblest and freest? For so they say of a generous man who cannot hold anything back, that he has his hands — as mine are — pierced. Am I not of all things the sweetest and most fragrant? Thus all the reasons why men ought to love you may find in me, especially if you love chaste purity, for none may love me unless she hold that dear" (*Early Middle English Verse and Prose*, 243; translation mine).

The author is not merely using convenient imagery. He alludes thus to a saying of Augustine's: "So great is the difference between God's approach and man's approach to woman, that a man's approach makes a wife of a virgin, but God's makes a virgin of a wife" (242). As the poetry of John Donne brazenly asserts, God's is a more, not less, potent penetration:

> Take me to you, imprison me, for I,
> Except you enthrall me, never shall be free,
> Nor ever chaste, except you ravish me.
> ("Batter My Heart," 12–14; orthography normalized)

What, then, is the relationship between God's love for man and the love of man and woman for each other?

Whom Do You Love?

THAT QUESTION DEEPENS AND enriches the opportunities for irony that a narrative of love will inevitably present. For man never fully knows his own heart: Romeo is certain, absolutely certain there never will be another woman for him besides the Rosaline who has rejected him. Then he sees Juliet, and we know the rest. In George Eliot's *Middlemarch*, Dorothea Brooke, idealistic and passionate and young and (because she is young) sometimes very silly, marries an old scholar because she thinks she will assist him in his prodigious compendium of world mythology. She does not see that he is not much of a scholar, and will prove even less of a husband. Then she meets his kinsman, a curly blond artist. The shepherd Silvius in *As You Like It*, hopelessly in love with a shepherdess who scorns him, is asked whether he will take her if she will be compelled to consent. His reply reveals what he doesn't see, namely, what such a marriage would actually be like. Says the gallant lover: "Though to have her and death were both one thing" (5.4.17).

Now suppose we have the same calls to love—the same madness and confusion, the same wanting what we don't want, and rejecting what we really want. Suppose too there is a third man walking on this lovers' lane to Emmaus: Christ, who pursues the lovers though they are unaware of it, and may be pursuing them in accord with their love for one another, or at cross-purposes to it, thwarting what they think they love, that they may enjoy what they love indeed.

Those dramatic ironies have undergirded Christian literature of love since the Middle Ages. Nor need we return to the tortured soul of Lancelot to find it. The twentieth century, surprisingly enough, produced a small treasure of Christian literature of eros, almost always richly ironic. The fundamental plot of Graham Greene's theological novels presents a soul in love with God (though the person seldom understands or even confesses this love), yet running away from God, or attempting to run away, all while God himself is using love, no matter how earthly or confused or disappointing or tainted with sin, to snare the sinner with his own passions. So in *The Heart of the Matter*, a good man, Scobie the Just as they call him at the British outpost where he is the chief of police, compromises his purity by one step after another, taken in pity for the wife he thinks he no longer loves, and for the benefit of the frail young woman castaway whom he thinks he loves best of all. He will be checkmated by his own actions and by what appear to be disastrous events beyond his control, until finally the only way he can free both women is by committing suicide, feigning a fatal heart attack. He believes he is in the grip of despair: "This was what human love had done to him—it had robbed him of love for eternity. It was no use pretending as a young man might that the price was worth while" (280). But all along he is being pursued, relentlessly, by a love that grows stronger in its weakness, for it is the sufferer Christ who calls. When at last he takes the pills that will kill his heart, his heart beats all the faster as the lover knocks all the harder at the door:

> Somewhere far away he thought he heard the sounds of pain. "A storm," he said aloud, "there's going to be a storm," as the cloud grew, and he tried to get up to close the windows. "Ali," he called, "Ali." It seemed to him as though someone outside the room were seeking him, calling him, and he made a last effort to indicate that he was here. He got on his feet and heard the hammer of his heart beating out a reply. He had a message to convey, but the darkness and the storm drove it back within the case of his breast, and all the time outside the house, outside the world that drummed like hammer blows within his ear, someone wandered, seeking to get in, someone appealing for help, someone in need of him. And automatically at the call of need, at the cry of a victim, Scobie strung himself to act. He dredged his consciousness up from an infinite distance in order to make some reply. He said aloud, "Dear God, I love . . ." but the effort was too great and he did not feel his body when it struck the floor or hear the small tinkle of the medal as it span like a coin under the ice-box—the saint whose name nobody could remember. (265)

Greene leaves Scobie's last moment ambiguous: the man never did finish his sentence, but the fragmentary groan strongly suggests a final turn of the heart to God. The novel ends a few days after his death, with a conversation between Mrs. Scobie and the priest, neither of them sure that Scobie died of natural causes, the wife bitter against her husband yet worried that he has damned himself. But no one knows the mystery of the human heart, says the priest, which is to say, no one, not even oneself, can fully describe what love binds that heart to God, or what love has been destroyed in rejecting God:

> "You think there's some hope then?" she wearily asked.
> "Are you so bitter against him?"
> "I haven't any bitterness left."
> "And do you think God's likely to be more bitter than a woman?" he said with harsh insistence, but she winced away from the arguments of hope.
> "Oh why, why, did he have to make such a mess of things?"

Father Rank said, "It may seem an odd thing to say—when a man's as wrong as he was—but I think, from what I saw of him, that he really loved God."

She had denied just now that she felt any bitterness, but a little more of it drained out now like tears from exhausted ducts. "He certainly loved no one else," she said.

"And you may be in the right of it there, too," Father Rank replied. (272)

Greene is by no means alone. In *The Knot of Vipers*, his contemporary, François Mauriac, gives us a narrator it should be easy to hate: a manipulative and filthy rich old sinner who hates his whole family, partly because his wife has raised his children in the Catholic faith (he is an atheist), partly because of his own cavernous loneliness, and partly because his wife and children (especially the children) are smug religious hypocrites, desperately worried that he will disinherit them all before he dies, as in fact he plans to do. He writes a diary meant to be read by his wife Isa when he dies, which, given the precarious condition of his heart, could be any day. In this diary he confesses that he had once loved her, but cries out that *she* rejected *him*, that she never really loved or understood him, and that he sees through the pretense that they care about anything concerning him besides his money. It is a diary laced with acid: but the Lord works a wonder that the "hero" Louis never expects: Isa dies first, while Louis is in Paris, in peril of his life, attempting to arrange to give all his money to an illegitimate son. The news breaks his heart, for now "she had died without knowing me, without understanding that there was more in me than the monster, the tormentor, she thought me to be, that behind the mask there did exist a totally different man" (395). And despite the continued venality of the children, who have plotted against him only to have him foresee their awkward moves well in advance, Louis suddenly feels no desire to disinherit them, no more vengeance against them: "I had always been deceived in the object of my wishes. We do not know what we desire: we do not love those whom we think we love" (404). Man's heart becomes, in sin, a "knot of vipers," and he grows accustomed to it, taking it as his central reality, when all along beneath that knot, so long as the Lord yet loves us, a heart of flesh beats still.

But Louis sees that the secret of love, the sword that will cut the knot, is not an intellectual theory, but a person, some One in whom he and his family might have been united. His death ever nearing, having forgiven his children who have by no means forgiven him, he begins to feel the presence of that One whom he always thought to flee, but whom he had always sought: "Stripped of everything, isolated, and with a terrible death hanging over my head, I remained calm, watchful, and mentally alert. The thought of my melancholy existence did not despress me, nor did I feel the burden of my empty years. . . . It was as though I were not a sick old man, as though I still had a lifetime before me, as though the peace of which I was possessed was Somebody" (419). He is at last reconciled with one granddaughter, whose silly and worthless husband had abandoned her for what *he* thought was love. They are alone in the vast old house, and he looks at the plain little woman and is moved by Love to love: "The lamp on the chimney-piece shone down on her heavy, crouching figure, while I wandered about among the mahogany and rosewood in the encumbered dark. Impotently I prowled around that lump of humanity, that bruised and beaten body. 'My child . . . ,' I began, but could find no words for what I wanted to say. . . . Something, as I sit to-night writing these lines, is stifling me, something is making my heart feel as though it would burst—it is the Love whose name at last I know, whose ador . . ."(423). Those are his last words. In the final irony of the novel, his diary is discovered by the children; and no one except the granddaughter can believe that he had turned his heart to God, not even when they learn that he had been seeing a priest to prepare for baptism. It is as Mauriac once said: we will be surprised to see not only the harlots and publicans enter before us, but even the persecutors and the atheists. Let us pray we will be in a position to enjoy the irony.

So it is in *Brideshead Revisited* by Evelyn Waugh: the narrator, Charles Ryder, utterly areligious and contemptuous of the Catholicism of the family of Lord Marchmain, is irresistibly attracted to that family nonetheless. He spends his adulthood as a second-rate artist painting pictures of great English country homes before they go on the auction block to be turned into apartments (or before they are requisitioned as barracks for World War II, as happens with the Brideshead estate). What he does not know, what he only comes to see in the end, is that he is searching for something far older than Brideshead, something permanent. His friendship with Sebastian—who turns into a ragged, drunken, ever-childlike beggar at a monastery in Africa, a man out of place in this dead modern world, good for nothing but the love of God—he sees as the forerunner of his love for Sebastian's sister, Julia. But Julia herself says that his love for her may be only the forerunner of a love for something else—the God whom Julia too has tried and failed to reject. In a tense scene near the end of the book, Lord Marchmain is dying, and Charles is scandalized by the children's attempts to have him confess his sins. He tries to prevent what he calls fables and magic, especially since Marchmain had long lived with his mistress, and had fled the Catholicism he accepted when he married. We think we are running far away from him, Waugh says, when one twitch on the rope in the end will bring us all the way back, if we love him. Charles cannot frustrate the will of God, and instead finds that he, too, is a lover being brought back by that twitch of the rope.

The person who thinks he hates his enemy (wife, mother, God) yet loves, and who thinks he is running away from God, but is running towards him or is about to be overtaken by him whether he likes it or not, figures prominently in the novels of Walker Percy (e.g., *Lancelot, The Moviegoer*); in many of the stories of Flannery O'Connor ("Parker's Back" is a poignant example, as is "Everything That Rises Must Converge"); in the novels of Mauriac; in *The Diary of a Country Priest* by Georges Bernanos; in C. S. Lewis's Space Trilogy and even, in places, in *The Chronicles of Narnia*; and in George Macdonald's Curdie novels.

But I wish to devote the next chapter rather to the irony of thinking that you love indeed, and only later learning by the grace of God that your love was but young and green. That is, though troubled marriages and sudden deaths and broken engagements may provide plenty of ironic turns, the most sublime irony of love is that the mad passion we feel actually does reflect something true and eternal. A love affair turned sour may prove ironic: we thought we knew, but we did not. But that is small change compared to the irony of Christian love that leads to marriage: we were mad with love then, but even we did not know how much we had been given to know—or how much we were yet to be given.

16

A Sonneteer in Love: Spenser's Amoretti

For the Christian, as we have seen, it is no embarrassment that God's love be described in intensely erotic terms. Such description is implicit in Paul's assertion that the church is the bride of Christ. But if the body may be used as a metaphor for the highest things of the spirit, so too, in Christianity, the Incarnation has forever blessed the things of the body. That blessing extends to marriage especially: Jesus worked his first miracle at a wedding feast, and the wedding feast is Jesus' most common metaphor for the kingdom of heaven—if metaphor it be. Perhaps, considering the wedding feast of the Lamb in Revelation, we had better say that the kingdom of heaven will indeed be nuptial, in ways we cannot now fathom.

If the love of man and woman has been sanctified by Christ, then in Christ that love will find its highest and most joyous fulfillment. Of all the English poets who have written of love, only Edmund Spenser has presented for us a drama of wooing which is at the same time a drama of turning in love towards Christ:

> So let us love, deare love, like as we ought:
> Love is the lesson that the Lord us taught. (*Amoretti*, 68.13–14)

So runs the concluding couplet of Sonnet 68 of Spenser's *Amoretti*, the Easter sonnet. Now this sonnet is not an occasional piece tossed into an otherwise "secular" sequence celebrating erotic love. Spenser's sonnet sequence — comprising eighty-nine sonnets, four "Anacreontic" poems about Cupid, and the twenty-four stanzas of the time-poem *Epithalamion* — is structured around the church year, particularly the movement from Lent to Eastertide. Sonnet 22, for example, explicitly mentions the onset of Lent, "This holy season fit to fast and pray." Taking that poem for Ash Wednesday, we see that the Easter poem falls on exactly the forty-seventh day thereafter, thus covering the forty days of Lent and the seven days of Passion Week. In addition, this block of forty-seven poems is situated exactly in the center of the *Amoretti* — of the sequence of "little loves" or "little Cupids" — with twenty-one sonnets before it, and twenty-one sonnets after. Most intriguingly, Sonnet 67, which announces with incredulous joy the decision of Spenser's beloved to yield to his wishes to marry her, repeats images from the Psalms used to celebrate the Easter Vigil and to usher catechumens into full communion with the church. So it is that to enter into full intimacy with the beloved is to enter fully and finally into the Body of Christ. I will discuss Sonnet 67 in some detail below; it is rich in ironies. The point is, if Spenser did not wish erotic love to be interpreted in the light of Christ's love, he made a grave architectural mistake. If he did, it is reasonable for us to ask, how? What is the relationship between the divine love and the earthly eros?

Spenser plays upon two sorts of irony; each depends upon the chasm between the divine and the human. In the first, the human is held against the divine and is found wanting. In the second, divine love sanctions, informs, and even propels human love, so that human love is not just a distant image of the divine, but actually becomes a means: 1. The narrator — and, to a lesser degree, the occasionally aloof beloved — must come to feel the stark contrast between eros and true Christian love; 2. The narrator and the beloved come to see that eros is redeemed in Christ and is, astonishingly enough, an avenue of grace.

These ironies are compatible. If the divine plan includes the procreation of children, it must not (or at least it does not) eliminate the desire that makes that possible. The problem is that in fallen man the desire arrogates everything to itself. It is insubordinate. In its vainglory it would command where it is called to obey. Call it the tendency for eros to resolve itself into lust. This problem is so common for man that even the well-intended reader can miss Spenser's celebration of a Christian eros in the *Amoretti*. Easter raises the human from the dead, and eros is a part of being human and possessing a sexual body. Thus, eros is redeemed by Easter, and not simply replaced with a desexualized benevolence, a sort of Enlightenment altruism, or a nauseating androgyny. The lesson the Lord teaches is not niceness or kindness or even liberality. It is not a dose of saltpeter. It is, in the full-blooded sense of the word, Love.

To see how these ironies work, let us turn to Sonnet 22, the Ash Wednesday sonnet. At this point in the sequence, the narrator is caught in the grip of a very conventional woman-worship. Such homage may be preferable to an equally conventional woman-scorn, but both are mistaken. Women are made for neither. If you use a fork as if it were a spoon, you will spill a lot of soup; so it is no surprise that the idolizing narrator feels thoroughly frustrated. Unredeemed eros will frustrate or disappoint. To make matters worse, the narrator has chosen for his beloved a woman who remains unimpressed by all the conventions of such eros. Thus, everything is topsy-turvy in the narrator's soul, as is illustrated by the sonnet's absurd theology:

> This holy season fit to fast and pray
> Men to devotion ought to be inclynd:
> Therefore, I lykewise on so holy day,
> For my sweet Saynt some seruice fit will find.
> Her temple fayre is built within my mind,
> In which her glorious ymage placed is,
> On which my thoughts doo day and night attend
> Lyke sacred priests that neuer thinke amisse.
> There I to her as th' author of my blisse,
> Will builde an altar to appease her yre,
> And on the same my hart will sacrifise,
> Burning in flames of pure and chast desyre.
> The which vouchsafe O goddesse to accept,
> Amongst thy deerest relicks to be kept.

If we want evidence of disordered or unruly passion, the sonnet provides it. First, the speaker wittily uses Ash Wednesday to establish his own rite or "service" of penitence, the sacrifice of his heart upon an altar inside "her temple fayre," an edifice he has constructed in his mind to facilitate his worship of the beloved. There her image is placed, as if she were a divine protectress, and there his thoughts, like dutiful priests, ever send up sweet incense to the "author" of his happiness. It is not clear why he should have to "appease her yre," other than that it is natural for so great a goddess to be angry when beset by the affections of a mere mortal. All he asks of her, as he dons his idolatrous sackcloth and ashes, is that she keep the remains of his holocaust, his burnt heart, perhaps in the sanctuary of that same temple, as "relickes." What makes such a woman a "sweet Saynt"? We cannot tell. She is so, it seems, because the speaker has determined to consider her so.

In the context of our passage from Lent to Easter, we can read this sonnet as Spenser's way of subjecting a certain sort of love to fairly obvious ironic commentary. One must not build temples to goddesses on Ash Wednesday. One must not pay homage to a young lady as if she were the author of blessedness. Young ladies are nice, but they are not goddesses. And one must not "fast and pray" by plunging oneself into self-sacrificing worship of one's desire.

Yet it may be objected that such a reading takes the poem too seriously. The idea of worshiping one's lady love is not to be subjected to theological analysis. It is a literary jest, as is clear from the poem's light and playful tone. Spenser's imagination is simply not working very hard here.

The objection touches upon some truth. The tone *is* lighthearted, and there is a sense in which the "idolatry," so conventional and predictable, is not to be taken wholly seriously. But that is not because Spenser's imagination was dormant. Rather, he is constructing an irony right on top of an apparently contradictory irony. If the fundamental irony of this sonnet is that we should not be turning young ladies into goddesses, the more sublime irony is that, after all, we *should*; nor do these positions contradict each other, once we understand the nature of true love and its relationship with Christ, the true Author of all bliss.

Here it might be helpful to suspend our discussion of *Amoretti* to show how two contradictory ironies can work, for self-contradictory irony is a hallmark of Spenser's style and vision. It comes naturally to an author whose didacticism is as maze-like as the paths of Faery Land. Or, better, Spenser's didacticism is not focused on propositions but on rhetoric. He wishes not so much to make us see the truth about a thing, as to make that truth rouse us to action. For such a purpose, he needs surprise. Even when we think we have solved Spenser's allegories and can settle back into an intellectual appreciation of the truths he presents, he shocks us out of our complacency by *seeming* to contradict himself. He does so to force us into a fuller and deeper commitment to the truth.

Take the matter of "excellence" in Book One of his epic *The Faerie Queene*. When our hero the Red Cross Knight enters the House of Pride, he sees the queen of that house, the aptly named Lucifera, embodying in herself the utter illogic and self-destructiveness of pride. The passage is so full of delicious invective that I quote it in full:

High above all a cloth of State was spred,
And a rich throne, as bright as sunny day,
On which there sate most brave embellished
With royall robes and gorgeous array,
A mayden Queene, that shone as Titans ray,
In glistring gold, and peerelesse pretious stone:
Yet her bright blazing beauty did assay
To dimme the brightnesse of her glorious throne,
As enuying herself, that too exceeding shone.

Exceeding shone, like Phoebus' fairest child,
That did presume his fathers firie wayne,
And flaming mouthes of steedes vnwonted wilde
Through highest heauen with weaker hand to rayne;
Proud of such glory and aduancement vaine,
While flashing beames do daze his feeble eyen,
He leaues the welkin way most beaten plaine,
And rapt with whirling wheeles, inflames the skyen,
With fire not made to burne, but fairely for to shyne.

So proud she shyned in her Princely state,
Looking to heauen; for earth she did disdayne,
And sitting high; for lowly she did hate:
Lo vnderneath her scornefull feete, was layne
A dreadfull Dragon with an hideous trayne,
And in her hand she held a mirrhour bright,
Wherein her face she often vewed fayne,
And in her self-lou'd semblance tooke delight,
For she was wondrous faire, as any liuing wight.

Of griesly *Pluto* she the daughter was,
And sad *Proserpina* the Queene of hell;
Yet she did thinke her pearelesse worth to pas
That parentage, with pride so did she swell,
And thundring *Ioue*, that high in heauen doth dwell,
And wield the world, she claymed for her syre,

> Or if that any else did *Ioue* excell:
> For to the highest she did still aspyre,
> Or if ought higher were then that, did it desyre. (*Faerie Queen*, 1.4.8–12)

All that glisters is not gold. Spenser has no sooner said that the "mayden Queene" is "wondrous faire," than he reports, with wonderful nonchalance, that she happens also to be the daughter of "griesly Pluto" and "sad Proserpina the Queene of hell." Furthermore, in her luxury and pride, Lucifera resembles the woman who has brought Red Cross here to the House of Pride: Duessa, personification of the (as Spenser thought) decadently wealthy Roman Catholic church, itself an embodiment of the Whore of Babylon. But how can we tell that the beautiful woman is evil? Forget the sinister name "Light-bearer" or *Lucifera*; forget also that she dwells in the House of Pride. Surely the clearest sign of her evil is her stupefying excess. Lucifera is so consumed with pride and envy that the brightness of her countenance seeks to dim the brightness of her throne, as if she and her regal chair were locked in combat for supremacy. Spenser stresses the absurdity by repeating the phrase "exceeding shone," followed by the explanatory simile comparing Lucifera to the vain boy Phaethon. He thought he could manage the steeds of his father, the sun-god Apollo, but in his foolish ambition he destroyed himself and nearly destroyed the earth. Such self-destruction is the reward for those who try to exceed themselves—a logical impossibility. So ought we to understand Lucifera's self-overleaping ambition. She wants to claim for her parentage the very highest, or, what is frankly silly, the even higher than the highest.

So it is with some queasiness that we view Red Cross Knight, in a soft bed in the House of Pride, tossing and turning before his scheduled duel with the "faithelesse foe" Sans Foy:

> The noble hart, that harbours vertuous thought,
> And is with child of glorious great intent,
> Can neuer rest, vntill it forth haue brought
> Th' eternall brood of glorie excellent. (1.5.1.1–4)

After the sight of Lucifera and her self-exceeding brightness, claiming a self-excelling parentage, it is not hard to see that Red Cross, for all his natural nobility, is behaving more like her than like a Christian soldier. Events bear out this fear. Red Cross will soon fall to the monster of Pride, and, rescued from that monster's dungeon, will nearly fall to the smooth talking of Pride's subtler counterpart, Despair. Only after a bitter and humbling stay at the House of Holiness, a combination of hospital and schoolhouse, will he grow fit to attack the dragon he had originally set out to slay.

Yet in describing the reborn Christian soldier, Spenser returns to the very language he seems to have flatly rejected at the House of Pride. Thus, the holy damsel Una encourages Red Cross Knight on the morning before the battle:

> The sparke of noble courage now awake,
> And striue your excellent self to excell;
> That shall ye euermore renowmed make,
> Aboue all knights on earth, that batteill vndertake. (1.11.2.6–9)

Why is Red Cross now "excellent," and how is it now praiseworthy to try to excel the excelling? The explanation is to be found in the change he under-goes at the House of Holiness, where he is instructed in the Christian faith. He learns to trust not his own prowess but Christ's. He dons the virtues of faith, hope, and charity. He is, in fact, ready for full communion in that one true church which Una represents. Thus, as the dragon will discover to his dismay, Red Cross Knight is not himself. He is, and is not, the Red Cross Knight. He is now in Christ, and Christ is in him. He can then say with Saint Paul, "I can do all things through Christ which strengtheneth me" (Phil. 4:13). In Christ he can indeed excel excellence. What was pride in Lucifera, in the newly instructed Red Cross is the glory and exaltation awaiting him who submits himself wholly to the Lord. To see how a man cannot, and yet can, vault him-self beyond excellence, is to distinguish subtly between glory and glory; that is, the vain glory of man, and the glory of the Lord, shed upon man. Paul does not exactly forbid boasting when he says, "He that glorieth, let him glory in the Lord" (1 Cor. 1:31)!

In the *Amoretti*, Spenser encourages a similar double-angled view of the events of the love affair. It is easy to see that Spenser pokes fun at his narra-tor, who celebrates Ash Wednesday by idolizing the woman he loves. What is harder to see, but necessary, if we are to make the most coherent sense out of the *Amoretti*, and if we are to learn all that Spenser wishes to show us about love, is that such idolizing, like Red Cross Knight's self-excelling, may be justi-fied, may even be holy, and not on pagan grounds but according to the very Christianity it appears to violate.

Such an interpretation becomes possible as soon as we allow that there must be some relationship between erotic love and the love of Christ. It is not the ardor or the coolness of the desire that makes it innocent. It is rather the right ordering of the desire that makes it *holy*. To put it simply, sexual desire is rightly ordered when it is seen as a gift from Christ, and when the benefits of the gift are offered to Christ in return. Although Sonnet 22 does not refer to Christ directly, still we can see hints that the speaker's love is not that of the typical sonneteer-lover. For one, his heart will burn "in flames of pure and chast desyre." Since there is no trace of lasciviousness in the *Amoretti*, and since the sequence ends in holy matrimony, I think we can take the narrator at his word. He is burning with a chaste love, and therefore with all the more passionate love. For, as Spenser elsewhere is at pains to tell us, the sinful desire for mere copulation rises no higher than the "dunghill"; it does not aspire to so high a passion as does chaste love. It is weak and cold:

> For loue is Lord of truth and loialtie,
> Lifting himselfe out of the lowly dust,
> On golden plumes vp to the purest skie,
> Aboue the reach of loathly sinfull lust,
> Whose base affect through cowardly distrust
> Of his weake wings, dare not to heauen fly,
> But like a moldwarpe in the earth doth ly.
>
> His dunghill thoughts, which do themselves enure
> To dirtie drosse, no higher dare aspyre,
> Ne can his feeble earthly eyes endure
> The flaming light of that celestiall fyre,
> Which kindleth loue in generous desyre,
> And makes him mount aboue the natiue might
> Of heauie earth, vp to the heauens hight.
> (*Fowre Hymnes*, "A Hymne of Love," 176–89)

Suppose, then, by "Goddesse" we mean something other than a literal deity: perhaps "the earthly ruler of my earthly desires," or "the person to whom, in Christ, I long to give myself wholly." Then not only would it be pardonable for the Christian speaker to attend to the temple of the glorious image of his beloved, but he might be to blame if he did not. Such devotion would be part of the divinely ordained desire he feels. He builds an altar to her "as to th' author of [his] blisse," not literally taking her for that Author, but considering her in the place of that Author, commissioned by the Author to bring him blessings. If that is how he thinks, there is no sin: he does not "thinke amisse."

Something of this pseudo-idolatry appears in several sonnets wherein the narrator tries to justify his pains and the time he has spent wooing the beautiful woman. His justification sounds like a theodicy—an attempt to justify the ways of God to man. Why must we suffer? A partial answer given by apologists is, we suffer so that heaven may be all the more joyful. Shakespeare's duke delays the happy moment when he will reveal to Isabella that her brother whom she thought dead is still alive, in order to "make her heavenly comforts of despair" (*Measure for Measure*, 4.3.110). This line of reasoning may sound merely cruel, or logically circular: if God is God, why can he not give us the full joy without the misery beforehand?

We should keep two important points in mind, points I have been arguing throughout this book, if this sort of theodicy is to make any sense. First, Christianity is not a set of propositions, but a story in which men play their part; and it is a mark of God's supralogical grace that the part we play is integral to the story and not just superadded to it. We are characters, not marginalia. We are allowed the dignity of aspiring, striving, failing, persevering, and succeeding. We make real choices, with real consequences, in the drama set before us, and *in Christ*—and only in Christ—we may "earn," as it were, the just rewards for our "merits." The second point is that God is the author and completer of the story, and it is only as a whole that the story can be judged. A part of the story derives its meaning only from the providence that guides and determines the whole.

With that in mind, we can see how Spenser can develop a theodicy of love. Things seem desperate for the poor confused narrator, who pleads impatiently that the beloved decide what to do with him once and for all. We may say he is pleading against time. But whenever he considers again the port he longs to find, he becomes willing to let time be, and submits himself to providence. For that haven will be the more heavenly the more he has had to endure to reach it:

> But yet if in your hardned brest ye hide
> A close intent at last to shew me grace;
> Then all the woes and wrecks which I abide,
> As meanes of blisse I gladly wil embrace.
> And wish that more and greater they might be,
> That greater meede at last may turne to mee. (*Amoretti*, 25.9–14)

Again, we must be sensitive to the gentle ironies of a fulfilled love. The narrator utters the conventional epithets: the beloved's breast is "hardened," he says, just as he will also insinuate, or will pretend to insinuate, that she is a "sense-less stone" (54.14) or that in her intransigence she will "to stones at length all frozen turne" (32.14). But the conventionality of the accusation suggests that Spenser is not serious about it. It is too obvious. If we take it at face value, we must assume, with many critics, that the *Amoretti* in places is just not very good. In this case, a little psychological perceptiveness, Christian or no, would help. This "hardness" of the woman's is but the speaker's hasty judgment upon her constancy, assuming that he wholly believes what he says, as he does not. Soon he will judge quite differently: "Thrise happie she, that is so well assured / Vnto her selfe and settled so in hart" (59.1–2). Constancy is not callousness, but steadfastness, a troth plighted and never to be revoked. The woman's ap-parent hardness is instead a loyalty to "just Time" and to Love. She knows when to give her heart, and knows that once it is given, it is given for ever: "Most happy she that most assured doth rest, / But he most happy who such one loues best" (59.13–14).

Indeed, the beloved may even now, during the "Lent" of the courtship, be harboring "a close intent at last to shew me grace" (25.10). The use of the word "grace" is psychologically and theologically apt. The speaker knows that nothing in him warrants so great a gift. It would be unmerited "grace" if the woman agreed to become his bride. But this "grace" is comprehended by the grace of God, of which it is an instance or manifestation. So the woman's "providence," her waiting until the right time, is in harmony with God's provi-dence, for God is providing for their love's fulfillment in marriage. The irony lies in the disjunction between the speaker now, as he suffers the pain of not-yet-fulfilled love, and the speaker as he sees himself in a still unclear future, having been rewarded for his persevering faith. This irony is framed by the larger irony of the language of theology used in the service of erotic love — si-multaneously absurd, even idolatrous, and yet most fitting and holy.

These two loves — the narrator's love for the woman, and Christ's love for all of us — merge in the climactic pair of Sonnets, 67 and 68. Here the theod-icy is completed. Here too we find the ironic paradoxes of Christian love: that we find freedom through binding our wills over to another in love, and that the way to gain one's life is to lose it in Christ.

First let us look at Sonnet 67:

> Lyke as a huntsman after weary chace,
> Seeing the game from him escapt away,

sits downe to rest him in some shady place,
with panting hounds beguiled of their pray;
So after long pursuit and vaine assay,
when I all weary had the chace forsooke,
the gentle deare returnd the selfe-same way,
thinking to quench her thirst at the next brooke.
There she beholding me with mylder looke,
sought not to fly, but fearelesse still did bide:
till I in hand her yet halfe trembling tooke,
and with her owne goodwill hir fyrmely tyde.
Strange thing me seemd to see a beast so wyld,
so goodly wonne with her owne will beguyld.

In the image of the deer quenching its thirst at the brook, Spenser alludes to Psalm 42, a psalm read during the Easter Vigil service: "As the hart panteth after the water brooks, so panteth my soul after thee, O God. My soul thirsteth for God, for the living God: when shall I come and appear before God?" (Ps. 42:1–2). The "hart" or deer (or the "dear," the precious one) is an allegory of the beloved, once "wild," now finally by her own will beguiled to enter into matrimony. But if we keep the psalm in mind, it is also an allegory of the soul's desire for union with God. Thus read, we see a stunning reversal in the psychology of the *Amoretti* sequence. Until now we have been looking at the theology of the speaker's love for the woman, his having to wait patiently until his prayers are answered. But here we see the theology of the woman's love for the speaker, her need, in the light of his prayers and his patient faith, to surrender herself to *him*. That surrender is placed in the context of quenching the thirst, precisely when the speaker has given up the chase. In other words, this thirst is presented as arising not from the immediacy of the pursuit, but from the beloved's own timely and irresistible desire. She thirsts, as does the soul: she thirsts for love. That is why she regards the speaker with "mylder looke," and that is why, in a moment of lovely self-sacrifice and submission, she allows him to become her husband, her head: "I in hand her yet halfe trembling tooke." She trembles, I take it, with the fearful joy of surrender.

Yet the image of the deer refers not only to the beloved or to the soul: traditionally it refers to Christ himself. Thus, the sacrifices of the lovers to one another, and here, more particularly, the submission of the beloved to her lover, must be seen in the context of Christ's sacrifice. If we read further in Psalm 42 we see why ancient Christian iconography used the deer as a symbol for the suffering Christ:

> I will say unto God my rock, Why hast thou forgotten me? why go I in
> mourning because of the oppression of the enemy?
>
> As with a sword in my bones, mine enemies reproach me; while they
> say daily unto me, Where is thy God?
>
> Why art thou cast down, O my soul? and why art thou disquieted with-
> in me? hope thou in God: for I shall yet praise him, who is the health of my
> countenance, and my God. (Psalm 42:9–11)

If Christ, the "suffering servant," is seen as the speaker in the psalm, we have
an instance of the same kind of theodicy as Spenser has suggested for the love
affair in *Amoretti*. Christ is beset with enemies; his spirit groans within him, he
seems to have been abandoned by God, yet he still places all his hope in the
Father. The enemies are time-bound, and see only the Son's temporary suffering, but hope looks forward, can project itself confidently to that serene point
from which all present sufferings shall have been vindicated. Hope can say,
with David, "Therefore my heart is glad, and my glory rejoiceth: my flesh also
shall rest in hope. For thou wilt not leave my soul in hell; neither wilt thou suffer thine Holy One to see corruption" (Ps. 16:9–10), or with Paul, "For I reckon
that the sufferings of this present time are not worthy to be compared with the
glory which shall be revealed in us" (Rom. 8:18). In this time we suffer, yet we
hope in the Lord of time: "For we are saved by hope: but hope that is seen is
not hope" (Rom. 8:24). But there will come a time, says Spenser at the end
of his *Faerie Queene*, when time itself shall cease to be, and then all shall be
changed, "in a moment, in the twinkling of an eye" (1 Cor. 15:52):

> Then gin I thinke on that which *Nature* sayd,
> Of that same time when no more *Change* shall be,
> But stedfast rest of all things firmely stayd
> Vpon the pillours of Eternity,
> That is contrayr to *Mutabilitie*:
> For, all that moueth, doth in *Change* delight:
> But thence-forth all shall rest eternally
> With Him that is the God of Sabbaoth hight:
> O that great Sabbaoth God, graunt me that Sabaoths sight.
> (*Faerie Queen*, 7.8.2)

If the worldly see only the present time, they also see only the surface of
things. The irony of Christian love is that it exists both in and beyond time,
and is expressed in the humblest and most physical ways, as in the most ex-

alted spirituality. For the former is an incarnation of the latter. Thus, the world accused the beloved of pride:

> The glorious image of the makers beautie,
> My soverayne saynt, the Idoll of my thought,
> dare not henceforth aboue the bounds of dewtie,
> t'accuse of pride, or rashly blame for ought. (*Amoretti*, 61.1–4)

Actually, this "Idoll" or "image of the makers beautie" knows that she is not meant to give herself away for less than she is worth, that is to say, for less than her Maker has made her worth:

> For being as she is diuinely wrought,
> and of the brood of Angels heuenly borne . . .
> what reason is it then but she should scorne
> base things, that to her loue too bold aspire? (61.5–6, 11–12)

Thus, too, a worldly point of view tempts the beloved to fear the bonds of matrimony:

> The doubt which ye misdeeme, fayre loue, is vaine,
> That fondly feare to loose your liberty,
> when loosing one, two liberties ye gayne,
> and make him bond that bondage earst dyd fly. (65.1–4)

Actually, matrimony is a bondage that sets free:

> Sweet be the bands, the which true loue doth tye,
> without constraynt of dread or any ill:
> the gentle birde feeles no captiuity
> within her cage, but singes and feeds her fill. (65.5–8)

The apparent aloofness of the beloved, her stateliness, goes hand in hand with humility; she will enter the church on her wedding day with "portly pace," like the goddess of the moon, yet when she reaches the altar she looks meekly to the earth:

> Her modest eyes abashed to behold
> So many gazers, as on her do stare,
> Vpon the lowly ground affixed are.
> Ne dare lift vp her countenance too bold,

> But blush to heare her prayses sung so loud,
> So farre from being proud. (*Epithalamion*, 159–64)

As for the deer's (dear's) loss of freedom, we need to look to the irony of Christ's sacrifice to explain what it means for a Christian to be free. According to Saint Paul, it is in baptism—in dying with Christ, and being regenerate through the waters of his suffering—that we rise again and become truly free:

> Know ye not, that so many of us as were baptized into Jesus Christ were baptized into his death?
> Therefore we are buried with him by baptism into death: that like as Christ was raised up from the dead by the glory of the Father, even so we also should walk in newness of life. (Rom. 6:3–4)

In that new life, no longer slaves to the Law or to the passions it fails to restrain, we are sons, and can cry "Abba, Father" (Gal. 4:6). In Paul's day, a man's sons would be given responsibility to take care of the father's estate. They would wield a subordinate authority in the household, and could exercise considerable initiative. The relationship then is not mother to baby, but father to mature and trusted family workers, both sons and daughters. This is the freedom within subordination, the "true filial freedom" that Milton ascribes to Adam and Eve, as we have seen. In any case, the Christian freedom is not only a negative one, a freedom from sin. It is also a positive freedom to choose to serve the Lord with all one's heart and mind and body. This is most appropriate for our sonnet sequence, since the *Amoretti* moves from courtship to marriage, the holy state within which man and woman, using the gift of sex, participate as agents of a creative providence, fulfilling the first command, which is also the first blessing: "Be fruitful, and multiply, and replenish the earth, and subdue it: and have dominion over the fish of the sea, and over the fowl of the air, and over every living thing that moveth upon the earth" (Gen. 1:28). The fulfillment of that command, as Spenser sees, has joyous and eternal consequences, for on his wedding night—that intersection of time and eternity—he will pray for children, "Of blessed Saints for to increase the count" (*Epithalamion*, 423).

The world sees this freedom as subjection, but what truly enslaves is the willfulness that looks like freedom. Allow me to offer the most grimly ironic illustration. At the bottom of Dante's *Inferno*, locked in ice, Lucifer flaps his wings forever, to no avail. Once angelic, now the wings are the scaly wings of a bat; once, when Lucifer served the Lord, they were instruments of swift and majestic flight, but now their very flapping does nothing but cause a gale to blow, freezing the river Cocytus, in whose icy grip Lucifer is caught forever. As it was his act of "freedom" from God—his willful pride—that earned him hell, so the wing-beating which was once evidence of his mighty freedom now imprisons him. He had freedom in God. Illogically wanting to be free of God, in whom all creatures live and move and have their being (Acts 17:28), he enslaves himself for eternity.

The ideal of Christian freedom is surely set forth by Sonnets 67 and 68, and has been craftily prepared for by Spenser, who from the beginning of the *Amoretti* has rung changes on words like "captivity," "bond," and "liberty." For one thing, the psalm read in the Sarum Missal for the Easter Vigil—Psalm 42, of the deer thirsting for the running streams—is also considered a psalm of baptism.[1] The imagery of the psalm makes that association natural enough, and in fact adult catechumens in the days of the church fathers were baptized into the church on the night before Easter. Thus they can, ritually and sacramentally, enter by baptism into Christ's death, to rise with him on Easter, freed of sin.

Thus, the love of one man for one woman is placed in the context of Christ's all-comprehending, all-sacrificing love for all mankind. Having won the consent of his beloved in the poem of Easter eve, Spenser shows both the depth and the meaning of his joy in Sonnet 68, devoted to Easter:

> Most glorious Lord of lyfe, that on this day,
> Didst make thy triumph ouer death and sin:
> and hauing harrowd hell, didst bring away
> captiuity thence captiue vs to win:
> This ioyous day, deare Lord, with ioy begin,
> and grant that we for whom thou diddest dye
> being with thy deare blood clene washt from sin,
> may liue for euer in felicity.
> And that thy loue we weighing worthily
> may likewise loue thee for the same againe:
> and for thy sake that all lyke deare didst buy,
> with loue may one another entertayne.
> So let vs loue, deare loue, lyke as we ought,
> loue is the lesson which the Lord vs taught. (68.1–14)

---

1. See Anne Lake Prescott, "The Thirsty Deer and the Lord of Life: Some Contexts for *Amoretti* 67–70," *Spenser Studies* VI (1986).

On Easter eve, as tradition held, Christ "harrowd hell," a harrowing that was symbolized by the purging of the soul in baptism. He captured and brought away captivity itself: "But unto every one of us is given grace according to the measure of the gift of Christ. Wherefore he saith, When he ascended up on high, he led captivity captive, and gave gifts unto men" (Eph. 4:7–8). What gifts is Paul talking about? Above all, the unity of Christian love:

> I therefore, the prisoner of the Lord, beseech you that ye walk worthy of the vocation wherewith ye are called,
>> With all lowliness and meekness, with longsuffering, forbearing one another in love;
>> Endeavouring to keep the unity of the Spirit in the bond of peace.
> (Eph. 4:1–3)

For Paul, the "prisoner of the Lord," the highest expression of this Christian love is in marriage:

> Wives, submit yourselves unto your own husbands, as unto the Lord.
>> For the husband is the head of the wife, even as Christ is the head of the church: and he is the saviour of the body.
>> Therefore as the church is subject unto Christ, so let the wives be to their own husbands in every thing.
>> Husbands, love your wives, even as Christ also loved the church, and gave himself for it;
>> That he might sanctify and cleanse it with the washing of water by the word. (Eph. 5:22–26)

Christ, who set the prisoners free, frees us also from the power of death and sin and therefore from all of the "former conversation" (Eph. 4:22) which prevents us from loving one another truly. Christ it is who enables us to love. Thus, in a sudden, well-prepared pun on the word "dear" (meaning "costly, precious," "beloved," but also "deer"!), Spenser associates the love of his dear/deer with Christ's inestimable love for us. In Christ alone will the lover and his beloved be truly free and irrevocably bound in love. Spenser understands that for a Christian, there can be no true love outside of Christ, for even love of neighbor flows from love of God: "As the Father hath loved me, so have I loved you: continue ye in my love" (John 15:9). Nor does love begin with us:

> Beloved, let us love one another: for love is of God; and every one that loveth is born of God, and knoweth God.

He that loveth not knoweth not God; for God is love.

In this was manifested the love of God toward us, because that God sent his only begotten Son into the world, that we might live through him.

Herein is love, not that we loved God, but that he loved us, and sent his Son to be the propitiation for our sins.

Beloved, if God so loved us, we ought also to love one another.

(1 John 4:7–11)

John's words and Spenser's poem teach us first to love God, and then to love one another for God's sake, since what God has bought so dearly—what was so "dear" to him that he, the sacrifical "deer," redeemed it by his death—should also be esteemed by us as "dear." Thus, the lessons of captivity and love go together. Christ shows that there can be no true love without utter surrender of the will, yet it is that obedience, as of a servant, that binds captivity captive and sets us free. To repeat Spenser's lines:

So let us loue, deare loue, lyke as we ought,
loue is the lesson which the Lord vs taught. (*Amoretti*, 68.13–14)

The result of such freedom is aptly described, in the final lines of Sonnet 65, as the rebuilding of Paradise, insofar as human beings still prone to sin can rebuild it on earth:

There pride dare not approch, nor discord spill
the league twixt them, that loyal loue hath bound:
but simple truth and mutuall good will,
seekes with sweet peace to salue each others wound:
There fayth doth fearlesse dwell in brasen towre,
and spotless pleasure builds her sacred bowre.

Perhaps, after such speculative heights, it would be well to imitate Spenser, who always brings his readers, with quiet, self-deprecating irony, back to the world of the homely, the small, and the physical. Shortly after the Easter sonnet, we have a delightful little poem that gives us a glimpse into the warmth and playfulness of the personalities involved in this love. The lady is knitting a teasing bit of embroidery: a design of a spider with a bee caught in his net. Of course, she compares herself to the bee and the speaker to the spider, and he takes joy in the comparison, even proceeding to show the lady how appropriate it is:

> Right so your selfe were caught in cunning snare
> of a deare foe, and thralled to his loue:
> in whose streight bands ye now captiued are
> so firmely, that ye neuer may remoue.   (*Amoretti*, 71.5–8)

So he says, perhaps weaving his arms about her. A gentle mock-accusation is thus answered by a gentle mock-sentence of doom. Yes, he agrees, you are right, you are never going to escape from me now! And furthermore, it is no prison but a bower of bliss you will dwell in, as your own embroidery proves:

> But as your worke is wouen all aboue,
> with woodbynd flowers and fragrant Eglantine:
> so sweet your prison you in time shall proue,
> with many deare delights bedecked fine. (71.9–12)

The final image is one of earthly and heavenly peace. Spiders and bees, we know, are natural enemies, but this spider and this bee will, unexpectedly enough, live in fine harmony:

> And all thensforth eternal peace shall see,
> betweene the Spyder and the gentle Bee. (71.13–14)

Thus Spenser echoes his own vision of the eternal Sabbath, the day of Resurrection which nature herself looks forward to, a day of peace:

> But time shall come that all shall changed bee,
> And from thenceforth, none no more change shall see.
> (*Faerie Queen*, 7.7.59.4–5)

So too does our poet, in a touching and lighthearted way, echo the beautiful vision of the peaceable kingdom that Isaiah said would be ushered in by the Savior: "The wolf also shall dwell with the lamb, and the leopard shall lie down with the kid; and the calf and the young lion and the fatling together; and a little child shall lead them" (Is. 11:6).

From the redemption of the human race, to the gentle flirting of a man with his bride-to-be as she stitches a handkerchief: the juxtaposition embraces a lovely Christian irony which, if we are caught up with false ideas of power and sex, we will not see. But "the foolishness of God is wiser than men; and the weakness of God is stronger than men" (1 Cor. 1:25). If it is foolishness to love—and who can doubt it?—then Christians are commanded to be fools. If it is foolishness to enter into bondage—and the world is certain of that—then Christians are commanded to ensnare themselves in the love of God and neighbor, in order to be set free.

17

Gerard Manley Hopkins and the Dangerous Love of God

"God is Love"

WE ARE USED TO hearing the biblical verse, "God is love" (1 John 4:8), and nodding knowingly to ourselves. "Ah yes," says the modern agnostic with a taste for religion. "I don't know whether God exists, but I do know that if he does, then he is love. So I will try to live according to love."

That's better than nothing. But we are too familiar with the verse. We no longer hear its thundering challenge to the entire Greek philosophical system. For if God is love and not necessity (since what is determined or compelled cannot be an act of love), then none of this universe need have been. Nor need it have been the way it is now. The belief that God creates from nothing, freely, is a logical consequence of believing that he creates from love.

But how can God love man? God needs nothing from man, not even man's love. Christians believe that God already is a communion of three persons bound by love, each distinct, yet each fully God. Man knows a trace of the love that moves God, or that is God's movement within himself: as he moves not from need, but from superabundance, from generosity, one might even say from playfulness. Man will cherish animals from which he derives nothing of use; he will potter about a flower garden for delight in the flowers; his heart will soar at the strains of music; he cheers at the sight of a big and boisterous family. Unlike every other creature on earth, man needs what he does not need, and loves where he does not lack—and he feels that he loves more fully from his plenty and strength, from his fascination with life, and from his will-to-beauty, than from his sense of incompleteness and insufficiency. In those high-hearted moments, man is close to God.

In no classical author do we find the great Zeus, father of gods and men, stooping to limn a blade of grass or smooth out a dewdrop. Such affairs would be relegated to some deity so low on the scale as to be nameless. But our God who made even the creeping things that creep upon the earth, who cares for the ostrich egg because the hen is too birdbrained to do it herself (Job 39:13–16), whose kingdom is as a mustard seed, and who decks the lilies of the field in such glory as would put to shame the tailors of Solomon, delights in his works. He enjoys them; he calls them good; he loves them. And, to paraphrase Jesus, if God so loves the grass, which is here today and tomorrow is thrown into the fire, how much more does he love us, us of the hard hearts?

We might think such things beneath our notice; but the incomparably great God notices them. Small as they are, they provide for the attentive a powerful way to draw closer to the heart of the Lord. Such was the insight of the Victorian priest-poet, Gerard Manley Hopkins. The more unusual the creature, the more it is peculiarly itself, the greater the delight. Consider this magnificent miniature sonnet on the beauty of all things great and small:

> Glory be to God for dappled things—
>   For skies of couple-color as a brinded cow;
>   For rose-moles all in stipple upon trout that swim;
> Fresh-firecoal chestnut-falls; finches' wings;
>   Landscape plotted and pieced—fold, fallow, and plough;
>   And all trades, their gear and tackle and trim.
>
> All things counter, original, spare, strange;
>   Whatever is fickle, freckled (who knows how?)
>   With swift, slow; sweet, sour; adazzle, dim;
> He fathers-forth whose beauty is past change:
>   Praise him. (*Pied Beauty*)

The bustling corral of things animate and inanimate defies category, exactly as Hopkins intends. No one really looks upon the sky and thinks of the splotches on a calico cow, probably because no one looks appreciatively enough at the sky and its cowishness, or at a cow and its reflection of a weathering sky. That odd second line brings heaven to earth with a delightful bump. The point, after all, is that heaven *can* be seen where no one sees it, especially upon the peculiarly beautiful things of earth—on the rosy stipples of a freshwater trout, for instance.

Not only there, though; Hopkins would never settle for being a dreamy little nature poet, a devotee of the pretty, and therefore a pretender of love. For how can you love weeds and thrush's eggs and not love man? If God delights in the making of chestnuts, the more does he delight in making beings who can delight also in his making of chestnuts and everything else. Therefore, man, his labor and his ingenuity, must also be praised; for the quirky beauty of man's own creativity, as evinced in sickles and ice-tongs and flails and adzes, reflects its source, the beauty of God. Fishing lures, wrenches, lathes, ropes and pulleys, pails of tar, seedbags and harrows, all in "trim," in order, share in Hopkins's hymn to muscular love.

But in the second stanza the poet leaves these particular things behind and turns his attention to their typical qualities: there is not one specific noun for the rest of the poem. That is because he wants to reverse the kaleidoscope: we shift our sights from the ever-changing and exuberantly various individual things to the never-changing God who made them. Now the ironic thing about this shift is not just that a never-changing God would create things which, since they are not God, would be subject to change. It is rather that God would delight in having his never-changing beauty pieced out among, refracted through, so many forms and so odd. Yet it is no derogation of his one and eternal beauty that it should be made manifest in the swift and the slow, the dazzling and the dim. For he does not simply make, as an artificer. He "fathers-forth."

We should meditate upon that phrase. It suggests neither the pantheism latent in earth-mother cults (whose goddess is identified with the mindless fecundity of nature), nor the fatalism latent in rationalistic theologies such as deism. God "fathers-forth"—the begetter and maker of what he did not have to beget or make. He has loved all things into being. Begetting them, he is to be found by means of them, whether the spiraling galaxy or the conch on the shore. Man's proper response, then, after he has paid his loving attention to trout and finches and things that show forth that breathless list of adjectives, is a quiet movement of the heart: "Praise him." Two simple words, for a simple act that does not change: praising the Maker of change, who dwells in eternal light.

Hopkins asserted with great ardor that man could approach his Lord by the inconsiderable trifles of the world, a love for irises and moths and falcons. His notebooks are crammed with the canniest descriptions, born of love, of what he called the "inscapes" of the things he saw, the peculiar inner fingerprint of a thing that made it itself and no other:

> Each mortal thing does one thing and the same:
>   Deals out that being indoors each one dwells;
>   Selves—goes itself; *myself* it speaks and spells,
> Crying *What I do is me: for that I came*. ("As Kingfishers Catch Fire," 5–8)

His term *inscape* is well chosen. It suggests a creation that delves deep within a thing, to its essence. The term is derived from the German *schoepfen* (to create) and *-schaft* (knowledge, as of a craft), and from the Anglo-Saxon *scieppan* (to shape or fashion) and *scop* (a shaper of verses, that is, a poet). Hopkins says the finding of inscapes is precisely what the world is for; all things are for man's beholding, that he may learn of his Maker and sing his praises.

Hence the typical irony of Hopkins's poetry. Knowledge is everywhere to be gleaned, but only by those who love. The fault line severs those who can read the signs, often in the most unexpected places, from those who cannot, because their love does not beat warmly enough. The double identity of the world—as heaven penetrates this smallish portion of the world that we misconstrue as the whole—comes across quite nicely in the following notebook entry, describing the first time Hopkins saw the northern lights:

> My eye was caught by beams of light and dark very like the crown of horny rays the sun makes behind a cloud. At first I thought of silvery cloud until I saw that these were more luminous and did not dim the clearness of the stars in the Bear. They rose slightly radiating thrown out from the earthline. Then I saw soft pulses of light one after another rise and pass upwards arched in shape but waveringly and with the arch broken. They seemed to float, not following the warp of the sphere as falling stars look to do but free though concentrical with it. This busy working of nature wholly independent of the earth and seeming to go on in a strain of time not reckoned by our reckoning of days and years but simpler and as if correcting the preoccupation of the world by being preoccupied with and appealing to and dated to the day of judgment was like a new witness to God and filled me with delightful fear. (Sept. 24, 1870)

Note that Hopkins senses a time-within-time, independent of the clicking minutes whereby we calculate our days in the countinghouse. But it is also a time above that time, steering it, leading it from the nothingness whence it came to the eternity whither it is going. He experiences the fearful sense of the provisionality of time, of its being embedded in God's time — against which our minutes seem to clash.

Bringing in the Sheaves

BUT IF OUR HEARTS are open, we will see. Then it will be as if the veil of creation had been torn in two. We will not see beyond creation, leaving it behind in disdain, but *into* creation, as into the mountains suggested in the depths of Niggle's picture. We will see even unto the dangerous and loving Creator who awaits within and beside and beyond. God is no mere object of love, but the Lover who will tear through cloud and sky to grip the heart of man. That explains the ironic reversals in one of Hopkins's loveliest hymns to natural beauty, "Hurrahing in Harvest":

> Summer ends now; now, barbarous in beauty, the stooks rise
> Around; up above, what wind-walks! what lovely behaviour
> Of silk-sack clouds! has wilder, wilful-wavier
> Meal-drift moulded ever and melted across skies?
>
> I walk, I lift up, I lift up heart, eyes,
> Down all that glory in the heavens to glean our Saviour;
> And, eyes, heart, what looks, what lips yet gave you a
> Rapturous love's greeting of realer, of rounder replies?
>
> And the azurous hung hills are his world-wielding shoulder
> Majestic — as a stallion stalwart, very-violet-sweet! —
> These things, these things were here and but the beholder
> Wanting; which two when they once meet,
> The heart rears wings bold and bolder
> And hurls for him, O half hurls earth for him off under his feet.

The first line of the poem leads, or misleads, the reader to believe that he is about to hear of the "barbarous" beauty of late summer. Hopkins echoes Shakespeare's famous line describing the sheaves brought in for the harvest, "Borne on the bier with white and bristly beard" (Sonnets 12.8). The "stooks" or ricks of baled corn are bearded and bristly—in that sense barbarous, punning on the Latin *barbatus* (bearded)—and of a rough and rustic thrusting into the sky.

But that is the last sight of an autumn harvest we have in the poem. For Hopkins casts his eye upward. Dante had called the world "this little winnowing floor" (*Paradise*, 22.151), alluding to Jesus' warning that at the Last Judgment the wheat would be winnowed from the chaff. Hopkins instead looks to the physical heavens—*there* is the harvesting, unbeknownst to the men who shock the grain on earth. The skies are "wind-walks" where the horses of the air march round (and there, not simply round and round but in the wildest streams) to power the fan to blow the straw free; the clouds are silky sacks of grain a-bursting; they spill the meal, flowing away in sudden runnels and siftings and scatterings.

It is no mere physical description. A real gleaning is going on, with the poet as gleaner, walking through the rows of grain: and his instruments are his heart and eyes. He is gleaning the Savior. That image is meant to evoke a theology of love. In most of the New Testament passages that refer to the harvest, Jesus is comparing the grain to the souls of the blessed (e.g., Luke 8:4–15), but in at least one place the soul's enjoyment of the kingdom of God is compared to a bumper crop at the harvest, "good measure, pressed down, and shaken together, and running over" (Luke 6:38). And why not? Since the life of Christ is the feast: he is the manna from heaven, the food that brings eternal life.

This is the paradox of Hopkins's poetry of love. God loves a world whose beauty should stir man to fall in love with it and with him. The more truly I love the meal-drifting clouds, the more truly I love God; because unless I see God in them, I do not fully see what they are. In the same way, Christ gives himself in the Eucharist that we may be gleaned by our gleaning: our taking him in is his own taking us up to himself, so that Aquinas properly says of the sacrament that it is not heaven that descends to us, but we who are raised to heaven.

No earthly love can match the fullness, even the violence, of God's love for man, when man lifts up his heart to God. Christ's is a "real" and a "round" reply, a halloo more reverberant than any man's shout of joy, a kiss more real and warm than the most passionate lover's embrace. Worship is not for the faint of heart. The hills above are the "world-wielding shoulder" of this royal hero—this God and man who is as "stalwart" (and as self-willed!) as a "stallion," yet mysteriously as sweet as "very-violet." Very God and very man, says *The Book of Common Prayer*; but Hopkins combines both natures in those superb images of royalty and approachable beauty.

Just as the northern lights seem to keep a time fixed upon eternity—a real time, a rounder time than what we know—so too the beauty of the harvest is and has always been ready for our seeing. Not the harvest of an Irish countryside, but in that harvest the harvest of oneself, in harvesting Christ. What is wanting? Only our attention: "the beholder." But we are here to behold it. Then it is our love that is wanting. But if that heart should once move in love, it will find ravishment, swept away by and from the beauty of the earth to the beauty of Christ. For "they that wait upon the Lord shall renew their strength; they shall mount up with wings as eagles" (Isa. 40:31).

Is Natural Man to Be Loved?

WHAT OF MAN'S BEAUTY? Hopkins is keenly aware of sin and the fallenness of a creation that "wears man's smudge and shares man's smell" ("God's Grandeur," 7). Yet in the poem "Spring," the "racing lambs," the falling blooms of the "glassy peartree," the liquid flute song of the wood thrush, even the lush and wheeling weeds, are all after-hints of Eden, earth's spring:

> Nothing is so beautiful as Spring—
>   When weeds, in wheels, shoot long and lovely and lush;
>   Thrush's eggs look little low heavens, and thrush
> Through the echoing timber does so rinse and wring
> The ear, it strikes like lightnings to hear him sing;
>   The glassy peartree leaves and blooms, they brush
>   The descending blue; that blue is all in a rush
> With richness; the racing lambs too have fair their fling.
>
> What is all this juice and all this joy?
>   A strain of the earth's sweet being in the beginning
> In Eden garden.—Have, get, before it cloy,
>   Before it cloud, Christ, lord, and sour with sinning,
> Innocent mind and Mayday in girl and boy,
>   Most, O maid's child, thy choice and worthy the winning.

But that was when man was in his springtime too, so the poem ends with a prayer, and again Hopkins invokes a time that most people cannot see and a youth that most people do not know. "Have, get, before it cloy, / Before it cloud," he begins his final sentence, and we think he is appealing to us: "Get this joy while you can!" But the word "cloy" should give the game away. It means either to turn sickly sweet, or to seem too sweet to the taste of one who has surfeited on sweets. Both senses work here, and apply to the sinner's repetition of the first sin in Eden, when sweet was not sweet enough. The "juice" is not something we taste, but that vintage we are, when we are young: and finer and sweeter than the thrush's eggs and the weeds.

We, then, though we fail to see it, are the goods to be gotten, and "Christ, lord" is the subject of the sentence. Hopkins is praying that Christ will take the young into his preserving care while the juice and the joy of Eden still run strong in their veins. We are led by the word order to suppose that we are being urged to gather Christ, but we gather him when he gathers us. He "gets," for his picking, the sweet blooms of May: "Innocent mind and Mayday in girl and boy." Appropriately so, since Christ himself advised us that unless we became as little children we should not enter the kingdom of heaven. And who is this Christ the Lord? A child of the springtime, the "maid's child," son of the innocent Mary, whose month is May, as is most fitting:

> This ecstasy all through mothering earth
> Tells Mary her mirth till Christ's birth
>   To remember and exultation
>   In God who was her salvation. ("May Magnificat," 45–48)

We think we love, but how slow and lukewarm our hearts are! How fortunate that salvation depends not on our love, but on God's. Hopkins seems to have been as naturally curious about other people as anyone alive, but he is honest about how far this love of neighbor takes him. Not far:

The Lantern Out of Doors

> Sometimes a lantern moves along the night,
>   That interests our eyes. And who goes there?
>   I think; where from and bound, I wonder, where,
> With, all down darkness wide, his wading light?
>
> Men go by me whom either beauty bright
>   In mould or mind or what not else makes rare:
>   They rain against our much-thick and marsh air
> Rich beams, till death or distance buys them quite.
>
> Death or distance soon consumes them: wind
>   What most I may eye after, be in at the end
>   I cannot, and out of sight is out of mind.

Christ minds: Christ's interest, what to avow or amend
  There, eyes them, heart wants, care haunts, foot follows kind,
Their ransom, their rescue, and first, fast, last friend.

Many a man would not travel with the lantern carrier to the end of the first stanza. But we are each of us that lantern carrier, traveling the darkness alone. And more: we *are* that darkness, too. For the physical or intellectual beauty of a man has to fight its way to us: it has to "rain" "rich beams" "against our much-thick and marsh air." Then we notice him, we of the dismal marsh: a beautiful man with a lantern, going somewhere.

Where does he go? The way of all flesh. He fades into death or, what serves as well for the speaker, into distance. With that, the speaker loses all interest. The metaphor is financial as well as psychological. Death or distance buys up everything we have invested, and then "out of sight is out of mind." Thus Hopkins says, with sadness, that even friendship is little more than the flickering interest kindled in us by a lantern swinging in the hand of a night traveler.

No, we do not know love from ourselves. That is the affront Christianity delivers to the sentimentalists who divorce the dignity of man from God. The sentimentalist will make a god out of love; Christianity asserts that you do not even know what love is unless in some fashion you know God, for it is *God* who is love, the Creator and no other. He chose us that we might choose him. We do not say he is our friend, deriving the image by analogy from human friendship. Rather we say that all human friendship is the far and shadowy reflection of God's true love for us.

For here in a world of night-foundered wayfarers, there is yet one who seeks us out. We may "wind our eye after" someone in whom we are interested, but we do not follow. Christ follows. Moving among us mind-misted people of the marsh, who half forget even as we begin to love, is one who not only remembers, but who loves and amends what he sees. We think we enjoy fellowship, says Hopkins, but that is but an interruption of our solitude. Yet in that same solitude, unseen by us and unsuspected, walks Christ. His interest does not flag, because his is the creature, as his are the winnings. He buys us back from death and distance; he loses, so to speak, that he may win. He alone is our "ransom" and "rescue." In the beginning, now, and evermore, Christ is ours before we know we are his, closer to us than we are to ourselves, our "first, fast, last friend."

The Shipwrecked Heart

WE MISTAKE IF WE believe that we can have the friendship of Christ on our own comfortable terms, whereby we desire only such intimacy with him as we would desire from the lantern carrier. We have heard in the poetry of Herbert that Christ asks for more: he asks for all. This love which the world resists is portrayed with terrifying intensity in several of Hopkins's poems. In particular, Christ is the "mastering me / God" of *The Wreck of the Deutschland* (1.1–2), who makes man and who, in fear-striking love, will unmake to remake. If we wish for a haven, Hopkins suggests, we must choose the God of storms, and maybe we will find our haven only after the shipwreck of what we thought we were. So the love of God is both port and tempest:

> The frown of his face
> Before me, the hurtle of hell
> Behind, where, where was a, where was a place?
> I whirled out wings that spell
> And fled with a fling of the heart to the heart of the Host. (3.1–5)

The speaker, a young priest who has said "yes / O at lightning and lashed rod" (2.1–2), confesses the terror inspired by Christ, whose love is more heart-hurling than any gale. For as in the Book of Job, the Lord knows the uttermost of our capacity, and the time for us to feel his might:

> Thou knowest the walls, altar and hour and night,
> The swoon of a heart that the sweep and the hurl of thee trod
> Hard down with a horror of height:
> And the midriff astrain with leaning of, laced with fire of stress. (2.5–8)

The ship, traditional symbol of the church, here becomes the side-straining heart of a man, hurled to the depths by the abyss of God's mercy. The man "leans" toward this "stress," this urgent pull, instinct in him, to seek God; but it is a leaning prompted by the "fire" of the stress, the work of the Holy Spirit within.

Storm calls unto storm: the perilous love God bears man is matched in man by a daredevil leaning and straining and longing. And that, says Hopkins, dates from the day of the Passion. It is no calm calculation that moves the brave man as he looks to Christ:

Hither then, last or first,
To hero of Calvary, Christ's feet—
Never ask if meaning it, wanting it, warned of it—men go. (8.6–8)

And God meets him with the love of a Creator who will have what he will have. God's tender mercies are ruthless, and his chastisements sweet. Mercy or chastisement, slow patience or sudden fire, it is all one to the faithful soul, who says, "Thy will be done," fashion me as you like, that I may be what I am meant to be, and not what I think I am:

With an anvil-ding
And with fire in him forge thy will
Or rather, rather then, stealing as Spring
Through him, melt him but master him still:
Whether at once, as once at a crash Paul,
Or as Austin, a lingering-out sweet skill,
Make mercy in all of us, out of us all
Mastery, but be adored, but be adored King. (10)

The stanzas I have quoted are part of the prelude to Hopkins's longest poem, a meditation upon the shipwreck of the *Deutschland*, carrying, among others who went to their watery graves, five Franciscan nuns exiled from Germany for their Catholic faith. They never reached shore. Rather they were vaulted in by the "dark side of the bay" of God's blessing (12.7); and he, Christ, both "lord of thunder" ("The Loss of the Eurydice," 109) and he who of all "can reeve a rope best" ("The Soldier," 10), would "reeve even them in" (*Wreck of the Deutschland*, 12.8) by means of the hero-making storm. For Christ is Lord over the storm and through the storm, and his heroism is to make heroes of men. One sailor, "handy and brave" (16.3), lashed to a rope, was pitched to his death trying to save a woman, "for all his dreadnought breast and braids of thew" (16.5), the cords of his muscles and the steadfastness of his heart. Not by such ropes were they to be saved, nor were they destined for the kind of salvation they sought.

The mother superior of the five nuns divined the terror to come, and the love. Lashed to the riggings, she called out to Christ, and her cry rang over the roar of the seamen and the wailing of women and children. For her and her sisters, the "martyr-master" (21.7) was at work, instructing them in their witness. What the passengers could see—the wild snowflakes—was only the vellum of the book she was being given to read. In Christ, this storm assumes the calm beauty of gilded miniature work fretting the capital letter of a chapter in Acts, let us say the same that described the shipwreck of Saint Paul:

> In thy sight
> Storm flakes were scroll-leaved flowers, lily showers — sweet
> heaven was astrew in them. (21.7–8)

In the sight of God, and that means in reality (could we but see it), the storm flakes were showers of lilies, symbols of virginity and of the Resurrection. Even the number of the nuns, five, is providential, reflecting the five wounds of the suffering Christ (22.1–2). Those five wounds were received by the founder of their order, Saint Francis, given him by an Eros-winged crucified Christ — Hopkins's astonishing line calls it "Lovescape crucified" (23.4). Such are the marks that Christ scores himself "on his own bespoken" (22.5), claiming them even here on earth as his, as he conforms them in love to his own suffering and conquering self.

The good nun cried out, "O Christ, Christ, come quickly!" (24.7). Does the world understand such love, Christ's love for us, and our self-devastating and therefore self-exalting love in return? "The cross to her she calls Christ to her, christens her wild-worst best" (24.8). Her cross is her Christ. She is not like the fearful apostles on the Sea of Galilee. She does not cry out for assistance, says Hopkins; no "we are perishing" comes from her (25.6; cf. Luke 8:24). She asks for nothing from her beloved, not the blessings of "pied and peeled May" (26.4), not ease for the "sodden-with-its-sorrowing heart" (27.4). It is neither horror nor stoic resignation that moves her, but something the poet finds too great to name. For in the end, Love sets us to stammer like a babe:

> But how shall I . . . make me room there:
> Reach me a . . . Fancy, come faster —
> Strike you the sight of it? look at it loom there,
> Thing that she . . . there then! the Master,
> *Ipse*, the only one, Christ, King, Head:
> He was to cure the extremity where he had cast her. (28.1–6)

"*Ipse*" — himself; that is all she wants. You who have cast me, cure me! In her rock-fast faith she is "the Simon Peter of a soul" (29.7), a woman of "single eye" (29.2), of whom Jesus said, "Blessed are the singlehearted, for they shall see God" (Matt. 5:8). She calls for Christ in the storm, and in the calm beyond the storm. For this same "mastering me / God" is, Christians affirm, the babe born painlessly to the Virgin in Bethlehem, "Jesu, heart's light, / Jesu, maid's son" (30.1–2). Hero and maker of heroes is he, but also the haven to which the hero longs to come, and the means of arrival. He is the "ark / for the listener" (33.2–3), and the dove sent by Noah to bring us the good news of the haven, for even when we linger, he "with a love glides / Lower than death and the dark" (33.3–4). His mercies pierce the walls of those "past-prayer, pent in prison, / The-last-breath penitent spirits" (33.5–6).

That is no contradiction. Love is as meek and as mild as the sweet babe in the manger; yet that Love is none other than "the Love that moves the sun and the other stars" (Dante, *Paradise*, 33.145). He is the homebody Christ shut in by the stars like a shock of grain:

> This piece-bright paling shuts the spouse
>   Christ home, Christ and his mother and all his hallows.
> ("The Starlight Night," 13–14)

And he is the hero who treads us down—whom we know not whether we love or resist, and whom we approach in the darkness of our resistance, thinking we have been abandoned, longing to be abandoned, yet wrestling all the same, lest he whom we love slip from our grasp:

> Cheer whom though? the hero whose heaven-handling flung me, foot trod
> Me? or me that fought him? O which one? is it each one? That night, that year
>
> Of now done darkness I wretch lay wrestling with (my God!) my God.
> ("Carrion Comfort," 12–14)

This Quintessence of Dust

WHAT IS MAN, THAT God should trouble to love him? It is one of the bitter truths of our age that we no longer sense the beauty of man, nor of woman, whom we incongruously dress as man, even in floppy outsized military uniforms. For us, man and woman are moderately handsome functionaries in a social machine of our making, or moderately intelligent animals on a planet spinning in the galactic backwaters. The strain of lyric beginning with the Provençal troubadours, making love close kin to religious wonder, has at long last petered out.

Hopkins might ask us what we had expected, we who have forgotten the beauty of Christ. It is no merely theological point. Christ is the pattern of physical, moral, and intellectual beauty:

> Our Lord Jesus Christ, my brethren, is our hero, a hero all the world wants. You know how books of tales are written, that put one man before the reader and shew him off handsome for the most part and brave and call him My Hero or Our Hero. Often mothers make a hero of a son; girls of a sweetheart and good wives of a husband. Soldiers make a hero of a great general, a party of its leader, a nation of any great man that brings it glory, whether king, warrior, statesman, thinker, poet, or whatever it shall be. But Christ, he is the hero" (From a sermon given Nov. 23, 1879).

The beauty of man, fashioned by Christ and for Christ, is never to be distinguished from Christ, who, though he is one and the selfsame, is "lovely in arms and lovely in eyes not his," playing "to the Father through the features of men's faces" ("As Kingfishers Catch Fire," 13–14). Everywhere in Hopkins we feel the attractiveness of human beauty, though we do not, he says, know why it draws us so powerfully. We think we see a sailor in uniform, smart and trim, and we admire the manly posture and the brown-skinned vigor; what we do not see is that he is an image of the all-sacrificing Christ. So when a young bugler comes to Father Hopkins to receive his First Communion—"Christ's royal ration" ("The Bugler's First Communion," 28)—the poet prays that the beauty of Christ may shine forth in the young man:

> As a heart Christ's darling, dauntless;
> Tongue true, vaunt- and tauntless;
> Breathing bloom of a chastity in mansex fine. (14–16)

When men are blind to the beauty of heaven, they cannot fathom the beauty of earth. But for Hopkins the farmer spreading dung and the woman with the slop pail are also images of the divine, and even the clop-clop of the plowhorse through the mud makes for the glistenings of heavenly beauty. So the swooping and diving falcon is the more beautiful for his descent; and the fire of Christ burns the brighter for his having been swaddled in a manger:

> No wonder of it: sheer plod makes plough-down sillion
> Shine, and blue-bleak embers, ah my dear,
> Fall, gall themselves, and gash gold-vermilion.
> ("The Windhover," 12–14)

The sad irony is that man asserts in defiance that he needs no Redeemer; he is lovely enough on his own. But after a brief noon of pride, he looks upon himself as little better than an animal or a machine. Hopkins's Christian vision affirms both the poverty of man and the richness to which he is called. Man is paltry and poor, but Christ divested himself of his riches to save man through poverty. Man is small and weak, but Christ became small and weak to save man, calling him to become even as a little child: "It leads one naturally to rhetorical antithesis to think for instance that after making the world He should consent to be taught carpentering, and, being the eternal Reason, to be catechized in the theology of the Rabbins" (from a letter to E. H. Coleridge, Jan. 22, 1866). Man is even less than the beasts, who act as they do by God-instilled instinct; more degraded, with a true sourness and spoiling. A machine rusts; man rots inwardly. But man is at the same time more than he knows. He has been granted an immortal soul, to be redeemed by One who became nothing, to bring to nothing the things that are.

The terrible depth to which man has sunk, and the beauty he has not quite lost, are thrown into startling juxtaposition in a poem with the ungainly title, "That Nature is a Heraclitean Fire and of the Comfort of the Resurrection." The philosopher Heraclitus had famously proposed that, because the world was a maelstrom of incessant change, its fundamental element must be fire, which is more variable than earth or air or water. You cannot step into the same river twice, says his famous dictum. And when Hopkins looks out upon the physical world, he sees the clouds, the "heaven-roysterers" (2) ganging up above, tossing and puffing and mingling, readying for the dazzling rain; and the "bright wind" (5) lashes and beats away at "yestertempest's creases" (6), as if every day or every year were a grand new storm to furrow its mark and then to have it wiped clean away by the storms to come. But the bustling wind and rain have other marks to efface—swelling to muddy dough and drying to dust the "manmarks" that adorn the earth, the footprints of "treadmire toil" (8).

Poor man here is as a beast of burden. He walks a *treadmill* that is a *quagmire*—superb image of ceaseless and profitless activity. It is the curse of Adam's sin: "In the sweat of thy face shalt thou eat bread, till thou return unto the ground; for out of it wast thou taken: for dust thou art, and unto dust shalt thou return" (Gen. 3:19). All is subject to change, yet nothing, essentially, changes; and man, sentenced to a drudgery whose very traces will fade as surely as he, is powerless to stop the change, or to change his fate: "Million-fueled, nature's bonfire burns on" (9).

But note that word *bonfire*: a "good fire," a fire for celebration. The fire of nature is meant to burn on—it has been kindled by God. The problem is not the fire but man's self-extinguishing in sin:

> But quench her bonniest, dearest to her, her clearest selved spark
> Man, how fast his firedint, his mark on mind, is gone!
> Both are in an unfathomable, all is in an enormous dark
> Drowned. O pity and indignation! Manshape, that shone
> Sheer off, disseveral, a star, death blots black out; nor mark
>   Is any of him at all so stark
> But vastness blurs and time beats level. (10–16)

Man is nature's "bonniest spark"—how finely humble and colloquial the adjective is! And he is most precious, because he is "clearest selved," by which Hopkins means that man possesses a beauty infinitely surpassing that of tree or bird or star. For man's intellect allows him to see and love the beauteous selves of other creatures, and to reflect in himself, and to desire union with, the beauty of God who made him. Man is both natural and beyond nature: the crown of nature, whose natural place is therefore not delimited. He shines "sheer off, disseveral," like a shooting star.

But what happens when this spark is quenched? In himself, man lacks the heart to love man, as we have seen in "The Lantern Out of Doors." He may see man's beauty, but the apprehension fades; it is no storm that beats last year's plough-ruts level, but only our sluggish and twilit minds that fail to grasp not a footprint in the mud but the veritable "firedint" of a man—as if each man should engrave himself with fingers and chisels of fire, and yet the engraving be flattened away once he had passed into the grave. Such was the darkness of heart that caused the Israelites to forget their God even as Moses was receiving the commandments, etched in fire.

Should man then finally be lost? Hopkins cries out, "Enough!" (16), and we might be tempted to suppose that he wants God to put out the bonfire. Nothing of it—let that fire burn on; we want not less change, but more. For the great change is yet to come, a change that shines with the fire of love:

> Enough! the Resurrection,
> A heart's-clarion! Away grief's gasping, joyless days, dejection.
>   Across my foundering deck shone
> A beacon, an eternal beam. (16–19)

Hopkins is punning here: the lovely *beacon* for the soul lost in darkness, the eternal *beam* of a fire that burns for the love of man, is a *sign* of stable meaning in and through this world of change. For, as Hopkins the linguist knew, *beacen* is the Anglo Saxon word for *sign* or *token*, as used in the brilliant poem *The Dream of the Rood*. And in that poem, as here, the sign is none other than the *sigebeam*, the victory-tree, the *beam* or *wood* of the cross. That tree alone burns and is not consumed. Burn on, then, fire of nature, cries the poet, and purge away the "mortal trash" of man! Let the fire burn all the hotter, for in this last pressure of heat and light will man become more than that sad one-time shooting star:

> Flesh fade, and mortal trash
> Fall to the residuary worm; world's wildfire, leave but ash:
> In a flash, at a trumpet crash
> I am all at once what Christ is, since he was what I am, and
> This Jack, joke, poor potsherd, patch, matchwood, immortal diamond
> Is immortal diamond. (19–24)

We are Jacks, jokes, broken scraps of pottery; not Job upon the dunghill, moaning his losses, as in his afflicted body he awaited the day when he would see his Redeemer. Nothing so noble as Job are we, but the sharp-edged shard of a pot with which he scraped his scabs and purulent sores. Such are we, no more substantial than a patch, no greater light to give than matchwood. But we are also immortal diamond, endowed with a soul that is, in its existence at least, past change. And Christ became man, even the loveliest of men, to make us the "immortal diamond" we essentially are. By the love of Christ, we become most ourselves.

The Language of Faith

HERE I WOULD LIKE to add a few comments concerning love and language. The single thing that all critics praise Hopkins for, his incredible originality of language, springs from the fount they prefer to ignore. For Hopkins never undertakes the struggle with words for its own sake. With all his strange archaisms and rope-twisting syntax, Hopkins is one of the least self-indulgent of writers. He never intends to be merely clever. Language must be jolted out of its ruts—must be anvil-set and hammer-dinted—to forge and flash forth the essence of the individual creature, the flame-drawing dragonfly, the mealed-with-yellow sallows, the piece-bright paling of the Milky Way.

Such excruciating, knuckle-cracking care is not spent in vain. If the things you wish to describe are not selves, but only arbitrary conglomerations of sense-impressions dependent upon the viewer's caprice, then there is no point trying to unlock their essence. They have none to unlock. Indeed, to speak properly, they are not *they* at all. Certainly they cannot be objects of genuine love.

But Hopkins did believe in the real and objective existence of beautiful and beautifully distinct things. That belief came to him from the source of his faith: God. To read the poet's notebooks is to glimpse an immensely active mind in love with God's creation: "The bluebells in your hand baffle you with their inscape, made to every sense: if you draw your fingers through them they are lodged and struggle/with a shock of wet heads; the long stalks rub and click and flatten to a fan on one another like your fingers themselves would when you passed the palms hard across one another, making a brittle rub and jostle like the noise of a hurdle strained by leaning against" (Journal, May 9, 1871). Now as I have argued above, Hopkins chose that word "inscape" wisely. An inscape is an in-shape, and that implies a Shaper, a bestower of form, a poet-architect.

Things are lovely because the God who is love loved them into being. They have an inscape, can be known by the eye and the heart in love, because they have been shaped, fashioned, formed by the God who saw them before they came to be. And we can wring our words to flash out some glint of that inscape, because words do signify, anchored as they are in the Word made flesh, the Word through whom all things were made.

Thus the single most powerful poetic innovator of the last 150 years of English poetry, whose small book of lyrics contains more diamonds than do decades of works by many greater names, would have been but a fair Victorian lyricist, were it not for his faith. The mystery of the Incarnation was that bonfire to heat the imagination of this priest white-hot. Let the world, if it pays attention, think that Hopkins banged the anvil under the influence of that faith. Let the Christian reader see the truth. Gerard Manley Hopkins loved because he was the object of God's love first. Many a frightful clank and hiss might we hear from that glorious poetic forge, but it was Hopkins himself who was being flinted out, fashioned into a curious and utterly selved tool for the praise and glory of the Love who rolled up his sleeves and set to work.

Part Five

The Mighty Child

18

A Meeting of Youth:
Dostoyevsky's The Brothers Karamazov

Two brothers are sitting at a table in the upper room of a tavern. Because of a father who saw his children as impediments to his debauchery, they were not raised in their own home, and are only now coming to know one another.

The elder, Ivan, has spent his last few years as a student, frequenting the salons of Saint Petersburg. There he has been exposed to the superstitions of the Enlightenment, wherein God was to be displaced by the goddess Reason, just as the revolutionaries of France had done in the Cathedral of Notre Dame in Paris. Jaded old Russian aristocrats, upon whose lips a broken and pretentious French is commonly heard, adopt the ideas to show how they can mingle among the most liberal young men in Europe—just as they adopt the newest style of collar or frock. They even free the serfs upon whose labor they rely to enjoy their imported wines and oranges; or would surely free them, were they ready to be set free. Ivan has heard these philanthropic ideas and rejects them, not because he believes in God—the fashionable atheism has fed his despair—but because he does *not* believe in man. He sees through the sentimentality of *that* religion. He is too old in experience, he thinks; he has observed too much of the mendacity and cruelty of man to believe that a benevolent God could have created our race.

The younger, Alyosha, has spent his last few years in what the enlightened European would consider the most retrograde institution imaginable: a Russian monastery. There, as a young man seeks out the hero, he has attached himself in youthful love to a saintly elder, one Father Zossima, now frail and dying. Such is the priest's reputation for spiritual discernment, prophecy, and healing that crowds visit him daily, and despite his weakness he listens to them, smiles upon them, rebukes them gently, and assists them on their pilgrimage. Besides his faltering voice, nothing about him betrays the pain he suffers. From his deathbed, Zossima will exhort Alyosha and the other monks to practice a childlike humility: they must embrace the earth in love, confessing that they are the greatest of sinners and are responsible for the sins of all mankind. Alyosha will soon hear the story of the youth of this remarkable man—bodily youth, for Zossima is more a child now than he was when he was a soldier long ago, with all the empty vices of that trade. The grace of God, by the example of a beloved brother who died young and in peace, brought him through. Alyosha knows that his elder will soon die, and he expects, with a naïve enthusiasm, that wonders will attend the saint's body and even his burial garb. It will not be so; God has in store for Alyosha a deeper childhood, a wiser naïvete. But the young man shines with the ardor of youth. He can believe in man, because he believes in Christ.

So these two passionate young men meet in that drab little tavern, to try to love one another as brothers, and to venture upon an intellectual and spiritual quest. They will discuss the existence of God, but not by ingenious proofs. Ivan winningly says that he has a "Euclidean imagination": he cannot follow justifications of God that set all things right at some point infinitely distant, like the non-Euclidean point where parallel lines meet. If God and this world are to be justified, they must be justified now, and we simple human beings must be able to understand it. Ruthless with both the theologian and the humanitarian, Ivan shines with a self-tormenting honesty. And at the heart of his disbelief in both God and man—at the heart of Dostoyevsky's vision in *The Brothers Karamazov,* and at the heart of the most astounding irony that Christians affirm—stands the child.

A Son Is Born to Us

WELL FOR IVAN THAT he should be haunted by the plight of children. Until Christ came to this wizened world, man had never heard that he was to grow old by growing young. "Suffer the little children to come unto me," said the Teacher, "and forbid them not: for of such is the kingdom of God" (Mark 10:14). "Verily I say unto you, Except ye be converted, and become as little children, ye shall not enter into the kingdom of heaven" (Matt. 18:3).

It is another saying we have heard too often. But it shook the continental shelf of man's stolid mind, this exaltation of the child (and of the mother, too, though many now forget). Granted, the moment was prepared for by the Hebrew Scriptures, and this too warrants notice.

The Book of Genesis is an epic of family destruction and social chaos, usually brought on by sexual sin. Lamech the boastful murderer is the first bigamist (4:19, 23–24). The daughters of men and the sons of God lust for one another, bringing about the wickedness that God will punish by the flood (6:1–4). Ham mocks the nakedness of his father Noah, and is cursed for it (9:22–27). Sarai, without child, begs Abram to sleep with her handmaiden, Hagar, but conceives an irremediable envy of her when Hagar bears a son, Ishmael (16). The men of Sodom attempt to have unnatural relations with the three angels of the Lord (19:1–11). Lot's daughters, living in a cave with their father, ply him with wine so that they may lie with him and bear his children, thus becoming the mothers of the idolatrous Moabites and Ammonites (19:30–38). Rebekah helps Jacob deceive his father Isaac, stealing from Esau the blessing that Isaac had intended to give him and dividing her family (27). Laban tricks Jacob into sleeping with Leah on the night of his wedding to Rachel, then coaxes him into an additional seven years of service, seven for each of the daughters he will have married (29:16–23). That is not to mention the rivalry of Rachel and Leah (30:1–13), the rape of Dinah and its consequences in treachery and bloodshed (34), Judah's fornication and Onan's perversity (38:1–10), Tamar's sleeping with her father-in-law (38:13–26), and the failed seduction of Joseph by Potiphar's wife, who then accuses him of rape (39:7–20).

Yet Genesis also bristles with the excitement of new life. The women burst into inspired naming whenever they bring forth a child. Abraham, Isaac, and Jacob all marry women whose difficulty in conceiving must be overcome by the merciful intervention of the Lord. The covenant with Abraham, that his descendants would be as numerous as the stars, seems often to rest upon the slenderest hope. And the book is interrupted—so we call it, who do not understand the point—by glorious lists of *begats,* as if the holiest and happiest thing men did in those early days was to bring more people into being. That is the natural way to look at it; theologically, in Genesis, fecundity is the gracious blessing and command of God. No doubt the naked pair in the garden would have obeyed that command! But even after they sin, the redemption promised by God is to come through their seed. So God curses Satan, in the person of the serpent: "And I will put enmity between thee and the woman, and between thy seed and her seed; it shall bruise thy head, and thou shalt bruise his heel" (3:15). The church fathers were unanimous in reading that verse, the so-called protevangelion or first good news, as a prophecy of the Messiah.

The pattern continues through the Old Testament: salvation comes through the birth of a child. The lad Joseph, sold by his brothers into slavery, remains faithful to God and becomes the most powerful man in Egypt. He it is, not Reuben, not Judah, who will save his brothers from the famine. When they come to Egypt looking to buy grain, they do not recognize in him the boy they wronged. But he recognizes them, and tests their honesty and love by pretending to keep their youngest, his full brother Benjamin, in his custody. Their willingness to give themselves up to save Benjamin, who is only a boy, shows Joseph that they are ready for forgiveness.

Many years later, long after Joseph and all his brothers have returned to the dust, the Pharaoh grows anxious about the fecundity of the Hebrews. He orders the drowning of their male babies. But one baby boy is saved in a wicker basket floated down the river to where the Pharaoh's sister and her maids are bathing. She "discovers" the boy, who will be given the Egyptian name of Moses. And he will become the greatest prophet in Israel, and the deliverer of the people from bondage.

Then comes the wild slayer of the Philistines, Samson the judge, born to a woman who had been barren; the angel promising his birth commands that he be consecrated to the Lord. A humble Moabite woman, Ruth, sets herself in the path of her deceased husband's kinsman, the wealthy Boaz; their tale of love and mercy ends in marriage, and the establishment of the Davidic line. David himself is but a youth and his father's youngest son when he gains renown in Israel, slaying the giant Goliath. Then we have the lads Samuel and Daniel, and the three young friends in the fiery furnace, and the seven defiers of King Antiochus Epiphanes. But the boy awaited by all Israel is the one of whom Isaiah speaks:

> For unto us a child is born, unto us a son is given: and the government shall be upon his shoulder: and his name shall be called Wonderful, Counsellor, The mighty God, The everlasting Father, The Prince of Peace.
> Of the increase of his government and peace there shall be no end,

upon the throne of David, and upon his kingdom, to order it, and to establish it with judgment and with justice from henceforth even for ever. The
zeal of the LORD of hosts will perform this. (Is. 9:6–7)

What Is the Child For?

HOW STRANGE IS THIS fascination with the child! Rome has her Hellenistic fables (postdating by centuries the story of Moses) about the twins Romulus and
Remus, exposed to die by their wicked uncle Amulius. But the gods had them
suckled by a she-wolf (whence Rome derived her warlike ferocity, for that is
the meaning of the fable), after which they were rescued and raised by a local
shepherd. Naturally, their royal blood flashes forth in heroic deeds when they
reach young manhood—heroic in cattle raiding and in protecting their own.
Finally they learn the truth of their parentage and slay the usurping uncle,
restoring the rightful king to the throne, and then founding the great city.

But the focus of that story is never on their being born. Indeed it would
have seemed indecent had Livy, who relates the story (winking at us, letting
us know that he does not believe a word of it), stressed the fecundity of Rome's
old republican families. For Rome, like China and Japan, honored age. A Roman boy grew up under the eyes of many generations of grandparents. Every
day he saw them watching him from the mantle above the hearth, in masks
made from waxen casts molded over their faces after death. Those ancestors
became the gods of the home and the hearth. Age, not childlike love, is our
destiny and aspiration.

In Greek mythology we do find exuberant lists of begats—when gods are
begetting. In Hesiod's *Theogony*, Mother Earth does nothing but produce, apparently without plan; and Zeus expresses his newly won authority by impreg-
nating every goddess or mortal woman he can lay his hands on. Yet those gods
themselves fear that a child will come to destroy them: so Uranus thrusts his
own children back into Mother Earth till his son Cronos avenges his siblings
by castrating him. Zeus in turn has to be hidden away from Cronos, who, once
he has gained authority over all the gods, swallows his children whole, lest one
should grow up to supplant him.

Zeus too would have been conquered by *his* son, according to a prophecy
that a certain goddess, no one knew who, would bear a child who would be
greater than his father. The details of the prophecy were known only to Prometheus, the clever and wayward Titan who had infuriated Zeus by helping

the sons of earth. He had given them the secret of fire, that key to the arts of civilization (cooking, baking brick, forging iron), allowing them to rise beyond the level of vermin. But Zeus wants to keep mankind lowly. He punishes Prometheus by chaining him to a mountain in the Caucasus, sending an eagle every day to pry his side open and feed upon his liver. Zeus relents in time, and Prometheus reveals his knowledge. Had he not relented he would have been overthrown, for he had been about to seduce the sea-goddess Thetis, the goddess named in the prophecy. To make double sure of avoiding the disaster, Zeus marries Thetis to a petty king in Thessaly, one Peleus, who becomes the father of the hero Achilles. And all the Olympian gods come to celebrate the wedding—and a birth that did not occur.

As for man, Greek mythology considers fecundity a mixed blessing. It may stir the gods to envy. King Priam is the most famously generative man in all the legends, but his fifty valiant sons and fifty lovely daughters mainly come to a bitter end in the Trojan War. They are lessons in the instability of fortune and the malice of the gods. Noble Hector would have lived out his days as a beloved prince had his brother Paris not stolen Helen away—or had Paris died in infancy, as his parents intended, exposing him on Mount Ida because of a prophecy that he would bring his people to ruin. Cassandra had cried out against the war, but because she had denied the love-stricken Apollo, he cursed her by inspiring her with prophecy and causing nobody to believe her. Agamemnon leads her off in chains to Greece, where she is murdered by his implacable wife, Helen's sister Clytemnestra.

Granted, the Greeks sculpted the beauty of youth, trying to capture its essence in stone. Their memorial statues of nude youths—*kouroi*—stand atop pedestals depicting young men doing what young men ought to do, in the happy vigor of manhood: gaming, wrestling, racing. But that a mere baby could be the hope of a nation never crossed their minds. Then, too, the Greek cultivation of youth grew diseased and unnatural. Greeks, and the Romans who first conquered them and then submitted to their vices, used boys as objects of sexual release. Even in Aristophanes, who for all his bawdy comedy is old-fashioned in his views, young boys are valued for their sexual appeal. So in *The Knights* one old veteran cannot help noticing, with embarrassed arousal, the impressions made by the boys' naked bottoms upon the dusty earth of the gymnasia. No trace of that vitiation of childhood can be found in scripture, unless it is among the Canaanite idolaters of the Baalim and the Ashtaroth, with their bathhouses and pretty-boys.

Romans and Greeks "exposed" their unwanted children, particularly the girls, who could not fight or dig a mine or plow a field, and might soon end up increasing the number of mouths to feed. Phoenicians and Canaanites made their children "pass through the fire to Moloch," charring babies beyond recognition in order to ensure a good harvest. These are not exceptions in human cultures.

Hebrews and Christians were not the first people to love their children. Romans were fond of them (and of dogs, too, by the way). But scripture does not talk about fondness. It turns our expectations inside-out. We think that the child is but an imperfect adult: we look not to what the child is, but to what the child will become. Jesus asks us to look to the child as the mysterious model for what we must become.

Aging Before One's Time

LET US RETURN TO the tavern. What is this Ivan like, who is about to prosecute his case?

He is young, yet his heart is rapidly aging. He is running away from his better self and does not know it. He recalls how Alyosha once loved cherry jam when he was a boy; in fact, he says he remembers everything about Alyosha until he went away to study in Moscow, after which he hardly thought of him at all. Now, planning to leave for good (though as it turns out he will be compelled to remain in Alyosha's care for the rest of his life, which Dostoyevsky suggests will not be long), Ivan aims to get to know his brother a little before he says goodbye. He is attracted by Alyosha's youthful steadfastness: "'The little man stands firm, I thought. Though I am laughing, I am serious. You do stand firm, don't you? I like people who are firm like that whatever it is they stand by, even if they are such little fellows as you. Your expectant eyes ceased to annoy me, I grew fond of them in the end, those expectant eyes. You seem to love me for some reason, Alyosha?'" (272).

We should not take Ivan entirely at his word. He does like Alyosha, but behind that gentle condescension—"little man"—lie respect and fear. In the conversation that follows, it seems that the elder is out to destroy the simple faith of the younger; but deep in his heart, Ivan both longs to possess that same faith and youth and is afraid of that possibility. Not for nothing do pagans slay their children: man suspects that the soft-skinned baby comes to be his executioner.

Alyosha replies that their eldest brother, Dmitri, calls Ivan "a tomb," associating him with age and death. But the child Alyosha (who has never witnessed duels, or haunted a brothel, or drunk vodka in a barracks, all those unfailing sources of wisdom) sees through the creases that are beginning to print their tracks on Ivan's soul. As Father Zossima had knelt before Dmitri, honoring the suffering and the unexpected holiness he foresaw in him, so now Alyosha appears to know Ivan better than Ivan knows himself. He sees in his brother an ardent, fresh youth, longing for the love of a woman, or the love of this old world:

> "I do love you, Ivan. Dmitri says of you—Ivan is a tomb! I say of you, Ivan is a riddle. You are a riddle to me even now. But I understand something in you, and I did not understand it till this morning."
> "What's that?" laughed Ivan.
> "You won't be angry?" Alyosha laughed too.
> "Well?"
> "That you are just as young as other young men of three and twenty, that you are just a young and fresh and nice boy, green in fact! Now, have I insulted you dreadfully?" (272–73)

Ivan isn't insulted at all. Closed-mouthed before Dmitri, whom he despises for his rashness and extravagant passion, cryptic and ironical before his father, as if he enjoyed witnessing the old man's degradation, seething with anger and love for the high-minded Katerina (the betrothed of Dmitri, whom Dmitri loves and hates), before this child and before no one else in the novel Ivan lays bare his heart. The child Alyosha reveals the child Ivan. But it is a youth that Ivan believes he must soon lose:

> "Do you know I've been sitting here thinking to myself: that if I didn't believe in life, if I lost faith in the woman I love, lost faith in the order of things, were convinced in fact that everything is a disorderly, damnable, and perhaps devil-ridden chaos, if I were struck by every horror of man's disillusionment—still I should want to live and, having once tasted of the cup, I would not turn away from it till I had drained it! At thirty, though, I shall be sure to leave the cup, even if I've not emptied it, and turn away— where I don't know. But till I am thirty, I know that my youth will triumph over everything—every disillusionment, every disgust with life." (273)

Such thirst for life is not base. It characterizes the Karamazov race, beating most warmly, and most unexpectedly, in the heart of Alyosha. But for Ivan it has no foundation. It is detached from both reason and faith. It is a surging of animal spirits that will subside with age. Such a childhood must die.

Ivan is a finer young man than he has any right to be, given his loss of faith; what he is not is exactly what he most prides himself on being. Ivan is not logical. He reasons acutely and precisely, but always athwart the truths his heart discerns: "'Though I may not believe in the order of the universe, yet I love the sticky little leaves as they open in spring. I love the blue sky, I love some people, whom one loves you know sometimes without knowing why. I love some great deeds done by men, though I've long ceased perhaps to have faith in them, yet from old habit one's heart prizes them'" (273). The problem is not pride, or not pride alone. Having suffered as a child and been neglected by his father, Ivan cannot become "like unto one of these little ones." He has witnessed man's brutality, never more brutal than when visited upon children. So although he says he is willing to accept God and his wisdom and his purpose, he cannot accept the world God has created.

Let us be clear about what Ivan does *not* mean. What he rejects in the world is not our physical weakness, but our wickedness. Thus, he is no easy materialist. He is not like the ancient Epicureans, for whom the child is simply weak, an object of pity:

> And then, a baby, tossed up like a mariner by
> Fierce waves, lies naked on the beach, dumb, helpless
> To save its life, when Nature has spilled it out
> Of the clench of its mother's womb to the shores of light,
> And fills the place with wailing—as is proper
> For one whom so much suffering awaits.
> (Lucretius, *On the Nature of Things*, 5.222–27)

Ivan does want to believe, and wants to be a child in truth:

> "I believe like a child that suffering will be healed and made up for, that all the humiliating absurdity of human contradictions will vanish like a pitiful mirage, like the despicable fabrication of the impotent and infinitely small Euclidean mind of man, that in the world's finale, at the moment of eternal harmony, something so precious will come to pass that it will suffice for all hearts, for the comforting of all resentments, for the atonement of all the crimes of humanity, of all the blood they've shed; that it will make it not only possible to forgive but to justify all that has happened with men—but though all that may come to pass, I don't accept it. I won't accept it." (279–80)

Ivan has lost his faith—meaning that he did once believe, and does still wish to believe. "'Dear little brother,'" he says, "'I don't want to corrupt you or to turn you from your stronghold, perhaps I want to be healed by you'"—and he smiles like a "little gentle child," a smile that Alyosha had never seen on him before (280).

It may seem foolish to go to a boy for the healing that philosophers have sought in vain, but Ivan's hope is well founded. The childlike hero of *The Brothers Karamazov* passes among its array of madmen, liars, lovers, and sinners—a drunken and vicious buffoon of a father, the desperate soldier Dmitri, a gang of schoolboys pelting their classmate with stones, the woman of ill repute for whom Dmitri will abandon his betrothed, the snide and cowardly "liberal" Rakitin. By his gentle presence and firm honesty he will recall to childlike simplicity all who wish to be called, and will move to derision and disgust those few who reject him. But Alyosha's faith must be strong, not milk-and-water sweetness. Zossima has sent him into the world to brave it. Here in the person of Ivan the world will fire its most dangerous weapons at Alyosha's heart.

A Child Does Not Love in Theory

IVAN BEGINS THE ASSAULT with a winningly frank confession: "'I could never understand how one can love one's neighbors. It's just one's neighbors, to my mind, that one can't love, though one might love those at a distance'" (281). The problem for Ivan is the face, the body, the gnarls and smells of incarnate man. Anyone can give to beggars so long as the beggars have the good grace to stay out of sight and smell. The reader senses that Ivan is partly correct; it is a devastating critique of the humanitarianism that Dostoyevsky so loathed. For we subscribe money for unseen natives far away—in what Dickens called "Telescopic Philanthropy" (*Bleak House*)—but neglect the poor whose bodies are embarrassingly present here and now. Children embarrass more than all, they who cannot take care of their humblest bodily needs. Ivan will not see the connection.

Dostoyevsky has been probing this failure of man's throughout the novel. He exposes quite a few lovers of mankind who hate their neighbors. Perhaps the noblest (and the shallowest) is the cousin of old Karamazov's first wife, one Miusov. It is the great boast of Miusov's life that when he was a young man in Paris he knew Proudhon and Bakunin, the most enlightened minds in France. In his age he magnified his importance to mankind: "He was very fond of describing the three days of the Paris Revolution of February, 1848, hinting that he himself had almost taken part in the fighting on the barricades. This was one of the most grateful recollections of his youth. He had an independent property of about a thousand souls, to reckon in the old style" (7). With what savage irony does Dostoyevsky lance the liberal self-image! He who pretends to have liberated France depends for his income on a thousand "souls," as the old euphemism for "serfs" put it. But Miusov thinks neither of serfs nor souls. They are too near. His reminiscences of youth, too, figure upon himself and his place in history, not upon a woman, nor the "sticky little leaves" that Ivan loves. Fittingly, his dealings with his neighbors now consist in upholding that self-image. He keeps up a feud with the monastery that borders his estate, the same where Alyosha has dwelt. It is an "endless lawsuit" concerning woodcutting or fishing rights, neither of which Miusov cares about; he merely wishes to oppose the priests. It never enters his mind that the ragged, the miserable, the debauched, and the grieving come to that monastery for help.

Miusov does rescue his cousin's son from old Karamazov. Not that the father had taken notice of the boy Dmitri. Were it not for the rough charity of Karamazov's servant Grigory, there would have been nobody "even to change the baby's little shirt" (7). Miusov insists that he be named guardian of the child and of certain revenues left to him by his mother. That done, he hastens back to France, leaving Dmitri in the care of a female relation. Miusov the high-minded is far more like his filthy neighbor Karamazov than he would care to admit: "It came to pass that, settling permanently in Paris he, too, forgot the child, especially when the revolution of February broke out making an impression on his mind that he remembered the rest of his life" (8).

Is the callousness of age then inevitable in man? Are we condemned to fool ourselves into thinking we were once young? Not if we live like the elder Zossima. But Ivan has turned his back upon Zossima's faith. Throughout the novel we find him shadowed by parodies of himself: desiccated intellects, weak and shallow and never young. Miusov is but the first and most risible of these, and Dostoyevsky places him beside Ivan in an early scene in the novel, as they and their father go to Zossima to ask him to arbitrate the strife in the Karamazov family.

We enter the elder's cell and see a startling union of age and youth. Two other old and venerable monks besides Zossima are present, along with Alyosha and a young divinity student with a "broad, fresh face" (42). In this same small and poorly accoutered room, Alyosha has slept for two years on a cot, beneath such holy pictures and engravings as might adorn the thatched hut of a peasant. As for Zossima, his looks bespeak a youth that glimmers even now, a few days before his death: "His face was very thin and covered with a network of fine wrinkles, particularly numerous about his eyes, which were small, light-coloured, quick, and shining like two bright points" (42). To the worldly, "mature" man who cannot see the child, it is a face to despise: "To all appearances a malicious soul, full of petty pride, thought Miusov" (44).

The conversation is delayed because Dmitri is late. That gives old Karamazov time to play the buffoon, to goad his hated neighbor Miusov into a rage. He accuses Miusov of having caused him to lose his faith by a slighting dinner reference to the *Lives of the Saints*—"'Yes, you were dining then, and I lost my faith!'" (50). It is a lie, but it captures enough of the haughty insolence of Miusov that the man cannot deny it. His only reply is a splutter of contempt against the neighbor: "'What do I care for your faith?' Miusov was on the point of shouting" (50). That outburst will be echoed by Ivan when Alyosha asks him how he thinks the murderous strife between their brother and their father will end: "'You are always harping upon it! What have I to do with it? Am I my brother Dmitri's keeper?'" (275). The words of Cain escape him before he is aware of it.

If only Miusov could have ignored his neighbor, he might have left the elder's cell no wiser, but at least no wickeder. But he descends from carelessness to disgust. Says he to Karamazov, who at least has a heart young enough for debauchery, "'You defile everything you touch'" (50). That too is echoed later by Ivan. Remarking upon the love shown by Saint John the Merciful, who breathed into the mouth of a sick beggar, "'putrid and loathsome from some awful disease'" (281), Ivan can only attribute it to "'the self-laceration of falsity.'" Even saintly love, in his heartless vision of man, is but the spreading of corruption.

Confronting the Children

FATHER ZOSSIMA HAS ENOUGH of the wearisome talk. While the arguers remain inside, still waiting for Dmitri, he goes out to meet his other visitors. Alyosha accompanies him, but not Ivan. We might say that these new visitors are children whose education has never given them the illusion of being intelligent or important. And "there is a silent and long-suffering sorrow to be met with among the peasantry" (53).

One weeping woman has come from afar to be counseled by the holy elder, as a child by a grandfather. Karamazov and Miusov were too preoccupied to care for Dmitri when he was little, but all this woman can think about is her child: "'It's my little son I'm grieving for, Father. He was three years old—three years all but three months. For my little boy, Father. I'm in anguish, for my little boy. He was the last one left. We had four, my Nikita and I, and now we've no children, our dear ones have all gone. I buried the first three without grieving overmuch, and now I have buried the last I can't forget him. He seems always standing before me. He never leaves me. He has withered my heart. I look at his little clothes, his little shirt, his little boots, and I wail'" (53–54). Her good husband Nikita has taken to drink; he comforts her by telling her that "'our son is no doubt singing with the angels before God'" (55), yet he weeps nonetheless. The poor mother longs for the flesh of her child, to hear "'his little feet,'" to hear his little voice cry, "'Mammy, where are you?'" And in her pain she no longer wishes to join with her husband in love: "'And what would our life be now together? I've done with him, I've done. I've done with them all. I don't care to look upon my house or my goods. I don't care to see anything at all!'" (54). How ardently her love shines through her ingenuous refusal ever to love her husband or her simple home again.

The elder's response embraces and affirms her suffering. He does not shrink from it. He does not explain it. He does not wish it away. He who is a child can treat this child-mother. "'Weep, but rejoice'" (54), he advises her, as she takes from her bosom her boy's sash and shakes with sobs:

> "It is Rachel of old," said the elder, "weeping for her children, and will not be comforted because they are not. Such is the lot set on earth for you mothers. Be not comforted. Consolation is not what you need. Weep and be not consoled, but weep. Only every time you weep be sure to remember that your little son is one of the angels of God, that he looks down from there at you and sees you, and rejoices at your tears, and points at them to the Lord God; and a long while yet you will keep that great mother's grief. But it will turn in the end into quiet joy, and your bitter tears will be only tears of tender sorrow that purifies the heart and delivers it from sin." (55)

It is the answer not of an intellectual but of one who has experienced the purifying of the heart that he holds out in hope for the woman. There is nothing theoretical about it. Zossima then asks the lad's name, that he may pray for him, and learns that he was Alexey (the baptismal name of Alyosha, too), named after Alexey, the man of God. Then he returns the grieving mother to the world, to her old life in the humble house she has abandoned, and to the husband whose sorrow she has not been patient enough to share. He returns her to her husband's bed; and perhaps there will yet be a child to come, to comfort them in their declining years.

The Child as Counterpoint

OF SUCH LOVE IVAN is not now capable. His excuse for not being such a child is, ironically enough, his love for children: but he loves them for their being free from the vices of grown-ups, and notes that he ceases to care for them after they reach the age of seven or so (282). Ivan dismisses the suffering of everyone else: "'Besides being disgusting and unworthy of love, they have a compensation—they've eaten the apple and know good and evil'" (282). In Dmitri and old Karamazov, he sees nothing childlike at all, and will express the hope that one monster will prey upon the other. That contempt will prevent him from saving his father's life; the failure will drive him mad with guilt. But children (at least before the age of seven) are another matter, and their suffering preys on his mind.

Like a prosecuting attorney, or like the Adversary among the Sons of God, Ivan amasses his evidence against man. It is prodigious. His macabre hobby is to collect newspaper clippings, anecdotes of man's hardheartedness or ferocity against children. There are the Turks, legendary for brutality, yet in their "artistry" and imagination enacting the cruelty men assign to beasts. They rip the unborn from the mother's womb, or toss a child in the air to spear it on a bayonet, or let a baby play with a pistol and then, in full view of the mother, pull the trigger. But Ivan has worse specimens from home, Europe. He relates the beheading of a thief and murderer named Richard, a bastard child hardly clothed or fed by the shepherds who "'raised'" him; and the spectacle of all the hypocrites of "'philanthropic and religious Geneva'" (285) coming forth to cheer his conversion to the Lord as he made his way to the scaffold. Or the "'well-educated, cultured gentleman'" (286) who with his wife beat his little daughter with a birch-rod, working himself and his wife to the pitch of sexual excitement. The man was acquitted in court. Or the little girl beaten and kicked by her middle-class parents, who locked her up in a privy one winter night because she wet the bed: "'They smeared her face and filled her mouth with excrement, and it was her mother, her mother did this'" (286).

Ivan cannot square the suffering of children with any harmony God may bring about in the end. A mother whose child was thrown to the dogs may embrace his murderer in love, but what of the child? "'It's not worth the tears of that one tortured child who beat itself on the breast with its little fist and prayed in its stinking outhouse, with its unexpiated tears to "dear, kind God"! It's not worth it, because those tears are unatoned for'" (290). Who has the right to forgive on account of that child? Would it be worth creating a universe, asks Ivan, if it meant that it was essential that such a child would suffer, for the harmony in the end to come about? Would the pious young monk consent to take his happiness under those conditions?

"'No, I wouldn't consent,'" says Alyosha softly (291). Alyosha will flash out with the answer to Ivan's riddle, the clue to solve the case. For Ivan's prosecution is like the case that the district lawyer will build against Dmitri, who will be accused of murdering his father. A concatenation of facts and testimonies and plausible interpretations of motive appears to lead inevitably to Dmitri's guilt; yet no single element in the chain is unambiguously true. Dmitri will be convicted, but he is *not* guilty.

Ivan's solicitude for children is an instance of this too-easy thinking. He says he cannot believe in God because he cannot accept a world in which children must suffer. But as vigorously as he may deny it, he was himself an unloved child whose response to the neglect was to turn away from childhood. For years he forgot about Alyosha; he cares nothing for Dmitri; and his conclusion that "there is no virtue if there is no immortality" (79) is the hinge upon which the novel's tragedy turns. Dmitri will hear it—Ivan seems to intend that Dmitri hear it, that it may corrupt him and bring about the much-desired death of their father. Not that Ivan is consciously a parricide, but life would be simpler for him if both Dmitri and old Karamazov were out of the way, the one in prison and the other in the grave.

As it turns out, the father's effeminate valet (and self-styled intellectual) Smerdyakov will hear Ivan's words and act upon them, with what he thinks is Ivan's tacit consent. The result of Ivan's philosophy thus turns against his presupposition. God does not exist; man is too bestial for that. But if God does not exist, then all things are lawful. If all things are lawful, then, in particular, it is lawful to rape an ugly idiot girl, "Stinking Lizaveta," as old Karamazov did, and beget a son upon her, the nicknamed "son of the stench," Smerdyakov. Then it is lawful to kill one's father, or to put one's brother in the way to kill him. Or it is lawful to engage in all the wickedness against children that Ivan has catalogued.

No reasonable man can say that he cannot believe in the objective Good because there is too much evil in the world, since with the notion of objective Good must fall the notion of evil. The most he can do, reasonably, is say that he cannot understand it, and in particular he cannot see how a good God could have created a world in which such a being as himself would exist. But as soon as you see that *you are* the problem of evil—that every time you pass in front of a mirror you behold the cause of despair in others—then you are a step away from humility. You will embrace the earth and beg its forgiveness, as Zossima urges his disciples to do. You need no longer despair at the suffering of children when you have become a child and will suffer beside them in love.

The Answer Is a Child

THAT IS A STEP that Ivan never takes; he is hobbled by his philosophy. But Alyosha takes the step. Many children suffer in the small town where the Karamazovs live, but Ivan does not notice. We never see Ivan near a child. That is remarkable in itself; more remarkable is what we see in Alyosha. For in this tavern, the intellectual has allowed his passions to throw his reason down, while the mere child will struggle, with all the might of his love for poor suffering man and with all his faith, to think clearly and, more than that, to love his brother Ivan. Even Dmitri will shock Alyosha with a mysterious parting plea: "'Love Ivan'" (727). No comparable plea comes from Ivan.

It would take an entire book to flesh out the role that Alyosha plays in ministering to the sufferings of children, not from the superior vantage of age, but from childlike honesty and love. Critics tend to ignore, as peripheral to the main plot, Alyosha's striving to befriend a pack of quarreling schoolboys and reconcile them to one another, but that digression—and not Ivan's justly famous fable of the Grand Inquisitor—shows what Dostoyevsky holds out as man's hope. Alyosha confronts the anger and betrayed love of a child who is sick and about to die; the pain and shame of the child's poor drunken father, and a patiently tended mother who has lapsed into feeblemindedness; the longings and the sins of boys who have already, as Ivan would have us believe, tasted the apple of wickedness; even the intellectual and spiritual aspirations of a young lad well on his way to atheism, who, but for the intervention of Alyosha, would have become another Ivan. By the end of the book, we shall see Alyosha at the head of this gang, now no gang but friends united in faith and in love for the deceased classmate they had hurt. They vow to remember their friendship even should the years (and sin) separate them. And they look forward in hope to the resurrection.

For there is a person who has the right to forgive the sufferings of the child. The answer is himself a child: "'No, I can't admit it. Brother,' said Alyosha suddenly, with flashing eyes, 'what you said just now, is there a being in the whole world who would have the right to forgive and could forgive? But there is a Being and He can forgive everything, all and for all, because He gave His innocent blood for all and everything'" (292). For Christ was a child, and never left off being a child. He suffered, and forgave; and to conform ourselves to him, as Alyosha strives to do, is to know the peace of childhood, in all this suffering and confused world.

19

Wisdom from a Child:
Dickens's A Christmas Carol

The Child as Hero

DOSTOYEVKSY STROVE FOR YEARS to portray the strange hero inspired by Christ: the child of a man, overlooked by the worldly-wise, but endowed with a vision of truth inaccessible to most. The contrast between the innocent who really does know things, and the sophisticate who really knows little, is central to Dostoyevsky's ironic vision in *The Brothers Karamazov* and *The Idiot*, and something of it glimmers in the darkness of the strangely childlike murderer Raskolnikov in *Crime and Punishment*, the boorish misfit of *Notes from the Underground*, and the pathetic "hero" of *A Ridiculous Husband*.

The Russian was not the first. Perhaps the most famous, and the wisest, child in all literature wears a pasteboard helmet, thinks a barber's shaving basin is "the helmet of Mambrino," promises his fat and faithful squire the government of an island, and spends entire nights awake in the cold and the dew, pining away for a local peasant woman, a dealer in hogs whom the good knight's loving imagination has transformed into Dulcinea del Toboso. When he is asked why he does not leave his master Don Quixote—seeing as he gets for his service mainly bruises, broken bones, bad rations, and embarrassments too numerous to list—Sancho Panza refers not to the knight's illusions but to his innocence: "'His soul is as clean as a pitcher. He can do no harm to anyone, only good to everybody. There's no malice in him. A child might make him believe it's night at noonday. And for that simplicity I love him as dearly as my heart-strings, and can't take to the idea of leaving him for all his wild tricks'" (*Don Quixote*, 2.13).

A holy simplicity, like that of Saint Francis, dwells in the knight of La Mancha. No doubt he is a sinner, too—Cervantes was no sentimentalist—but we might wish for some of the knight's folly. The irony of that book turns finally against all those who see only irony. It is not quite correct to say that Don Quixote seems foolish but really is wise. The man indeed *is a fool*, as we should all be. For the author too loves his knight as dearly as his heart-strings, and so will give him good company for his knighthood. Sancho and his master meet some men taking statues to town for a religious play they are to present. When the knight asks to see the icons—for he is winningly curious about everything and everyone, like a child—he is shown Saint George, "mounted on horseback with his lance thrust through the mouth of a serpent" (2.58). Says Don Quixote with wonder: "This knight was one of the best errants in all the Heavenly Host," and "he was an especial defender of maidens" (2.58). Of Saint Martin of Tours: "This knight too was one of the Christian adventurers, and I believe he was even more generous than valiant," as witness his parting of his cloak with the beggar. His praise of Saint Paul is unmatched for simple eloquence: "'This was the greatest enemy our Lord God's church had in his time, and the best defender it will ever have—a knight errant by his life and a peaceful saint in his death, a tireless labourer in the vineyard of the Lord and teacher of the Gentiles. He had Heaven for his school and Jesus Christ Himself for his professor and master'"(2.58). Shipwrecked and stoned, whipped and beaten, arrested here and sent packing there, taken up into the heaven of heavens to see what tongue could not utter nor the mind of man conceive, Saint Paul committed the folly of faith, traversing the Roman world, winning souls for Christ.

If this be folly, who would not be a fool? Christian literature abounds in "children" who are the heroes and the sages of their tales, from whom no one but the wisest and most childlike themselves expect anything of value. Such is the "fool" in the plays of Shakespeare, a dramatic innovation we now take for granted, but surely inspired by the ironies of his Christian faith. Lear's Fool, whom at one point the king addresses humbly and affectionately, as a child

("In, boy; go first" [3.4.26]), is the only man who can poke fun at the king's folly to his face, and even sets to school the wise and faithful Kent (2.4). So too the one character in *Twelfth Night* who sees through everyone's pretenses and can, more or less, get along with everyone anyway (even while counterplotting the plotter Malvolio), is Feste, the clown. Touchstone, Launcelot Gobbo, Dogberry, even the ass-translated Bottom are all granted moments when they are wiser than their masters, or when through their own humble means some injury is averted or some wrong is set to rights.

Erasmus had already, in *The Praise of Folly*, suggested, in a double-reversing irony, that though all those who give their lives to riches and power and fame are fools, the biggest fools of all are Christians, bless them. For Christ gave thanks that the Father "had concealed the mystery of salvation from the wise, but revealed it to babes and sucklings, that is to say, fools. For the Greek word for babes is fools, which he opposes to the word wise men" (140). He who slighted the company of lawyers and doctors of theology delighted in "little children, women, and fishers," preaching the foolishness of the Cross, and inspiring the foolishness of the martyrs: "Lastly there are no sort of fools seem more out of the way than are these whom the zeal of Christian religion has once swallowed up; so that they waste their estates, neglect injuries, suffer themselves to be cheated, put no difference between friends and enemies, abhor pleasure, are crammed with poverty, watchings, tears, labors, reproaches, loathe life, and wish death above all things; in short, they seem senseless to common understanding, as if their minds lived elsewhere and not in their own bodies."(143–44). Any kind of religion appeals most to those who are not known for their wisdom: "Consider first that boys, old men, women, and fools are more delighted with religious and sacred things than others, and to that purpose are ever next the altars; and this they do by mere impulse of nature" (143). Yet, though their visions will surpass their ability to describe, these simpletons will see what Plato only dreamed of, even a foretaste of what is promised in scripture: "The eye hath not seen, nor the ear heard, nor has it entered into the heart of man to consider what God has provided for them that love Him" (151). Such a vision in any case must render us no better than an infant, as Dante says:

> Even for these few memories I've confessed,
>   my words are less than what a baby says
>   who wets his tongue still at his mother's breast. (*Paradise*, 33.106–8)

And Christian authors themselves have rejoiced in the sheer fun of Christian folly, the childlike wisdom that abounds in irony: for we can, as with the starry-eyed knight of La Mancha, laugh heartily at the follies of the Christian fools, and laugh more heartily, and sadly, at the follies of everyone else, and wish that we might tilt at a few windmills too. It is an irony that such as Voltaire could never touch: Candide is an innocent, but there is no wisdom in that ingenuousness; and his tutor Doctor Pangloss is a pretentious idiot. How different is the grand Parson Adams of Henry Fielding's romp *Joseph Andrews*: an old man so silly as to believe that he can just walk to London with a sheaf of sermons and sell them to a publisher; yet also so silly, in a Christian way, as actually to have important things in those sermons to say about charity and the Christian life to a semi-Christian world that knows better and will not hear. The good Parson Adams is a child—delighting in stories, racing a coach on foot, spoiling for a fistfight against ruffians, and snapping his fingers in an ecstasy when a stroke of good fortune for someone else tickles his heart.

Adams survives in all kinds of manifestations, especially in the work of Charles Dickens: gleeful and sharp-eyed Tommy Traddles in *David Copperfield*; the circus performers of *Hard Times*; the hard-laughing Mr. Boythorn who never outgrew his youth in *Bleak House*. He survives in the hero of Myles Connolly's *Mr. Blue*, a modern Saint Francis (a fool himself); Father Brown in Chesterton's theological detective tales; Samwise Gamgee of Tolkien's *Lord of the Rings*; the manly and innocent Curdie of the romantic fables by George Macdonald; the good priests of Willa Cather's *Death Comes for the Archbishop*—and in too many other works to list, even works written by authors who reject any formal Christianity but retain its deep wellsprings of hope. So Italo Calvino celebrates a wise and hapless clown of a laborer in *Marcovaldo*, or a boy who in defiance against his staid old aristocratic parents climbs a tree on their estate and for the rest of his long life never comes down again, but manages from up there to fight for Italian independence anyway, leaping from tree to tree, brandishing sword and pistol and pondering the ideals of the Enlightenment (*The Baron in the Trees*).

The Child Who Teaches

BY THE VICTORIAN AGE, the teacher-children were often children indeed, whose innocence is powerful enough to bring to life the dead souls of their "wise" elders. That is the plot of *Pollyanna* and *Heidi*, but it is also the plot of such psychologically subtle works as George Eliot's *Silas Marner* and *The Mill on the Floss* and Charlotte Brontë's *Jane Eyre*. For that saying of Jesus remained, "that unless we become as little children, we shall not enter the Kingdom of Heaven" (Matt. 18:3). It was the leaven in the lump. The Incarnation alone—think of the feast of the Nativity—ensured that Christians could never look upon children as their pagan predecessors had. What that little babe is now, my Lord and Savior once was. Beyond that, though, lay the suspicion that Jesus was not speaking metaphorically. Somehow we are to aspire to the character of a child. It is as if an adult were but an imperfect boy or girl.

The result for Christian art is a unique emphasis on the child, not only as object of instruction (as in Plato's *Symposium*, *Republic*, and *Meno*), but slso as teacher. Sometimes the child instructs by a wisdom granted through God's direct intervention; more often it is by the child's indirect example. The folklore of every Christian people in Europe is full of tales wherein the child is nobler than the parent, or wherein a young lad or maiden plays, sometimes unconsciously, the redeemer (as do the dying Ilusha and Markel in *The Brothers Karamazov*). And the most ironic thing of all, the thing that the adult least expects, is that the child will teach him how to be a child again.

A child again? I have miscast the matter. If we are to become like God, then we are to grow young: not young *again*, but truly young for the first time. Jesus did not speak of salvation as our refreshment or rejuvenation, but as our being *born again*. Without Christ, we are like the young shepherd in Shakespeare's *Winter's Tale*, who in the midst of a terrible storm witnesses the destruction of a brave vessel and the deaths of all the wailing sailors aboard, while nearby a ravenous bear kills and feeds upon the nobleman who did not make it back to the boat. "'Thou metst with things dying,'" says his father, when he returns to tell him of it. But that old man has found a little baby girl exposed to the elements, and a box of treasure nearby. "I met with things newborn," says he (3.3.111). To meet with things newborn: for the Christian, that is the hope that burns brightly at Christmas, and Pentecost, and Easter.

The Caroler Dickens

IT IS ODD THAT Charles Dickens should be the one Christian author most attached to the mystery of the Christ child. He is confusedly unitarian, harboring a deep and poorly considered detestation of all theological distinctions, including that which asserted the divinity of Christ, coeternal with the Father.

Nonetheless, Dickens called Jesus "Our Savior," and he meant it, cherishing Jesus' words and working the lessons of the Gospels into all he wrote.

In fact, much of Dickens's work is a narrative meditation upon Christian ironies. Most prominent among these is that the Son of man came not to be served but to serve, and that therefore he who wishes to be greatest in the kingdom of heaven must be as the least, and serve his brothers. That pattern is borne out with wonderful psychological accuracy (for the Savior says nothing which is not also true in our world, though people prefer not to admit it) by many of Dickens's most beloved characters. We have the cheerful Sam Weller, rakish and roguish and yet devoted to his good and sometimes addled master, Mr. Pickwick (*The Pickwick Papers*); the ever-whistling Mark Tapley, whose brand of dour evangelicalism sits so ill upon him that he blames himself for never meriting anything, so great is the pleasure he derives from lending a hand to a disease-ridden family or helping his callow master navigate the illusion of fortune-hunting in America (*Martin Chuzzlewit*); the bluff and (when her wrath is aroused) formidable Miss Pross, who knows only that she must delay Madame Laforge as long as she can, with her own body if need be, and who goes deaf from the gunshot that accidentally results (*A Tale of Two Cities*); the helpful and openhearted Cissy, who cannot keep in her head the hard "facts" taught in her patron Mr. Gradgrind's school, but who does remember such things as goodness and love, and who enlists the assistance of her old friends in the circus to save Gradgrind's son, a monster of amorality, from the law (*Hard Times*); and Newman Noggs, inoffensive and unassuming, employed by a wicked master, yet endangering himself to assist his master's young nephew (*Nicholas Nickleby*).

Then there are in Dickens those who risk their lives, or who lay them down, in imitation of Christ—all for love. Sydney Carton drugs his look-alike, Charles Darnay, to smuggle him out of a French prison and take his place, awaiting the guillotine, while Darnay will be returned to his wife, the woman to whom Carton has declared the only redeeming love he has ever known (*A Tale of Two Cities*). Esther Summerson exposes herself to smallpox, and goes temporarily blind from it as she tends to her poor chambermaid, an orphaned girl she had saved from the streets, while the man she loves, who thinks he has lost all hope to win her hand in marriage, sets out on a dangerous voyage as a ship's doctor, and returns to minister to the most destitute of the filthy streets of London (*Bleak House*). The manly and jilted Ham takes on all the most perilous work on the shore of Yarmouth, knowing that other men are married and have children to support and that his own life is dispensable. Thus, in the midst of a wild storm he dies trying to rescue someone in a sailboat foundering offshore: Steerforth, as it turns out, the selfish daredevil who had seduced Ham's betrothed (*David Copperfield*).

These meditations in Dickens often focus on the figure of a child. Sometimes it is a childlike adult from whom a most unexpected salvation comes. Joe Gargery, who cannot read or write and who spends most of his married life being cowed by Mrs. Gargery, saves the ambitious Pip from destruction, and does so despite his pained memory of Pip's ingratitude (*Great Expectations*); the half-wit Barnaby is the unwitting instrument for unraveling the secret of an old murder (*Barnaby Rudge*); the loyalty of the one-armed old tar, Cap'n Cuttle, and of a poor brain-blasted scholar of Latin by the name of Toots, combine in the most absurd and touching ways to save the innocence of a helpless young woman (*Dombey and Son*). Sometimes it is the child himself who stands as a sign of the sins of his elders. He returns, in the providence of God, to claim restitution or punishment, or to be the innocent revealer of the evil done to him. Such an agent of providence is the cripple Smike in *Nicholas Nickleby*, and the orphan Oliver in *Oliver Twist*. Or he dies on the streets and communicates to others the dread disease to which they have exposed him, as does the poor single-named Jo in *Bleak House*. Sometimes the child *is* the teacher, as Cissy in *Hard Times*, Esther in *Bleak House*, Paul and Florence Dombey in *Dombey and Son*. And then sometimes the child is one's own, a reproach against one's sins, yet an undeserved call to return to nature, in effect to become a child all over again (*Little Dorrit, Dombey and Son*).

All they who hold fast to their own purposes, come Who may, conclude by murdering the child. So did Herod, and so did the inflexible Mr. Murdstone, who prided himself on a firmness as cold as death—firm enough, apparently, to crush the life out of a frail young widow, a very child of a woman (*David Copperfield*). But Dickens shows that Herod is a kind of suicide, too. For the sake of such cramped and degraded life as a Herod knows, he will shrug off or destroy the child sent by God to make him young. That is, he will destroy himself. He will grow sickly-hearted and ancient before his time.

An Old Man We Think We Know Well

DICKENS'S MOST POPULAR WORK—his admirer Chesterton called it his greatest—is so well loved that we may be tempted to take it for granted. But long before he wrote *A Christmas Carol*, Dickens had pondered the birth of the Savior in a humble stable, laid to sleep in a manger.

Dickens knew what he was about. His miser Ebenezer Scrooge is no child. He is an old man, as Saint Paul defines age:

> But now we are delivered from the law, that being dead wherein we were held; that we should serve in newness of spirit, and not in the oldness of the letter. (Rom., 7:6)
> Put off concerning the former conversation the old man, which is corrupt according to the deceitful lusts;
> And be renewed in the spirit of your mind;
> And . . . put on the new man, which after God is created in righteousness and true holiness. (Eph. 4:22–24)

But, like many an old man, Scrooge cannot see his age. Without the grace of God, how can he? He is too upright to see it. We should not suppose that Scrooge ever engaged in *illegal* seizure of goods. He, like Shylock, will have his bond. He stays securely within the pale of legality and respectability, if a cold, grasping mind be legal and respectable.

There are plenty of aged characters in Dickens who mellow in the cheerfulness of their honest hearts, growing young and green for heaven. My favorite is the perfectly nicknamed "old girl" Mrs. Bagnet (*Bleak House*). Of her, Dickens says that she has grown slightly plump as she has gotten on in years, so that the ring she wears for Mr. Bagnet will never come off again, not till ring and finger be resolved into the dust. But Scrooge is old: everything about him suggests a skeletal skinniness, constriction, confinement, the dreary routine of sin, a walking death. So our introduction to Scrooge is as the "chief mourner" at the funeral of his old business partner, Jacob Marley, seven Christmas Eves before the events of the novel. They were collectors of bad debts, those two: buying a creditor's rights at wholesale, then exacting from the debtors as much as they could by law. It never occurs to him that *he* might owe a hefty debt; his moral imagination has been worn away by the respectable and routine. He is, as he calls himself, a good man of business.

Of course, there was no true mourning in Scrooge's heart that day of Marley's funeral. He showed up as the chief mourner because that is what partners in business do to fulfill all righteousness. If there was a glimmer of a tear, Scrooge himself was unaware of it. He knew Marley was dead, and after that death he was oblivious to anything concerning Marley: "Scrooge was his sole executor, his sole administrator, his sole assign, his sole residuary legatee, his sole friend, and his sole mourner. And even Scrooge was not so dreadfully cut up by the sad event, but that he was an excellent man of business on the very day of the funeral, and solemnized it with an undoubted bargain" (9–10). In his confinement from anything beyond the walls of his countinghouse self, Scrooge is a blast of cold against what remains of the springtime of our fallen nature. Like most sinners, he toils hard in the traces:

> Oh, but he was a tight-fisted hand at the grindstone, Scrooge! a squeezing, wrenching, grasping, scraping, clutching, covetous old sinner! Hard and sharp as flint, from which no steel had ever struck out generous fire, secret, and self-contained, and solitary as an oyster. The cold within him froze his old features, nipped his pointed nose, shrivelled his cheek, stiffened his gait, made his eyes red, his thin lips blue, and spoke out shrewdly in his grating voice. A frosty rime was on his head, and on his eyebrows, and on his wiry chin. He carried his own low temperature always about with him; he iced his office in the dog-days; and didn't thaw it one degree at Christmas. (10–11)

Scrooge's age in sin must be construed closely with his vaunted independence, his being his own man. To be old as Scrooge is old, as Dickens saw it, is to choose a thin gruel of a life, to kill oneself slowly with loneliness. It is therefore a serious mistake to suppose that Scrooge's chief sin is greed. For there is in Scrooge a sin deeper than greed, and it compels the rejection of everything helpless and humble in our sad comedy of a life.

To see this sin, let us recall the first conversation we overhear in the book—we who sit listening, like the clerk Bob Cratchit in his miserable little tank. A young man bursts into the countinghouse:

> "A merry Christmas, uncle! God save you!" cried a cheerful voice. It was the voice of Scrooge's nephew, who came upon him so quickly that this was the first intimation he had of his approach.
> "Bah!" said Scrooge. "Humbug!" (13)

Scrooge's nephew Fred is one of those sensible fools, those holy scapegraces, to be found ever marrying the prettiest girls in Dickens's novels. He is a regular David, his face "ruddy and handsome" (13). We should not take his words as mere convention. Fred wishes—in the form of a prayer—that his uncle will have a merry Christmas (as, by grace, he will), and that God will save him (as, by grace, *He* will!).

The arrival of Fred is like a Christmas, then, as sudden as the spirits who will appear, and as unmerited as grace. But Scrooge has shut the child out of his heart. Here let us note a clash between what Scrooge says about Christmas and how he argues its worthlessness. When Scrooge calls Christmas "humbug," he seems about to dismiss it as fairy-tale, as many Victorian intellectuals had done. But he argues against it on brutely utilitarian and personal grounds. The Savior was never born in the flesh centuries ago, and why not? Because the holiday has never put a shilling in his pocket. Scrooge hates Christmas because it has brought him no happiness; in effect, he hates it because by rejecting it he has made himself old and miserable. Scrooge justifies his contempt by asserting that all Christmas does is leave Fred one year older and no better off. He brings up the dead reckoning of a year's bills, like a dreary Last Judgment from which the poor man, a fool as Scrooge calls him, will find no redemption: "'Out upon merry Christmas! What's Christmas-time to you but a time for paying bills without money; a time for finding yourself a year older, and not an hour richer; a time for balancing your books, and having every item in 'em through a round dozen of months presented dead against you?'" (13)

The fact is, Scrooge wants desperately to believe that the only book-balancing for man will be the sort he knows in his business. Christmas is a painful reminder that it is not so. When Fred protests that Scrooge, far from keeping Christmas ill, does not keep Christmas at all, the uncle's response tolls his own death. It identifies his sin: "'Let me leave it alone, then'" (14).

"It is not good for the man to be alone," said the Lord God, who cast a deep sleep upon Adam and fashioned from one of his ribs the woman, the helpmeet and object of Adam's desires. This one at last, says Adam, is bone of my bone and flesh of my flesh (Gen. 2:23). He called her Eve, says Scripture, because she was to be the mother of mankind. Critics say that that verse of joy (Gen. 3:20) has been misplaced by a careless redactor. But critics assume they know more than they do; that is their occupational hazard. Whether or not God used a careless redactor for his purposes, it is fitting that the verse *follow* the account of the Fall—as if Adam understood that even with the loss of Eden, man's redemption must come from motherhood and fatherhood through the child that is to be. Scrooge has, then, pitched himself into Adam's curse while rejecting Adam's blessing. He wants to increase and multiply his accounts. Otherwise he has willed himself into solitude. He is his own.

That solitude is what the nephew seizes upon in his spirited reply. Fred does not wish to engage Scrooge in a theological argument, for it is bad old-fashioned sin, not argument, which has turned Scrooge into the Christmas atheist. Nor does Fred make light of the birth of Christ, as might a modern hawker of sentiment; he expressly says that nothing belonging to Christmas can be separate from that birth. Instead he argues on Scrooge's own terms. The birth of the Child does men good, because they rediscover one another in it. Christmas is "'the only time I know of, in the long calendar of the year, when men and women seem by one consent to open their shut-up hearts freely, and to think of people below them as if they really were fellow-passengers to the grave, and not another race of creatures bound on other journeys. And therefore, uncle, though it has never put a scrap of gold or silver in my pocket, I believe that it *has* done me good, and *will* do me good; and I say, God bless it!'" (14). As if to provide evidence for his assertion, Fred shows that he has come to invite Scrooge to Christmas dinner. The old miser declines, saying, with a horrid oath, that he would see Fred in some unmentioned extremity first. The young man finds that anger inexplicable and sad:

> "But why?" cried Scrooge's nephew. "Why?"
> "Why did you get married?" said Scrooge.
> "Because I fell in love."
> "Because you fell in love!" growled Scrooge, as if that were the only thing in the world more ridiculous than a merry Christmas. "Good afternoon!"
> "I want nothing from you; I ask nothing of you; why cannot we be friends?"
> "Good afternoon!" said Scrooge.
> "I am sorry, with all my heart, to find you so resolute. We have never had any quarrel, to which I have been a party. But I have made the trial in homage to Christmas, and I'll keep my Christmas humor to the last. So a merry Christmas, uncle!"
> "Good afternoon," said Scrooge.
> "And a Happy New Year!"
> "Good afternoon!" said Scrooge. (15–16)

A Child's Loneliness

INTO THIS CONVERSATION DICKENS has compressed much of Scrooge's life. From the Ghost of Christmas Past we will learn that Scrooge has one important reason to love Fred. He is the son of a kind and beautiful woman, Scrooge's little sister, Fan. When we meet her she is running into the schoolhouse where young Ebenezer has been left alone. Old Scrooge himself, accompanying the Ghost, has been incongruously remembering his "hopes, and joys, and cares long, long forgotten" (43), even to the point of shedding a tear. He has heard again the whoops of boys riding away for the holidays. He was once one of those boys, yet not one:

> "The school is not quite deserted," said the Ghost. "A solitary child, neglected by his friends, is left there still."
> Scrooge said he knew it. And he sobbed. (44)

Indeed, the loneliness of the boy—interrupted by fairy-tale flights of imagination, as he "sees" his companions Ali Baba and, most poignantly, the island-stranded Robinson Crusoe—is but a reflex of the child-murdering going on in young Scrooge's own family. So we gather from little Fan, who rushes onto the scene to greet her brother:

> "I have come to bring you home, dear brother!" said the child, clapping her tiny hands, and bending down to laugh. "To bring you home, home, home!"
> "Home, little Fan?" returned the boy.
> "Yes!" said the child, brimful of glee. "Home, for good and all. Home, for ever and ever. Father is so much kinder than he used to be, that home's like Heaven! He spoke so gently to me one dear night when I was going to bed that I was not afraid to ask him once more if you might come home; and he said Yes, you should; and sent me in a coach to bring you. And you're to be a man!" said the child, opening her eyes, "and are never to come back here; but first, we're to be together all the Christmas long, and have the merriest time in all the world."
> "You are quite a woman, little Fan!" exclaimed the boy. (47–48)

Their home is like heaven? Can we suppose it is so? Evidently Ebenezer was to be apprenticed; but we can hardly believe that the hard-hearted man who fathered a hard-hearted son had suddenly grown kind. Instead we lend our attention to Fanny. She was never strong; yet she it was, a child, who was sent to bring Ebenezer *home*, and has been sent on the same errand now, if Scrooge could but see it:

> "Always a delicate creature, whom a breath might have withered," said the Ghost. "But she had a large heart!"
> "So she had," cried Scrooge. "You're right. I will not gainsay it, Spirit.

God forbid!"

"She died a woman," said the Ghost, "and had, as I think, children."

"One child," Scrooge returned.

"True," said the Ghost. "Your nephew!"

Scrooge seemed uneasy in his mind and answered briefly, "Yes." (49)

In rejecting Fred, and the Child to whom Fred will be paying homage on the morrow, Scrooge has rejected the sister who was the brightest light of his own childhood, and who, as seems implied in the text, gave her life in giving birth to her son. Scrooge does not hate Fred; he cannot help feeling, even in the scene at the countinghouse, a growly and disgruntled *something* that shrivels before it becomes affection. Instead he looks down upon him as a fool, a child. The contempt allows him to keep Fred's faith at a distance. When Fred leaves, exchanging cordial greetings with the clerk Bob Cratchit, Scrooge delivers himself of this piece of worldly wisdom: "'There's another fellow,' muttered Scrooge, who overheard him; 'my clerk, with fifteen shillings a week, and a wife and family, talking about a merry Christmas. I'll retire to Bedlam'" (16). Note that Scrooge is aware that Bob has a wife and family. We will learn that he is ignorant of exactly who makes up that family. It is clear that Scrooge considers these familial appurtenances to be mainly a drain upon one's resources; or perhaps, would he care to admit it, a forcible prying open of one's solitude, a call against one's growing comfortably old in selfishness. In this regard the words of Jesus ring through the novel, as we too are meant to praise the Lord of heaven and earth, who denies his wisdom from the wise, and reveals it unto fools and children.

Bachelor Scrooge

SCROOGE NEVER MARRIED—or did he? Recall that A *Christmas Carol* opens by asserting the absolute certainty of the death of Jacob Marley, Scrooge's old partner in business. Scrooge was the only man there as official mourner at Marley's funeral—as we are told there will be no one to mourn Scrooge when he in turn shall die. But Dickens presents us with a strange union of the two ancient men, a "marriage" neither in flesh nor in soul but in coin, in financial arrangements, in business: "Scrooge never painted out old Marley's name. There it stood, years afterward, above the warehouse door: Scrooge and Marley. The firm was known as Scrooge and Marley. Sometimes people new to the business called Scrooge Scrooge, and sometimes Marley, but he answered to both names. It was all the same to him" (10). How odd, this affair of the interchangeable names. It is as if Scrooge and Marley had merged their identities into a "partnership" that dissolved the individuality of each. When, later on this same night, Jacob's ghost visits Scrooge to warn him of the arrival of three spirits, we find a flicker, and it is only a flicker, of the friendship that might have flourished between the two men, had each not padlocked the strongbox of his heart: "'I am here to-night to warn you, that you have yet a chance and hope of escaping my fate. A chance and hope of my procuring, Ebenezer'" (32). It is one of the rare moments when old Scrooge is addressed simply by his Christian name.

A wife and family, not a partner in misery: that is what Scrooge could have had. So the Ghost of Christmas Past shows us. After the scene between the boy Ebenezer and his sister has melted into the mist, we find ourselves in the office where Ebenezer was apprenticed: the business of old Mr. Fezziwig. It hardly needs mentioning that the Fezziwig place of employment is a burst of firelight and song as compared with the dank, cold countinghouse of Ebenezer Scrooge. The point is not that Christmas Eve will be celebrated there, but that its celebration renews the youth of all who attend. People are gathering in friendship—and young love. All about Fezziwig is young and foolish:

> "Yo ho, my boys!" said Fezziwig. "No more work to-night. Christmas Eve, Dick. Christmas, Ebenezer! Let's have the shutters up," cried old Fezziwig, with a sharp clap of his hands, "before a man can say Jack Robinson."
> You wouldn't believe how those two fellows went at it! They charged into the street with the shutters—one, two, three—had 'em up in their places— four, five, six—barred 'em and pinned 'em—seven, eight, nine—and came back before you could have got to twelve, panting like racehorses.
> "Hilli-ho!" cried old Fezziwig, skipping down from the high desk with wonderful agility. "Clear away, my lads, and let's have lots of room here! Hilli-ho, Dick! Chirrup, Ebenezer!" (50)

Fezziwig calls his prentices "boys" and "lads" because that is what he is, as we see when he dances with the matronly (and irrepressibly young) Mrs. Fezziwig, "worthy to be his partner in every sense of the term" (52). And the Fezziwig "partnership" has produced more than a bustling business: "In came the three Miss Fezziwigs, beaming and lovable. In came the six young followers," adds Dickens, with a jocular jab at the sweet follies of youth, "whose hearts they broke" (51). Scrooge himself is by no means alone in this scene: his fellow prentice, Dick, apparently would have been a close friend. Something seems to have intruded; Scrooge's words suggest that Dick has for a long time not been seen upon this earth: "'Dick Wilkins, to be sure!' said Scrooge to the Ghost. 'Bless me, yes. There he is. He was very much attached to me, was Dick. Poor Dick! Dear, dear!'" (50)

The Marriage That Should Have Been

WE SEE IN YOUNG Ebenezer and his friend Dick a trace of what Dickens is careful to suggest throughout the novel, lest the conversion of Scrooge be not only incredible but unsatisfying or odious. Evil is, after all, but the twisting and rotting of a genuine good. And there is, or there ought to have been, something attractive about Scrooge. We see it in the sensitive child and the friendly prentice; there remains a bit of the wag in the conversation of the old sinner; even in his physical and moral old age, we can trace the fallen outlines of a just man. For Scrooge once managed to win the love of a beautiful woman—one of those creatures, now all too rare, who remind us in their very beings and by the gentleness of their bodies that the "business" of this life must always return to the child.

Here lies the great tragedy of the novel. A man grows older and wiser, and forgets that in doing so he is to grow younger and more foolish. As a young man Scrooge knows (and he is no cad; his manners are gentlemanly) that he is to provide for the woman he loves. But he forgets the woman for the provision. In the toil of the man he forgets the play of the child. What might have been admirable in him is curdled:

> For again Scrooge saw himself. He was older now, a man in the prime of life. His face had not the harsh and rigid lines of later years, but it had begun to wear the signs of care and avarice. There was an eager, greedy, restless motion in the eye, which showed the passion that had taken root, and where the shadow of the growing tree would fall.
>
> He was not alone, but sat by the side of a fair young girl in a mourning-dress, in whose eyes there were tears, which sparkled in the light that shone out of the Ghost of Christmas Past. (55)

What death has fallen? We are not told. Perhaps Belle's father and with him Belle's hope of a dowry. But we are watching what might have been the very moment of a death, had it not been for the intervention of the spirits, that is, the intervention of God's grace. In this interview Scrooge decides to put to death, or at least to try to put to death, the love in his heart. He has shouldered Belle aside in favor of the abstract, unreal love of gain. Says Belle, with a grim prophetic irony, "'Another idol has displaced me; and if it can cheer and comfort you in time to come, as I would have tried to do, I have no just cause to grieve'" (55).

Scrooge protests that even though he has changed (for the better, he says, since now he is wise in the old world's ways), he has not changed towards Belle. He seeks no release from their engagement. It is important to recognize that Scrooge does not wish to undo the betrothal they had contracted when they were both poor. His love for Belle—as, we have seen, his love for Fanny and his affection for old Fezziwig and Dick Wilkins—was never quite extinguished. That love is, amazingly enough, more than the "unprofitable dream" (57) that Belle suggests it will come to appear to him; and old Scrooge hears these words again, in the midst of a dream that will prove most profitable indeed!

But young Scrooge's judgment upon what he was when he and Belle were first betrothed is quite accurate, in a way that he has ceased to understand. Says Belle:

> "Our contract is an old one. It was made when we were both poor, and content to be so, until, in good season, we could improve our worldly fortune by our patient industry. You *are* changed. When it was made, you were another man."
> "I was a boy," he said impatiently. (56)

Exactly. He was a boy. *Puer nobis nascitur*, sings the old hymn: a boy is born to us. Scrooge cannot hear. How he longs now that he had been more the boy and less the man; that would have made him more of a man, and a better man.

Scrooge pleads with the spirit to spare him any more pain; he would not wait till the "good season" then, and cannot bear to wait for grace now. But the spirit is relentless. He compels Scrooge to see that Belle would have given him the greatest gift man can enjoy on this earth, short of becoming a child again. That is the gift of children:

> They were in another scene and place, a room, not very large or handsome, but full of comfort. Near to the winter fire sat a beautiful young girl,

so like that last that Scrooge believed it was the same, until he saw *her*, now a comely matron, sitting opposite her daughter. The noise in this room was perfectly tumultuous, for there were more children there than Scrooge in his agitated state of mind could count; and, unlike the celebrated herd in the poem, they were not forty children conducting themselves like one, but every child was conducting itself like forty. The consequences were uproarious beyond belief; but no one seemed to care; on the contrary, the mother and daughter laughed heartily, and enjoyed it very much; and the latter, soon beginning to mingle in the sports, got pillaged by the young brigands most ruthlessly. What would I not have given to be one of them! (58)

There they are, the rough-and-tumble flock, the sweaty and cowlicked increase and multiplication that God blesses us with; how can a wise man take himself seriously either doing the foolish and beautiful act that brings children into being, or dwelling among the foolish and beautiful things that children are?

Their gleeful sport is animated by some wonderful event about to befall the eldest daughter: her waist is being measured, possibly for a wedding dress. It is a moment that bridges the generations, for, God willing, that comely matron will soon be dandling another baby in her arms. So lovely is this girl that the narrator himself, allowing the boy in him to triumph, interrupts the scene with exclamations of his own desire to kiss her, to look into her eyes, or to undo the braids of her hair: "'In short, I should have liked, I do confess, to have had the lightest license of a child, and yet to have been man enough to know its value'" (59).

All at once the door is flung open, and in comes the man Scrooge should have been, the father of this boisterous brood, attended by a porter heaped high with Christmas presents. When the glee subsides into contentment, this "master of the house"—a true household, and not a garret for bad debts, and thus truly obeying the laws of the household, that is, economics—sits with his daughter and his wife at his own fireside. A far cry it is from the cold ashy grate that this evening had warmed Scrooge's gruel to a sour tepidity. Scrooge perceives the youth-in-age he has missed: "When he thought that such another creature, quite as graceful and full of promise, might have called him father, and been a springtime in the haggard winter of his life, his sight grew very dim indeed" (60).

But Dickens will not let Scrooge rest, even in that sorrow. The vision is of Christmas Eve, exactly seven years ago, and the husband has noticed something on his way home:

> "Belle," said the husband, turning to his wife with a smile, "I saw an old friend of yours this afternoon."
>
> "Who was it?"
>
> "Guess!"
>
> "How can I? Tut, don't I know?" she added in the same breath, laughing as he laughed. "Mr. Scrooge."
>
> "Mr. Scrooge it was. I passed his office window, and as it was not shut up, and he had a candle inside, I could scarcely help seeing him. His partner lies upon the point of death, I hear, and there he sat alone. Quite alone in the world, I do believe." (60)

"What is a man profited," says Jesus, "if he shall gain the whole world, and lose his own soul?" (Matt. 16:26). And even that world he thinks he gains is a cheat.

The Human Infestation

SO MUCH, AND FAR more, does Dickens prepare for in his opening scene in the countinghouse. Let us quickly return to it again. After Fred leaves, two more fools enter the house, philanthropists who request from Scrooge a Christmas contribution for the poor, though Scrooge be as destitute of any real wealth as the most ragged beggar is in copper and woolen cloth to keep out the cold. Well-known is Scrooge's steering of their conversation away from the realities of human beings and their simple bodily needs (the "common comforts" and "common necessaries" to which the philanthropists delicately refer (17) to the illusory solutions proposed by the grim political economy of his day. The treadmills, the workhouses, the prisons, and the Poor Law: all these deny the household, the place where mother and father care for children. Underlying Scrooge's partisanship for such false solutions is a willingness that people who cannot fend for themselves, or who cannot endure the privations of the prisons and workhouses, should die. For the specter of the child looms over the whole question of overpopulation, the child whom the disciples of Thomas Malthus metamorphosed into an all-eating monster.

Thus it is a child we meet next. The boyish Fred was more than a match for his argumentative uncle. The good old philanthropists will also, on the morrow, be found celebrating the birth of the Child. But what about a little boy, who does not even open Scrooge's door?

The owner of one scant young nose, gnawed and mumbled by the hungry cold as bones are gnawed by dogs, stooped down at Scrooge's keyhole to regale him with a Christmas carol; but at the first sound of

> *God rest you merry, gentlemen,*
> *May nothing you dismay,*

Scrooge seized the ruler with such energy of action, that the singer fled in terror, leaving the keyhole to the fog and even more congenial frost. (20)

It is the Christmas carol of the novel, the carol that Scrooge will not bear to have sung to the end. Let us finish the verse:

> For Jesus Christ our Savior
> Was born on Christmas Day,
> To save our souls from Satan's power
> When we were gone astray.
> O tidings of comfort and joy, comfort and joy,
> O tidings of comfort and joy.

It is a carol both solemn and joyful. It confesses the darkness of man's heart, and the dawn of the Child, without whom there would be only dismay for man in the power of Satan. For we were all gone astray, "as sheep having no shepherd" (Matt. 9:36). The message comes like a note of grace through the last keyhole that man has forgotten to caulk solid. But Scrooge, the man, holds to his purposes. The little boy is crushed.

Scrooge will remember the lonely little caroler when he sees himself in the lad—himself, that is, as he once was, the abandoned boy in the school-house. But of course that boy only prepares Scrooge to meet Tiny Tim, the boy at the heart of Scrooge's conversion.

When the Ghost of Christmas Present takes Scrooge to the Cratchit home, we meet an out-at-elbows version of the bustling home of Belle (and, by the way, of the Christmas party at Fred's house, complete with one Topper cheating at blind-man's buff and, with the conspiratorial aid of Fred and his young bride, cornering her sister in a stairwell and pressing so close to her that he manages to slip a ring on her finger). A mother and four children are busy preparing Christmas dinner. They are happy, but the worries of poverty hang like a pall over their holiday. The eldest girl, aptly named Martha, comes home late, having been kept overtime in the seamstresses' sweatshop. The family had feared that she night not make it home—a reasonable enough fear for the children to play upon to tease Bob, for they ask Martha to hide when they hear their father's footsteps approaching.

Bob carries a frail lad on his shoulder: "Alas for Tiny Tim, he bore a little crutch, and had his limbs supported by an iron frame!" (74). After the children give up their joke—Bob's face fell when they told him that Martha wasn't coming—they hustle Tim off to the washhouse, a humble place for a humble pleasure, "that he might hear the pudding singing in the copper" (75).

That gives Mrs. Cratchit a chance to ask Bob about how Tim was in church. To accuse Dickens of sentimentality here is to show one's own insensibility. The lad is named "Tiny" Tim not for the euphony or for the emotional tug, but for the wisdom of it. It is the heartbeat of the New Testament: "And base things of the world, and things which are despised, hath God chosen, yea, and things which are not, to bring to nought things that are" (1 Cor. 1:28); "Ye are of God, little children, and have overcome them: because greater is he that is in you, than he that is in the world" (1 John 4:4); "The stone which the builders disallowed, the same is made the head of the corner" (1 Pt. 2:7). Nor is it implausible that a child should suffer in cheerful patience the trouble that would bring a grown man or woman to the edge of despair; for children are ever aware of the smallness and the weakness that grown men and women forget.

The Child comes to sing a carol through the keyhole of our hearts. He is dangerous; he brings great tidings. He may cause us to see, who are accustomed to blindness; he may cause us to remember, who sleep in oblivion. He may heal the leprosy of our souls that we may again mingle with our fellow men, when for so long neither we nor they desired to press the flesh. So here the child becomes the teacher. In his littleness and his patient suffering—not in his clamor for a miraculous cure, or for the chimerical promises of science—he points us towards his own Teacher:

> "And how did little Tim behave?" asked Mrs. Cratchit, when she had rallied Bob on his credulity, and Bob had hugged his daughter to his heart's content.
>
> "As good as gold," said Bob, "and better. Somehow he gets thoughtful, sitting by himself so much, and thinks the strangest things you ever heard. He told me, coming home, that he hoped the people saw him in the church, because he was a cripple, and it might be pleasant to them to remember, upon Christmas Day, who made lame beggars walk and blind men see." (75)

So says the child Timothy, in the role of an inconsiderable apostle, the least, the tiniest. Bob tries to cheer himself by imagining what would in fact be miraculous: his "voice was tremulous when he told them this, and trembled more when he said that Tiny Tim was growing strong and hearty" (75).

Bob does not know it, nor will the narrator intrude with a comment, but a miraculous cure *is* being effected. The Child who made blind men see is opening the eyes of Ebenezer Scrooge, that moral cripple, and that is a more astonishing miracle than the healing of a little lame boy. In fact, the lameness of the boy is the occasion of grace: it opens the way into Scrooge's heart. Not for sentiment's sake, then, does Dickens assign to Tiny Tim—etymologically, that tiny boy who honors God—the all-embracing extension of his father's blessing at table:

> "A merry Christmas to us all, my dears. God bless us!"
> Which all the family re-echoed.
> "God bless us, every one!" said Tiny Tim, the last of all. (78)

By now, Scrooge has seen himself as a boy, a boy now lost; has seen Fanny, lost; Dick Wilkins, lost; Belle, to him forever lost; all the young boys and girls of Belle's household, lost. He has seen no one of them die—but watches intently as Bob holds Tim's "withered little hand in his, as if he loved the child, and wished to keep him by his side, and dreaded that he might be taken from him" (78–79).

There Are Children, and There Are Children

THAT IS TOO MUCH for Scrooge. He asks whether Tiny Tim will live. The spirit answers by referring to the family; to the loving care of father and mother and brothers and sisters for the least among them: "'I see a vacant seat,' replied the Ghost, 'in the poor chimney-corner, and a crutch without an owner, carefully preserved. If these shadows remain unaltered by the Future, the child will die'" (79). When Scrooge protests, the spirit hurls his own words back at him: "'If these shadows remain unaltered by the Future, none other of my race,' returned the Ghost, 'will find him here. What then? If he be like to die, he had better do it, and decrease the population'" (79). For the wisest in the ways of the world are fools even on their own worldly terms. They are of the world, but not *in* it, unaware of the realities about them. As the spirit says, "'it may be that in the sight of Heaven you are more worthless and less fit to live than millions like this poor man's child'" (79).

But there will be children, whether we like or not—if not children of God, then the children of men. The spirit hides beneath his robes two abject and terrible creatures:

> "They were a boy and a girl. Yellow, meager, ragged, scowling, wolfish; but prostrate, too, in their humility. Where graceful youth should have filled their features out, and touched them with its freshest tints, a stale and shriveled hand, like that of age, had pinched and twisted them, and pulled them into shreds. Where angels might have sat enthroned, devils lurked, and glared out menacing. No change, no degradation, no perversion of humanity, in any grade, through all the mysteries of wonderful creation, has monsters half so horrible and dread" (94).

Christians are called to be born again, to become new creations; but man's sin withers the heart of childhood and corrupts it with age. Does anything in our day so fully reveal our corruption than our itch to usher little children into a precocious knowledge of the carnal? There is more than one kind of destitution, and more than one way to hate the child.

The boy in particular is a figure of Antichrist: he has "Doom" written on his brow, "unless the writing be erased" (95). The horror of it moves Scrooge to wish that something—of course, with man it is always something vague and faraway—be done:

> "Have they no refuge or resource?" cried Scrooge.
> "Are there no prisons?" said the Spirit, turning on him for the last time with his own words. "Are there no workhouses?" (95)

The Way of All Flesh

BUT, HAPPILY FOR SCROOGE, we are not done with the Boy born on this holy night. The Ghost of Christmas Yet to Come will show Scrooge the "business-men" who jest about his death, men of great importance who hardly exchange a word about the dead man they sneeringly call "Old Scratch" (101). One of these, though it is Christmas Eve, is too old to be beguiled into small talk about skating. Scrooge will see the thieves who filch his bedclothes and shirt as he lies in rigor mortis (one of whom, in an unwitting and wicked parody of scripture, compares Scrooge to the self-sacrificing Christ, for Scrooge "'frightened every one away from him when he was alive, to profit us when he was dead'" (107). Scrooge will see a husband and wife relieved by the news, for no creditor to come could ever be as heartless as Scrooge was. After all this horror, this sloughing of a human life as if it were a pestilent disease, Scrooge longs for some tenderness connected with a death. So the spirit returns him to the Cratchit home.

No bustle any more. Mother and daughters are sewing in silence. Peter reads a book aloud: "'And he took a child, and set him down in the midst of them'" (cf. Mk. 9:35). Scrooge wonders how he can have heard the words—for the boy could not continue. Nor can the mother. She puts her hand to her face, pretending that the color of the fabric has hurt her eyes.

Bob is late coming home. His pace is slower than it used to be. His heart is broken. Once he was boyish enough when he carried Tim upon his shoulder, but then, says Mrs. Cratchit, Tim was light to carry, "'and his father loved him so, that it was no trouble'" (113).

When Bob enters and sits down to take his tea, all the children gather round to comfort him. He tries in turn to cheer them, but on this Christmas Eve he has visited the graveyard, a green and comforting place, not like the ghastly tomb preparing for Scrooge. He breaks down as he tries to talk about it. "'My little, little child!' cried Bob. 'My little child!'" (113).

Except ye become as one of these, warns Jesus; but on the other side of that warning stands the promise, for of such is the kingdom of heaven. Only that hope can reconcile us to the death of a child. Bob is reconciled, and the conversation resumes, with the husband teasing his good wife, praising the kindheartedness of Fred, who had offered him genuine condolences. He even suggests that Fred can get Peter a better situation (and that gives one of the girls a chance to tease Peter, who must soon then be falling in love!).

But Bob ends the grieving and surviving and hoping by raising Tiny Tim as a teacher to them all. Tim shall be the heart of their family, not the good father and the good mother, but that little child:

> "But, however and whenever we part from one another, I am sure we shall none of us forget poor Tiny Tim—shall we?—or this first parting that there was among us?"
>
> "Never, father!" cried they all.
>
> "And I know," said Bob—"I know, my dears, that when we recollect how patient and mild he was, although he was a little, little child, we shall not quarrel easily among ourselves, and forget poor Tiny Tim in doing it."

"No, never, father!" they all cried again.

"I am very happy," said little Bob—"I am very happy!" (115)

Only his faith in the Child born this night can allow "little" Bob to utter those last words in what might have been a tragedy, not for him but for the unseen witness, Ebenezer Scrooge.

We all know the end of the story. The lessons of the spirits strike to Scrooge's heart, and the writing on his tombstone will be sponged away. Scrooge makes restitution to the philanthropists, considering it not charity but the partial payment of his own forgotten debts. Then he sends an enormous turkey to the Cratchit house, anonymously, lest his left hand know what his right hand is doing. After walking nervously up and down the street, he musters the courage to enter his family again, ringing Fred's door, hat in hand. "'Will you let me in, Fred?" he asks (126). He goes to church; he keeps Christmas in his heart, the day of Christ's birth.

Also the day of Scrooge's birth. Says he on that fine morning: "'I don't know what day of the month it is,' said Scrooge. 'I don't know how long I have been among the Spirits. I don't know anything. I'm quite a baby. Never mind. I don't care. I'd rather be a baby'" (120). A baby. *Puer nobis nascitur.* So may we all become, and rejoice as foolishly, and as wisely, as the frosty-haired boy, the good Ebenezer Scrooge.

20

The Child at the End of the Journey: Pearl

With what work should I end this book on Christian irony? Names of renowned authors come to the fore. Bunyan's *Pilgrim's Progress* is premised on the disjunction between the wisdom of the world and the foolishness of God. C. S. Lewis's Space Trilogy, in particular *That Hideous Strength*, illustrates the disjunction between man's perception of historical time and God's unfolding plan. The suffering child—and the redeeming child—is central to the stories of Hans Christian Andersen. Flannery O'Connor may be the finest ironist in English literature of the last fifty years, especially in her scorn for those rags we call our righteousness. T. S. Eliot's "Hollow Men" shrink in fear from the most terrible vision a man can see: the eyes of a blessed woman. The *Fowre Hymnes* of Spenser are a crazy-quilt crisscross of analogies and distinctions between earthly love, earthly beauty, heavenly love, and heavenly beauty, concluding with a vision beyond the tongue of man to describe.

But I am choosing a poem, *Pearl*, which unites all the ironies I have been discussing. The narrator does not understand the strength of the humble. He cannot separate himself from his time-bound vision. He loves, but imperfectly, and cannot fathom the wild generosity and self-sacrifice of perfect love. He imagines that heavenly hierarchies are based on merit gained by one's hard work on earth, and does not see that they might be other than what we expect. His teacher is a child, and, to make it all the more painful, his own child: a little girl, teaching a grown man. And all of these ironies reveal the person of Christ, the Lamb.

Thine Be the Glory

PEARL IS, TO MY mind, the greatest religious lyric in English. But we do not know who wrote it. That is a common enough plight for the historian of the Middle Ages. The lacework of glass and stone that we know as the Gothic cathedral—whose were the hands that cut the marble, that fired the glass, that brewed the stains for the petaled windows, that hewed the rafters, that chiseled into the downspout the leer of the gargoyle? Who were the master builders? For the most part we have no idea.

Many of the masons were illiterate, but that hardly explains it all. Once again, we have grown used to a marvel. We do not know who dragged the blocks of stone on sledges up the diagonals of the Egyptian pyramids; but those pyramids were built by the sweat and muscle of slaves, and they look it. By contrast, hardly a corner of a medieval cathedral or church remains untouched by skill and cleverness and sheer play, not to mention devotion and genius. Is it possible that man attained this peak of architectural beauty not *despite* the anonymity and the "smallness" of the workmen and the designers, but *because* of it? And is that not appropriate for buildings erected to honor the One who saved mankind by becoming the stone which the builders rejected? If Christ is the cornerstone, why should the architect intrude his name upon the base?

Of course I know that I have signed *this* work, though I am not sure the work is the better for it. It is at least reasonable to suggest that the greatness of *Pearl* depends upon its author's never having troubled about how great he was. Our author sought to delight and instruct, and so placed his prodigious linguistic and architectonic talent in the hands of God.

Something of this vanishing from the stage survives in much Christian literature. In *The Canterbury Tales*, Chaucer assigns his narrative voice to one "Jeffrey," a pilgrim slow on the uptake, whose "Tale of Sir Thopas" is, ironically and also appropriately, the silliest tale told on the journey to Canterbury, its meter such a jog-trot that the Bartender in charge of the tale-telling begs him to stop! That is not just a clever joke. Humility is essential to the pilgrimage. In the end, after the Parson (who also insists, with genuine humility, that he cannot rhyme at all) delivers his sermon on penance, the same Jeffrey makes an act of contrition. That involves a retraction—an acknowledgment that all his art is as nothing compared with the glory of the One who gave him the art. Thus, the narrator, though Chaucer himself no doubt has a twinkle in his eye, apologizes for his books of worldly vanity, including those of the *Canterbury Tales* that show a sinful tendency, "and many a song and many a leccherous lay." But he thanks God for everyhing else he wrote, and begs that he may be granted true penitence, confession, and satisfaction, "thurgh the benigne grace of hym that is kyng of kynges and preest over alle preestes, that boghte us with the precious blood of his herte; so that I may be oon of hem at the day of doom that shulle be saved" (10.1090). And the final words on the manuscript, whether placed there by Chaucer's instructions or by the pious love of the man who put the book together, express the humility for which this man of genius prayed:

> HERE IS ENDED THE BOOK OF THE TALES OF CAUNTERBURY, COMPILED BY GEFFREY CHAUCER, OF WHOS SOULE JHESU CRIST HAVE MERCY. AMEN. (10.1091)

Ovid ends his *Metamorphoses* by boasting that he has fashioned one thing that will not suffer metamorphosis, namely his great poem about change. Horace echoes him at the end of his third book of odes, claiming that he has erected a monument for himself. How different is Spenser's ending of *The Faerie Queene*, that vast epic of love and sin and redemption and church polity and statecraft and virtue and friendship and change and time and eternity, a poem whose complexity makes Ovid look like a boy rolling for skittles. As we have seen, he ends the poem perfectly by ending it imperfectly, for only God can bring this whole creation to its perfection. The narrator's last words are a prayer: "O that great Sabaoths God, grant me that Sabboth's sight" (7.8.2.9).

The greatest literary genius who ever lived, arguably the greatest genius of any kind, ends his career with an epilogue that confesses the inadequacy of his final play, and begs the audience's forgiveness: "As you from crimes would pardoned be, / Let your indulgence set me free" (*The Tempest*). Thomas Aquinas was so prolific that at one time he dictated four books to four separate secretaries, *simultaneously*. Yet shortly before he died, he had a vision of the glory of the Lord that, as he said, made everything he had written seem as straw. Nor did he write another word, unless, perhaps, this holy man wrote the eucharistic hymn with the verse beseeching the Lord to raise him to the glory of a common criminal:

> Godhead alone was hidden on the Cross,
> But here humanity is hidden too.
> Believing and confessing both, I seek
> What the repentant thief then sought from you. (*Adoro te devote*, 9–12)

Michelangelo's only self-portrait can be seen in the apse of the Sistine Chapel, in *The Last Judgment*: it is as a loose skin from which hangs a face of anguish and piteous ugliness, with heavy brow, broken nose, and rough black hair. The skin is held as evidence of martyrdom by Saint Bartholomew, who was flayed alive. At the Last Judgment, the artist prays, let me be numbered among the blessed, if only as the sloughing of a saint far surpassing me. Caravaggio paints himself as one of the tormentors in *The Crucifixion of Saint Peter*. Tolkien had no ambition to become a great writer; he said that he longed to be able rather to farm three feet square of land, and tend it perfectly. All he did was to write the greatest British novel of the twentieth century.

It is ironic, but also understandable, that the author of *Pearl* should be unknown. It is even more deeply ironic that, as opposed to what the world considers sensible, a poet should attain greatness by means of the same humility that caused him never to bother to sign his work. Had we known who he was, he might not have written the poem to make us care to know who he was.

Perfection and the Flaw

THE *PEARL*-POET'S GREATEST WORKS, by their architecture, allude to the sublime irony of the Christian faith, that of the *felix culpa*. As the chant for the Easter Vigil puts it, "O happy fault, O necessary sin of Adam, that brought for us so great a redeemer!"

Now we must be careful lest we suggest that Adam's sin was a good thing, or that God willed that there be evil in the world, that he might triumph over it with an even greater good.

First, Scripture is unmistakeably clear that the sin of Adam, brought death into the world, not slowly but with devastating speed. Immediately after Adam and Eve are driven from Eden, we are told of how Cain slew his brother Abel out of envy. Murder, bigamy, lust, pride, perversion, and treachery soon follow.

Second, we must recall the error that plagued the young Augustine. Christians cannot assign to evil a quantity, to be outweighed on some big scale by a counterpoise of good. Evil, as Augustine insists, is not a thing in itself, but a negation or privation, a falling away, a warping of what ought to be straight. God redeems man by straightening the warp: so Dante's mountain of purgatory straightens the souls "made crooked by the world" (*Purgatory*, 23.126). Yet God does more than restore to man his lost innocence before the Fall. Christ takes on human flesh and suffers the indignities of fallen man, culminating in his unjust condemnation, his cruel Passion, and his death. We do not die with Christ to rise with prelapsarian Adam: we die with Christ to rise with Christ. What is reaped, says Paul, is not what is sown. We reap not a deathless earthly life, but union with the life of God himself (1 Cor. 15:35–58).

Was sin necessary for such redemption? Let us watch our words. It could not be necessary, if we suppose that God required it that he might raise us to glory. But in fact, in our sorry history we did sin, and in that history—speaking always from man's time-bound view—the redemption has come as a merciful answer to sin, its remedy. So the *fault* or *flaw* has proved to be *happy*—not in itself, but as the redeeming God has willed.

A Flaw and a Pearl

SO, THEN, THE PEARL-POET writes poems with deliberately placed flaws. He incorporates these flaws so cunningly into the whole that the beauty and the perfection of the poem rely upon them. He "sins" artistically, to teach us about holiness; he mars his work, to teach us about perfection.

He has read his Dante, and knows of the ten times ten *canti* of the hereafter. He knows that ten is a triangular number (being the sum of 1 + 2 + 3 + 4; think of ten blocks stacked in a triangle); and he knows that it is the sum of the squares of trinity and unity (9 + 1). He understands Dante's attempt to render poetically the perfection of God's justice and mercy. As we have seen, far from boasting that he has erected an everlasting monument to himself, Dante ends by claiming that the vision so far exceeds his poetic powers that he is left as helpless as a babe "who wets his tongue still at his mother's breast" (*Paradiso*, 33.108). Our poet makes his humility manifest not only by confession but by architecture.

To see how, let us consider briefly the structure of another of his masterpieces, *Sir Gawain and the Green Knight*. There the poet explores the divergence of worldly glory from heavenly glory. Ironies abound: we see, without the poet's having to spell it out for us or set brimstone a-smoking, that a gallant knight is not always a gallant knight. The courtliness of the Round Table rings hollow: it does not bode well that the adulterous Guenevere is prominent at the feast that begins the poem. The true courtliness of the Christian knight will be seen elsewhere. The court of the world boasts its derring-do, yet in the poem the knights of the Round Table achieve nothing except to conceal the sin of Guenevere and Lancelot. Sir Gawain, however, knows he is the weakest and most feeble-witted of Arthur's knights (354), and will attain his renown in an adventure that shows him he is not perfect; in fact, that he is weak and feeble-witted. Therefore he is strong and wise, in that he comes to know how utterly he must depend upon the mercy of God.

Here, briefly, is the delightful plot of *Sir Gawain*. It is New Year's Day at Arthur's court. The king is about to commence the feast, when a hulk of a man rides straight into the hall on horseback. His beard is bright blond; he casts a cunning eye on the crowd; he carries a prodigious axe. He and his horse are gaily accoutered with gold and green. This man under any circumstances is strange enough to strike fear into the heart, but the poet whimsically waits till the end of a stanza to deliver the bold stroke:

> Men were stunned at his hue,
> So plainly to be seen:
> He moved as elves will do,
> And was all as green as green. (147–50)

This burly representative of the demonic looks all about Arthur's court, that palace of chivalry, and asks whether there is any bold knight around who will play a little holiday game with him. The knights are struck dumb. Lest his court lose its reputation, Arthur agrees to play. The game is simple. You take my ax, says the Green Knight, and strike me with it once on the neck, as hard as you can. (The ax has a haft four feet long, and a blade to match.) Then you will bide the same from me, if I am around to deliver it, exactly one year later. Obviously, one blow from such an ax should ensure that the bottom of the inning is never played; but then, a fully green knight on a green horse is not exactly in the natural run of things.

If you play, then, you risk your life. But just as Arthur is about to commit himself, Gawain speaks up and offers his services, not because he is brave, but because, as he says, his death would mean the least loss to the Round Table. The Green Knight is pleased, and repeats the rules. He bows his head and clears his locks away from his neck. Gawain strikes as hard as he can, cutting the head clean off, the ax biting into the wood floor. But the Green Knight stands right back up, gropes around for the head, turns and says, pleasantly, that he'll be seeing Gawain next New Year, and rides out. Now *that* is an adventure, agree the company! And they finally begin their feast.

But the year turns with terrible swiftness; in the midst of life we are in death. Before Gawain knows it, the whole round of church feasts has come and gone, and on All Hallows he makes his way into the wilderness, determined to keep his word as a true knight and seek his green foe at some mysterious green chapel. He goes forth to die, a lonely young man suffering hunger and cold and the attacks of giants and other creatures of the woods. At last on Christmas Eve he prays that he might be graced to hear Mass somewhere on the morrow with fellow Christians, and sure enough he looks up to see a marvelous castle. There he is welcomed by all, including a burly blond lord of the castle (he is *not* green) and his lovely wife. The lord feasts Gawain for several days, assuring him that he knows where the Green Chapel is and that he will have him taken there on the appointed day. Meanwhile, he proposes a holiday game: he will go out to hunt, and will give Gawain whatever he wins; and Gawain will stay indoors, and give the lord whatever *he* wins.

Gawain is too courtly and brave to ruin everybody's holiday by telling them what challenge he will have to endure. He keeps to himself the knowledge that he is about to die. That knowledge makes him unbearably lonely in the midst of the festivities. And to make matters more painful, when the lord leaves for his hunt, his lady enters Gawain's bedchamber for *her* hunt, with the game not a stag or a boar or a fox, but a human soul. She professes love for Gawain, and on three successive mornings the poor man must find some way to deny her without committing the discourtesy of insulting a woman. He must also keep his promise to the lord without revealing the wife's treachery. He struggles, in other words, to reconcile his courtly code of honor with the law of God—and it is clear that the courtly code is not a perfect thing after all.

In the end, Gawain manages to keep his soul clean of the mortal sin that must damn him should he soon die unrepentant. But he does take, a tad grudgingly, one "favor" from the lady: a green belt that she says will make him proof against any wound. Gawain is grasping for anything that might help. He is not at all confident that it will, nor does he tell the lord about it in the evening.

Gawain thus breaks the rules of the game. He tells a lie; he wants to save his skin. He sins—and who would not sin, in his circumstances? But that is the poet's point. Gawain bears a shield that celebrates a purity that man, of himself, cannot attain. Its device is a pentangle:

> It is a symbol that Solomon some time ago set
> As a token of truth, that it has by title,
> For it is a figure that holds five points,
> Each line lapping over and locking the other,
> Everywhere endless, and in England called,
> As I hear, over all, the endless knot.
> And it befits this brave knight and his bright arms,
> For faithful ever in five ways, five times,
> Was Gawain known as good and, like refined gold,
> Void of all villainy and adorned with virtues. (625–34)

The "endless knot" of the pentangle is proper to Gawain, who sets his mind to embody the purities it symbolizes: he is "faultless in his five wits" (640), has never "failed in his five fingers" (641), he rests all his trust in the five wounds of Christ (642–43), in the heat of battle he thinks upon the five joys that "the courtly queen of heaven had in her child" (647), and, for the fifth five, practices frankness and fellowship, cleanness and courtliness, and the surpassing virtue of mercy (651–54). On the inner half of his shield, not his testimony to the world but his reminder to himself and his aid in time of trouble, he has had painted the figure of Mary.

No one can live up to this shield of purity. No one can live up to the holiness of Jesus (and of Mary, made pure by the grace of her Redeemer). The poet knows this full well. Jesus calls us to be "perfect, even as your Heavenly father is perfect," knowing that we cannot fulfill the call (Matt. 5:48). So we must press on bravely *and* humbly; we must pray; we must (the poet is of course a Roman Catholic) seek the sacraments, God's humble conduits of grace; must be "Mary's knight," as the poet says of Gawain.

The victory will not be ours, but Christ's, who then will make it ours in his mercy. That sublime irony is evident in Gawain's "flaw." For when he trudges off to that dreadful Green Chapel—an unholy mound of earth, with nary a cross in sight—though he has resisted his loneliness, the advances of a lovely woman, and the temptation to renege on his word of honor, and though he has prayed fervently that the Lord would keep his soul free from mortal sin, yet he relies, ever so slightly, upon that supposedly magic green girdle.

Ironically, it is his acceptance of the girdle—an understandable and pardonable failing, given his fear of the terrible death approaching—that brings Gawain to harm however slight, and, through that harm, to what the poet celebrates as his glory. For the Green Knight swings once, but withholds his stroke at the last instant when Gawain flinches. He swings a second time, but again checks himself, to make sure that Gawain will not flinch, and to torment him a little. When he swings the third time, the blade nicks Gawain's neck, and that is all. When Gawain springs up and hollers that the game is over, that he has fulfilled to the letter his vow to endure the stroke of the ax, the Green Knight roars with merry laughter. For he is the same lord of the castle whose wife tempted Gawain to sin the mortal sin of Guenevere. Truest knight alive, Gawain did not fail those tests, but did come up short on the third day by receiving the girdle and lying to the lord about it:

> "For it is my weed you are wearing, that woven girdle;
> My own wife wove it for you, forsooth, I know well!
> And the kisses too I know, and the kind gestures,
> And the wooing by my wife—I worked it myself.
> I sent her to sift you, and it seems to me truly
> You are the most faultless fellow that ever went on foot.
> As the more price has a pearl than a white pea,
> So has Gawain, in good faith, than the other gay knights.
> But you lacked a little here, sir, and fell short of the law,
> But not for wanton work was it, nor for wooing,
> But that you loved your life—and I blame you the less." (2358–68)

Gawain fell just a little short of the law, or of his loyalty, depending on how you translate the Middle English *lewte*. Both senses of the word are in play: Gawain was not entirely firm in his faith. Now all of this is taking place on January 1, the feast we know as New Year's. But the poet is fond of setting his poems in both seasonal time and salvation time. Here in the heart of winter we celebrate Christmas and the dawn of a new law. That dawn is heralded on New Year's, the Feast of the Circumcision: "And when eight days were accomplished for the circumcising of the child, his name was called Jesus, which was so named of the angel before he was conceived in the womb" (Luke 2:21). In being circumcised, Jesus shed the first drops of blood for our redemption: his life of suffering dates from that morning. He fulfilled the terms of the old covenant God made with Abraham (Gen. 17:10–14) and confirmed by the law of Moses. But Saint Paul advises us that under the law we are all condemned:

"By the deeds of the law there shall no flesh be justified in his sight: for by the law is the knowledge of sin" (Rom. 3:20). No one is sinless; no one can fulfill the demands of the most holy Lord. Everyone fails the test the Green Knight poses. It is Christ who fulfills the law for us, and who institutes the new law of charity: the forgiveness of sin, and our relinquishing all our hopes in the magic girdle, the illusory works of man. Thus, the poem begins and ends, appropriately, with an allusion to Troy, whence came the legendary founder of Britain, one Brutus. Troy, we remember, was burnt to the ground.

The true sacrament is a brave victory by surrender: it is the death that baptism brings, the circumcision of the heart: "Know ye not, that so many of us as were baptized into Jesus Christ were baptized into his death? Therefore we are buried with him by baptism into death: that like as Christ was raised up from the dead by the glory of the Father, even so we also should walk in newness of life" (Rom. 6:3–4). And that is what Gawain experiences. When he returns to Camelot and tells his story, the good lords and ladies respond by instituting the Order of the Green Garter as a mark of the highest honor. They are right to do so. But for Gawain the garter is a perpetual reminder of his weakness, his proneness to sin. He determines to wear it in humility and penitence. He too is right to do so.

The flaw has been folded into glory. In this poem that celebrates the five senses and the five clean fingers and the five wounds of Christ and the five joys of Mary and the five courtly virtues, five fives of purity, the "flaw," the nick on the neck, the circumcision, becomes the key to the fulfillment of the whole. For our poet has written not 100 cantos but 100 + 1 stanzas, suggesting the excess of sin, the overreaching of Adam. That 101 is surely an imperfect number. But 101 gives him the opportunity to weave his fives into his own poetic endless knot, concluding where he had begun. For there are exactly 2530 lines in *Sir Gawain and the Green Knight*—2,525 + 5; the "bob and wheel" at the end of each stanza is a five-line device that, for all we can say, the poet never used elsewhere. Line 2,525, "After the siege and the assault had ceased at Troy," repeats line 1, "Since the siege and the assault had ceased at Troy," giving us a 2,525-line poem, or 5 x 5 x 100 plus 5 x 5. That leaves the last five lines linked to the rest yet also hanging by themselves, another "flaw" perhaps, that bursts out of the poem just as mankind hopes to burst out of a world of sin that begins with Troy and ends with Troy:

> Surely,
> Many adventures in days of yore
> Have befallen such as this.
> He who bore the crown of thorn,
> May he bring us to his bliss! Amen. (2526–30)

No circumcision now, but all the terrible wounds of Christ, whose righteousness alone redeems us from our weakness. To bear the wound of the Green Knight's ax is to know one's insufficiency, and in this knowledge that bears fruit in faith, we are made "more than conquerors" (Rom. 8:37).

Measure, Weight, and Number

In *Pearl*, the poet has incorporated a similar flaw into a structure of cathedral-like precision and virtuosity. The Lord "ordered all things in measure, and number, and weight" (Wis. 11:21), and the Christian artists of the Middle Ages and the Renaissance honored that harmony by reflecting it in their work. In *Pearl*, the harmony is not that of a static universe, but of the dynamic history of the salvation of mankind and of an individual human soul.

Let us tarry to examine this structure. Though the poet wields it effortlessly, the rhyme scheme, for English, is extraordinarily difficult: ABAB / ABAB / BCBC, with one rhyming sound, B, used six times, linking the three quatrains that make up the stanza. Yet the link is striking and powerful, as the B sound suddenly is used for the *first and third* lines of the final quatrain. The result is that the first two quatrains, with identical rhyme schemes, hang together, but the third is both connected with the first two and noticeably different. In fact, the poet will often introduce an ironic turn in the argument precisely at line 9. The quatrains themselves are supple, with the poet frequently crossing their boundaries with sentences that spill over from one to the next; and very often he will separate the last two lines for the effect of a powerful concluding couplet (e.g., 1.2.11–12). Sometimes the last line will stand alone, like an exclamation point (e.g., 2.4.12). In short, we are in the presence of a master of metrical form.

That mastery extends from the smallest units of his poetic universe to the greatest. The individual lines, for example, are tetrameter: there are four strong stresses to each line, with a variable number (two, one, or the stunning zero) of unstressed syllables between them, allowing for an astonishingly broad range of musical, emotional, and rhetorical effects. (Our poet likes combinations of four: the stanzas of *Patience* and *Purity* are four lines long, as is the "wheel" device of *Gawain*.) But these stresses are holdovers from the old-fashioned Anglo-Saxon poetry of alliterative half-lines, with usually two stresses in each half-line, and alliteration to bind them across the divide. The Middle-English poet does not use the half-line, but there is a small yet noticeable breath in the middle of each: "My soul forsook / that spot in space"(2.1.1), with alliteration, in wild variety from line to line, almost always forming a bridge between. Out of the first sixty lines, two do not alliterate at all, nor do ten additional half-lines. But 106 out of the 120 half-lines do alliterate, and in the broadest range of patterns, with A A / X A the poet's favorite, setting up a strong alliteration in the first half-line and delaying its completion until the very end.[1] Both the alliteration and the half-line structure conduce to irony. Alliteration allows the poet to link words we might not suppose should be linked, forcing us to consider a connection deeper than the surface. The first line of the poem, "Pearl, that a Prince is well content," suggests that the Pearl has something to do with the Prince; and indeed the message of the poem is that the Pearl only becomes a Pearl by submitting to the "paye" (Middle English, M.E. hereafter) or delight of the Prince. That truth is not obvious in the opening line; we are led to think only of a beautiful pearl that a prince would like to place in a lovely setting. The full meaning of this piece of alliteration will only be revealed to us when the line is repeated at the end of the poem.

Half-lines, in turn, allow the poet to play one item against another, linked but not quite linked; so that the second half of a line may cut slightly against the first half. For example, in the line "[She] profered me speche, that special spyce" (4.5.7; M.E.), we are startled into conceiving what the words of the Pearl have to do with a "special spyce"—as if the lesson she is about to teach the speaker were incense, offered to the Lord.

But our poet is still cracking his knuckles, warming up. For the stanzas themselves exhibit this ironic pattern of apparent separation and deeper connection. The poet links his stanzas by ringing changes on the final line, and by repeating a key word from the final line in the first line of the next stanza. For instance, the final lines of the first five stanzas are:

Of that secret pearl without a spot
My secret pearl without a spot

---

1. Unless noted, I will provide not the original Middle English lines, too difficult for the general reader, but the fine translation by Marie Borroff.

> From that precious pearl without a spot
> Of my precious pearl without a spot
> On that precious pearl without a spot

The first lines of stanzas 2–5 repeat the key rhyming word "spot," thus:

> Since in that spot it sped from me so
> That spot with spice must spring and spread
> To that especial spot I hied
> Before that spot with head inclined

And the pattern continues unto the first line of stanza 6:

> My soul forsook that spot in space

We may think of the repeated line as a rhyme across the stanzas—each stanza "rhymes" with the others in its group of five (for those groups, see below), because they all end with the same "sound"—not the same line exactly, but the same rhyming word in very similar lines. That allows the poet to develop or deepen the meaning of the climactic line—or to comment ironically upon it, changing it slightly or placing it in a new context. For instance, the speaker first describes his "perle" as "privy," that is "secret," "private," belonging to him alone; he will learn, as the poem goes on, that its price, what makes it "precious," is that it belongs rather to the prince alone, and only thus can be restored to the speaker.

Similarly, the repeated keyword is a sort of alliteration across the top of the stanzas, and an immediate link from the end of one stanza to the beginning of the next. The poet uses this device with great cunning. In the final lines of the first group of stanzas, "spot" translates Latin *macula*, the blemish associated with sin; but "spot" in the initial lines means "place," in particular, the place where the speaker lost his Pearl. He blames that spot—yet blames it wrongly, as we will see; for spices spring from it, and it will bring him a vision of glory. In this sense too, the "spot" that mars the Pearl—in itself spotless—is a happy fault that gives the speaker "oght for noght," something out of nothing (5.3.10).

I have given the reader a glimpse of the first five stanzas, because in fact *Pearl* is composed of groups of five stanzas each. These groups preserve the identical final rhymes in nearly identical lines, and the keyword from the final line is repeated in the first line of the following stanza. But that is not all. For the groups themselves bear forth a division that must be bridged. The first line of the first stanza of each group of five will repeat the keyword from the last line of the last stanza of the previous group of five; then a new rhyming line and a new keyword will be used in turn for the new group. Thus, the keyword "spot" is repeated in the first stanza of the second group (stanza 6):

> My soul forsook that spot in space

And a new final rhyme is provided for the new group of five:

> Such rich and rare embellishment

That provides the new keyword, "embellishment," for the first lines of stanzas seven through ten, completing the second group:

> Embellished were those hills in view
> Amid those hills embellished bright
> So all embellished was the land
> Embellishing those waters deep

Then the repetition ends with the first line of stanza 11, linking the second group to the third:

> Embellished with such wondrous grace

This device too is a fine one for irony, in two ways. First, when the keyword moves from one *group* of stanzas to the next, the poet may lend it a new meaning, even one that seems to contradict what it had suggested before. For instance, in the third group of stanzas the speaker describes a vision of paradise that causes him to long to see more and more, until he finally sees something—someone—that seems to him to bring the vision to its climax. But the next time he uses the word "more," as a word in the first line of the fourth group of stanzas, it is to express his growing dread. Appropriately so, since, as we will see, this speaker has quite a lot to learn, especially about how to want more and how to want enough.

But the group-connecting keywords, so prominent and easy to remember, also allow the poet to return to them later in the poem, to reexamine what they mean, and to show the reader that what he thought they meant was not quite right, or not quite all. The poet does this most strikingly with the related words "more," "nevertheless," and "enough" (keywords for groups 3 and 10, 15, and 11), and with "pearl" (keyword for groups 1 and 4, and almost for 13).

But how do you end such a poem, when the last line will clearly not link to anything to come after? Easy, when you possess the genius of the poet of *Pearl.* Just as the end of time was foreseen by God in the beginning, though time moves by passing away, so the passage of the poem brings us back to the beginning. The last line of *Pearl* links to the *first* line of *Pearl*— and the keyword is, surprise, "pearl." Thus, all the groups, all the stanzas, all the lines come round full circle, like a pearl, perfectly round, without spot.

A Spot of Genius

EXCEPT THAT THERE IS a spot. Actually, there are two places where the poet deviates from his intricate design. At the beginning of section 13, the keyword "right" from section 12, meaning "right" or "by right" or "righteousness," is not repeated. Instead the poet begins with the name of the only man who possessed perfect righteousness by his own power:

Jesus on his faithful smiled

The change is fitting, since Pearl has been warning the speaker against believing that men should try to win salvation by their own merits. In the passage thus introduced, she will remind him that Jesus told his apostles that unless they became little children, they should not enter the Kingdom of Heaven (Matt. 18:3).

The second deviation really is the happy flaw. At a crucial moment of spiritual and intellectual conviction, the speaker confesses his need to submit to the wisdom of God. He does so in an extra stanza, at the end of section 15. Thus the pattern of five stanzas per section is broken. We know from *Gawain* that the poet used the number five to symbolize purity; the number six, however, is the traditional Christian number for sin or at least *imperfection*, since man was created on the sixth day (and, if we believe Dante, sinned on the sixth hour after noon on that same day [*Paradise*, 26.139–42]). Six is also one shy of the "perfect" number seven, perfect because it is the number of consummation, the Sabbath day of rest. Man is but "mokke and mul," muck and dust, the speaker concedes, as he submits his will to God's (cf. Job 40:4, 42:1–6).

Thus, the imperfection of man is woven into the structure of a poem that discusses the imperfection (and incomplete vision) of man. Yet the flaw is redemptive; not in itself, but when taken up into the mercy of God. For that one stanza in excess—itself a stanza of concession—gives the poet exactly 101 stanzas for the poem, as many as he used in *Sir Gawain and the Green Knight*. And just as in *Gawain* he used the number of stanzas to give him 2,525 lines (plus a five-line prayer), so now he uses the "imperfect," the too-many 101, to give him exactly 1,212 lines. And that number is poetically perfect. It is intended to suggest the 12 x 12 thousand servants of God in the Apocalypse (cf. Rev. 7:4), one of whom addresses the speaker; and the 12 x 12 x 12 mile City of Peace, the twelve-jeweled, twelve-gated New Jerusalem, its trees bearing twelve fruits of life (cf. Rev. 21:12–21). The poet goes so far as to make the references explicit, in case we should miss them (14.1.6, 17.2.8–9, 17.4.7–8, 17.5.10–12, 18.1.3, 18.4.10). The poem is perfect, then, because its structure mirrors its subject, the perfecting by Christ of imperfect, sinful mankind. We see a flaw; but the faithful will exclaim with the church at Easter, "O happy fault, O necessary sin of Adam, that brought for us so great a Redeemer!"

A Pearl Not Found, but Lost

NOW THAT THE READER has some idea of its magnificent and playful architecture, let us turn to the narrative of the poem. *Pearl* alludes most obviously to these twin parables of Jesus:

> The kingdom of heaven is like unto treasure hid in a field; the which when a man hath found, he hideth, and for joy thereof goeth and selleth all that he hath, and buyeth that field.
> The kingdom of heaven is like unto a merchant man, seeking goodly pearls: Who, when he had found one pearl of great price, went and sold all that he had, and bought it. (Matt. 13:44–46)

As the poem opens, we have these parables only dimly in mind. The speaker has not found a pearl, or a treasure in a field, but has lost it. It is, he says, his secret pearl, his very own pearl, without a spot. We soon learn, with rising poignancy, that "Pearl" is the name he gives to a beloved: "Pearl" was enclosed in a jewelry box, that is, a coffin. (Her name is likely Margery or Marjory, meaning "pearl.") "Through grass to ground away it shot," he says, reversing the event of the first parable. The Pearl is lost because it has entered the ground.

When we finally meet Pearl, we see that she is but a child, a "maiden child of mortal mold, / A gracious lady gowned in white" (3.4.5–6), who died before her second birthday (9.1.3), before she could pray her *Pater Noster* or the creed. In other words, this is a poem about a father's terrible sorrow at the loss of his little girl.

The speaker longs to have his Pearl again. All he considers is the person of that lovely child:

> So comely in every ornament,
> So slender her sides, so smooth they were,
> Ever my mind was bound and bent
> To set her apart without a peer.
> In a garden of herbs I lost my dear;
> Through grass to ground away it shot;
> Now, lovesick, the heavy loss I bear
> Of that secret pearl without a spot. (1.1.5–12)

He mourns, understandably enough, that the earth should mar the beautiful Pearl; yet even here he sees that the loss of Pearl is not simply a loss. The earth rejoices to fold her in its bosom. It is not earth that mars her, but she who ennobles the earth, bringing forth sweetness and life:

> That spot with spice must spring and spread
> Where riches rotted in narrow room;
> Blossoms white and blue and red
> Lift now alight in blaze of noon. (1.3.1–4)

Yet he does not understand what that sweetness signifies. So he misquotes the Gospel of John:

> Flower and fruit could never fade
> Where pearl plunged deep in earthen tomb,
> For the seed must die to bear the blade
> That the wheat may be brought to harvest home. (1.3.5–8)

The speaker sees that in the natural course of things, life must spring from a seed that "dies" in being burst open. If it does not die, then we have no wheat to store in our barns. But that is the metaphor Jesus uses to describe the entry into eternal life: "Except a corn of wheat fall into the ground and die, it abideth alone: but if it die, it bringeth forth much fruit" (John 12:24). The death Jesus refers to is not only physical death (which is not the last word for us, since he *is* "the resurrection and the life" [John 11:25]), but death to the hard cold kernel of self-will, the old Adam dwelling within us. We want what we want, here, now, exactly as we would have it, but Jesus says, "He that loveth his life shall lose it; and he that hateth his life in this world shall keep it unto life eternal" (John 12:25).

The words of Jesus blare like a trumpet, proclaiming the folly of the world by what seems folly in its own right. Whoever would save his life must lose it. That is a moral law of human life. Without that death, no life: only the static, small, dead grain of self. Except that corn of wheat fall to the ground and die, it abideth alone, solitary, ossified in will. The speaker in our poem mourns the passing of Pearl, but we who hear the allusion to Jesus' words in the gospel—spoken shortly after he raised Lazarus from the dead—now begin to question the full wisdom of his mourning. We will see that Pearl lives, and that it is the speaker who must die, not only in the body when the time shall come, but to the will, now. We think the poem is about the death of a child, but instead it relates the painful death and rebirth of her sorrowing father.

Only in Adventure Is There Security

THE FATHER VISITS THE flowering field where he lost his Pearl—the graveyard. There he falls asleep and is granted an "aventure," a finding, a something-chancing, by the grace of God. In the Cistercian *Quest of the Holy Grail*, adventures only come to knights who are spiritually prepared to receive them; all others wander as if in a desert, achieving nothing, and sometimes killing one another unwittingly. Our courtly father here is not about to fathom the depths of the mysteries of the Eucharist, as is granted to Galahad at the end of the *Quest*. Nor, like that gallant knight Saint Paul, is he about to be rapt to the heaven of heavens (2 Cor. 12:1–6). He needs tenderer food. So he is brought in a vision to the threshold of heaven, as he stands atop what we come to recognize as earthly paradise. A broad and deep river—and what that river means and whence it comes, we have yet to learn—separates him from heaven. In a stunning reversal of the imagery we expect, the poet has his speaker gaze *down* into what looks like the bejewelled and changeless heavens:

> Embellishing those waters deep,
> Banks of pure beryl greet my gaze;

Sweetly the eddies swirl and sweep
With a rest and a rush in murmuring phrase;
Stones in the stream their colors steep,
Gleaming like glass where sunbeam strays,
As stars, while men of the marshlands sleep,
Flash in winter from frosty space. (2.5.1–8)

That very separation causes him to want to bridge the gap. He wants *more*, as is natural. To see heaven, but not to be in heaven, is to be fired with longing for more than you now enjoy. It is to long for the fulfillment of your being, made by God for himself. Yet the speaker tells us that he is like a man on whom fortune has smiled. Any such man favored by fortune, he says, will forever long to have "more and more" (3.1.12). Now that is *not* simply natural. To enjoy good gifts and to wish even more of them is sometimes to be peevish and ungrateful. Most of the poem will play upon the ironic differences between the two meanings of wanting more: for the speaker at first treats the bliss of heaven as something that can be quantified and doled out according to earthly standards of fair play.

But as he looks over the water to the shimmering cliffs, the stream glinting with gems, the deep green forests loud with birdsong, and as his heart yearns for more and more of the leaping joy the wild scene lends him, he sees something more beautiful than all. Says the speaker, in a simple and aching understatement, "I knew her well, I had seen her before" (3.4.8).

Then "more" means only to have the beloved again, with or without all the beauties of earthly paradise that pale before her. It is all too human. Even heaven is forgotten in his anticipation of reunion. The longer he looks upon her, "the more and more" is his heart stung with love. At first we may be led to believe that he wants too much; we will see instead that he wants too little.

The little child is herself a pearl, wearing pearls embroidered in her gown, and a single large pearl upon her breast. It is the pearl of great price, clean and clear and pure. By her life she represents the joy of the kingdom of God, for to win this pearl is to be marked with the pearl, to be made like unto the pearl. "He abides in me, and I in him," says Jesus of the faithful believer; to dwell in the City of God is to have been made a fit temple for the Lord to dwell. None of this does the speaker consider. He sees Pearl approach, and reveals to us for the first time who she was: "She was nearer to me than aunt or niece" (4.5.5). Pearl is his daughter. The "spice" she gives him is her acquired wisdom, as she bows to him in womanly fashion: she who died before she could say her prayers, and who manifests the delicate humility of a gracious woman, becomes the teacher. For "wisdom is better than rubies" (Prov. 8:11).

The speaker bursts into a fully human lament. He almost repeats the first line of the poem, but he mistakes the possessor, addressing her as his own:

> "O pearl," said I, "in pearls of price,
> Are you my pearl come back again,
> Lost and lamented with desolate sighs
> In darkest night, alone and in vain?" (5.1.1–3)

Who can blame him? But we are not our own. We are God's, as are the pearls we call our children. The "Prince's paye," the delight of the prince, governs all. The speaker misses that truth, or if he sees it, he considers only that the Pearl is what a prince may take from him. If the prince has one more, then I have less. I have no pearl at all.

The Dimness of Man's Imagination

MAN SEES, AND DOES not see. Isaiah puts it thus: "For my thoughts are not your thoughts, neither are your ways my ways, saith the Lord. For as the heavens are higher than the earth, so are my ways higher than your ways, and my thoughts than your thoughts" (Isa. 55:8–9). In "Caliban upon Setebos," Browning examines this irony from the other end, as the monster projects upon his deity Setebos the cruelty and frustration of his own heart. But scripture stresses that we are made in the image and likeness of God, and not that God is to be imagined as like ourselves. Hence the severe prohibition against making cultic graven images. It is nonsense to suggest that the Hebrew prophets inveighed against idolatry merely because they were partisans of their own God. For to worship any other god is to fall down before a human creation, a totem, a stock or a stone.

The speaker in *Pearl* is no idolater, but in his self-involved grief and in the weakness of his flesh he cannot imagine heaven as anything other than a more pleasant and enduring version of the joys he has known on earth. To paraphrase Jesus, he would save his life, and is not willing to lose it. But Pearl admonishes him straightaway:

> But, jeweler, if your mind is bound
> To mourn for a gem in solitude,

Your care has set you a course unsound,
And a cause of a moment maddens your mood;
You lost a rose that grew in the ground;
A flower that fails and is not renewed. (5.3.1–6)

The poor man busies himself, vexing his mind, as Jesus urged his followers not to do, over the transient things of earth. It is the nature of all such things to be born and to die:

All flesh is grass, and all the goodliness thereof is as the flower of the field:
The grass withereth, the flower fadeth: because the spirit of the Lord bloweth upon it: surely the people is grass.
The grass withereth, the flower fadeth: but the word of our God shall stand for ever. (Is. 40:6–8)

But there is a "kynde" (M.E.) above "kynde," a nature above the nature of things that die. Consider the chest wherein Pearl was placed. We have seen that the poet portrays the coffin as a treasure chest or a box of spices. Has a coffin transformed the summer's rose into the precious pearl?

Something else must do that, some other box, especially a box that can ferry you across the flood. That box is the true ark of Noah, the ark of the new covenant. It is Mary who bore Christ in her womb; it is the church, the Body of Christ. Eight people were saved in that ark, and eight is the number of the Resurrection, because on the eighth day, the first day after the sabbath, Christ rose from the dead (cf. 1 Pet. 3:20–22).

Thus the death of the little girl has been no "thief," as the speaker thinks. He misses his beloved, but the real thief is the devil, who would steal the sheep from the fold. What thief is it who, more than restoring you your own good, exalts it and saves it forever? Pearl tries to remind the speaker that he has gained, not lost, a pearl; God has made something eternal from the next-to-nothingness of our passing days. "More" is exactly what the speaker has been given, and is offered.

Yet he still knows only that he sees his little daughter again:

"Now I have found it, now shall I rest,
And live with it ever, and make good cheer,
And love the Lord and his laws revere
That brought me the blissful sight of her.

> Let me once cross and behold you near,
> And I am a joyful jeweler!" (5.4.7–12)

He would live with Pearl in the beautiful dark woods of terrestrial paradise, worshipping God and rejoicing in her love. What he wants is a painless return to the time before the fall of Adam, a restoration rather than a redemption. He wants Eden, not heaven; the peace he can understand, rather than Christ our peace, the peace that passeth understanding. He is like Mary Magdalene after the Resurrection, recognizing her Teacher and longing to embrace him, as if she could have his friendship in the same old way, on earth; she wants Christ revived, not risen. But as Christ must return to his father, that we may know we are to be one with him there, so the way to Pearl lies only through the waters of death and Resurrection (6.1.5–6). In the meantime, says Pearl, we must admit the limits of our judgment (6.1.11–12), and abide what the Lord sends us:

> "Better to cross yourself, and bless
> The name of the Lord, whatever he send;
> No good can come of your willfulness." (6.4.5–7)

I Am But Dust

WITH THAT REBUKE THE speaker confesses his folly. The poet has portrayed him with a masterly subtlety: he is not an ignorant wretch, only a poor man who means well, and who tries to worship the Lord aright, despite his short-sightedness and confusion. So in his reply to Pearl he gently reminds her of his suffering and the part she has played in it: "'You gave me a heavy grief to bear, / Who once were ground of all my bliss'" (7.1.11–12). She has been in fact both his bliss and his sorrow, and more sorrow than bliss. But he wishes for no more dispute, not now, for "'we meet so seldom by any milestone'" (7.2.8). In his humility he echoes the submission of Job, whom God addresses from the storm, not explaining his suffering, but reminding him that he is God. He will provide; but man will not know his inmost secrets. Says the speaker, "'I am of earth, and speak amiss'" (7.2.10; cf. Job 40:4, 42:6).

Here is the first turn in the poem. Socrates was not the only man to see in humility the door to enlightenment, or to see its barricade in pride. Jesus says that light follows upon obedience: "He that hath my commandments, and keepeth them, he it is that loveth me: and he that loveth me shall be loved of my Father, and I will love him, and will manifest myself to him" (John 14:21).

It is not the reverse: we are not advised to defer obedience until we understand. Ready obedience is the mark of the virtuous child, who knows only what the Father wishes; and this child is what the speaker must suffer some pain to become.

Pearl softens; she welcomes her father and allows him to walk at his leisure on the near side of the dividing stream. That meekness is proper, not because the Lord is a tyrant, but because in fact he is "My Lorde the Lamb" (7.4.11, M.E.). He it is, says Pearl, who, young as she was, took her in marriage when she was lost to her father on earth, and crowned her a queene "in bliss to stay / Forever and ever glorified" (7.5.7–8). The sum of her bliss is expressed in one half-line of utter simplicity and love: "I am holy hysse" (7.5.10; M.E.).

Now there are two things Pearl has said that the mortal speaker cannot fathom. Both involve an earth-bound understanding of justice. First, the father wonders how Pearl can call herself a queen, when Mary is the queen of heaven. Unique is the Virgin Mother, elevated to her high station by grace:

> "Yet as none is lovely like unto her,
> We call her Phoenix of Araby,
> Sent flawless from the artificer
> As was our Queen of courtesy." (8.1.9–12)

Call his error an anticipation of the equalitarian heresy, whereby God must love all men equally, grant them equal grace, and raise them to equal rank, since more for you means less for me, and greater power granted to you is quite positively an infringement of my dignity and rights. Conversely, if I am entitled to a position of singular honor, as Mary is, then it is an act of *lese majeste* to derogate from that honor by honoring anyone else with it. Yet, as I have argued, Christ revealed that there will be hierarchical order among the blessed (though not the order we might expect, since the first shall be last, and the last shall be first). Even the mystery of the Trinity shows that hierarchy and equality are not contradictory.

In reply, Pearl kneels to acknowledge Mary her superior. Then she gives her father the same insight that Piccarda gives Dante in the *Paradise*. There in the lowest sphere of heaven, the Moon, reserved for those whose inconstancy caused them to neglect their religious vows, Dante asks Piccarda whether she and the others desire a higher place, "to see more, know more, and be held more dear" (3.66). Piccarda's reply shows that "less" and "more" lose their earthly meanings in the fire of charity, for every soul in heaven is filled with bliss. Indeed it is nothing but bliss for Piccarda to be blessed as she is, and to see that others are blessed more highly. Charity makes gifts to others *our* joy, a joy the world finds hard to understand. Says Piccarda:

> "Brother, the virtue of our charity
>   brings quiet to our wills, so we desire
>   but what we have, and thirst for nothing else.
> If we should feel a yearning to be higher,
>   such a desire would strike disharmony
>   against His will who knows, and wills us here.
> That cannot catch these wheels, as you shall see:
>   recall love's nature, recall that Heaven is
>   to live in loving, necessarily.
> For it is of the essence of this bliss
>   to hold one's dwelling in the divine Will,
>   who makes our single wills the same, and His,
> So that, although we dwell from sill to sill
>   throughout this kingdom, that is as we please,
>   as it delights the King in whose desire
> We find our own. In His will is our peace:
>   that is the sea whereto all creatures fare,
>   fashioned by Nature or the hand of God." (3.70–87)

Charity does not insist upon its own, says Saint Paul. Graced with the profoundest depth of charity, Mary more than any soul would desire that all who arrive at the court of the kingdom of God (how different this, from earthly courts of ambitious scramblers) be crowned queen or king. As Pearl puts it, the souls wish—if such a wish were possible, which it is not, since nothing is lacking in heaven—that instead of one crown, the *other souls* should receive five!

A Day's Wages

To ILLUSTRATE THE EQUATION-DESTROYING logic of heaven, Pearl relates the parable of the workers hired for a day's pay to labor in the master's vineyard. The parable is an ironic commentary on flawed human expectations:

> For the kingdom of heaven is like unto a man that is an householder, which went out early in the morning to hire labourers into his vineyard.
> And when he had agreed with the labourers for a penny a day, he sent them into his vineyard.

And he went out about the third hour, and saw others standing idle in the marketplace,

And said unto them; Go ye also into the vineyard, and whatsoever is right I will give you. And they went their way.

Again he went out about the sixth and ninth hour, and did likewise. And about the eleventh hour he went out, and found others standing idle, and saith unto them, Why stand ye here all the day idle?

They say unto him, Because no man hath hired us. He saith unto them, Go ye also into the vineyard; and whatsoever is right, that shall ye receive.

So when even was come, the lord of the vineyard saith unto his steward, Call the labourers, and give them their hire, beginning from the last unto the first.

And when they came that were hired about the eleventh hour, they received every man a penny.

But when the first came, they supposed that they should have received more; and they likewise received every man a penny.

And when they had received it, they murmured against the goodman of the house,

Saying, These last have wrought but one hour, and thou hast made them equal unto us, which have borne the burden and the heat of the day.

But he answered one of them, and said, Friend, I do thee no wrong: didst not thou agree with me for a penny?

Take that thine is, and go thy way: I will give unto this last, even as unto thee.

Is it not lawful for me to do what I will with mine own? Is thine eye evil, because I am good?

So the last shall be first, and the first last: for many be called, but few chosen. (Matt. 20:1–16)

Note that the master of the vineyard instructs his steward to pay the latecomers first. That causes the others to expect that they will be paid more. Their reasoning is strictly quantitative, thinking that justice demands an equal hourly rate. It does not occur to them that the Lord might, without offense to them, be generous to others; they forget that their own pay is fair and is what they agreed to in the first place. We may go farther and say that the "pay" is not pay at all, but a gift, nor do we deserve it. We "merit" bliss, as it were, by the gracious will of God who works within us; our Father will accept the little return we make, even compromised by our failings and weakness, exclaiming, "Well done, good and faithful servant!" (Matt. 25:23).

But the early laborers are blind, and are in for an instructive disappointment. The parable is intended first as a warning to Jews who stand too confidently on the externals of their covenant. To them, in their pride, John the Baptist has choice words to say: "God is able of these stones to raise up children unto Abraham!" (Luke 3:8). Or the early workers may stand for all those who are sure they are righteous and full of labors; to whom Jesus says, "Verily I say unto you, That the publicans and the harlots go into the kingdom of Heaven before you" (Matt. 21:31). They who bank upon the kingdom already will never sell all they have to buy that pearl of great price.

Another common interpretation links this parable with the account of the repentant thief: no matter how late it is when we turn to the master of the vine, the same feast will be ours in the kingdom. Mauriac says that most souls will turn to God only in the aridity of old age and approaching death, after all the cheats to which they have lent their hearts have disappointed them or been taken away (*The Son of Man*, 27). All three interpretations highlight the "unreasonable" grace of a Lord whose justice gives us infinitely more than the paltry pennies that we imagine are our just wages.

It is the third interpretation that the poet plays upon, with a glance at the other two. Pearl did not repent upon her deathbed, but she died early, too early for her to do any work in the vineyard—so early, that she could not even say her prayers. How can God twist so far wrong? She might be made a lady, perhaps, or a countess—but a queen, and on the "first day"? "'[It] is too dere a date'" (9.1.12; M.E.).

Within that word "date" is enveloped a rich theology of the permeation of time by eternity. The word means "goal" or "end," a fulfilling limit; it also recalls the Latin *datum*, "something given," and by the time of this poem's writing it had come to mean what we know as a "date," that is, the right time for a work to be done. The speaker sees only the costliness of the aim or goal—to be crowned queen in heaven. It is as if he considered it an end that could be worked for, were one granted enough time. He does not consider it a gift given from beyond time yet at the right time, or in "the fullness of time."

So Pearl seizes upon that word and asserts, "'Ther is no date of [his] goodness'" (9.2.1; M.E.), no limit to it, but also no circumscribing time. It works in time, yet is from eternity. Thus when the Lord is about to hire the vineyard workers, he considers the time of year, seeing that "'to labor vyne was dere the date'" (9.2.12; M.E.).

The little child, whose time on earth was so brief, reminds her father that time is in God's hands, not ours. God's gift of eternal bliss surpasses anything we think we can deserve by our temporal works. The "date" of the day—its setting, its passage into reward, is nevertheless not to be severed from that passing day, nor is it an extension of the passing day.

The Lord of the vineyard recognizes the "'date of the daye'" (10.1.1), says Pearl, and assembles the workers before him for that parable of final judgment. He who knows the end of time knows the purpose of time, as we who dwell within time can but dimly perceive. And what is the "date" whereon this vision, and this discussion of dates, occurs? The speaker has given us a clue: it is "'in August at a festive tide / When corn is cut with scythe-edge keen'" (1.4.3–4). It is almost certainly August 1, Lammastide, the Feast of the Lamb. The laboring for the harvest, then, is reflected by the labor of the vineyard workers in the parable; and that harvest refers both to time and to eternity. For the Lord has ordained a season for reaping, and a time for the final reaping, when all the good grain will be gathered into bins, the "barns" for the wheat whose seeds fall into the ground and die, while the tares or the chaff will be destroyed in fire (cf. Matt. 13:30).

As for Lammastide, the gospel reading for that day is the account of the Transfiguration, and the feast applies to the poem in several interesting ways. The Transfiguration foreshadows the Resurrection of Christ the Lamb of God: Jesus appears atop Mount Tabor before Peter, James, and John, mysteriously transfigured, his garments as dazzling as the snow, so bright that "no fuller on earth can white them" (Mk. 9:1–3). Beside that Lamb stand his forerunners, the prophets Moses and Elijah, representatives of the old covenant. They do not insist upon their primacy, but pay homage to him whom they foretold. Looking upon the three in awe, Peter blurts out—as a man would whose understanding of time is limited to his experience of night and day—"Master, it is good for us to be here: and let us make three tabernacles; one for thee, and one for Moses, and one for Elias" (Mark 9:5). Peter wishes to preserve, on that mountaintop, an earthly moment of bliss, not seeing that the life he longs for lies on the far side of Calvary, the cross he will later warn Jesus against, earning a stinging rebuke for his solicitousness (Matt. 16:23). Then a voice comes from heaven, encouraging and admonishing: "This is my beloved Son: hear him" (Mark 9:7), the same words spoken as when John baptized Jesus, the "Lamb of God, which taketh away the sins of the world" (John 1:29). Sin and death must be conquered, not averted or deferred; and the conqueror is the Lamb.

The speaker is like Peter: he knows how good it is to be with Pearl, but he does not understand the way of the Lamb, which is the way of the cross. It is only through that victory of the Lamb that baptism becomes Resurrection.

In misjudging time, then, he misjudges time's end: both the setting of this life's little day, and the end or purpose towards which time moves. He is like the grouching vineyard worker who has labored since the morning: "It seems to us we should have more" (10.1.12). More what? Two pennies instead of one? A longer stay atop Mount Tabor? Pearl for twenty years instead of two? The irony is that the Lord, who is Love, the love to which, as Mauriac says, we have so often repeated the words of Peter, "Depart from me" (*The Son of Man*, 18; Luke 5:8), wishes to give us more, of what we neither expect nor deserve:

> "More of ladyship here is mine,
> Of life in flower and never to fade,
> Than any man in the world could win
> By right and right alone," she said. (10.4.1–4)

When the father persists in complaining that the girl's tale is "unresounable" (10.5.2; M.E.), she must shift the discussion away from more and less to the unfettered freedom of God's kindness, for "the grace of God is enough for all" (11.1.12).

Enough—not less, not more, but enough; not some niggardly "only enough," but a sufficiency that fulfills all God's purposes and all our desires. It is not unreasonable, but it does defy our cramped calculation of our deserts, that a little water at baptism should graft the baby onto the church:

> "But grace enough have the innocent:
> When first they see the light of day
> To the water of baptism they are sent
> And brought to the vine without delay." (11.3.1–4)

Why not? Redemption itself is "unresounable." The Babe in the manger, representing in his very ignorance God's utter freedom from evil, is more powerful than all the Herods of our dark world. He will defeat them, but not by their means—not by the brute force that Herod employs to ferret out the threat, leaving thousands of babies dead by the sword. He will defeat them in defeat! Hell without respite is what man deserves: an eternity in such a world as man would make of it, were he allowed to live forever apart from God's grace, spreading his pollution and hating his own works. But where sin abounds, there grace above grace abounds: and the medicine is the water and blood, the baptism and the Eucharist, flowing from the side of the Crucified:

> "But then there came a remedy right:
> Rich blood ran down rood-tree tall
> And with it flowed forth water bright:
> The grace of God was enough for all." (11.4.9–12)

It behooves us then to claim entry into God's kingdom not by our labor but by a battering ram more potent than all the armies of the world: the innocence of the Lamb.

What Is a Child?

THINK AGAIN OF THAT Child in the manger, sleeping. He *is really a child*, not some tricky deity in disguise. He the Word does not know how to speak a word. He the Redeemer is peacefully unaware of the human evil he has come into the world to redeem:

> Upon the straw of Bethlehem He is still "He who is"; not the Child-God but the God Who has become a Child: the God-Child, a child who is like a river uncontaminated by human sinfulness.
>
> Trembling with joy, kneeling over the common graves of Europe and carrying within me the memories of concentration camps, the charred cadavers of children and women in the ruins of French, German, Russian, and Japanese cities, I adore Him. *I believe in you, God-Child, because you are a love that is still blind, that is still ignorant of innumerable crimes.* (Mauriac, *The Son of Man*, 20)

What can it mean for a Christian to become like a little child? We who have lived past childhood have felt the waves of human cruelty and lust and hard-heartedness and sloth wash over us, yet when we see a child we know somehow that we were once so innocent and so full of life. The child we are to become is Christ; he is the little Child who welcomes his own, they whom he has raised up as "little children," into the kingdom. Then there can be no worry for those baptized children who die before they know what man has made of his world. "But Jesus gathered them round his knee" (12.5.9) when his disciples with important work to do in the world tried to keep the children away from him (12.5). Those children — mirroring the innocence of Jesus — are what we must become, "Harmless, steadfast, undefiled, / Unsullied bright to gaze upon," without a "mascle" ("blemish," M.E., 13.1.5–6). To buy the "perle was mascelles" (13.1.12; M.E.), without spot, is to become such a pearl, like unto the kingdom of heaven and the king who reigns there. He is "makelles," "matchless," because he is in himself "immaculate," without spot:

> "This immaculate pearl I tell you of,
> The jeweler gave his wealth to gain,
> Is like the realm of heaven above;
> The Father of all things said it plain.
> No spot it bears, nor blemish rough,
> But blithe in rondure ever to reign,
> And of righteousness it is prize and proof:
> Lo, here on my breast it long has lain;
> Bestowed by the Lamb so cruelly slain,
> His peace to betoken and designate;
> I bid you turn from the world insane
> And purchase your pearl immaculate." (13.2)

On earth we bring gifts to the wedding feast. In heaven we are given the gift, we our ourselves are wedded, and the gift is the Lamb.

And this raises another question for the father. How can Pearl be espoused to Christ? For when Pearl departed from her father's world, she was courted by the Lamb with gentle gallantry and courtliness:

> "When I left your world of rain and sleet
> He called me in joy to join him there:
> 'Come hither, my dove without deceit,
> For you are spotless, past compare.'" (13.4.5–8)

"Come hither, my love, to me," Christ sings, from the Song of Songs — sings it to a little girl as she passes from death to life. The father can see only a marriage of one and one, misunderstanding the nature of the church, the Bride of Christ. If you are Christ's bride, he asks, what about all the rest? But the generous lover, whom Pearl calls "'my jewel dear, my joy's sole source, / My Lamb, my lord, my love, all three'" (14.2.3–4), would have more than one. He would espouse the 144,000 virgins revealed in the Apocalypse (14.1.6), a number suggesting endlessness, beyond reckoning. He whose beautiful face was buffeted for our sins (14.3.5–6), the handsomest and purest of men, the meekest of sufferers, has unto his bride all those souls that have been polished as white and pure as he. And what hindrance of one's joy is it, that more should enjoy the Lamb's love? Says Pearl, turning her father's objection upside-down with a wonderful turn on a humble proverb:

> "And though he fetch a score each day
> No strife is stirred in our citadel,
> But would each brought four others as well —
> The more the merrier in blessedness!
> Our love is increased as our numbers swell,
> And honor more and never the less." (15.1.7–12)

It is as Jesus said, the second commandment is like unto the first. Thou shalt love thy neighbor as thyself. Not simply because God so commands; but because love of neighbor is implied in love of God. If God is love, how can we otherwise love him than to desire to become like him? To be a member of the Body of Christ is to rejoice when there are more to rejoice over: the more the merrier! Finally the narrator capitulates, all his objections set aside. He is like Job, but happier than Job. The old Hebrew was admonished to be patient, but this poor muddled Christian father is granted a vision of the bliss that awaits all who humbly accept the marvelous gifts of God. So in that "extra" stanza (15.6) he accepts Pearl's wisdom, then asks her to bridge one more divide: she says she dwells in Jerusalem, but isn't Jerusalem in the Holy Land?

The father, our man of earth, thinks of Jerusalem as the city of David, founded a long time ago, just as the old covenant was established in time. Pearl reminds him that the old Jerusalem was the place where "the old guilt was canceled clean" (16.3.6), as Christ canceled the old sin of Adam by paying the penalty of the old Law. But the new Jerusalem fulfills its name:

> "Two holy cities I figure forth;
> One name suits well with both of these,
> Which in the language of your birth
> Is 'City of God,' or 'Sight of Peace.'" (16.4.1–4)

The eternity and infinity of this city is suggested by its gemlike construction: its twelve adorning jewels, its twelve gates. Time, there, is past — or is itself the Lord. So remarks the father, as he beholds his Pearl as part of a great pageant celebrating the Lamb:

> Sun and moon were far surpassed;
> The Lord was their lamp eternally,
> The Lamb their lantern ever to last
> Made bright that seat of sovereignty. (18.2.1–4)

Nor is there church or temple there, as all are the church: "The Almighty was their place of prayer" (18.3.7). Nor was there sacrifice or meal, but only the Lamb to refresh them: "The Lamb, the sacrifice all to restore" (18.3.8). So beautiful is the vision, that if anyone should confront it in the body, says the speaker, not all the wisest clerks and physicians in the world could cure him (18.5), for who can look upon the face of the Lord, and live?

A Friend Benign

THE FATHER SEES THE virgins approach in procession, "mild as maydenes seme at mas" (19.2.11; M.E.), walking onwards in great delight, led proudly by the Lamb. When they sing to that "jewel" (19.3.8), the Lamb in glory, the music of their love seems as if it could pierce through earth to hell. It certainly pierces the father's heart, for now he falls into a love-longing, not, as at the beginning of the poem, for *his* Pearl, little Margery, but for *the* Pearl of great price:

> To share his praises in citadel
> My heart indeed had great delight. (19.3.11–12)

Christ—not his daughter—is now "blythest, and moste to pryse" (19.4.3; M.E.), and it fairly breaks his heart to see the wound in His side, wide and wet with blood. It is a love-wound, and it moves the speaker to love: "'O God,' thought I, 'who had such spite?'" (19.4.10). And at last he sees his "little queen" (19.5.7)—and all the lessons fly from his memory, such is his love-longing.

He tries to cross the river—the river all men must cross. But that river flows from the side of the pierced Lamb. Only at the Lamb's pleasure, then, can it be crossed, and only by dying with the Lamb. It is not the father's time to cross. He tries, but "'[It] was not at my Prynces paye'" (20.1.12; M.E.). He wakes instantly from the vision and finds himself again in the graveyard, at the spot where his Pearl slipped into the ground. Now a wiser man, instructed by a child on how to become a child, he sighs, "'Now al be to that Prynces paye'" (20.2.12; M.E.). If Pearl's words are true, he says, "'Then happy am I in dungeon drear / That he with you is well content'" (20.3.11–12). Thus he alters what he had said before, when he met Pearl after having missed her for so long: not well for him that he sees her again, but well for him that she pleases the prince. The father knows he has lost the vision because of his own folly, the madness of wanting more than God gives, which is always less than what God intends to give, even nothing.

For this is the same Lamb who descends so far as to give of himself in the Eucharist. Then how can he be a difficult prince to please? He is the omnipotent Lord, yet nearer to us than we are to ourselves, and he wishes to bring us boundless joy by making us into what pleases him. Except a corn of wheat fall to the ground and die, it abideth alone. The heartsore father of *Pearl* learns that the good Christian is not alone. For if we die with Christ, will we not also rise with Christ?

> To content that Prince and well agree,
> Good Christians can with ease incline,
> For day and night he has proved to be
> A Lord, a God, a friend benign.
> These words came over the mound to me
> As I mourned by Pearl so flawless fine,
> And to God committed her full and free,
> With Christ's dear blessing bestowing mine,
> As in the form of bread and wine
> Is shown us daily in sacrament;
> O may we serve him well, and shine
> As precious pearls to his content.
> Amen. Amen. (20.5)

Conclusion

There's a charming moment in one of the vignettes in Italo Calvino's *Cosmicomics*. The whole universe, you see, is crammed into a single point, the point before the Big Bang: all the matter that would become nebulae and mountains in France and beryllium isotopes, along with all kinds of rather grouchy characters underfoot, always gossiping and sniping, especially at the expense of a so-called "immigrant" family with camp beds, mattresses, and baskets. "It was," says the narrator with cosmological hilarity, "what you might call a narrow-minded attitude, our outlook at that time, very petty" (44). Yet one character, a Mrs. $Ph(i)Nk_0$, inspired devotion in everyone, so that even after all these years, should the narrator meet one of his old point-fellows, say at an international dentists' convention, the conversation inevitably comes round to her, the lovely and gracious. For she it was who one day said, "'Oh, if I only had some space, how I'd like to make some noodles for you boys!'" (46; italics mine). And that did it: they imagined the space for her floured and oiled arms working back and forth with the rolling pin, and the space for the wheat fields, and for the mountain streams to water them, and for the rain, and for the sun to ripen the wheat, and the galaxies to hold the sun in place. . . . And there it was, the universe, born of "a true outburst of genuine love" (47).

Calvino had abandoned his Catholic faith, yet he remains steeped in a world where the least is the greatest, where love is stronger than force, where time works out its surprising purposes. What I hope to have shown in this book is that the teachings of Christianity give to irony a richer constellation of possibilities than the pagan world could have supposed existed. So rich is it that now, after two thousand years, even though Europe reels upon the verge of oblivion, abandoning first its faith and then its reason and its artistic patrimony to boot, it is nearly impossible for us to imagine a world in which irony never takes the part of the Poor Soul, never shows victory budding on the scorched sides of Mordor, never strides into a nation's capital and conscience with a vision-led minister followed by no armies but those whose hope is in the Lord. Not only our churches and our parliaments, but our very *laughter* has been formed by Christ. But as the faith goes, so will that exalted irony go; and then, I fear, irony will decline again into that sardonic half-deceit that made Socrates hated, and that caused Thomas Aquinas to inquire as to whether it was a deadly sin.

In the meantime, it is still with us, and like dew on a parched land, the irony of faith winks in the sun. It has not been difficult for me to find subject matter for this book. More difficult have been the decisions on what to omit. I hope the reader will find the analyses here fruitful also for understanding countless writers who have received short treatment, or who have been by-passed altogether. These I have left out sometimes because I wished to present a range of literary genres and ages, or because their forms of irony might have led me into new fields and thus swelled the book beyond manageable limits, or because, on account of my own deficiencies, I thought it best to leave discussion of their ironies to others. Chaucer deserves several chapters; so does *Piers Plowman*. Sidney's *Arcadia* is a tapestry of providential ironies, revealing the folly and the grandeur of love. I have unconscionably neglected John Donne, Henry Vaughn, and Richard Crashaw. Milton's sonnets are small masterpieces of irony. Then come Swift and Dryden and Pope, and the inimitable Doctor Johnson, not to mention their wise and demure admirer, the deeply Christian Jane Austen. I might go on in this vein for a long time; I might also note that the ironies of faith that animate Christian poetry also animate Christian art and sculpture and music. What I have said about Graham Greene will apply to Caravaggio and Rembrandt; what I have said about the precise turns of expectation in George Herbert will apply to Bach.

The world may mock, but a mockery is hollow laughter. The Christian faith teaches that the last laugh is on the world, because that grim old world, taking itself so seriously that even its laughter is a sneer, that same world will be redeemed. It will be made spanking new, whether it likes it or not, and if I know the world, and for better and for worse I am well acquainted with it, I wager that it will *not* like it at all, and will kick up quite a fuss before that consummation. But the end will not be a silent heat-death, or a shadowland below.

It will be laughter as bright as the stars in their earliest glory. It will be wholly unexpected, and wholly right; it will fulfill all times, and time itself, and the time after time. It will be as quiet as a still small voice, and will crack open the hardest material in the universe, the heart of man. It will still our questions, and stir our wonder with love. Nor can love allow the lowliest among us to be forgotten; not when Man himself sits upon the throne, Son both of Man and God. "Behold," says He, "I make all things new."

Works Cited

The following is a list of the editions of those works whose lines or passages have been cited directly in the text. In general, the method of citation is numerical. For most ancient texts, book and chapter numbers are given; e.g., *Confessions*, 1.12, or, for the works of Plato, the traditional manuscript numbers: *Phaedrus*, 203b. For poems, the numbers given are as follows: book, canto, stanza (if numbered), lines. Thus *Faerie Queene*, 7.7.59.1–4 denotes the seventh book, seventh canto, stanza fifty-nine, lines one through four. Plays divided into acts and scenes are referenced by act, scene, and line number: *King Lear*, 3.1.10–15. Works divided by section and paragraph number are referenced thus: *Commentary on the Song of Songs*, 3.3. All other works are referenced by page numbers.

Augustine. *The Confessions of Saint Augustine*. Trans. John K. Ryan. New York: Doubleday, 1960.

Beaumont, Francis, and John Fletcher. *The Knight of the Burning Pestle*. Ed. Michael Hattaway. London: A.&C. Black, 1986.

Bernard of Clairvaux. *Commentary on the Song of Songs*. In *Bernard of Clairvaux: Selected Works*, trans. G. R. Evans. Mahwah, NJ: Paulist Press, 1987.

Blake, William. *Complete Writings*. Ed. Geoffrey Keynes. Oxford: Oxford University Press, 1984.

Browning, Robert. "Andrea del Sarto," from *Men and Women* London, 1855). In *The Selected Poetry of Robert Browning*, ed. George M. Ridenour. New York: New American Library, 1966.

———. *The Ring and the Book.* Ed. Richard D. Altick. New Haven, CT and London: Yale University Press, 1971.

Calvino, Italo. *Cosmicomics.* Trans. William Weaver. San Diego: Harcourt, Brace, Jovanovich, 1968.

Campanella, Tommaso. "The World and Its Parts." In *European Metaphysical Poetry*, ed. Frank J. Warnke. New Haven, CT, Yale University Press, 1961.

Cervantes, Miguel de. *Don Quixote.* Trans. J. M. Cohen. Harmondsworth: Penguin Books, 1950.

Chaucer, Geoffrey. *The Canterbury Tales.* In *The Complete Poetry and Prose of Geoffrey Chaucer.* Ed. John H. Fisher. New York: Holt, Rinehart, and Winston, 1977.

Dante. *Inferno.* Trans. Anthony Esolen. New York: Random House, 2005.

———. *La Vita Nuova.* Trans. Mark Musa. Bloomington, IN, and London: Indiana University Press, 1973.

———. *Paradise.* Trans. Anthony Esolen. New York: Random House, 2005.

———. *Purgatory.* Trans. Anthony Esolen. New York: Random House, 2004.

Dickens, Charles. *A Christmas Carol.* New York: Airmont, 1963.

Donne, John. *Poetry and Prose.* Ed. Frank J. Warnke. New York: Random House, 1967.

Dostoyevsky, Fyodor. *The Brothers Karamazov.* Trans. Constance Garnett. New York: Random House, 1955.

Erasmus, Desiderius. *The Praise of Folly.* Trans. John Wilson. Ann Arbor, MI: Michigan University Press, 1972.

Genesis A. Cited selection from "The Sacrifice of Isaac."In *Bright's Old English Grammar and Reader,* 3rd ed. Eds. F. G. Cassidy and Richard N. Ringler. New York: Holt, Rinehart, and Winston, 1971.

Greene, Graham. *The Heart of the Matter.* New York: Penguin, 1962.

Herbert, George. *The English Poems of George Herbert.* Ed. C. A. Patrides. London: J. M. Dent & Sons, 1974.

Homer, *Iliad.* Trans. Richmond Lattimore. Chicago: University of Chicago Press, 1951.

Hopkins, Gerard Manley. *Poems and Prose of Gerard Manley Hopkins.* Ed. W. H. Gardner. New York: Penguin Books, 1953.

Lewis, C. S. *That Hideous Strength.* New York: Simon and Schuster, 1996.

———. *The Lion, the Witch, and The Wardrobe.* New York: HarperCollins, 1978.

———. *The Screwtape Letters.* New York: Macmillan, 1959.

Lucretius (Titus Lucretius Caro). *On the Nature of Things.* Trans. Anthony Esolen. Baltimore: Johns Hopkins University Press, 1995.

Manzoni, Alessandro. *I Promessi Sposi.* Harvard Classics, no. 21. New York: Collier, 1937.

Mauriac, François. *A Kiss for the Leper. The Knot of Vipers.* In *A Mauriac Reader,* trans. Gerard Hopkins. New York: Farrar, Straus, and Giroux, 1968.

———. *The Son of Man.* Trans. Bernard Murchland. Cleveland: World Publishing Company, 1960.

Middle English Lyrics. Ed. Maxwell S. Luria and Richard L. Hoffman. New York: Norton, 1974.

Milton, John. *Paradise Lost.* In *John Milton: Complete Poems and Major Prose,* ed. Merritt Y. Hughes. Indianapolis: Bobbs-Merrill, 1957.

Moliere, Jean-Baptiste. *Tartuffe and Other Plays.* Trans. Donald M. Frame. New York: Penguin, 1967.

Nietzsche, Friedrich. *Ecce Homo: On the Genealogy of Morals.* Trans. Walter Kaufmann New York: Random House, 1967.

Njal's Saga. Trans. Magnus Magnusson and Hermann Palsson. New York: Penguin Books, 1960.

Plato. *Symposium.* Trans. Michael Joyce. In *Plato: The Collected Dialogues,* eds. Edith Hamilton and Huntington Cairns. Princeton, NJ: Princeton University Press, 1961.

Pearl. Trans. Marie Borroff. New York: Norton, 1977.

Rule for Anchoresses (Ancrene Riwle). In *Early Middle English Verse and Prose.* Eds. J. A. W. Bennett and G. V. Smithers. Oxford: Oxford University Press, 1974.

Shakespeare, William. *The Complete Signet Classic Shakespeare.* Ed. Sylvan Barnet. New York: Harcourt, Brace, Jovanovich, 1972.

Sidney, Sir Philip. *Selected Poems.* Ed. Catherine Bates. London: Penguin, 1994.

Sir Gawain and the Green Knight. Trans. Marie Borroff. New York: Norton, 1977.

Sienkiewicz, Henryk. *Quo Vadis.* Trans. Jeremiah Curtin. New York: Grosset and Dunlap, 1925.

Sophocles. *Oedipus the King.* In *The Theban Plays,* trans. E. F. Watling. Baltimore: Penguin, 1970.

Spenser, Edmund. *The Faerie Queene.* Ed. Thomas P. Roche, Jr. New York: Penguin, 1978.

— — —. *Amoretti and Epithalamion. Fowre Hymnes.* In *Spenser: Poetical Works.* Eds. J. C. Smith and E. de Selincourt. Oxford: Oxford University Press, 1912.

Tacitus, Publius Cornelius. *The Complete Works of Tacitus.* Trans. Alfred John Church and William Jackson Brodribb. Ed. Moses Hadas. New York: Random House, 1942.

Tasso, Torquato. *Jerusalem Delivered.* Trans. Anthony M. Esolen. Baltimore: Johns Hopkins University Press, 2000.

Tolkien, J. R. R. "Leaf, by Niggle." In *The Tolkien Reader.* New York: Ballantine, 1966.

Virgil. *The Aeneid of Virgil.* Trans. Robert Fitzgerald. New York: Random House, 1990.

Index

About the Author

Anthony Esolen, Professor of English at Providence College, is the editor and translator of the Modern Library edition of Dante's *Divine Comedy*. He has published scholarly articles on Spenser, Shakespeare, Dante, and Tasso in various journals and is a senior editor and frequent contributor to *Touchstone: A Journal of Mere Christianity*.